EXPERIMENTAL FOUNDATIONS

OF GENERAL PSYCHOLOGY

EXPERIMENTAL FOUNDATIONS

OF GENERAL PSYCHOLOGY

Willard L. Valentine

Late Editor of Science

AND

Delos D. Wickens

Professor of Psychology • Ohio State University

THIRD EDITION

HOLT, RINEHART AND WINSTON

NEW YORK

PREFACE

The character of this book, as it now stands, differs considerably from the character of the first edition. In his second edition, Dr. Valentine had dropped one chapter, had added a considerable amount of interpretive material to most chapters, and the internal arrangements of many of the chapters had been reorganized. He was materially assisted in this work by advice from Professors Charles Bird, Ernest Hilgard, and John McGeoch. Mrs. Marjorie Lisle had aided him in simplifying the presentation of some technical matters.

Dr. Valentine had begun the third revision of this book just before his death. He had completed a new first chapter, and this has been included, unchanged. It expresses something which had concerned Dr. Valentine for many years: the fact that even today there are so many misconceptions about the nature of psychology and psychological phenomena. I have tried, in revising the remainder of the book, to keep this point of view and at the same time add some new materials which play an important part in determining the theoretical structure of modern psychology.

One new chapter has been added. This is the last chapter of the book and it samples some of the problems in the field of personality. The chapter on Perception is almost completely new; it is increased in length and contains only one of the experiments described in the previous editions. The chapters on Conditioning and on Learning were also changed rather drastically in an effort to point out some of the theoretical principles that seem to form an important part of modern psychological theory. Additional experiments have been added to almost every chapter.

In several instances I have omitted former experiments and substituted others which identify the same principle. When I have done this, it is because the newer experiment is technically more precise, or because it used a kind of material which might be of greater interest to the student.

I have tried to include in the book experiments which are indicative of more recent trends in the field. The new chapter on Personality has been added for this reason, and, although there is no

v

single chapter on Social Behavior, I have included in other chapters various experiments which are social in nature. I have also made use of a number of experiments conducted by the psychologists who worked with military problems during the war.

I should like to express my appreciation to a number of persons who assisted greatly in this revision. Dr. Claude E. Buxton has sent me a very thorough criticism of the previous revision, and this has been most helpful. My wife, Carol Wickens, has aided me with a critical reading of several of the chapters. I am indebted to Mrs. Mary E. Gilbert for patient secretarial work with the manuscript. Several of my colleagues, particularly Mr. Lawrence T. Alexander, Mr. Frank P. Gatling, Mr. Richard A. Littman, and Mr. L. Starling Reid, have assisted me in one way or another.

D. D. W.

Columbus, Ohio
June, 1949

PREFACE

TO THE FIRST EDITION

This book was written to help supply the need in a first course in psychology for reviews of contemporary experimental work, presented in such a way that the beginner can understand them. This contribution is neither an exhaustive nor a critical review for professional psychologists; controversial issues have therefore been avoided. It is concerned mainly with the application of the scientific method to behavior problems, an area of major concern among the generally recognized objectives of the first course. The book reviews a sample of the literature in each of the subject-matter fields traditionally treated in the first course. It discusses details of experimental procedure in each area, and attempts to give some insight into the enormous amount of labor behind the formally written reports of experiments. Each chapter purposes to digest enough material to show why the generalizations that are made in the text appear reasonable in the light of our present knowledge.

I have had to select the material rigorously. There are innumerable excellent experiments that contribute to so small a part of the total picture that they could not be included. Many others were eliminated because they were too technical for beginners, or because they treat of phenomena so remote from everyday experience that they remain incomprehensible to the beginner even though the instructor may labor valiantly to point out their significance. On the other hand, some relatively trivial experiments were included because they have proved over a period of years to be of interest to beginners, however little they appeal to the professional psychologist. The present integration of materials appear to me the best possible integration of the interests of both student and teacher.

The experience of a single person imposes a severe limitation on the accomplishment of such an integration, but in the case of this book this restriction has been relieved by counsel from many colleagues. Dr. Frank Stanton prepared the chapter on *Market Research,* and Dr. Donald B. Lindsley wrote the section on "Brain Waves." Dr. F. C. Dockeray selected some of the material and criticized some parts of the manuscript. Dr. Charles Bird, who read all the manuscript, made innumerable useful criticisms, as did Dr. Frank A. Pattie, Jr. Two of my students, Milton M. Parker and Robert Harper, read the rough draft from the student standpoint, and their aid helped to clarify many of the statements made here. Mr. Harper and Mrs. E. W. Senderling worked assiduously with the proof. To all of these colleagues and friends I owe a debt of gratitude.

It is a pleasure to acknowledge the cooperation of many authors, editors, and publishers in granting permission to use the longer quotations. In each instance appropriate credit is given in the text.

W. L. V.

Columbus, Ohio
May, 1938

TO THE STUDENT

In this book we shall be concerned principally with psychological facts and principles on which there is a majority, if not a universal, agreement. The experiments that are referred to by no means exhaust the list. If he had the patience to do it, one could rewrite this whole volume and arrive at exactly the same conclusions in each chapter, mentioning not a single specific item, with a few exceptions, that I have chosen. I have left out great sections of material that have traditionally appeared in psychology texts. In the selection of the material that appears here my criterion has been its utility to a young person who in all likelihood will have only one course in psychology. To that end there is frequent reference to the practical application of the principles developed.

This book is not designed to prepare a person for an advanced course in any special branch of psychology, nor is it planned to give him any rigorous system of psychology. Above all it is not a handbook for graduate students.

It will find its most useful purpose in providing some insight into how a psychologist goes about collecting the information he needs and what he does with it after he collects it. It also attempts to show why professional psychologists make some of the investigations that seem so important to them, but which to the outsider look like busy work without purpose.

This book will find its greatest value if it is used in conjunction with one of the standard texts, which will furnish the framework for understanding and for systematizing the items of information contained in this volume.

INTRODUCTION

When a person learns a poem by heart, decides to take a blonde to dance rather than a brunette, expresses himself in favor of the United Nations, changes roommates because he can't get along with the one he is leaving, fails an examination, or enters a law school, there is a reason for his action. These are only a few examples. Everything that he has ever done, is doing now, or ever will do is caused by something else. No action is ever spontaneous—uncaused. Even if a person honestly cannot give a reason for making a choice, there is no proof that it had no cause. Many forgotten conditions affect us: others that affect us now we cannot identify, however obvious they are to others. Some that are perfectly obvious to us cannot ever be detected by others however hard they may try to penetrate our privacy.

For a long, long time some people have believed that the relative position of the planets on the date of one's birth had a major effect in the determination of one's destiny. But to substantiate this view there has never been offered any evidence that would stand close examination.

The length of certain lines in one's palm has been credited with indicating how long he will live, whether he will marry and how many times, and with what success. But again the evidence offered is shaky and the reasoning processes used in arriving at the prognostication violate practically every known rule of ordinary logic.

The height of one's forehead, the length of his nose, the size of his mouth and the shape of his ears, the length of his fingers and the breadth of his hand, together with every other known item of physiognomy, have been shown time and time again to bear no relation to temperament, attainment, aptitude, vocation, or economic condition. But more about this in Chapter II.

These pseudo determiners of destiny are considered so silly by psychologists that most textbooks do not even mention them. What the positive factors are will depend for exact statement upon the particular author one is reading, but no one of them would quarrel with this: The factors which determine a person's behavior are (1) his heredity; (2) his biography—the things that have happened to him; (3) his surroundings and his internal condition at the moment under consideration. Nothing is said about stars, or luck, or charms, or curses, and there is no place to fit these things into the psychologist's blueprint. On the other hand, physique—length of fingers and so on—does pretty definitely belong in the hereditary category. And if, as we have already suggested, these factors are not pertinent ones, then they will have to be eliminated on an entirely different basis from the first-named group. There is no single specific condition that can have an effect on behavior which cannot be placed in one or more of the categories mentioned. *These categories are not intended to be mutually exclusive.* Suppose we wanted to determine the effect that one grain of caffeine sulphate has on a person's behavior. There is no question (as has been proved experimentally) but that how much caffeine he was in the habit of taking in coffee, tea, and soda-fountain drinks would have its effect. This fact would come pretty definitely in the personal biography category. But his reaction would also be conditioned by various physiological factors which are both conditions of the moment and which are also affected by a remote hereditary determiner.

Perhaps one reason why there is practically no disagreement on the threefold classification above is because it is too broad. Were we to become more specific, objections would be forthcoming. The elaboration of the specific elements of these topics is the burden of the remainder of this volume.

CONTENTS

LIST OF FIGURES

xxi

EXPERIMENTAL FOUNDATIONS

OF GENERAL PSYCHOLOGY

CHAPTER ONE

MAGIC AND SCIENCE

When we use the word "magic" today in ordinary conversation, we usually first think of a sleight-of-hand performance by a magician, or recall a paper-bound catalog of magical devices offered for sale, a book we sent for when we were ten or twelve years old. Magic, in this sense means stage performance, tricks with cards or coins, wands, boxes with false bottoms, costumes with hidden pockets, and the like.

But "magic," as we use the word in this chapter, is a serious business. It has more sober goals. At one time in the history of the world, every item of learning or wisdom was thought to be magically inspired. The very word in English comes from wise men of the East, the Magi, described in the New Testament. To the unlearned all learning is magic.

If we want to explain how a person can throw an image onto a wall, or a white cloth, from a box with a lamp in it, we can call it magic, as people did in calling the first crude projectors "magic lanterns." The effect could be obtained, they thought, only through the agency of the supernatural; a man would have to be allied with some unearthly force to get an effect of this kind. Today we know that a sounder "explanation" in terms of projection lenses, condensing lenses, focuses, is not magic, but science. But a knowledge of any one of these constituent elements would only a few centuries ago have been called "magical knowledge," and even today we say of a new device based on known engineering principles or a new drug based on known pharmaceutical information, "It works like magic."

Here we might as well distinguish between science and magic: And it is not easy to do. Some have said that magic is an "attempt to gain control over things and people," implying that science is not interested in controlling. Actually scientific knowledge does bring control in many areas, and in many instances scientific procedures have been undertaken expressly to direct and control hitherto unmanageable events.

It will help us to make the distinction if we describe a practice in another society than our own. We have become so used to our own practices that we don't question them. In New Guinea, it has been observed, certain magical rites are practiced when seed is planted and gardens are cultivated. The native believes that the garden will not grow if he does not observe these rites, which we need not describe. Still he builds fences to keep animals out of his garden, he hoes it to keep the weeds down. He plants the seeds, he doesn't just throw it on the ground, and he takes other practical measures to ensure a crop. If a crop does not result, he blames the trouble, *not on natural causes,* but on the more powerful magic of one of his enemies, or on some displeasure of the gods. If some jungle animal breaks through his fence and ruins his crop, he makes his fences stronger; if seeds wash out of the ground, he plants them deeper; these relations he can observe and accept, *but magical explanations are used to explain otherwise unaccountable mishaps or failures.*

In some societies the medicine man or magician claims that by injuring, defiling, or "killing" a small clay or wax likeness of a person he can bring injury, torment, or death to the person whose image it is. The image has to be made in a particular way, according to a long-established rite, which is different in different cultures, and has to be accompanied by a charm or curse which must be voiced according to ritual.

Although there are many interesting details to this particular form of magical practice, the feature that interests us here is that people who believe in it hold that somehow there is an *identity between the image and the person it represents.* The identity is obtained by *naming* the image. Because the two things, person and image, have the same *name,* they are held to be identical so that harm done the image becomes, by that fact, harm done to the person.

Not all magic need be bad; so, by the same token, a curative treatment applied to an image is expected to be effective in the person who bears the same name as the image. But so real is the fear that someone seeking to harm you may name an image after you, that over wide parts of the world people have secret names which must be known to the shamen before his magic can be effective. The ordinary names that people answer to every day are looked upon as pseudonyms.

As this chapter will show later, there are many things and events we, in our own culture, hold to be identical because they bear the same names. We are as guilty of magical belief as the untutored "savage" at whose practice we laugh.

Let us take another example which is more closely related to our own culture. Among the ancient Greeks it was common to arrange dots in certain forms to represent numbers. Thus 1 is .; 2, ..; 3 is 1 + 2 or ∴.; 6 is ∴∴.; 10 is ∴∴∴∴. These numbers and all others that fit into the system were called "triangular numbers." But certain numbers could not be arranged in a system of this kind. The first ones are 4, 9, and 16. They can, however, be arranged in squares ∷ ⦂⦂⦂ ⦂⦂⦂⦂ and were for this reason called "square numbers." Today we know that whether numbers can be arranged in a triangular form or in a square is not important, although we still use "square" to indicate certain useful relations between 2 and 4, 3 and 9, 4 and 16, 5 and 25, etc. We do not use the reference "triangular numbers" any more.

Through analogous processes the Greeks developed notions like these:

odd	even
good	bad
male	female
light	dark
straight	crooked

Now, if we know very little about numbers, the fact that they can be arranged in triangular or square forms might be very striking and that they can be thrown into two series, even and odd, is also striking, but magic enters when we identify other properties such as "goodness" and "badness," "straightness" and "crookedness" with these series.

Another example may help in making the magical practice clearer. In the University of Pennsylvania Museum there are two Sioux shields, one made from buffalo hide having a certain decoration. This shield is a good one. The hide is tough enough to offer substantial protection to the warrior carrying it. The decoration, while pleasing enough in adorning the piece, was held to bear the additional function of protecting the warrior who carried it in battle. The other shield has precisely the same design but is constructed only of thongs. The warrior who carried it would be protected only by the magic symbol. It was thought that he needed no other protection than the magical properties of the design.

In a boys' book on early people, a writer recounts an imaginary but instructive incident. After a hard chase, it is related, a band of hunters, hot and tired, finding a cool cave, rested and slept on the ground leaving one of their number to watch the game. This young fellow sat on a stone outside the cave and felt sorry for himself because he had to sit up while his comrades slept. Next morning all of the band except the watcher were sore in joint and muscle and sniffling with colds. According to their thinking, his magic protected him. In trying to account for the difference between their magic and his, they found only one symbol; the watcher had a deep scar on his left arm. They had none. To have a noticeable scar in that position they thought must be powerful protective magic; so they all gouged themselves deeply in the left arm with stone knives to produce the same happy protection against sore muscles and sniffles. Today the story might be told in terms of vitamins, to say nothing of the charms and symbols or rituals that some people hold to be magically protective.

Magical rites and beliefs rest on faulty observations. If error of observation could be eliminated, there would be no room for magic in our world. It is the business of science to substitute accurate and comprehensive observations for inaccurate and restricted ones. But this is no easy task and, in general, it becomes harder the nearer we get to the everyday affairs of human beings.

It is estimated that today several hundred millions of dollars are spent each year on various fraudulent schemes for analyzing character and personality based on the size of a person's cranium, the type of his profile, or the shape of his hands. The way in which some of these schemes are used is described by Dorothy H. Yates in a book, *Psychological Racketeers*. Every student will want to read this little volume which is a record of a teacher's visits, sometimes in the company of her students, to the various quacks that prey on the gullible.

Most of these quacks are fairly sincere persons. They themselves believe in the doctrines they promote, just as the primitive medicine man believes in his charms, or a mother believes in her home remedies. Lee Steiner makes this interpretation in her book *Where Do*

People Take Their Troubles? (Houghton Mifflin Company, Boston, 1945.)

Most modern befuddled procedures for guidance trace their ancestry to a famous Viennese physician, Franz Joseph Gall, who

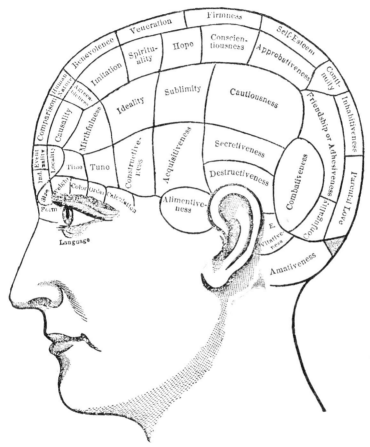

FIG. 1.—A phrenological chart. (After Spurzheim.)

lived a century ago. Dr. Gall's greatest work was a set of books which in some editions ran to six volumes and contained one hundred plates. The title of this voluminous treatise was the *Anatomy and Physiology of the Nervous System, Together with Observations on the Possibility of Determining Mental and Moral Qualities in Men and*

Animals by the Contours of Their Heads, a title almost as detailed as the six-volumed text itself. It contained some sober anatomical investigation. There are parts of the central nervous system that are still known by Gall's name just as there is a Strait of Magellan or a Hudson Bay. At the time Gall worked it was not unreasonable to investigate the *possibility* that mental qualities were related to the contours of skulls. This assumption that there is a relationship between skull contours and personality is called *phrenology*. But Gall soon forgot that he was investigating a possibility. Or, what is truer, he never really comprehended that a belief is only a hypothesis, subject to confirmation or denial in view of the observations.

His first observations of a phrenological kind were made when he was nine years old. He said he had observed that if boys in school had good memories they also invariably had bulging eyes. The "brain," which to a nine-year-old was obviously responsible for the good memories, was back of the eyes and therefore must be pushing them forward.

Aside from his own uncritical observations at age nine, Gall was doubtless influenced by the teachings of the Swiss priest Lavater whose books on physiognomy[1] were widely read about 1800. Physiognomy differed from Gall's phrenology only in ascribing potency to the face rather than to the skull. And Lavater, in turn, was influenced by Theophrastus, pupil of Plato and friend of Aristotle, who wrote of thirty "types" of people in ancient Athens. But Lavater was responsible for a very clear statement of the position of the phrenologists when he wrote, "The cavity of the skull is visibly fitted to the mass of substances it contains and follows their growth at every age of human life. Thus, the exterior form of the brain, which imprints itself perfectly on the internal surface of the skull, is, at the same time, the model of the contours of the exterior surface." Lavater's assertion "sounds" reasonable, but what he did not comprehend is that the assertion is also a hypothesis. It can be tested; he never thought of doing it, but a student today can examine a few skulls in any modern collection in an anatomy department to see that there is no relation

---

[1] Physiognomy has a history extending back to Aristotle, who believed that the principal characteristics of animals were exhibited by human beings whose faces resembled the animal; this is sheer magic, of course.

between the external surface contours and the formation of the brain within. Figure 2 shows how the thickness of the skull wall varies in two different specimens. Figure 2 is of particular importance because

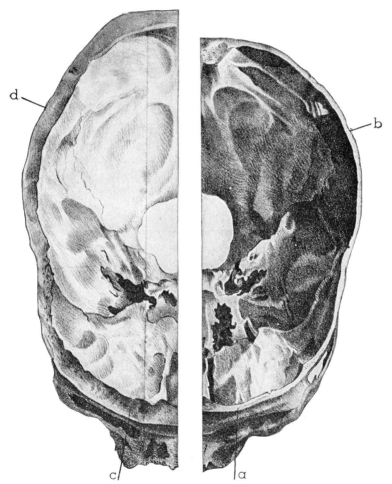

FIG. 2.—A section through a thick-walled skull on the left; a thin-walled skull on the right.

it is taken from a book published in 1839, before there were anatomical collections to make observation easier.

Some further insight into the logic of phrenologists is revealed in Gall's discovery of the seat of what he called "attachment" or

7

"friendship" (Figure 1). He once knew a woman, he said, who was noted for the many friends she had. Since there was a bump at the back of her skull, he believed that the back of the skull must be the determiner of a person's "adhesiveness," as it came to be called. This kind of evidence could be continued for the twenty-odd "organs" that Gall thought he had discovered and the score that were added by his followers. Modern observation shows that there is positively no relation between the *assumed* functions of various parts of the brain and the actual function.

If we refer again to Figure 1 and try to interpret what we see in terms of modern anatomical research, we note no correspondence. Remember that the areas shown in Figure 1 are drawn on the outside of the skull, but the functions of the brain parts immediately underneath are something like this: For Parental Love read "seeing"; for Secretiveness and Destructiveness, read "hearing"; for Hope read, "movements of the toes and feet."

Phrenological advice today, as a hundred years ago, is offered without reservation. A phrenologist just can't be wrong. For example, physicians are said to require "large perceptive organs so that they may study and apply a knowledge of anatomy and physiology with skill and success; full destructiveness, lest they shrink from inflicting pain; large constructiveness, to give them skill in surgery; large combativeness, to render them resolute and prompt." This is only part of the list, but the rest reads in the same vein. *Not a single acceptable shred of evidence is offered to support any of these contentions.* You are expected to believe that the phrenologist, because of some studies about which he is terribly vague, is competent to advise you on what vocation you are best suited for. Suffice it to say here that any psychologist worth listening to is extremely reluctant to offer vocational predictions. He is not able to predict by *any* method, with certainty, how successful a person will be on any job. A beginning has been made on this problem, but there is no certainty about it (see Chapter Four).

In some fields of scientific activity magic has been almost completely eliminated. In astronomy, for instance, where we study events that are farthest removed from human activity, the names of the constellations alone remain to remind us that at one time these constellations were thought to be potent spirits and controlling destinies over human beings. In general, as science steps into a field of inquiry, magic steps out. But not gracefully or willingly.

Magic depends on tradition and belief. It does not welcome observation, nor does it profit by experiment. On the other hand, science is based on experience; it is open to correction by observation and experiment. More detailed knowledge revealed by improved observation becomes the basis of more exact classification and description. These descriptions often contradict everyday experience. They do so because everyday experience is usually based upon superficial and biased observation. Science thus finds itself frequently at odds with common sense.

Science, although a full-grown, mature method of inquiry now, has not always been so. The early scientists established *some* scientific facts, but they also made some horrible misinterpretations of their observations and their scientific honesty was not beyond reproach. In the attempt to transmute the baser metals into gold they were not above adding tiny pellets of real gold to their concoctions in order to impress people with their alchemy. But at the same time their mortars and pestles, their furnaces, their retorts, their methods of crushing, grinding, burning, boiling, and decanting finally resulted in detailed information about the physical properties of natural substances based on accurate observation. They could not have used these methods for long without ultimately finding some scientific truth.

In a general way, whatever we accept as true depends on the methods we choose to ascertain the truth. What appears to be true using one method of inquiry may turn out to be false when we use a different method of "arriving at the facts." It is for this very reason, that *method* is so important, that his book was written. In it we attempt to go back of the statements made in textbooks to find how the textbook fact was determined in the first place. Most texts for practical reasons can spend but little time on methods, so that when a student finds a fact that is contrary to his previous instruction or belief in a book, he resists the new and contradictory fact until he satisfies himself that the new fact is based on some sound method of procedure. Most of the time he will find that his previous belief was based on what is called "common sense," what "seems reasonable," what he was told by somebody, or what "everybody knows."

In the field of human interrelations—the area in which psychologists concern themselves most—magic is today being crowded out of the picture only slowly. The pressure of scientific achievement in the field has increased tremendously since the turn of the century, but the accomplishment based on sound observation is by no means final.

There are really two problems: one is to educate, to inform people about what is known; and the other is to push the frontiers of sound knowledge further ahead. This book is devoted to both of these problems. It is addressed to college students, a group of people highly selected from the general population. It cannot, therefore, achieve any substantial effect on the outlook and practices of the large body of our people, but it does propose to inform the few who will be in a position of influence and authority tomorrow. At the same time it is designed to point to areas in which knowledge is not complete, and from the few who read the book one or two may perceive the dimensions of the job ahead and find some satisfaction in matching their professional stature against its proportions.

CHAPTER TWO

PSYCHOLOGY AND THE METHODS OF SCIENCE

In the previous chapter it was stated that the method used in collecting our data or "facts" is all-important. Now we shall go even further and state that the makings of a science are not in the materials it studies, but in the very methods it uses in studying these materials.

The early alchemist, working over his charcoal blaze with mortar and pestle and retort, was not a scientist, though he was working with chemicals. The tribal medicine man with his drums and masks and incantations cannot be placed in the same catagory as Pasteur, though he, like Pasteur, was trying to find a cure for illness. The medieval scholars who turned to the books of Aristotle to settle their disputes about the nature of the universe instead of turning to the universe itself, may have been educated men and brilliant men, but they were not scientists. Science comes to a subject matter only when those who are interested in this subject matter are willing to investigate its characteristics by employing certain methods and techniques.

What is the nature of these methods of science? Actually they are not in themselves either mystical or abstruse as some of the movies would lead one to suspect. They sound like common sense, but unfortunately common sense neglects them more often than not.

In the first instance the scientific procedure requires some systematic approach to the problem to be solved. Ordinarily this systematic approach takes the form of a hypothesis or theory. The theory should be specifically stated in such terms that predictions of concrete events can be made from it. The theorist should be able to state that, according to the theory, and under the stated conditions, such and such an event or relationship should occur; and also, such and such an event or relationship should *not* occur. Once such statements can be made, the theory can be put to a test.

In the process of testing this theory one must start by making a careful and objective collection of *all* the data which are considered appropriate to the theory. This apparently simple demand is too often disregarded. People become so wrapped up in their own theories that they want very much to prove them true. There is nothing wrong in this except that what we see is often governed by what we want to see. The result is that a person may disregard data which cannot be explained by his theory, and except only the material which fits into it. He may not know he is doing this, but he may do it, nevertheless. It is for this reason—that our biases can easily determine what will be seen—that a science requires the experimenter to collect *all* the data, and to employ an objective and impersonal method of collecting it. Only in this manner can we be sure that the report reflects what has truly occurred and not what some theorist expects should have occurred.

The group of experiments which are presented in this chapter illustrate this objective method of collecting data. For many years assertions about the relationship of personality traits and certain physical characteristics have been made. Much argument both pro and con has occurred, but no clear answer could be given as long as the methods of evaluating the theory were muddled and ambiguous. The first two experiments of the chapter show how modern psychological methods of investigation can attack this controversial problem and give an answer which can be accepted with considerable confidence. The third experiment turns to an entirely different field—the field of aviation—and illustrates how scientific methodology can be used to increase human efficiency by decreasing flying hazards. The student, as he reads these experiments, should contrast the methods they employ with the happy-go-lucky sort that he may have been inclined to use in the past. The definite superiority of the scientific approach to an unsystematic collection of data will be obvious.

1. BLOND AND BRUNET TRAITS

Another effort to find an easy short cut to the very complicated task of describing or predicting personality is similar to Gall's phrenology in its assumption of the existence of a parallel between psychological and physical traits. It was briefly mentioned in the previous chapter and it is called *physiognomy*. It is a more sophisticated system than phrenology. Today the phrenologist is apt to be a fly-by-night who rents a vacant store for a week, hangs his oilcloth phrenology chart in the window, and plies his art for a modest fee. The physiognomist fares better; he may even reach the status of a personnel consultant in a reputable business. His system does not rest solely upon skull shape, but on the assumption that all types of bodily characteristics, but especially of the face, are associated with certain psychological traits. He might hold that a coarseness of skin texture is associated with coarseness of character, and fine texture is paralleled by fine-grained feelings; or again, that close-set eyes are a sign of the thief.

Paterson and Ludgate[1] found one physiognomist[2] who described traits supposed to be related to color of the skin and hair with such detail that the traits and alleged relation to complexion could be studied experimentally. Most physiognomists are not consistent. Their work will stand no careful comparison of what is said on one page with what is announced on another. Blackford held that blonds "always and everywhere" are positive, dynamic, driving, aggressive, domineering, impatient, active, quick, hopeful, speculative, changeable, and variety-loving. Brunets present just exactly the opposite of these traits: They are negative, static, conservative, imitative, submissive, cautious, painstaking, patient, ploddy, slow, deliberate, serious, thoughtful, and specializing. On the basis of these and other physiognomical relations, Blackford made sweeping generalizations relating to vocational guidance.

In order to subject these claims to experimental test, Paterson and Ludgate prepared a sheet of paper on which the twenty-six traits were listed in random order. These papers were given to a group of students who were asked to select from among their acquaintances two blonds and two brunets. In four separate columns, one for each person rated, they were to place check marks if it could be said that the person under consideration could be described by the adjective supplied. In this way judgments were made on 187 blonds and 187 brunets.

After these sheets were collected the results were tabulated and percentages computed as shown in the table.

[1] Donald G. Paterson and Katherine E. Ludgate. "Blonde and Brunette Traits: A Quantitative Study," *Journal of Personnel Research*, 1922, 1, 122-27.
[2] Katherine M. H. Blackford and A. Newcomb, *The Job, the Man, the Boss*, 1919, p. 141.

	Per Cent Required by the Hypothesis		Per Cent of 187 Actually Who Were Said to Be Described by the Adjective	
	Blond	Brunet	Blond	Brunet
Blond traits				
Positive...............	100	0	81	84
Dynamic...............	100	0	63	64
Aggressive..............	100	0	49	50
Domineering............	100	0	36	36
Impatient..............	100	0	56	51
Brunet traits				
Negative...............	0	100	16	17
Static..................	0	100	28	31
Conservative............	0	100	51	61
Imitative...............	0	100	39	40
Submissive.............	0	100	25	26

We reproduced only part of the data. The remainder tells the same story. In order for the hypothesis to be substantiated in the positive and dogmatic way in which it is stated, it is necessary that we have numbers closely approximating one hundred under the word "Blond" for the five blond traits. In this same column these numbers should drop to very close to zero with a corresponding rise in the brunet column and they should be very close to zero in the upper right-hand quarter of the table. None of these conditions obtains. *We must conclude that there is no relationship between the adjective that a group of judges will use to describe a person's behavior and the kind of complexion he has.*

For several years this little exercise was required of beginning Ohio State University students and in no instance was a relationship between complexion and behavior shown to exist. Paterson and Ludgate's results are uniformly substantiated; Blackford's claims are uniformly negated.

In a more complicated study Cleeton and Knight[3] were able to

[3] G. U. Cleeton and F. B. Knight, "Validity of Character Judgments Based on External Criteria," *Journal of Applied Psychology,* 1924, 8, 215-29.

examine intensively the relationship between the physical characteristics of face and hand, and the behavior that would be described as
judgment, leadership, originality, or impulsiveness in thirty different
subjects. These psychological investigators ran into the problem of
measuring "psychological traits," like frankness, that the physiognomists so glibly talk about as though there were complete agreement on
what these labels refer to. Just what is a "frank" person? What kinds
of things do frank people say and do that establish their frankness?
How completely do people agree in their judgments on abstract
qualities of this kind? Cleeton and Knight solved their problem by
allowing only intimate acquaintances to make the ratings. They
then pooled the ratings of several different raters in such a way that
they were fairly certain that another group of raters describing individual John Jones, one of their thirty subjects, would say the same
things about him. *Technically this procedure is known as establishing
the reliability of their ratings.*

They secured 122 physical measures on each of their thirty subjects and then made comparisons between the ratings and the 122
physiognomical signs. In all the 201 comparisons which they could
make from their data not a single relationship could be found. In
fact, their data were so monotonously regular in exhibiting no relationship that we will not reproduce them here.

2. GRAPHOLOGY

The same use of analogy that we have seen in phrenology and
physiognomy is evident in the work of people who claim to be able
to read a person's character by the kind of handwriting he exhibits.

"Graphology" is a word used to refer to three distinct kinds of
activity. First, it is commonly used to label the persons who are
interested in detecting forged documents and the like. That is a
story entirely apart from psychology. Then, those who consider handwriting a kind of expressive movement, like the gestures that a
person uses, have used the word to cover their special interest. That
story is the interest principally of the social psychologists.[4] Although
the experimental work from this angle is of the highest caliber, we

[4] G. W. Allport and P. E. Vernon, *Studies in Expressive Movement*, The Macmillan
Company, New York, 1933.

cannot go into it here. The third, the oldest, and the most common use of the word "graphology" is as a label to the unproved assertion that the character and handwriting are related. This kind of graphology may hold that ambition is related to lines that slope upward; pride is related to lines that slope downward; bashfulness to fine lines; force with heavy lines; perserverance with long bars on t's; and reserve with closed a's and o's. The use of the crudest kind of analogy here is self-evident.

Hull and Montgomery[5] have subjected these latter claims to experimental test, using as subjects seventeen members of a medical fraternity at the University of Wisconsin. Each man was asked to write in his own manner, in his own room, at his own desk, and with his own pen, a paragraph from a popular magazine.

When he had finished writing, each subject was supplied with a set of sixteen small cards, each containing the name of one of the other subjects. The subject was directed to arrange the cards in the order in which the sixteen subjects ranged according to ambition, putting the most "ambitious" person first and the least ambitious last. The rank thus accorded to each of the other subjects was recorded by the experimenter. Then the cards were carefully shuffled and given to the subject again. This time he ranked his fraternity brothers in "pride."

From the seventeen rankings obtained in this way, an average position for each subject on each of six traits was obtained. These measures constituted the best estimate that could be made of the graphologist's traits of ambition, pride, bashfulness, force, perseverance, and reserve. It remained to measure the slope of the line, the fineness of the lines, the length of the t's, and the open or closed character of the o's and a's and to relate these measures to the character ratings.

When these comparisons were made *there was not a single item that showed any consistent relationship to the estimates of character by seventeen judges who were intimately acquainted with the people they were judging.*

[5] Clark L. Hull and Robert Montgomery, "An Experimental Investigation of Certain Alleged Relations between Character and Handwriting," *Psychological Review*, 1919, 26, 63-74.

The only conclusion possible is that the graphologists who assert a relationship between handwriting and character or behavior traits based on analogies of the one with the other are sadly in error. In order to protect one's self against the charlatans in this field it is only necessary to ask for an objective demonstration of the relation which the graphologist asserts. If the only evidence forthcoming is the authority of the graphologist, one may safely conclude that he doesn't know what he is talking about, however persuasive he may appear.

Summary of the two experiments. Efforts to understand human nature have not always been scientific. The systems of phrenology, physiognomy, and graphology that we have examined in this and the previous chapter typify any pseudo-scientific system—under whatever name—advanced by whatever self-styled psychologist today. These systems are nonscientific because they make no use whatever of the scientific method. Their proponents do not develop hypotheses which can be tested for truth, nor do they make any effort to formulate the kinds of hypotheses that are susceptible to testing. They assume the truth of their hypotheses at the outset: their hypotheses become dicta backed only by the authority that the charlatans are able to muster.

To the uncritical and the untrained this authority always carries a good deal of weight because it is supported by what seems to be an exact accuracy of statement. But this accuracy turns out to be a pseudo accuracy accomplished in three ways: first, the generalizations are so broad that they have to be true to a degree; second, the generalizations are flattering, never critical; third, they are supported by selecting cases that demonstrate or illustrate the dictum—other specific cases that do not fit are glossed over or ignored. By the proper selection of instances one can prove anything at all true provided somebody doesn't ask, "And how about all these other instances?" The charlatan has to evade this question.

The charlatan employs principally the logical method of analogy. There is nothing wrong with the method, but the analogies are made on the basis of superficial resemblances between nonexistent psychological traits like "force" and immaterial properties like "breadth of stroke" in handwriting.

The modern psychologist with adequate training in the scientific method would urge, as a substitute for these engaging short cuts to understanding human nature, the long and rigorous road which scientific method and principles provide. Science is a hard taskmistress.

3. EVALUATION OF AIRCRAFT INSTRUMENTS

The development of almost any modern piece of equipment is often a gradual process of moving from the simple to the complicated. Modern aircraft has shown such a history as the first plane of the Wright brothers gradually evolved into the modern four-motored bomber or transport. Associated with the increased performance of the modern plane there is, of course, an increase in the number of controls that the pilot must operate. His attention can no longer be limited to stick, rudder, and throttle; it must shift, rapidly and accurately, from one control to another. He is often required to reach toward a group of closely bunched levers and select the appropriate one while his eyes are turned in another direction. Errors of choosing the wrong control have produced many accidents, the most common of which results from confusing the landing flaps and landing gear controls.

Such confusion is inevitable if we require persons to make hurried responses to stimuli which are not readily distinguishable. The fact that instrument panels have been developed which do not take adequate account of the limitation of human capacity simply means that proper scientific psychological methods were not employed in choosing the instrument design. The decision as to what sort of design to use was not based upon scientifically collected data, but on common-sense guesses.

In the following experiment by Jenkins[6] we have an example of how the application of scientific methods in psychological research can result in designing a psychologically better control which might mean the difference between life and death.

Method. A group of twenty-five different plastic shapes of a size that could be used as knobs on levers were mounted on a turntable. The

[6] W. O. Jenkins, "The Tactual Discrimination of Shapes for Coding Aircraft-Type Control." Army Air Forces Aviation Psychology Program Research Report. Psychological Research on Equipment Design Report No. 19, Paul M. Fitts (ed.), U.S. Government Printing Office, 1947, Washington, D. C.

shapes and their mountings are shown in Figure 3. The subject was seated, blindfolded, and presented with one of the knobs which he felt for one second. The turntable was then rotated to a predetermined location, and the subject felt knob after knob until he found one

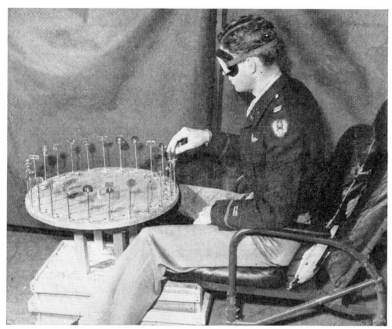

Fig. 3.—The experimental setup used in determining the degree of confusion between various knob shapes. (Courtesy of Dr. P. M. Fitts.)

which he thought was the test knob. Each of the shapes was tested in this fashion, once with bare hand and once with a flying glove on. Forty Army Air Forces pilots were tested, twenty being first tested under the gloved condition, and twenty taking the first test with bare hands.

Results. The record which the experimenter obtained consisted of the number of times a shape was confused with other shapes, and what were the particular shapes with which it was confused. When these errors are plotted in the systematic manner that is shown in Figure 4, a precise evaluation of each shape is possible. The figure is

19

read in this way: knob 16 is confused twice with knob 20, three times with knob 7, and so on. Shape 2 is confused once with shape 3, fourteen times with shape 20, and so forth. The two heavy squares in the figure mark off a group of eight knobs which are seldom con-

	16	2	6	17	15	1	13	14	4	10	3	20	25	8	7	9	24	11	23	22	18	5	19	21	12
16											2				3				1	1			2		
2											1	14				1							1	1	1
6											1					5									30
17												4				11		21				1			
15					1					18	2											11	2	23	1
1					1					2	2			28			1			1				1	1
13		1										7				9		4	1				1	1	
14	1	1	1							10						2			2		2				
4					1			3								8					2	17	3	9	4
10		1	1	16	1	1										1					2	5	5	32	
3				1																25	2	1	1	1	6
20		29												2			6	4				1			1
25		2	1		2				1							1		11	1	1					
8	2		1		15						2										2	1		1	2
7	2	6	1								2			2		1		2				2			
9			5		14					2			1			1		16							
24			1		2					7	1												7		3
11			1	15	1				4	1			5	1	1	2							1		
23	3	1							2	2	2			6		1		1		2	1	1		1	
22		1	1		2					36	1											1	7	1	7
18				1	1	3				12	8			1		1	6			3			2	6	2
5				11	1					1	27					2				1	1	4	7	5	2
19		1	1		3		1	1	1	4	1		1				1	1		7	3	7	4	2	1
21			1	1	36					1	33									3	1	2	7	1	
12	1	1	25							12	1				7	1		1		2	3	1	1	1	1

Δ560-AML

Fig. 4.—A graphic representation of the results of the experiment. (Courtesy of Dr. P. M. Fitts.)

fused among themselves. The group in the upper left-hand corner is the best; for no knob is confused with any other more than once. The middle square is not quite so satisfactory.

Summary of the experiment. The results of this rather simple experiment show how the method of science can be applied to a problem of human efficiency. By selecting the appropriate family of knobs it would be possible to set up aircraft levers so that errors of identification could be reduced. The pilot could distinguish one control from another not only because it was in a slightly different position, but because the shape of one knob differed from another. This potential improvement in efficiency was achieved by systematically recording all the responses to the group of knobs. With these data available the experimenter *knew* which knobs were confusing and which were not. Had such a planned experimental procedure been used years earlier, confusion between certain controls could have been predicted, and many costly accidents might have been avoided.

Summary of the chapter. It is hoped that this chapter will serve to give the reader some appreciation of the great power of the scientific method of collecting data completely, and in such a way that the personal bias of the experimenter is removed. In the experiments on physiognomy and graphology all subjects were rated on all traits. In the Cleeton and Knight and also the Hull and Montgomery experiments the persons who measured the physical characteristics were not the same ones as those who rated the psychological characteristics. In this manner a bias either for or against the theory could not affect the results. This might have happened if a person held a strong belief one way or another about the theory and then rated both the physical and the psychological characteristics. Under the objective and unbiased scrutiny that this experiment affords, the presumed relationship between these physical and psychological traits vanished.

The last experiment partly indicates how society has only belatedly come to use the methods of science in its evaluation of human capacities. The aeronautical engineer would not fail to test a new kind of spark plug or cable, but he might make an instrument that the pilot could not use efficiently. When scientific psychological principles are applied, however, it is possible to give the pilot a more efficient environment in which to work, just as it is possible to give him more efficient engines for his craft. By the use of these methods guesswork can be eliminated and replaced with experimentally determined predictions in which we can place confidence.

CHAPTER THREE

THE PRINCIPLE OF CONTROL

The materials of the previous chapter may have led the student to believe that all the scientific psychologist needs is to collect data in an objective and unbiased manner. This is not enough; he must go a step further. He must arrange the circumstances under which the data are being collected so that an unambiguous interpretation of the reasons for the trends in the data can be reached. Consider this example:

The intelligence tests which were given to the American soldiers during World War I indicated that certain races and nationalities were markedly inferior to others in their test performance. Furthermore, investigation of these races and nationalities showed that the environment in which most of them had been raised was inferior to the average American environment both economically and culturally. Is the inferiority due to some hereditary characteristic associated with the race and nationality, or is it due to the poor environment in which these groups had lived? Since the groups differed from the American population both in racial or national origin as well as in home environment, it is impossible to state which of these factors is responsible for their lower intelligence-test performance. Here we have an instance where the data are objective in the way they were collected and scored, but where the circumstances under which they were obtained make it impossible to determine the reason for the trend in the score.

The reader has probably arrived at the conclusion that the solution to the why of the obtained differences in intelligence in the above example could be reached only if these races or nationalities were brought up in an average American environment. Another way of saying this is that we must control or eliminate every other condition except race or nationality that might make for a difference in intelligence.

If the statement is generalized so that it does not refer only to intelligence or races and nationalities, but to any other psychological condition, it is a fairly good description of what the psychologist tries to do when he sets up an experiment.

In the technical language of science we employ two words which are of considerable importance in experimentation. One is "variable" and the other is "control." The term "variable" is similar to the word "cause" as used by many people. You might say that crime is caused by neglectful parents, poverty and the social and physical environment of the slums, low intelligence, or some sort of personality abnormality. In scientific language one would say that crime is a function of the following variables: neglectful parents, poverty, slum environment, low intelligence, or personality abnormality. The term "variable" is preferable to "cause" for many reasons which cannot be explained here.

Now in the ordinary course of events any particular kind of behavior arises in a very complex environment. Criminals may come from poverty-stricken homes, from slum areas, from families where the parents are neglectful or low in intelligence. They may also come from homes which are poorly painted, or from an environment whose atmosphere is heavily laden with soot. It is very likely that someone could make an analysis of the atmosphere from areas which have high delinquency rates and by comparing it with the atmosphere in low-delinquency areas, show that crime was related to atmospheric conditions. He could even support his facts with a fine theory of how the blackened air had blackened the residents' hearts and turned them to crime.

To most of us his fact finding and statistics would appear utterly ridiculous. We would point out that the results were simply due to the fact that slum areas tend to be located near industrial activities with their inevitable soot and grime. We would say that the nature of the atmosphere is not a real cause of crime, but it just happens to occur along with many other important factors. However, the soot theorist could continue to collect data showing high delinquency rates in sooty areas, and you could argue against his theory until you were blue in the face without convincing him he was wrong.

The only manner in which you could prove a point against him would be to conduct an experiment in which a *control group* was introduced. Your real argument is that soot is not a real variable of delinquency but that it just happens to be associated with other true variables. You would wish to find an area wherein all the other conditions—poverty, crowded housing, irresponsible parents, and so forth —are present but soot is absent, and compare that with an area which has all these and soot in addition. You would then be controlling the variable of soot and determining whether it alone is necessary for delinquency. You could control it also by finding a situation in which soot alone is present, without any of the other conditions, and determine the crime rate there. If, then, you found that soot could be present without crime, or that it could be eliminated from certain areas or types of areas without decreasing the crime rate, then you could show that it is not a pertinent variable in the production of crime.

In the following sections of this chapter several experiments showing different uses of the control will be presented. It will be worth the reader's time to try to predict the type of control group which should be run for each experiment before the description of the control is given. It will also be a good lesson to him in scientific thinking to recall the many instances in daily life when he has named one variable as the cause for a certain kind of behavior when several others could also be operating.

1. LATIN

It is frequently observed, and correctly, that students who take Latin in high school are abler than those who don't. But to go a step further and say that they are abler *because* they take Latin is not justified. This inference was shown to be false by a study made about thirty years ago.[1] (This is not the only evidence available, but it is one of the simplest demonstrations.) The grades received in English by Iowa City High School students who were taking Latin or German, but not both, were compared. There were 184 in the Latin group and 120 in the German group. The grades were first converted into points and the median number of points in English for the 184 Latin students was computed for the first year's work. This turned out to be somewhat above a B, in the A B C D E system of marking. The same

[1] J. M. Wilcox, "The Effect of Latin on High School Grades," *School and Society,* 1917, 6, 58-60.

operation for the German group gave a number midway between a B and C. This result was for the first year's work. For the second and succeeding years the same condition obtained. These results can best be shown by a graph, from which it is clear that the Latin students as a group are superior in English marks to the German students, *and*

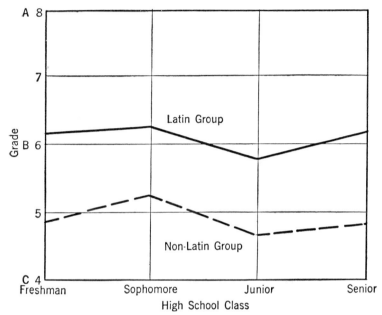

Fig. 5.—The difference between the median grades of high school students who are taking Latin and those who are not. Notice that the same difference that is present in the senior year is also obvious in the freshman year.

that the superiority does not increase as the four years are completed. It is, we should agree, a reasonable expectation that if Latin is effective in making English grades better, then more of it should have more effect. No such condition was demonstrated. The superiority found in the freshman year extended unchanged through the senior year; it did not become greater as time went on. This can only mean that a selected group decided to take Latin in the first place.

This little demonstration illustrates one of the first principles of scientific procedure as applied to psychological problems: the most *obvious factors are not always the effective ones in producing a result.*

In this case a hidden cause, the selection of abler people, was the factor which produced the superiority, not the Latin experience itself. We have to be constantly on the lookout for hidden factors of this kind. For instance, it has been asserted recently that certain kinds of nursery-school and kindergarten training actually heightened the intelligence level of the children who take part in these activities. The controversy over whether this is true or not has hinged on the adequacy of the control over this selective factor. It may be that more intelligent children are enrolled in nursery schools to begin with. If anyone wants to determine which one of these alternative explanations accounts for the fact that nursery school children *do* score higher in general on intelligence tests, he will have to be particularly careful to obtain a comparable group of children who are not in nursery school but who are equal in ability to the nursery-school group at the beginning of the experiment.

2. THE DEVELOPMENT OF WALKING

A very important area of research in psychology is directed toward determining the extent to which the development of a skill—walking, for example—is dependent on learning and exercise, and the extent to which it is simply the product of a growing nervous system and a muscular system. To answer such a question experimental procedure would demand that a group of children be brought up with little or no exercise and tested to discover when they would begin to walk. Their score could then be compared with that of a group of children who were not restricted in this manner, and the answer obtained.

Such a procedure is hardly feasible in our society, but a method of child rearing which results in considerable restriction of movement is found in some Hopi Indian villages. This method involves the use of the cradle board. The child is strapped securely to the board soon after birth, and spends most of the time on the board, being released only a short time each day for bathing and changing.

Dennis and Dennis[2] reasoned that a study of the age of onset of

[2] Wayne Dennis and Marcina G. Dennis, "The Effect of Cradling Practice upon the Onset of Walking in Hopi Children." *Journal of Genetic Psychology,* 1940, 56, 77-86.

walking in these children would give some indication of how exercise operated in determining the age at which walking would occur. Accordingly they went to a Hopi village and obtained data on the average age of occurrence of walking for sixty-three children. This proved to be 14.95 months. This is several months later than the age for the average American population.

Had the Dennises terminated their study at this point, they would probably have concluded that restriction of movement retards walking. However, they went on to obtain data from an adjacent Hopi village where the cradle-board practice was no longer employed. For this group of forty-two children the average age was 15.05 months, or essentially the same as that for the group which had its movements restricted in early life. This new group is called a "control group," and it is like the "experimental group" in all respects except that no cradle board was employed.

The Dennises were forced to conclude that the amount of restriction of movement that the cradle board entailed was not sufficient to retard walking. If the control group had not been available they might, using the average American norms as their base line, have rashly concluded otherwise.

Just why their two Hopi groups were slower in developing the skill of walking cannot be said. Their diet is different from the usual American diet, they live in a higher altitude, and, of course, they come from a different racial stock. Any of these, all of them, or some other unidentified variable may have caused the difference.

Summary of the two studies. Aside from the factual outcome of these two studies, we have also learned two fundamental methodological principles. First, *the most obvious factors in a situation are not, simply because they are obvious, the effective factors* in accounting for a result. As a matter of fact, it might be said that *all science everywhere has been concerned principally with discovering the non-evident causes of natural phenomena.* To be scientifically sophisticated means, among other things, to be skeptical about any generally accepted cause which is supposed to be self-evident and therefore not to require rigorous proof. To elaborate on this point would take us too far afield, but as we proceed to present the many experiments that make up this book it would be well to consider each of them in the light of this generalization.

The second principle we have learned can be called the *Principle of Control*. In planning an experiment we must have some basis of comparison. This usually, but not always, means that a control group has to be organized. *The control group has the same properties as the experimental group except one, that one being the factor under consideration.*

These principles are easy to learn, but to apply them is a difficult accomplishment. The selection of a control group is not easy, a fact upon which we shall comment from time to time. The principal difficulty is that we never can be *absolutely certain* that the control is sufficiently similar to the experimental group to be considered identical with it.

3. LEARNING TO RECOGNIZE AIRCRAFT

The control groups which were employed in the first two experiments served a function which was primarily negative in nature. They showed that the results were not due to the most obvious psychological variable—the study of Latin or cradle-board restriction. Control groups are not always employed in this fashion. Oftentimes in science we make a prediction from a theory that if conditions were arranged in a certain way a certain kind of result would occur. We might predict that under these conditions the subjects would learn better or worse, their intelligence-test performance would increase or decrease, their ability to discriminate colors would improve, or that they would turn to the right rather than to the left in a maze.

When such predictions are made it is necessary to set up an experiment to test their validity. The design for such an experiment will involve two separate groups of subjects or, in some cases, more. The *experimental group* will be trained or tested under the condition that will result, according to the theory, in some increase or decrease in performance. The *control group* will be trained or tested without this condition. A comparison of the performance of the control and experimental groups will show just how effective this particular condition—it is the *variable*—is. In this manner the theory is put to test. A study which was conducted during the past war demonstrates this type of experiment.[3]

This experimenter's task was to discover the most efficient ways of training future pilots in the recognition of aircraft. Of course it was not possible to fly all the different kinds of planes, both Allied and enemy, so that the future pilot could learn to recognize them in that manner. Instead slides and motion pictures were used. A common training technique employed during the latter stages of the war was to call out the name of the plane, then show a slide of it for a period of several seconds while the name of the plane was called out again. The instructor would then pass on to another plane and treat it in the same manner.

Now psychologists have reason to believe that one of the most effective ways of learning is to require the subject to make a response and then to discover almost immediately whether the response was correct or incorrect. The above-mentioned method of training does not force this behavior on the subject; he is not required to guess what the plane is but can sit back passively and be told what it is. The theory which this experiment puts to test is that learning will be better if the subject has been required to guess the plane and then discover whether he was right or wrong.

Method. The individuals who served as subjects in the experiment were aviation trainees at an Army air base. They were divided into two groups, a control and an experimental group. A group of twenty slides showing various foreign planes which were unfamiliar to the men was selected. Actually the extent to which any of these planes were known by the men was checked before the experiment began and anyone who knew as many as two was not used in the experiment.

The group of twenty plane slides was presented a total of four times for both groups. The first presentation was alike for each group. The name of the plane was called out and the slide was shown for five seconds while its name was called again. This same procedure was used with the control group on trials two and three. The experi-

[3] Army Air Forces Aviation Psychology Program Research Reports. "Motion Picture Testing and Research," Report No. 7, James J. Gibson (ed.), U.S. Government Printing Office, Washington 25, D. C., 1947.

mental group, however, was treated differently during these two trials. The plane was shown for 2.5 seconds and after this each subject tried to identify the plane. Then it was presented again for 2.5 seconds and its name was called out by the instructor. The fourth trial was the same for both groups. The slide was shown for 2.5 seconds and the men wrote down the name of the plane they thought it to be. This gave the experimenters a measure of what each group learned. The plan of this experiment is shown in the table below. You will notice that the two groups were treated *exactly* alike except for the variable of making the experimental group guess the plane's name during trials two and three. The initial period of introduction was the same, the total amount of time the plane was shown was the same, and the test situation was the same.

Trial One	Trial Two	Trial Three	Trial Four
Control Group a. Name b. Plane (5 sec.) with name	a. Name b. Plane (5 sec.) with name	Same as in Two	a. Plane (2.5 sec.) b. Written response
Experimental Group a. Name b. Plane (5 sec.) with name	a. Plane (2.5 sec.) b. Response attempted c. Plane (2.5 sec.) with name	Same as in Two	a. Plane (2.5 sec.) b. Written response

Results. The results of the experiment supported the prediction of the experimenter that forcing a response by the subject and confirming or correcting it immediately will result in superior learning. This is shown in the following table.

	No. of Individuals	Average Correct Score	Per Cent of Men Getting All Slides Correct
Control group............	149	10.49	2.7
Experimental group........	131	14.56	13.7

4. LEGIBILITY OF NEWSPAPER HEADLINES

One of the quickest ways to start an argument in a newspaper office or a printing plant is to deny that a line set in capital letters is more legible than the same line set in capital and lower-case characters. Everyone dealing with type faces and sizes seems to have his favorite size and style. One of the common beliefs is that newspaper headlines ought to be set in all caps because they are large and will be more readily seen.

Breland and Breland,[4] working at the University of Minnesota, have made a hypothesis out of this belief and have subjected it to experimental test. They prepared 120 five-word single-column headlines taken from *The New York Times* for comparison by having them set by a printer first in capital and lower case and again in all capitals.

Headline No.	Set Aa	Set aA
1	PARAGUAY OBJECTS TO BOLIVIAN PLAN	Paraguay Objects to Bolivian Plan
2	Cocker Spaniels Lead Breed List	COCKER SPANIELS LEAD BREED LIST

The headlines were printed on cards which were placed in a common laboratory device called a tachistoscope which shows them to a subject for a fraction of a second, in this case 1/20. The apparatus is used to assure that the subject will get "a glance" at the headline, but a measured "glance," and the same measure for each subject.

The odd-numbered subjects—there were twenty-two altogether—saw Set aA and the even-numbered subjects saw Set Aa, containing the same text, but with the opposite members in solid capitals.

The results were so distinctly in favor of the lower-case, or small-letter headlines, that there is no question about the interpretation.[5]

---

[4] K. Breland and M. K. Breland, "Legibility of Newspaper Headlines Printed in Capitals and in Lower Case," *Journal of Applied Psychology*, 1944, 28, 117-120.

[5] Students in advertising and journalism particularly will be interested in finding the more elaborate details of this and other experiments on legibility in D. G. Paterson and M. A. Tinker, *How to Make Type Readable*, Harper & Brothers, New York, 1940, especially pp. 22-25. Also see D. G. Paterson and M. A. Tinker, "Readability of Newspaper Headlines Printed in Capitals and Lower Case," *Journal of Applied Psychology*, 1946, 30, 161-168.

31

Since the difference was in favor of the lower-case type, which was admittedly smaller, there did not seem to be any reason to use a larger type size, in order to make the lower case about the same size as the capitals. *Even with the size difference in favor of the capitals there was a loss of legibility of 18.9 per cent.*

This simple experiment presents two problems of control: First, a comparison had to be provided between the capitals and lower-case characters. This means that the headlines had to be made up of the same words but printed differently. This constitutes the first control. But if a single subject had read the headline once, in either style he would automatically be disqualified from serving as a subject for the other style, because he would be getting a "second glance."

This necessitated a second control, the division of the twenty-two subjects into two groups so that the group as a whole would be seeing the identical headlines in the two styles, but paradoxically no individual member of it would be seeing the same thing twice. The fundamental assumption here is that the eleven subjects composing the odd-numbered members are sufficiently like the eleven composing the even-numbered half that the *groups* can be compared even though the *individuals* composing them could not be.

Summary of the two experiments. Although both of these experiments employed control groups, the particular way they were formed differs in the two experiments. The first experiment is simple and straightforward; the control group was composed of one group of men, and the experimental of another. When such a method is employed, it should be noted that the experimenter makes the assumption that the basic abilities of the two groups as a whole are alike. If both groups learned under the same conditions, the experimenter would assume that they would obtain the same average score. When a fairly large number of persons are used in each group there is nothing wrong in making such an assumption. Sometimes we even use devices to make fairly certain that the two groups are equal; we might equate the groups for intelligence, age, knowledge about planes, or whatever is pertinent to what we are measuring.

In the second experiment each subject contributes data to both the experimental and the control condition. He reads some headlines which are all in capitals and some which were in lower case, for these are not really two groups, but the same subject performing under two conditions. Such a method avoids any assumption about equality of the two groups. This type of control is frequently used in tests of the effects of drugs or oxygen deprivation, the subject being tested first in one condition then in another. Offhand this method would seem to be superior to the first, but that is not always so. Many times it is very cumbersome and time-consuming. Furthermore, in many instances it cannot be used if testing in one condition will influence performance in the other. Suppose we wished to discover how some variable affected the rate of learning of a particular skill such as walking. Once the subject has learned to walk, he cannot be used again, for he already possesses the skill. In this case groups composed of different subjects are essential.

There is one other point that should be discussed before we leave these experiments. Both were carefully planned before they were done. Everything which occurred during the experiment was determined by the experimenter. In this respect they differ from the experiments on Latin and on the development of walking, for in these studies the experimenter simply made use of events which had previously occurred. Typically our laboratory experiments have the characteristic of being planned and controlled in advance, though when we study behavior in the natural life situation we are often required to work with the experimental situation that the natural course of events has given us.

5. ROD DIVINING

The four examples described above have made use of groups of people, but not all experiments are of this kind. Sometimes a single person is studied in considerable detail. The following experiment illustrates this fact and further elaborates the Principle of Control. Here an experimenter, Foster,[6] made a detailed study of the claims of a rod diviner. A rod diviner, or dowser, is one who claims to be able to locate water and minerals under the surface of the ground

---

[6] W. S. Foster, "Experiments on Rod Divining," *Journal of Applied Psychology*, 1923, 7, 303-311.

by the dipping of a branch held in his hands.[7] Generally a Y-shaped branch of a willow tree is used. Held in the two hands by the two shorter parts, it is extended horizontally in front of the diviner. As he moves across the area where it is hoped water will be found, the rod suddenly dips at a fairly precise spot and the well diggers are instructed to go ahead. The diviner claims that he has no part in the movements of the rod, but that, under the influence of subsurface conditions, it bends sharply downward in ways that he cannot control.

A seventy-year-old diviner called at the Psychological Laboratory of the University of Minnesota and asked that his "powers" of divining be subjected to experimental test. He had documentary statements from engineers and others in Wisconsin, Minnesota, West Virginia, and Texas covering a period of forty-five years attesting to the success of his method in locating not only water, but oil, natural gas, iron, gold, and silver. Here is an example of a phenomenon which a newspaper reporter, a novelist, or even a lawyer would accept as true, without further examination, based on the man's story supported by documents of a long career of successful divination. Documentary evidence of this kind, however, finds no ready acceptance in scientific circles.

The explanation that will usually occur to a layman is that the man must have some special power that ordinary people do not have. Let us see how the psychologist proceeded in examining the claims and in explaining the phenomenon.

On March 26, 1923, in the presence of two other psychologists, R. M. Elliott and Donald Paterson, and with their cooperation, Foster made the following experiment. It was first determined that the rod would move downward for a cardboard box which contained a few coins. The diviner reported greater vigor in the movement when two gold watches and a silver watch were added. Of course, the diviner knew when the box was empty, and he knew what and how much was added at these preliminary preparations. This is an important point.

[7] "The Divining Rod—A History of Water Witching," *U.S. Geological Survey Pamphlet*, p. 416, 1917.

T. Besterman and W. F. Barrett, *The Divining-Rod and Experimental and Psychological Investigation*, London, 1926.

Accuracy of the positive judgments. A large table was moved to the center of the laboratory and chalk marks were made on it in such a way as to provide fourteen squares, each twenty by twenty inches. Each square was numbered. The floor directly under the table was marked in squares corresponding exactly in number and design to those on the table top. The area under the table was shielded from sight on all four sides by a wall made of cardboard.

The experimenter placed the box containing the metal on the floor on one of the squares. Then he left the room and another experimenter brought the diviner in.

The diviner mounted the table and walked slowly over the squares until, by a system of checking in both directions, he finally indicated where he thought the box was located on the floor beneath.

He was not told whether he was right or wrong. As a matter of fact, the experimenter who recorded the judgment did not know himself where his partner had placed the box, so that he was unable to communicate, by his facial expression, by the sound of his voice, or by his manner, any pertinent information.

These precautions are all *part* of the observation of the Principle of Control. There were thirty-two trials made, two for each of the fourteen squares, *and four in which the box was not on the floor at all.*

These four negative trials were made without the diviner's knowledge, of course, and his response on these trials was just as prompt, just as positive, as it had been in the twenty-eight times the box was actually there. In these twenty-eight trials the correct square was indicated only once. By the laws of probability he should have gotten two of these twenty-eight right by mere guessing, so that his performance in this part of the experiment must be considered a flat failure. The Principle of Control is observed here by instituting the trials in which there was nothing on the floor. *There is no evidence at all that he could locate a box of metal under these conditions although he was positive of his success outside the laboratory in locating hidden and lost watches by this method.* And, it must be remembered, he had documents to support his claim.

A second test was begun at once. None of the three people concerned knew as yet how the first test had come out, because the two experimenters had not compared their independent records of placement and judgment.

In the second test, the diviner stood on top of the table and attempted to judge how much metal was in the box when it was placed out of sight under the table on which he was standing. The judgments were made in terms of "nothing, weak, fair, strong and very strong," depending on the vigor of the rod movement. He had in the preliminary preparation, when knowing what was going into the box, been able to judge with ease whether only coins, or coins plus one, two, or three watches were in the box. He said that the difference between these steps was pronounced. But under the test conditions, when the box contained nothing five times and each one of the four positive amounts five times (making twenty-five trials in all) he was successful only six times. If he had been guessing, we might expect that he would get five right, anyway, so that his success here, considering that there were only twenty-five trials, can be said to be no better than random guessing.

We might really expect that the diviner would have done much better in this test, because in order to conserve his energy (he was seventy, remember, and had already climbed upon the table thirty-two times in the previous experiment) he was not required to leave the room between trials this time. Although he could not see the experimenter, it is conceivable that small noises made in changing the amounts in the box, placing the box on the floor, or the tone of the experimenter's voice in calling "Ready," however careful the experimenter might have been, could have been a source of considerable information.

Tests made out of doors. Another test was made out of doors and more closely resembled the conditions in which diviners usually work as they locate water and minerals. In this test he was required to identify the probable course of water mains leading to two campus buildings. An experimenter who knew the true locations accompanied him and recorded the observations on a rough map. Two probable courses were recorded. One missed an actual water main by fifteen feet at one end and fifty feet at the other. The length of the course was about two hundred and fifty feet and connected two buildings.

The second course missed a sewer outlet by about the same amount.

In the case of the second building a course of eighty feet was indicated correctly, but it ended in a hydrant that anyone could see! Any observant person could have done as well without a rod. A second water main leading into the building was passed over without any indication from the diviner. These results indicate that *where surface cues are available and where inadvertent signs from people who know the true locations are possible, diviners are more successful than under laboratory conditions.*[8]

Although we shall not examine it now, there is evidence that people can take advantage of barely perceptible signs or cues in directing the course of their behavior without being aware that they are using them. Not all diviners are charlatans.[9] Like this man, they are honestly convinced that they have some capacity that ordinary people do not possess.

Like most of us, they do not count their failures and they attribute their successes to the wrong factors. What these factors are can never be learned by interviewing the people involved or by collecting documents, however wholeheartedly they may be attested. *To obtain evidence that will stand the test of mature reflection concerning psychological matters, trained investigators must control all possible factors by special provisions.*

To a person who has not been trained in psychology these provisions, safeguards, or controls seem to be unimportant—a waste of time and energy.

6. MIND READING

The tiny changes in facial expression or posture on the part of one person, which are used as signals for directing the behavior of another, were suggested as part of the effective factors which enable the diviner to perform with more accuracy outside the laboratory than within. No actual demonstration of the efficacy of these factors

[8] F. A. Barrett, *Proceedings of the Society for Psychical Research,* 1897, 13, 2, 280; 1900, 15, 130-383.
[9] Charlatans resist a scientific examination of their claims. In this connection the student will find McComas's *Ghosts I Have Talked With,* Williams and Wilkins, Baltimore, an interesting account of investigations of spiritualistic mediums.

was made in the preceding example. It remained for Stratton[10] to show in another experiment just how effective they can be.

A young Moravian known as Eugen de Rubini appeared in San Francisco in about 1920 and impressed a social gathering at which Stratton was present with his ability to find hidden objects.[11] A common object was carefully hidden while de Rubini was out of the room. Then a person who knew the location of the object held onto one end of a delicate watch chain while de Rubini held the other. A handkerchief would have done as well. The guide thus led him to the proper location of the object, although he disclaimed any direct knowledge of having done so. The guide could be selected from the members at random. There was no collusion between two partners as there frequently is in stunts of this kind. After a few warming-up trials, the watch chain could be successfully discarded.

The most obvious cues, visual and auditory, were not necessary for de Rubini, who, in fact, told the guide on several occasions to stop giving him these perfectly obvious signs. He was also unusual as a public performer in that he made no claim of being able to read minds. He had to be assisted, he said, to the hidden object as a blind man would have to be. There must be, by the guide, continual mental correction of his false movements and a corresponding assent when his movements were right. His manner was wholly unfurtive; according to the descriptions of the psychologists who observed him, he was dreamy and receptive rather than aggressively on the lookout for cues.

Since he was willing to serve as a subject in an experiment, an experiment was made in an effort to find out just what the cues were.

He was first asked to take a brass bowl from a table in front of him and place it on one of two chairs to the right and left of him as directed "mentally" by the guide. The results of the experiment, which was repeated ten times, are shown in the following table.

[10] G. M. Stratton, "The Control of Another Person by Obscure Signs," *Psychological Review*, 1921, 28, 301-314.

[11] This story is only an example of a phase of human activity which seldom gets into psychological journals. The participants are usually Middle Europeans who are connected with organized entertainment in the sense that they have booking agents who secure radio or night-club bookings for them, or who sometimes arrange publicity appearances. There is always some recent example which will occur to the wide-awake student.

Number of trial	1	2	3	4	5	6	7	8	9	10
Direction intended	R	R	R	L	R	L	R	L	L	R
Direction taken by de Rubini	R	R	R	L	R	L	R	L	R	R

Except for the next to the last trial the directions were all as intended. Hence the subject was 90 per cent right. This is impressive, or rather would be impressive in a social gathering where more than ten trials, if that many, would seldom be required.

The next experiment, however, which was very similar to the first, gave somewhat different results. In it, de Rubini, as the subject, was required to place a small vase on either one of two small books about fifteen inches farther from him and to the right and left respectively. This time, without going into detail, suffice it to say that he got only three correct placements, an accuracy of only 30 per cent where 50 per cent might have been expected from a random placing.

In another experiment ten small volumes were placed flat, side by side so that they formed a row about six feet long. The subject was to designate which volume the guide was thinking of. The subject could pick up and handle any of the books in making a decision, but the one that was opened counted as his choice. Under these conditions chance success is very markedly reduced. When there are only two possible choices, random guessing should result in 50 per cent accuracy if enough guesses are allowed. But where any one of ten things can be right, we would expect the subject to get only one book right in ten trials if he were just guessing. Since he actually got thirteen right in twenty trials, he wasn't just guessing.

In order to find out just what he was doing, it was necessary to eliminate the possibility that he was receiving slight cues by any of the sense organs. He was reluctant to be blindfolded, but he had no objection to having his ears plugged. All of the auditory controls that were instituted seemed to have no effect on his accuracy. He was finally persuaded to wear blinders which eliminated his peripheral vision, not only on the sides but above and below as well, leaving only a restricted field in front of him.

Under these conditions there was a marked reduction in his successes. In other experiments the guide was screened from the subject; in still others he stayed so close behind that the subject could not see

39

him. In all of these experiments in which vision was interfered with, there was a marked reduction of the number of successes until in a total of sixty trials they did not exceed what might have been expected on the basis of chance alone. On the other hand, in all cases where no special precautions were taken to guard against visual cues, the successes ran definitely above chance expectation.

In one series in which the subject wore blinders and ear plugs and where the guide was completely screened, *there was not a single success in ten trials.*

Stratton concludes: "De Rubini received visual aid from signs."

Summary of the chapter. The principal purpose of this chapter has been to show how impossible it is, without the use of an experiment, to know what is really causing the behavior we observe. An experiment is a way of controlling our observation so that we can determine whether or not a particular condition is responsible for the behavior. This is what an experiment does in physics, chemistry, biology, or psychology. The usual day-to-day situation is a complicated one, a number of conditions occurring, each of which might be responsible for the form of behavior that arises. We are prone to look at these conditions and choose the particular one which agrees with our bias. If an experiment is properly done, and the appropriate control group is used, we are forced to see the behavior in its true light.

CHAPTER FOUR

APTITUDES

Whenever a person can learn a thing quickly and effectively, he is said to have an aptitude for it, or a special ability with respect to it. Whenever his learning is unusually rapid, he is said to be talented in the particular field under consideration. Talents are most frequently thought of in connection with artistic, literary, or professional fields; but the term really expresses only the notion of extraordinary excellence and may be applied to the more mundane fields of mechanical art, athletic activity, or even clerical skill.

Our very language preserves an important misconception. When we say, as we did in the preceding sentence, "talents are most frequently found," the implication is that "talents" are things, and if we were going to discover them we would look a person over as we would scrutinize him for moles or birthmarks. In this process we might find a "talent." People who believe that talents are things seldom take this crude view. They usually put the talent somewhere under the skin, usually in the nervous system or brain. Needless to say, neurological research has never turned up a talent in the central nervous system, nor anywhere else for that matter.

Heredity and aptitude.   There have been many unjustified assertions about aptitudes, special abilities, and talents conceived as things, and heredity. *Talents and aptitudes have been held to be wholly hereditary "gifts" of a special kind.* The phrase "gifted musician" or "gifted artist" means that the person in question has been endowed by his heredity with special talents of an artistic kind. The expressions "He wasn't cut out to be a physician" or "Teachers are born, not made" reflect the same notion of behavior causes— human nature is what it is because of special hereditary endowments or ineptitudes along specific lines.

Almost any novel we chance to pick up illustrates this belief, e.g., . . daughter of a doctor who had been forced by his family to go into medicine instead of being allowed to study music as a profession,

Lawrence had inherited her father's love for it, and her parents realized that even as a child she had an uncommon talent. . . ." *Lawrence Vane,* Angela du Maurier, 1946.

When we say that a person has a special ability as a public speaker, or is particularly adept at mechanics, we are not explaining why he is facile in these fields. The name cannot be the cause; it is a short description of the condition,[1] or simply a label.

If a boy wants to become a physician it is common to search through his ancestral tree to try to find the reason. Rather than fall back on a poorly understood inheritance of special ability as the *sole* cause, we should investigate alternative possibilities of explanation. A boy may *conceivably* become a physician because he is motivated to be like his family doctor. The occupation of a physician may have appealed to him because he observed that a doctor is a highly respected man in a community. Such early interest in medical practice could conceivably be as important in determining his vocational choice as his hereditary background. *We cannot state with any finality or even with any accuracy to what extent a successful career as a physician is dependent upon inherited structures as contrasted with acquired tastes, aptitudes, or skills.* But fortunately we do not have to face this problem in order to understand the nature of aptitude. *What a person has learned in the past both because of his genetic characteristics and his environment and the degree to which he has learned it is indicative of what and how quickly he will be able to learn new things in the future.*

What we call a "high aptitude for medicine" in a technical course in psychology is not some poorly understood inherited capacity but an evaluation of a person's present knowledge, habits, training, background, and interests that make learning medical facts and procedures easy for him. The same is true of "aptitude for law" or for any one of the many professions.

Highly competitive conditions in professions introduce other factors, economic and social, which determine who is actually going to enter medical school or law school. But before entering upon

---

[1] For centuries logicians have recognized this error in thinking. They say we "hypostasize" when we attempt to explain a phenomenon by giving it a name rather than by seeking out its cause.

42

discussion of the complicated professional fields and the special abilities which are usually accepted as being paramount in persons who succeed in them, let us see how one goes about determining the nature of talent in a simpler situation.

1. CLERICAL APTITUDE

Considerable success has been attained in separating clerical workers from nonclerical workers by the use of tests for what is called "clerical aptitude."[2] These tests are not concerned with whether an individual is a blond, whether his fingers are long, or how he dots his *i*'s and crosses his *t*'s. In the construction of a clerical aptitude test the first prerequisite is a careful description of the clerical occupation. This is called technically a "job analysis." Its purpose is to determine, if possible, the most important phases of clerical aptitude, and the essential abilities which they seem to require.

The job analysis shown on page 44 for the clerical occupations shows that they require at least four *different* kinds of abilities:

1. The ability to observe words and numbers and to perceive instantly what is on the paper.
2. The ability to make correct decisions regarding the questions these symbols raise.
3. The ability to handle the tools of the trade with facility.
4. An ability with elementary schoolroom skills of adding, multiplying, spelling, punctuating, capitalizing, and understanding the meaning of words and expressions.

Measuring clerical aptitude. The most hopeful attempt to measure these abilities has been made within very recent years by the Minnesota Employment Stabilization Research Institute. The test constructors have rather closely followed the above outline of abilities in preparing a collection, or a battery, of tests designed to measure clerical ability. The first test of the battery, as dictated by the job analysis, is a test of number- and name-checking performance. The speed and accuracy with which a person can perceive similarities

[2] Dorothy M. Andrew, "An Analysis of the Minnesota Vocational Test for Clerical Workers," *Journal of Applied Psychology,* 1937, 21, 18-47; 139-172.

JOB ANALYSIS OF CLERICAL OCCUPATION

Much of a clerk's work has to do with papers: memoranda, correspondence, and records. On the papers are words, symbols, numbers. These he reads, compares, classifies, transcribes, or passes judgment upon, and in the course of so doing makes decisions which, except in the more routine operations, may require a high order of technical knowledge and good sense. The tools of his trade include the pencil and the pen, and sometimes the slide rule, the typewriter, the duplicator, the bookkeeping or calculating machine, the filing cabinet, the card index, and similar aids in classifying, cataloguing, finding, rearranging, identifying, copying, computing, or otherwise manipulating for a purpose the papers and symbols used in recording and communication. It must be remembered, however, that a clerical worker's speed and accuracy in the mechanics of using these tools, essential though they are, rank lower in value than the correctness of his thinking about the problems which the papers present. A clerk may be called upon to do other kinds of work also, such as to use the telephone, receive visitors, make purchases, organize and supervise the work of others in the office. But as a clerical worker, the abilities indispensable to the effective performance of his duties are those which enable him to handle the problems arising in connection with his paper work judiciously as well as rapidly.[3]

[3] W. V. Bingham, *Aptitudes and Aptitude Testing*, Harper & Brothers, New York 1937, p. 151.

and differences between pairs of numbers and names is obtained. These are some sample items:

307–309
4605–4603
2063849102983–263349102983
Hulme Co.–Hulne Co.
L. T. Piver–L. T. Piser
Keely Institute–Kelly's Institute

The direct relation between these operations and the job requirements is perfectly obvious. The operations are identical. No vague "ability" is to be measured. If a person has learned to make promptly the discriminations required of him, he can make a good score on the test. This learning is presumably definitely limited by the physiological structure one possesses. But as we have pointed out, the problem of inheritance does not have to be faced in a practical problem like this. A clerk of considerable experience may not be superior to a person who has much less experience. But just why in terms of his brain, and just how the central nervous system is involved, we do not need to know.

The second requirement—that of being able to understand relationships between symbols and to make decisions regarding them—is met by the use of one of the standard "intelligence" tests. These tests really measure how well one can understand the meaning of words and symbols as we shall see in a later chapter. The particular tests used at Minnesota as part of the clerical battery were the Pressey Senior Classification Test and Senior Verification Test. Both of these tests are heavily loaded with items that overlap with the fourth requirement, a mastery of simple schoolroom skills. They test how well the skills of spelling, punctuating, capitalizing, and so on, have been mastered as well as what is usually called "intelligence."

The third requirement is measured by the performance on three kinds of manipulation tests. The first is called the Minnesota Rate of Manipulation Test. Sixty wooden disks about 1½ inches in diameter have to be placed in just slightly larger holes in a board. The placing has to be done in a specified way and the time required is a measure of hand and arm dexterity. Dexterity in handling the same objects with the fingers is measured when the subjects are required to pick the disks out of the holes with one hand, turn them over with a thumb-and-finger movement, transfer them to the other hand, and replace them in the same hole.

Finger dexterity is measured by the O'Connor Finger Dexterity Test. The time required to place small metal pegs, three at a time, in one hundred small holes, is the score. This is a task which is different from, though related to, what is demanded in the Rate of Manipulation Test. The small size of the objects demands a finer coordination of the small muscle groups of the fingers.

The ability to use a small instrument, a task requiring even finer discrimination and coordination, is tested by means of the O'Connor Tweezer Dexterity Test. The same pegs that are used in the Finger Dexterity Test must be inserted in somewhat smaller holes, one at a time instead of three at a time, and with a small pair of tweezers instead of with the unaided fingers.

Thus we see that there is nothing mysterious about a "test." In a testing situation the subject is merely active with respect to certain stimulating objects that are placed before him. He is constantly doing that anyway, whether or not he is being tested. It is true that the objects and symbols placed before him are of very highly selected kinds. The subject's reactions may be circumscribed or restricted in various ways, and there may be the pressure of finishing in a certain time limit. All this irritates some people and creates in them an unfavorable attitude toward tests and testing, but such an attitude should not keep us from learning the advantages of testing procedures. Of course, there are good tests and poor tests. *The ultimate standard by which tests should be judged is whether they prove to have high validity.*

The meaning of validity. Briefly, *when we determine the validity of a test we are finding out how accurate the title or label at the head of a test really is.* If a test constructor asserts that a score a person makes on his test is indicative of some property or attainment or ability that he has, he has to prove it. He proves it by determining the validity of the test.

Questions of validity do not generally arise in tests for simple

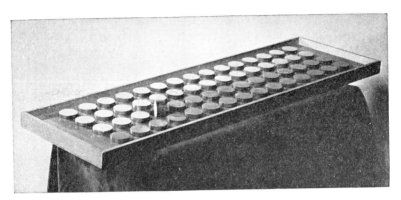

The Minnesota Rate of Manipulation Test

The O'Connor Finger Dexterity Test

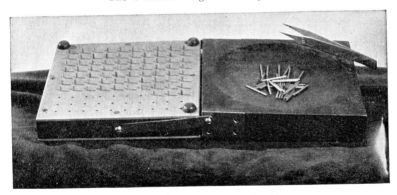

The O'Connor Tweezer Dexterity Test

FIG. 6.—(Courtesy of the University of Minnesota Press. From Paterson and Darley, *Men, Women and Jobs,* facing p. 10.)

schoolroom skills. A test of spelling involves the same activity that one is testing; one doesn't have to prove that it is a spelling test. Everybody would agree that a spelling test is a spelling test, or that an arithmetic test really tests what the label says it does.[4]

But if a psychologist asserts that he has an instrument which will select the people who will make the best salesman out of all the people who want to become salesmen, then he has to *prove* the assertion by showing that people who are already successful salesmen score high on his test and others who have been discharged or are about to be discharged or who have become discouraged and have quit because they were not successful in selling or did not like it, make low scores. The production in selling is called the *criterion,* and if it is highly valid, the test must agree with the criterion all the way down the line and not just differentiate the extremes (cf. page 57). Parenthetically, no such test for salesmanship exists.

The validity of the clerical battery. In keeping with these principles a person who designs a battery like these clerical tests *has to demonstrate that the battery does actually discriminate between persons who succeed in the clerical occupations and persons who are successful in other occupations that require different abilities.* This procedure is a marked contrast with that of the phrenologist or graphologist, to whom the necessity for this kind of proof would never occur. From our discussion of experimental and control groups in Chapter Three, it is obvious that the individuals in the contrasting occupational groups should be the same age, same sex, of the same social level, and so forth, except for occupation. The profile shown in Figure 7 exhibits the average performance of two adult groups of workers—garage mechanics and men office clerks. The mechanics are only slightly above the mean of an unselected adult population in all of the tests that we have used for measuring clerical aptitude, while the clerks are distinctly above the mean in the same tests. For women a similar condition exists when retail saleswomen are compared with women office workers. Thus the validity of the battery is demonstrated. The nature of aptitude generally is further elucidated by the addition to the men's battery of a "mechanical assembly" test

[4] This assumption is open to challenge, but we do not want to pursue the question any further here.

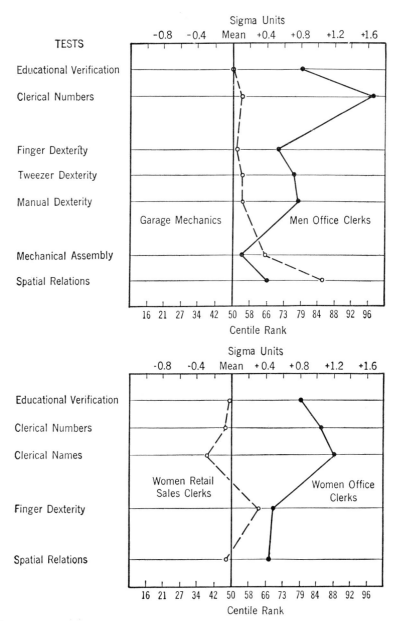

49

and a "spatial relations" test. These are tests of "mechanical ability" and, for our purpose, it is not necessary to describe them. They show that the garage mechanics are not simply generally of lower attainment than men office workers. When tests are used that tap the abilities they exercise in their occupations then they become superior. For the women, although there is a clear-cut difference for the clerical battery, i.e., the first three tests, no tests were used which permitted the retail saleswomen to show in what respects they were superior to the women clerks.

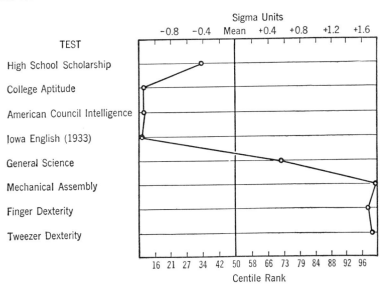

FIG. 8.—The profile of an individual student. This is an unusual case because thi boy stands in the lowest 10 per cent in three of the tests and in the topmost 3 or per cent in three others.

2. INDIVIDUAL DIAGNOSIS

As a digression from our main theme at this point, let us conside Figure 8, which exhibits a profile of a single student.[5] He stands ver near the bottom of the distribution in a college aptitude test, in th American Council Test, and in the Iowa English Examination. H high school scholarship record is also below average. If we had on

[5] Adapted from E. G. Williamson, *Students and Occupations*, Henry Holt ar Company, Incorporated, New York, 1937. Every student should consult this helpf volume.

50

these tests, we would be forced to conclude that his ability generally was very low, but the inclusion of a general science test and the dexterity and mechanical assembly tests shows that we have here a case in which there is a special ability in dexterity and mechanical assembly. In this case rank incompetence in the abilities required for scholastic success is associated with a manipulative ability that puts most college students in the class of "also rans." This case, however, is not typical.

Popular belief to the contrary, it is not true that low ability in the intellectual fields is invariably associated with high ability in the mechanical field. The patterns of aptitude and ineptitude must be determined for every individual. *There is no generalization that will permit us to predict what we will find in behavior segments which are as yet untested, from the results of tests in areas that are not closely allied with these.* This problem will be discussed at greater length in a later section of this chapter.

The meaning of the labels in Figures 7 and 8. It is necessary at this point to make still another digression from our main theme in this chapter. The careful student has observed the labels "Sigma Units" and "Centile Rank" in Figures 7 and 8. Since both of these units are used extensively in psychological work, an understanding of them is essential. They are both units for comparing the performance of one person on several different tests or of many people on the same test in order to find the comparative standing of individuals or groups. Whenever we have the problem of making this comparison, we need to state a given person's standing on a test with considerable precision. In comparing heights, for instance, we could say that a given man is 5 feet 10 inches, and that this is somewhat above the average. The use of centile ranks, however, would allow us to be more precise in our statements, because we can compute that a height of 5 feet 10 inches is in, say, the 75th centile. Interpreted, this means that 75 per cent of all men are of this height or below. Out of every one hundred unselected men we should expect twenty-five to exceed the height of the man we are studying.

If we want to find this same person's standing in weight we may use the same process. Our man may weigh 190 pounds, which might turn out to be in the 90th centile. Therefore we could say that this man was further removed from the central tendency in weight than in height.

The real value of this technique is not apparent, however, until we are confronted with the necessity of comparing several different measures on the same person or on groups of people. In comparing the garage mechanics with the male office clerks we have seven different measures on each group. In the first two tests the scores are in terms of points—the number of correct items resulting from the testing procedure. The finger, tweezer, and manual dexterity tests, however, are scored in terms of the time required to perform the various tasks. Now to try to compare the scores directly—points with seconds—results in having to deal with incommensurables, an error which any high school student should be able to recognize. By transferring the raw scores into ranks, the ranks can be compared without consideration of the units which determined them. Even when the units of measurement are the same—seconds, for instance—to compare them directly leads to ridiculous conclusions. A much longer time is required to complete the tweezer dexterity test than the finger dexterity test, but since this is true for everyone the total time is not important. The relative standing, or rank, however, is.

The same interpretation could be made from sigma units although the procedure is less direct. Each system has some technical advantage that we will not discuss here. Notice, also, that nothing has been said about the method of computing either derived unit. Our emphasis is on interpretation rather than on computation. For the latter the reader is referred to some standard text in psychology or elementary statistics.[6]

What is an ability? The results of a test of any kind are stated in some units of performance. One cannot observe an aptitude directly: what one does observe are marks on paper symbolizing the selection that was finally made out of a whole series of possible

[6] There are many sources: Three recent ones are Henry E. Garrett, *Statistics in Psychology and Education*, Longmans, Green & Co., Inc., New York, 1940; E. F Lindquist, *A First Course in Statistics*, Houghton Mifflin Company, Boston, 1938 Allen Edwards, *Statistical Analysis for Students in Psychology and Education* Rinehart & Company, Inc., New York, 1946.

responses. In non-paper-pencil tests, movements of fingers and other members are the processes under observation. These symbols (pencil marks) and coordinated movements constitute performance. Performance, however, needs to be explained. When there are observed relations between different performances, for example, it becomes useful scientifically to assume an underlying ability which is responsible for the fact that the relations obtain. This underlying ability is an abstraction. It cannot now be observed nor will it ever be observed in the future regardless of how sensitive our tests are made, because it is an abstract concept and not a "thing" which can be observed.

The difference between an aptitude and an accomplishment. Some tests are labeled "aptitude tests" and some are labeled "achievement tests." The difference between them is not very clear cut in practice. In an aptitude test the acts that are tested may differ quite widely from those in the job itself, but because there is a relationship between performance on these acts and on the job itself we are able to predict from aptitude test to job. In an achievement test we are always trying to sample directly what has been learned after opportunity to learn. The test always implies direct previous experience with the kind of materials out of which the test is constructed. The aptitude test does not. The aptitude test tends to look forward to predict achievement, but the achievement test usually looks backward to measure progress made. Actually there are times when we have constructed aptitude tests by having the subject perform a sample of the job itself.

3. ACHIEVEMENT AND APTITUDE

The degree to which a person has achieved a mastery of certain school subjects can sometimes be taken as an index of his aptitude for them, and for similar subjects when other techniques for the measurement of the more fundamental components are not available.

This is the condition that exists in the selection of candidates for many of the professional fields today. One can take advantage of the similarity of the professional subject to the preprofessional requirements where the job requirements have not yet been analyzed sufficiently to make true aptitude testing possible. Consider medicine, for instance. We would like to know how to test the aptitudes required for success in medical school, but an adequate description of just what is demanded for this success has not yet been worked out with the same precision and detail that has produced such favorable results for clerical positions. Among the requirements that have been mentioned are a facility for learning the Latin and Greek polysyllables that make up so much of medical nomenclature, an aptitude for exacting detail, and a few other specifications which are so general that they cannot be measured. It has further been said that:

Surgeons and dentists are craftsmen in addition to being medically trained. Clearness of eye, delicacy of tactile discrimination, steadiness and strength of hand, dexterity of fingers, are obvious necessities. Quite as indispensable is aptitude for visualizing vividly in three dimensions; for it is necessary to see in their true positions and to manipulate the forms observed in a dentist's little mirror or in a laryngoscope; also to picture correctly the highly complicated unseen structures beneath the body surface—arteries, nerves, muscles, tendons, joints, glands, vital organs—perhaps at the end of a probe. Add to these abilities the grit and steadiness of nerve as well as of hand, without which surgeon, oculist, or dentist is prone to disastrous slips at critical junctures, and we have the aptitudes most commonly mentioned as more essential for surgery than for general medical practice. It is, however, hard to imagine how any practicing physician can do his work without frequent resort to the exercise of these same abilities in at least some degree, if he ever has to remove a child's adenoids, drain a suppurating fester, reset a dislocated shoulder joint, deliver a baby, or take a sliver from an eyelid.

So far as the professional schools are concerned, it is, to be sure, in the dental school rather than in the medical that a seriously large number of failures are directly traceable to lack of manual and mechanical aptitudes Students who successfully pass the first two years of basic biological, physiological, and anatomical courses, not infrequently have to be dropped in the third year because they cannot master both the mechanical intricacie and the manual techniques of dental practice. . . .[7]

In a search for a better method of selection than is available in the premedical grades, the American Association of Medical College has sponsored what has come to be known as a Medical Aptitude

[7] W. V. Bingham, *Aptitudes and Aptitude Testing*, p. 184.

Test. Changed every year, the test comprises generally about six parts which are designed to measure

1. Comprehension and retention
2. Visual memory
3. Memory for content

4. Logical reasoning
5. Scientific vocabulary
6. Understanding of printed material

There is much in common between this test and a general intelligence test, but a knowledge of the subject matter of premedical courses is required for any passable performance. As an "aptitude test," its approach is very indirect. Involving, as it does, so much highly specialized information, it would be more appropriate to call it an achievement test.

The results of its use have been surprisingly good, notwithstanding this criticism. Only 40 per cent of the lowest decile were graduated, while 100 per cent of the top decile finished their four years in medical school.

In fact, the medical aptitude test score is of better predictive value than the grades in premedical subjects, but it is probably a better instrument for measuring the actual mastery of premedical subject matter than are the premedical grades themselves. Cramming or cheating might conceivably be more of a factor in determining grades than they are in determining test scores.

APTITUDE TEST SCORES

ABOVE 200: THE HIGHEST TENTH

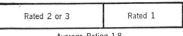

Average Rating 1.8

Does the medical "aptitude test" predict success after graduation? The superintendents of hospitals having three or more interns who had taken the test were sent rating scales to apply to the interns under their supervision. The ratings were to be made on a scale from 1 to 5; 1 was the highest and 5 the lowest

APTITUDE TEST SCORES

BELOW 100: THE LOWEST TENTH

Average Rating 2.3

FIG. 9.—Medical aptitude and rating of success as an intern. (After Moss.)

rating. The definitions of these ratings given to the superintendents were:

(1) means "comes up to the best intern the hospital has had"
(2) means "is good, above average, but not equal to the best"
(3) means "is equal to the average intern the hospital has had"
(4) means "is below the average intern, but better than the poorest"
(5) means "is among the poorest interns the hospital has had."[8]

The chart shows the results of this survey. The average rating of those who were in the highest tenth of the Medical Test Performance was 1.8. As a group they were "above average." Forty-two per cent of them were rated "1." The others were rated either "2" or "3." None was rated either "4" or "5." Those in the lowest tenth present a contrasting picture. Barely 10 per cent were rated "1." Thirty-eight per cent were rated "4" or "5." This study shows that as far as the extremes are concerned, the aptitude test can be used to predict how well *groups* of students will do as interns. The factors which are required for success as an intern still remain to be discovered. When they are, it is obvious that the prediction of success will be improved if they are taken into consideration.

The lack of a criterion.   We have been skirting a problem which is discussed in the technical literature under the topic "criterion." *A criterion is an objective measure of the mastery of one's job.* In some occupations, particularly those of a mechanical nature, the establishment of a criterion is relatively simple. The number of finished castings; the number of relays assembled; the number of soldered connections made—have all been used as criteria. In selling life insurance, the amount of insurance sold has long been a firmly fixed criterion of success in the occupation. In schoolwork grades have been used as the criterion; in other cases the attainment of some goal like graduation has been used. But after entrance into the legal and the medical professions, as well as into other professions, standards of this kind do not exist, so that in order to establish a criterion the tester has to resort to the use of rating scales in an effort to get quantitative measures of the subjective estimates of supervisors and colleagues.

As unsatisfactory as these scales always are and in spite of the fact that they may be a great deal less valid than the test score itself, there

8 F. A. Moss, "Medical Aptitude Tests," *Journal* of the American Association of Medical Colleges, 1936, 11, 275.

56

would never be any way of finding out whether these criticisms were true unless there were an objective criterion with which both the ratings and the aptitude scores could be compared. It is felt that in some fields the objective standards do not and cannot exist. Consider, for instance, the number of obscure painters, who even if they had been known well enough by their colleagues to be rated, would certainly have been placed at the lowermost category, and who at some later time have been recognized as masters of their craft. Numerous writers have been neglected or reviled by their colleagues, but later generations have turned the tables completely. Thus, by the very nature of artistic accomplishment, standards are constantly changing so that aptitudes can hardly be said to exist except with reference to a particular time in a particular culture.

4. APTITUDE FOR FLYING—The Criterion.

The importance of a criterion of performance appeared with remarkable clearness during World War II when so many young men were selected and trained as pilots. In the years immediately preceding the war, time and time again psychologists had tried to predict flying success, but they inevitably came up against the stubborn fact that a student pilot who would have been rated satisfactory, or even good, in one training school would have been "washed out" in another.

Each pilot instructor seemed to have his own standards of performance against which he tried to measure his students, but the standards of one instructor were completely different from those of another, so that although planes flew, they were flown in a variety of styles that were as individual as the pilots themselves. This variety in final performance makes the prediction of success an impossible task in flying as in other occupations.

In addition to styling, each flying instructor seemed to have a private notion of what marks mean. Some had in mind, as a standard, a kind of abstract, perfect pilot performance which no human being could ever achieve, and their students were rated in some kind of vague percentage scale according to the proportion of perfection they were able to achieve. Under this scheme nobody ever got 100.

For others the standard was some mythical "average" so that students were rated above and below this mark. Still others seemed

Student Pilot's Name _____

A SCALE FOR RATING PILOT COMPETENCY

No opportunity to observe

1. Considering his training, how skillful is he in carrying out precision maneuvers (spot landings, figure eights, etc.)?

very skillful — high average — average — low average — very poor

2. How does he handle the controls?

greatly over or under controls — considerably over or under controls — some over or under control — handles controls fairly smoothly — very smoothly and correctly

3. How carefully does he check his plane and engine before taking off?

very carefully — carefully — reasonably carefully — not carefully enough — does not check it

4. As compared with the other students you have trained, how readily does he "catch on" to your instructions?

very fast learner — fast — average — slow — very slow

5. To what extent does he have the feel of a ship?

unusually well — well — fairly well — poorly — not at all ... flies mechanically

6. Does he show respect for a ship and its motor?

takes excellent care — takes good care — shows reasonable respect for both — tends to be careless — no regard at all

7. How tense or relaxed is he when flying?

extremely tense — rather tense — slightly too tense — almost sufficiently relaxed — ideally relaxed

(Developed at Purdue University under grant from NRC Committee on Selecti

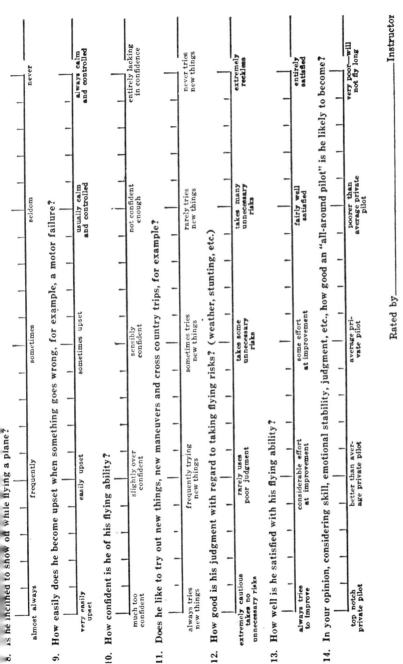

8. Is he inclined to show off while flying a plane?

almost always — frequently — sometimes — seldom — never

9. How easily does he become upset when something goes wrong, for example, a motor failure?

very easily upset — easily upset — sometimes upset — usually calm and controlled — always calm and controlled

10. How confident is he of his flying ability?

much too confident — slightly over confident — sensibly confident — not confident enough — entirely lacking in confidence

11. Does he like to try out new things, new maneuvers and cross country trips, for example?

always tries new things — frequently trying new things — sometimes tries new things — rarely tries new things — never tries new things

12. How good is his judgment with regard to taking flying risks? (weather, stunting, etc.)

extremely cautious takes no unnecessary risks — rarely uses poor judgment — takes some unnecessary risks — takes many unnecessary risks — extremely reckless

13. How well is he satisfied with his flying ability?

always tries to improve — considerable effort at improvement — some effort at improvement — fairly well satisfied — entirely satisfied

14. In your opinion, considering skill, emotional stability, judgment, etc., how good an "all-around pilot" is he likely to become?

top notch private pilot — better than average private pilot — average private pilot — poorer than average private pilot — very poor—will not fly long

Rated by _____ Instructor

d Training of Aircraft Pilots with funds from CAA. Courtesy of M. S. Viteles.)

to think the poorest student they ever had offered some kind of absolute zero against which all other students could be ranked.

A deviation from the personal standard of one instructor which would result in a major catastrophe for the student would not be considered an important, or even noticeable defection to another instructor.

It should be clear that to speak of "flying aptitude" under these conditions is completely hopeless. Those habits which could satisfy one instructor and result in the judgment "This man has flying aptitude," would not be demanded by another pilot instructor, and consequently would give an entirely different meaning to the concept of flying aptitude.

Parenthetically, it might be said that the student who has read "college instructor" for "pilot instructor" in the discussion above, has made an important analogy. As long as college instructors have so many different concepts of what constitutes good college work, as they have today, it is almost hopeless to talk of "aptitude for college work" and the accuracy of prediction of scholastic success based on test results is not likely ever to be much better than it is today.

The marvel is that test constructors having so little to build on have been able to do as well as they have.

Pooled judgment. In the case of the flying instructors, the first task was to get agreement on the really important phases of flying and to get accurate ratings on the essential features by groups of instructors. To this end various rating schemes were developed. One of these is shown on pages 58 and 59.

Standard flight. As soon as the rating blank was developed the need for some kind of standard performance, while flying, became evident to the instructors. When we are trying to judge how well one person does compare with another, it becomes evident to anyone, as it did to the pilot instructors, that we need some kind of uniform performance if we are to compare people. In music we could hardly compare a conventional rendition of "Yankee Doodle" with symphonic music; yet, that is what flying instructors were trying to do! Not in musical terms, but in terms of the final tasks they gave to their student pilots. Suppose we were trying to compare "achievement in history," and in order to test it we gave one person an examination on "Hispanic America" and somebody else an examination on "The Balkans." How is there any hope that they will be able to show that they have "historic achievement"? Specific knowledge, yes, but not "historic" knowledge. The demonstration of "achievement" or "ability" depends on some opportunity to show what has been learned. And if one person is going to be compared with another, the two must *do* the same thing, so that they can be compared.

If we set a standard, then we must have a standard performance. This requirement resulted in the careful development of a standard pattern of flight on which students had to fly under the surveillance of observers who rated them with respect to each other and not with respect to some imaginary perfect pilot. These ratings established the criterion.

Summary. This work was undertaken because of the paramount necessity of obtaining an accurate measure of performance in a task if we are to develop precise aptitude tests for the task. Until an accurate criterion is developed the predictive value of the aptitude test will always be limited. This study has indicated that an approach to accurate evaluation can be chieved by standardizing the task and the way of measuring efficiency of performance in it.

5. APTITUDE FOR FLYING—Prediction of Performance

As might be expected, one of the first problems assigned to psychologists in the AAF during the World War II was to predict, on the basis of tests given before flying instruction, which men would later become the most successful pilots. In devising an approach to the problem some twenty tests were developed; fourteen were of the paper-pencil variety and six were tests of coordination and speed of decision which required apparatus. The combined scores on these tests classified the student pilots into nine groups called "stanines," a coined word from "standard nines." Thus the entire range of scores was divided from high to low into nine groups.

The first results are shown in Figure 10 where the test scores of 185,367 men are represented in the horizontal bars. Of all these men

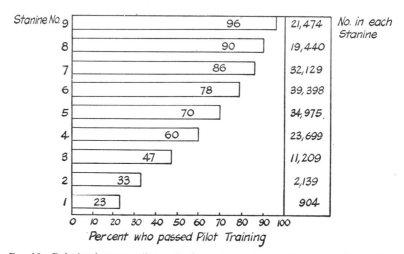

FIG. 10.—Relation between pilot aptitude stanine and per cent passing pilot training in the Army Air Forces. (After J. C. Flanagan, "Scientific Development of the Use of Human Resources," *Science*, 105, 1947, 57–60.)

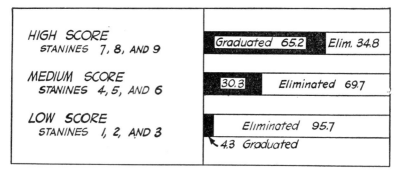

FIG. 11.—Results in a special experiment in which 1,017 were admitted to training, regardless of their test scores. (After J. C. Flanagan, "Scientific Development of the Use of Human Resources," *Science*, 105, 1947, 57–60.)

62

24 per cent were eliminated in the training for one reason or another, so that 140,878 men were made into pilots. This number and more were needed at the time (1943). If, however, the situation had been such that only about 20,000 had been needed, then those in the top stanine alone could have been selected for training at a loss of only 4 per cent.

In situations of this kind there is always a practical limit to which the use of tests can be put. We could get almost another 20,000 successful pilots by including stanine 8, and if the practical need is great, stanine 8 will be included even if in doing so we more than double the number of failures. But somewhere there is a balance between the number needed and those to be trained, at which the percentage of elimination becomes significant. Remember, there is another group waiting to be trained, waiting for the facilities that are wasted on the 77 per cent in stanine 1!

By the fall of 1944 the demand for pilots was so low that only those having scores of 7, 8, and 9 were admitted to pilot training. The practical considerations that led to the decision to eliminate the lower groups need not be reviewed here. What is important from our standpoint is that the decision destroyed the apparent efficiency of the tests. Only fourteen in one hundred failed in the lowest test group. The group that would presumably have been only 23 per cent successful was not included.

The practical use of tests in which some kind of critical score is set so that no one scoring below that point is accepted for training or employment always makes the test appear at a disadvantage in a subsequent appraisal of its merits. Since those who are poor in the tests never appear in the record, there sometimes is little difference between the test scores of those who do well and those who fail.

To show how effective the tests really are, it is necessary to make an experiment in which a group is admitted for training regardless of the test score. This was done in the AAF in the summer of 1943 when a sample of 1,017 men was admitted if they could pass the medical examination regardless of their test scores. The men were scattered in various schools throughout the country and their test scores were not sent to the training command, so that the training officers did not know whether a given student ranked high or low. The results are shown in Figure 11.

Individuals in the group making the highest score have about a two-to-one chance of success; the middle group reverses these chances, being about two to one for failure; while the lowest scoring group have about only one chance in twenty-five for success.

Summary. The work of the psychologists with the AAF has indicated that it is possible to develop a battery of tests which could predict with fair accuracy those who would fail in primary training. In this wartime situation the skill required to become a successful flier varied according to man-power needs. As a result, the same group of tests would superficially appear to be better at one time than another. Such, of course, was not the case. Obviously this means that the aptitude for flying is not something which exists in the abstract but something which is significant only with respect to the social needs.

6. ARTISTIC ABILITIES

Ability in music, painting, sketching, the plastic arts, dancing, decorating, architecture, and poetry has long been considered to be solely the product of hereditary endowment. Genetic charts have been made which purport to prove that since artistic talent runs in families, it must be inherited.[9] People who make assertions of this kind are a great deal more enthusiastic than the geneticists, who generally hold that a talent in the artistic field is so complex that it defies genetic analysis. It must be true that here, as in all fields, a structural substratum is necessary for the development of artistic talents. But the "necessity" for a structural foundation has to be developed from theoretical considerations rather than from observable items of information. If there is any difference in the brain or the ears or the muscles of a competent musician which distinguishes him from people who are inept in music, we don't know now what that difference is. *To assert that the possession or the absence of these talents is wholly determined by structure is entirely without foundation.*

[9] H. M. Stanton, "The Inheritance of Specific Musical Capacities," *Psychological Monographs* 1922, 31, 157-204. The same kind of charts would "prove" that tuberculosis or pellagra is inherited.

It also goes without saying that no attribute of physique, like long tapering fingers, holds any consistent relation to artistic skill. The old-time belief that long fingers and artistic temperament are related is just so much nonsense, because we have no notion of what artistic temperament is: we have no criterion for it.

Musical aptitude tests. There are several tests available which purport to measure musical aptitude. Since the test items are auditory stimuli, instead of being printed on paper as most tests are, they are presented by means of a phonograph. One of the best known is the Seashore Test,[10] named after its originator, for many years Dean of the Graduate School at the University of Iowa. There are six double-faced records comprising the test. The first test presents one hundred pairs of tones alike except for a difference in pitch. Beginning with easily observable differences, they come closer and closer together and consequently become harder to discriminate as the test proceeds. The second test measures how well the subject can discriminate between tones of different loudness. He has to say, of each pair, whether the second is louder or softer than the first. As in the pitch test, there are one hundred such pairs to be discriminated. The remaining three tests are more difficult to describe and should be heard in a demonstration for a more complete understanding of the task required of the subject. Suffice it to say here that they are aimed at testing how well the subject can judge time, discriminate consonance, and discriminate rhythmic patterns and recall melodies. It is clear from the nature of these tests that Seashore considers the complex musical aptitude to be made up of simpler abilities which can be tested. His job analysis includes more factors than the five comprising the test, but tests for the others have not yet been developed.

These tests have been studied by several investigators, prominent among whom are Hazel Stanton, L. H. Lanier, and Paul Farnsworth. One of the problems which concerned these people is that of reliability.[11] Any test, whether for musical aptitude, clerical aptitude, general

10 C. E. Seashore, *The Psychology of Musical Talent,* Silver Burdett & Company, Newark, 1919.
11 For a summary of all this literature see Paul Farnsworth, "An Historical, Critical, and Experimental Study of the Seashore-Kwalwasser Test Battery," *Genetic Psychology Monographs,* 1931, 9, 291-393.

intelligence, or for some school subject, must be reliable. *High reliability means that people who take the test for the second time rank in approximately the same way that they did the first time they took it.* If there is little relationship in the relative standing of people between two administrations of the test, then the reliability is low, and, of course, the test is worthless. The data on the reliability of the Seashore Test is ambiguous. Some investigators have reported satisfactory indexes of reliability: others, working with different groups of students of differing ages, have found low reliabilities. *One must conclude that these tests are still in an experimental stage.*

If one withholds a musical education from a child who does not do well on these tests, there is the possibility that a serious blunder is being made. On the other hand, a high score does not by any means ensure success in choosing music for a career, or even for a satisfactory avocation. Notwithstanding, Hazel Stanton[12] has found that a combination of the Seashore score and a score from a standard intelligence test is useful in predicting the success of students in the Eastman School of Music. At the Ohio State University, however, these scores have not proved to be valuable.[13] When we have contradictory evidence like this it usually turns out that there is a difference somewhere in the two situations. It is possible that the objectives of the two schools of music are entirely unlike, so that a test that satisfactorily predicts an outcome in one place will be useless in another. Since medical education is much more standardized than musical education, the outlook for developing even more adequate aptitude tests is much more favorable in the former field.

Improvability of pitch discrimination. Writing in 1910 Seashore said: "What a blessing to a girl of the age of eight, if the music teacher would examine her and if necessary say, 'Much as I regret it, I must say that you would find music dull and difficult, and I would advise you to take up some other art.' What a blessing if that child

12 Hazel M. Stanton, "Prognosis of Musical Achievement," 1929, University of Rochester, Eastman School of Music.

Hazel M. Stanton, "Psychological Tests—a Factor in Admission to the Eastman School of Music," *School and Society,* 1929, 30, 783-891.

13 M. E. Wilson, "The Prognostic Value for Music Success of Several Types of Tests," *Music Supervisors' Journal,* 1930, 16, 71-73.

could be started right; but current theory and practice is against her. There is too much faith in what music lessons can do for a person without native capacity. If we are to have musical ears, we must be born with them."

It is quite clear from the foregoing that he considered his musical talent tests to be measures, although imperfect, of some basic aptitudes of a physiological or anatomical kind. The pitch test, for instance, is aimed at making a measure of one aspect of having "musical ears." This was a perfectly reasonable assumption or hypothesis in the light of nineteenth-century biology, but it was not subjected to experimental test until recently.

Ruth Wyatt[14] selected sixteen students, eight from the music school and eight from the arts college at Northwestern University. Prior to training both groups would have been classed as poor with respect to their relative populations, although the music-school group was fairly proficient in singing. The arts-college group was composed of students who had experienced difficulty with pitch discrimination. One reported that he had been excluded from grade-school music classes because he could not carry a tune and that his singing was still the butt of many jokes. A girl had been told she could never learn to sing because she was a "monotone."

The "special training" consisted of explanations and demonstrations of what pitch means to a musician. Without such training differences in loudness are often confused with pitch differences. The subjects were encouraged to try to reproduce a tone they heard by humming and singing. An instrument called the Conn stroboscope was employed so that the subject could see as well as hear and "feel" when he was either sharp or flat or in unison with a standard tone.

After several training sessions the Seashore Pitch Test was again administered and both groups had improved; the "music" group changed its status from "low average" to "excellent," and the "non-music" group changed from "low average" to "good." The rank of the non-music students was higher after the training than the rank of the music students before training began.

Although there was more improvement on the tone on which the

14 Ruth F. Wyatt, "The Improvability of Pitch Discrimination," *Psychological Monographs,* 1945, 58, No. 270

subjects were trained, there was also transfer to tones an octave above and an octave below the training level.

Wyatt concludes that the Seashore Musical Talent Test, or at least the part of it on which she worked, has a real value, but its value is not to measure "musical capacity." She feels that *it can reveal deficiencies in pitch discrimination but that they are remediable: that special, individualized training can mend the deficiency.*[15]

From this experiment we cannot know how the pitch deficiency ever came about in the first place, but there is no justification in pinning the whole matter on an irremediable lack of "capacity."

Summary of the chapter. Aptitudes are abstractions. They are inferential constructs, like "gravity" or "force" in physics, which are used to explain behavior. Being abstractions, they never can be observed directly. Neither can they be inherited; one doesn't inherit an abstraction. Nor can they be learned, and for the same reason. The structural and maturational features of an organism, together with its past experiences, determine its behavior. The sum total of all these features determines whether one is to exhibit this or that kind of behavior. Theoretically, a deficiency in one of these aspects can be compensated for by a substitute function from some other area, at least within certain ill-defined limits. But the knowledge of the characteristics that a person has now can be used in predicting the kind of person he will be later after a certain course of study or a training period in the acquisition of certain skills and attitudes. Not all features of his present attainment are equally valuable in making a prediction. Which ones are significant can be determined only by testing the items that are thought to be important on a priori grounds. This testing involves the use of a criterion and a comparison between the criterion and test results. In the mechanical and clerical fields some progress has been made, but in the professional and artistic fields, progress is less satisfactory. This lack of progress is due to the fact that as yet no satisfactory criteria in the latter fields have been established.

---

15 There still are individual differences in performance after training in this and other functions. Some of the problems in connection with the relation between training and individual differences will be discussed later.

CHAPTER FIVE

INHERITANCE

Few problems are older than those pertaining to the relative importance of heredity and environment in determining human behavior. Few have more practical significance. If it is true, as some hold, that man's personality is wholly determined by heredity, then education in its broadest sense should merely allow growth to proceed with the least possible interference from people and circumstances. If it were possible to determine accurately what a person is innately best fitted for, his training should take place along these lines and no others. Since, according to this view, environment offers only an opportunity for inborn traits to develop, the only hope of racial improvement lies in allowing only those persons of unusually gifted hereditary backgrounds to have progeny. Some even argue that a gifted person will grow into superlative achievement in spite of environmental handicaps of the harshest sort, and contrariwise, opportunity is wasted on those who are innately incapable. This is an extreme hereditarian's viewpoint.

Another opposed view throws the burden of responsibility onto the environment. Opportunity, it is said, is the fundamental determinate of human behavior. People fail to achieve useful, wholesome lives, not because their germ plasm is defective but because poverty and restriction have so limited their horizons. One should concentrate on eliminating poverty and on equalizing opportunity, rather than on mating selectively if he would improve national well-being. This is an extreme environmentalist position.

The tremendous social impact of these two opposed ideas is obvious. The first fits in with an aristocratic political philosophy, and people who think in aristocratic terms have done all that they can to foster it. The second view fits the democratic ideal of equal opportunity for all and the more recent extension of this notion to include abundance and wealth of opportunity rather than half-open doors. Slum elimination projects have their origin in social beliefs of this kind.

What is the answer? Which group is right? What compromise position can be worked out which is best in accord with the facts?

The scientific way to approach a problem of this kind is to marshal whatever facts we are reasonably certain of and to arrive at some sort of an hypothesis that can be tested by an experiment. It has been suggested that the relative merits of these opposing beliefs could be evaluated if we transferred a group of American boys to some remote primitive tribe and allowed them to grow up in a preliterate environment, and conversely with a group of primitives. Just to *suppose* what would happen if we transplanted a group of Hottentot boys to central Illinois and took an equal number of Illinois boys to central Africa is outlawed at the beginning because the rules of the scientific game demand that we actually try out our bright ideas, and not just talk about them. It isn't at all likely that we ever could actually make an experiment of this kind because public opinion would be opposed to it. But frequently what would be morally outrageous as a planned experiment actually does take place as a result of circumstances beyond the control of organized society. An example of this kind of occurrence will be described shortly when we relate the story of the Wild Boy of Aveyron, but let us examine first an experiment with animals as subjects which was designed to test the view that hereditary factors can influence learning ability.

1. ANIMAL EXPERIMENTS

The experiment was conducted by R. C. Tryon, a psychologist of the University of California.

One hundred forty-two rats chosen at random were required to traverse a long and complicated pathway nineteen times. At the end of the path the animals were rewarded by finding food. A system of pathways like this is known as a maze. It is an instrument of wide use in psychological investigations, because it presents a series of alternative paths to food. Some of these are more direct than others. Hungry clever animals soon learn to take the most direct route in the shortest possible time, but hungry, dull, and stupid animals take the wrong turns on many more occasions, and in doing so require a longer time to go from the starting point to the food. The number of

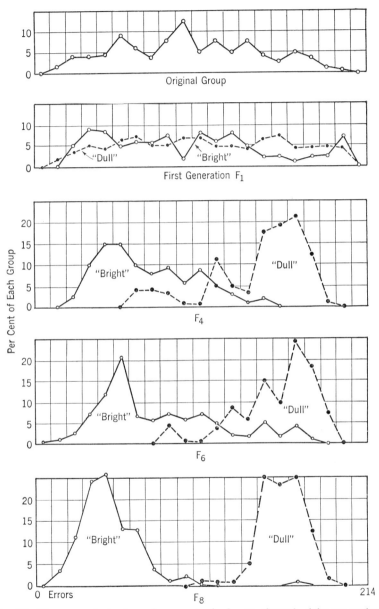

Fig. 12.—The errors that rats made on a standard maze through eight generations of selective breeding. The "brightest" and the "dullest" rats in each generation were inbred, a procedure which in eight generations produced two distinct "types" of "bright" and "dull" rats with little overlapping.

blind alleys they enter in successive attempts to get from one end of the maze to the other is taken as an index of how quickly they are learning.

The total number of blind-alley entrances for each rat in its nineteen trials showed that the rats, like humans, differ in the quickness with which they learn a new task of this kind. Some rats entered as few as seven or eight blind alleys. Others, with equal opportunity to make errors, entered as many as 214 cul-de-sacs. The remainder ranged between these two extremes.

When this part of the experiment had been completed, the bright rats were segregated and bred together as a group, and the dull and mediocre rats were bred together as another group. Their progeny were kept separately and required separately to run the same maze that had served to divide the preceding generation into bright and dull performers. Reference to the F_1 (first generation) progeny in Figure 12 shows the records made by these individuals when each had completed nineteen trials. The horizontal axis of the graph refers to the total number of blind alleys entered, a number which ranged from close to zero to approximately 214. The figures on the vertical axis refer to the percentages of bright and dull groups respectively, according to the total number of errors committed.

If we examine the series of graphs, one for each successive generation, we see that in the F_1 progeny there is little difference between the records made by the bright and dull groups. However, as the process of selective breeding is continued, and bright individuals are consistently mated with each other, while the dull individuals are also inbred, we observe that the curves for the respective groups become more and more distinct and separate from each other. Finally in the F_8 individuals (or eighth generation) there is practically no overlapping in ability between the two groups. In Figure 12 the intervening generations F_2, F_3, F_5, and F_7 are not shown.

One can see how impossible it would be, from the standpoint of time alone, to make an experiment involving several human generations. To make such an experiment with human subjects would take something like two hundred years. But aside from the time required there are many other practical considerations which make this type of experimentation with human beings impossible. Although our principal interest is in people, not rats, we can only infer that something very much like this would happen if we were rigorous in our selection of human subjects over many generations.

In the absence of experiments with people, there have been attempts to gather information about old families whose social and political history is known. One of the most famous of these is an early study by Goddard called *The Kallikaks*. It recounts the known history of two lines of the descendants of Martin Kallikak, a revolutionary war soldier. One of these lines had its origin in the mating of Martin and a normal woman, the other through an illicit affair that Martin had with a feeble-minded girl. The genealogy shows clearly that there is more feeble-mindedness, poverty, and social viciousness in the illegitimate line than in the other. But how much of this asocial conduct and general worthlessness is due to the fact that the line started with a feeble-minded girl and how much is due to the social level and economic insecurity of this branch of the family cannot be determined. Observations on other families, like the Edwards family of New England, which show an unusually large number of successful people, are likewise ambiguous in this respect.

The only conclusion which we may draw from Tryon's experiment with the rats is that two so-called "pure lines" have been produced through selection. *Inbreeding among the bright individuals results in bright progeny, and inbreeding among the dull individuals results in dull progeny.* Experimental evidence of this kind serves to establish the fact that the ability of the rat to learn the maze has a biological basis and, further, that the differences in this ability are genetically determined. Differences in ability to learn a thing, among human beings as well as among rats, are probably determined by many hereditary factors. *But because Tryon's animals learned promptly in this maze does not necessarily mean that they will learn all other things with as much facility as we find here.*

2. THE WILD BOY OF AVEYRON[1]

In the year 1799, a group of sportsmen found a lad roaming in a French forest who later came to be known as "the wild boy of

Adapted from W. N. Kellogg and L. A. Kellogg, *The Ape and the Child,* McGraw-Hill Book Company, Inc., New York, 1933. Used by permission.

Aveyron." [2] When discovered he was naked, scarred, and unkempt, and sought to resist capture by hurriedly climbing into a tree. Although he appeared to be fully eleven or twelve years old, he was quite unable to talk and was without knowledge of the most rudimentary habits of personal cleanliness. He was taken to Paris and subjected to a long period of methodical and painstaking education by a young French physician, Itard. Despite the fact that considerable progress was made toward fitting him for the complexities of civilized life, the training on the whole was regarded as unsuccessful.

The hereditarian explanation of the boy's behavior. The customary way of explaining the fact that a human being of this kind does not respond well to the efforts of those who would civilize and educate it is to say that he is feeble minded. It is inferred that even if such children had lived under civilized conditions, they would still have failed to duplicate the accomplishments of normal individuals. This reasoning carries with it the assumption that because these children were not up to the average for their ages when their re-education was discontinued, there must have been something wrong with them in the first place. In fact, going one step further, it is often argued that the "wild" children were probably abandoned *because* they displayed idiotic or imbecile tendencies at a very early age.

The environmentalist explanation. But there is a second way of accounting for the behavior of the wild boy. He may actually have learned, in a literal sense of the word, to be wild in the same way that a Caucasian child reared among Chinese grows into the Chinese customs and language, or a baby that has been kidnapped by gypsies knows in later years only the gypsy manner of living. He need not originally have been feeble-minded. He may have been so profoundly impressed with the experiences of his earlier years that the later efforts to teach him the reactions of the average educated child did not bear full fruit. *He had passed the age where the learning of civilized commonplaces was easy and natural, and had already consumed the most formative years in learning other things.* The wild animal cannot be thoroughly tamed unless its taming starts soon

2 Jean-Marc-Gaspard Itard, *The Wild Boy of Aveyron.* Translated by George and Muriel Humphrey, D. Appleton-Century Company, New York, 1932.

after it is born, which, paradoxically, is before it has actually become wild. Heredity, in this explanation, becomes of secondary importance; education and training are the powerful causal factors.

Here, then, are two complete but entirely distinct methods of accounting for the same phenomena.

Which view is correct? We can never know for certain which of these views is the correct explanation of the behavior of abandoned children. We could get a clue as to which is more likely to be true if we knew something about the hereditary background of a new case, but we should have to place a normal human infant in uncivilized surroundings and observe and record its development *as it grew up in this environment.* Since an experiment of this kind can not be carried out with a child, we must fall back on animal subjects.

3. THE APE AND THE CHILD

It would be both possible and practical to reverse these conditions. Instead of placing a child in a typical animal environment, why not place an animal in a typical human environment? Why not give one of the higher primates exactly the environmental advantages which a young child enjoys and then study the development of the resulting organism? [3]

If such an experiment were to produce dependable results, it would admit of no halfway measures. To carry it out in any comprehensive manner one would have to obtain an infant anthropoid ape, as young as possible, and rear it in every respect as a child is reared— even to the most minute detail. The animal subject would have to be bottle-fed, clothed, bathed, fondled, and given careful human treatment in every phase of its daily existence. It would have to be placed in a perambulator and wheeled. It would have to eat with a spoon as soon as it was able to feed itself at all. Its mistakes would be gently and persistently corrected as are the mistakes of a child. It would have to be made a thoroughly humanized member of the family of the experimenters, who would serve respectively in the capacities of adopted "father" and "mother." Many of the highly developed customs of our society might thus become integral parts of its be-

[3] W. N. Kellogg, "Humanizing the Ape," *Psychological Review,* 1931, 38, 160-170.

havior equipment in much the same manner that they are built into the human baby. As far as its immediate surroundings are concerned, the animal must never be given the opportunity to learn any other ways of acting except the human ways. This means that the *psychological* as well as the *physical* features of the environment must be entirely of a human character. That is, the reactions of all those who come in contact with the subject, and the resulting stimulation which these reactions afford the subject, should be without exception just what a normal child might receive.

Things we must avoid. Instances of anthropoid apes which have lived in human households are of course by no means unknown. But in all the cases of which we have any knowledge the "human" treatment accorded the animals was definitely limited by the attitude of the owner and by the degree of his willingness to be put to boundless labor. If an organism of this kind is kept in a cage for a part of each day or night, if it is led about by means of a collar and a chain, or if it is fed from a plate upon the floor, it is not unreasonable to suppose that these things must surely develop responses which are different from those of a human being. A child itself, if similarly treated, would most certainly acquire some genuinely *unchildlike* reactions. Again, if an organism—animal or human—is talked to and called like a dog or a cat, if it is petted or scratched behind the ears as these animals are so often treated, or if in other ways it is given *pet stimuli* instead of *child stimuli,* the resulting behavior may be expected to show the effects of such stimulation.

The incidental nature of the proposed training. The training of the ape must be what might be called *incidental* as opposed to *systematic* or controlled training. What it would get from its surroundings it would have to pick up by itself just as a growing child acquires new modes of behavior. It would be necessary to avoid deliberately teaching the animal, trial by trial, a series of tricks or stunts which it might go through upon signal or command. The things that it learned would have to be its own reactions to the human stimuli about it, not meaningless rituals elicited by a sign from a keeper. The spoon-eating training, to take a concrete example, according to the plan should be taken up only in a gradual and irregular manner at mealtime, as the subject's muscular coordination fitted it for this sort of manipulation. There could be no attempt to labor mechanically through a stated number of trials, rewarding or punishing the animal as it might succeed or fail. Such a proposed procedure, it will be readily seen, is loose and uncontrolled in that it precludes the opportunity to obtain quantitative data on the number of trials necessary to learn, the number of errors made, or the elapsed time per trial. It has the advantage, nevertheless, of being the same sort of training to which the human infant is customarily subjected in the normal course of its rearing.

Conclusions that could be drawn. At the completion of our experiment we should be in a position to make definite inferences regarding the two organisms:

(1) If the chimpanzee had failed to develop as did the child but remained instead on a subhuman level, then we could say that hereditary factors were dominant and that training did not seriously affect the resulting organism. Development along divergent lines within the same environment would show the importance of heredity. It could be maintained, should such results be secured, that the ape, given full opportunities to acquire a complete repertory of human reactions, had progressed only part of the way.

(2) If the chimpanzee in the human situation acquired many characteristically childlike responses, such results would show the importance of the human stimuli upon its growth. The extent to which the subjects learned to react in the same ways *despite their different heredities* would demonstrate the effect of the common cultural environment.

(3) In addition to showing environmental influence, the presence of identical responses in the ape and the child would also show that the heredities of the two, although different, were at the same time similar enough to permit like reactions to the same stimulation. Yet without the special influence of the civilized environment to serve as an activating cause in bringing out these likenesses, they would surely never come to light.

This plan was actually executed by Professor and Mrs. W. N.

Kellogg of Indiana University. Now no one, we hope, will be foolish enough to suppose from reading a proposal of this sort that either of the Kelloggs had so far lost his senses as to presume that one could make a human being out of an animal. There are obviously many natural differences between man and the apes which no amount of environmental equalizing can overcome.

The accomplishment of the experiment. It is difficult to appreciate the detailed nature of the preparations required for the accomplishment of an experiment like this. The experimenter had to obtain a leave of absence from the University of Indiana, where he was teaching, and move his family to Florida for the duration of the experiment. This arrangement involved the cooperation of numerous colleagues and administrative officers. Few college professors are wealthy enough to be able to take a year away from teaching without salary. As is true in most cases of this kind, an appeal was made to a foundation for the necessary money to furnish living expenses. The demands made on foundations are so numerous that each request must be carefully scrutinized. This involves convincing other people of the merits of the proposal. When all of the arrangements had been completed and the Social Science Research Council had agreed to grant Dr. Kellogg a fellowship there was already a history of several years' preparation that one never hears about in the formally written reports on experiments.

On June 26, 1931, a young female chimpanzee in the colony of the Anthropoid Experiment Station of Yale University at Orange Park, Florida, was separated from her mother, in whose cage she had previously been living. This little animal, named Gua, had been born in captivity in the Abreu Colony[4] in Cuba on November 15, 1930. She was turned over to the Kelloggs following the separation and was soon thereafter taken to their home, where her humanizing

[4] The story of a colony of great apes maintained by Mrs. Abreu, a wealthy resident of Havana, is found in R. M. Yerkes, *Almost Human* (1925). Mrs. Abreu's interest in apes was principally sentimental, but she did allow interested and qualified persons to make scientific studies of her animals. These studies by Yerkes and Bingham were responsible for the opening of the Orange Park Station of Yale University. The station is now known as the Yerkes Laboratories of Primate Biology and is jointly operated by Harvard and Yale. Karl Lashley is the present director.

was begun. Her age at that time was seven and a half months, or almost exactly two and a half months less than that of the Kelloggs' only child, Donald, who had been born August 31, 1930.

These two individuals lived together as companions, playmates, and members of the same household until March 28, 1932. Their surroundings and treatment were as nearly alike as it was possible to make them. At that time, nine months after the initiation of the research, Gua had attained the age of sixteen and a half months, while Donald was nineteen months old. The experiment was then discontinued and the ape was returned by a gradual habituating process to the more restricted life of the Experiment Station. During the nine months a continuous series of tests, comparisons, observations, and experiments made upon the two subjects covered nearly every phase of their structure and behavior for which there was measuring facilities.

We select for digest here only a few of the observations made during the study; for the complete account the student is referred to *The Ape and the Child*.

By the end of the first week Gua was always dressed in diapers and shoes, and on one or two occasions she had been clothed in a romper suit as well. Within the same period she began to sleep in her crib (although at first without a full equipment of bedding), and she was regularly fed from a spoon and a cup in her high chair. By the end of the second week, she permitted the cutting of her fingernails and before the fourth was over she was daily submitting to the application of a toothbrush.

General description of play activities. The human infant served as Gua's most intimate playmate for nearly nine months, and she in turned filled a similar role with regard to the child. It is safe to say that Gua was the first playmate Donald had ever had, aside from his parents. He correspondingly became the first playmate of the little animal, excepting only her mother, with whom she lived during her earlier cage existence. The initial reactions of the subjects toward each other should for this reason be of particular significance.

From the moment they first entered each other's presence there was evidence of curiosity and interest on the part of both. The interest seemed to be more marked in the case of Donald than of Gua. When they were seated side by side, the child reached for the ape and touched her, although at that early stage she would make no corresponding advances. They were not subsequently brought into close proximity for several days, but continued to eye each other from a distance. Donald, as before, seemed to persist in this behavior more than the chimpanzee. As soon as they had been moved together for the second time, she immediately *extended her lips in a series of exploratory kisses* which touched the child upon his face and lips. At first he seemed startled but made no avoiding reactions and subsequently cooed his pleasure.

Mutual attachment of the two infants. As examples of the mutual attachment which grew up after their initial meetings, it may be pointed out that Gua almost always, if not prevented, would make her way in some manner to the child. She would go to him if he was in his walker, climb into his lap if he was seated in his high chair, and frequently sit upon his foot or his leg if he was on the floor. She would even follow him away from the protection of those who cared for her. If he had not yet awakened from his nap when she awoke from hers, she could hardly be kept from the door of his room, to which she would go, and, during the later months, which she would open.

Once, during an unavoidable absence on the part of the two observers, the subjects were left at home taking their noonday naps in charge of a maid who was new and somewhat strange to Gua. The ape, then ten and a half months of age, awakened before either of the experimenters had returned. A report of her activities as obtained from the attendant is as follows: When Gua awakened and found herself alone with the strange person she began screaming and ran from one room to another as if in search of a familiar face. Her cries aroused Donald, to whose door she had not yet gone. Immediately upon hearing the noise he made, she rushed to the door of his room and hammered on it with both hands. When she was permitted to enter, she became quiet at once and remained in the presence of the child without further disturbance.

On another occasion, about two weeks after this incident, when the subjects were playing beside each other in the same room with both the adults, one of the observers without warning accidentally upset a chair. This made a sharp clatter near Gua as it struck the floor. Instead of running toward either of the grownups—a reaction to be expected under such circumstances—Gua rushed to Donald, threw both arms around him, and hugged him tightly, crying the while.

On his part, Donald began to toddle to Gua as soon as he was dressed and put down on the floor in the morning. His first act was then to greet her by stooping forward and hugging her. The same procedure would usually be repeated whenever she had been scream-ing or even if she had only been scolded. The little animal in her turn began about this time to take what appeared to be a protec-tive attitude toward the child, particularly if the two were out of doors. When they held hands as they walked together, it was Gua at first who did the actual holding. If their grip broke for an instant, it was she again who stopped, waited for Donald, or went after him and seized his hand in hers, although the child became the aggressor in this act at a little later date. When Donald would cry, she would run to him, and if he was being carried by someone she would often slap the holder.

The kinds of things they learned.   At the age of ten months the chimpanzee released a door latch by turning the doorknob. Her first success in such a task was accidental, however, since she was hanging by one hand from the knob at the time so that the torque-like pull of her weight on one side of the handle caused it to turn. Just when accidental door opening, which thereafter became quite common because of her increasing tendency to hang upon door knobs, gave way to deliberate door opening, it would be difficult to say. For some months Gua was more likely to cry, or to lie down on the floor and look beneath a door, to put her fingers under it, or to slap it, than she was to manipulate the knob itself. The child never succeeded through-out the entire nine months in releasing a single door latch, possibly because of the shortness of his reach. He would, nevertheless, touch the knobs with his fingers and rattle them almost whenever he approached one.

By the time the ape had attained the age of thirteen and a half months, she was observed to unlatch the front door of the house in a manner which appeared anything but accidental. This she accomplished by climbing upon a small piece of furniture beside it, reaching from the furniture to the knob with her right hand, and turning the knob successively to the right and to the left by extending and flexing her arm. As soon as the latch was released she pulled the door open at once.

Gua also formed a connection between electric light switches and the appearance of the light. The response, which she picked up without instruction or assistance, consisted in hooking the index finger over the movable part of the toggle switch and pulling it downward. Yet neither could extinguish the light by pushing the switch upward for more than a month, when Gua alone achieved this result. Donald tried frequently, but he was never successful, probably because his hands and fingers were not sufficiently sturdy.

The child proved, on the other hand, to be much superior to the chimpanzee at the game of pat-a-cake, for Gua was here a hopeless failure. Toward the last she would slap the extended hands of one of the adults when told to pat-a-cake but she never learned to respond with typical hand clapping. Her inability to acquire such a simple reaction is all the more surprising in view of the fact that she was given almost daily opportunity for such play for several months, while the human infant was not so persistently encouraged.

Miscellaneous observations of this sort are obviously conflicting with regard to the relative learning ability of the two subjects, so that we must turn to more precise experimental techniques in order to throw light on this important comparative problem. In this connection it is to be noted that probably the most exact and certainly the most persistent training through which the average human baby is conducted is in learning to control the bladder and bowels. Such training is begun usually at the age of less than a year and may continue as long as three or four years. If properly managed it is an invariable, methodical, day-and-night procedure which few subsequent endeavors in the lifetime of the individual can equal in either regularity or extensiveness. Here, then, should be an excellent field in which to compare the learning abilities of the two organisms,

July 5, 1931.

Donald placed in baby pen. Gua is on floor outside of pen. She goes towards him, reaching through the bars with her right hand. *They hold hands.* Donald seems delighted. She touches him gently on the abdomen with her closed fist. He gets hold of her hair and pulls it. She reaches through the bars with her right hand, and extending her index finger she touches his hand lightly. She loses her balance while sitting and falls back. . . . Donald soon afterwards falls likewise from a sitting position to his back, and cries.

July 10, 1931.

He stands in his play pen holding the rail. He is apparently so delighted when she approaches that he lets go with one hand as if to reach for her and nearly loses his balance. He laughs with almost every breath. . . . Gua goes to side of pen. Donald falls down, first to a sitting, then to a lying posture. He is picked up and placed again in a sitting position. He leans forward towards her so far that he falls forward. Raises his head while lying prone and looks through the bars at her. She reaches in to him, pulls his head down and kisses it. She touches his face and hands. . . . Both seem to be very interested and strive to get nearer to each other.

July 11, 1931.

He is so excited he pants, vocalizing at each exhalation. He repeatedly stands up in his walker and then sits down again stamping his feet in this manner. He seems to like to see her fall down and invariably laughs aloud when she does. She is very active, moves rapidly and awkwardly, and probably falls oftener than usual. She moves towards him, bites at the counting balls on his walker, and pushes the walker with her hand. He reaches for her head and touches it. He evidently attempts to go after her in his walker as she moves away but jumps up and down in his excitement and pushes the walker backward instead. He cannot push it forward very well as yet.

July 13, 1931.

They are placed on a bed together. Donald reaches towards Gua. She "smiles." Seems very complacent and friendly. He puts his finger in her eye.

He then gets upon his stomach and while in this position he slides himself backward by pushing with his hands. He accidentally slips off the bed by this means before he can be caught. He is not hurt but cries loudly. Gua appears terrified at the noise and excitement and although she utters no sound, she rushes to me and buries her head in my lap.

She continues to kiss Donald frequently on approaching him. This is usually the case when she climbs up in his high chair, making contact with his bare foot which she kisses.

without modifying their ordinary childlike surroundings or conducting them through unusual or irregular processes of training.

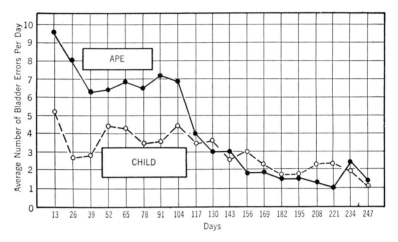

Fig. 13.—Average number of bladder errors per day for the ape and the child. The points plotted are the averages of 13-day periods. (After Kellogg.)

Throughout the nine-month period of training in both bladder and bowel control, nearly 6,000 responses of the ape were tabulated, of which a little over 1,000 were errors. The child, in his turn, reacted more than 4,700 times, of which about 750 were errors.

Manual dexterity. In manual dexterity, particularly with regard to the grasping of small objects and the making of fine, coordinated finger movements, the ape, it is well known, is inferior to man. The finest prehensile movements of which Gua was originally capable were made with the lips. In getting a morsel of food from the tray of her high chair, or in picking up such a minute object as a pin, her reactions at the beginning were invariably to stoop forward and use the mouth. There are good reasons why this should be the case: (1) The lips of the chimpanzee form an important tactile organ with an apparent capacity to feel and manipulate small objects considerably surpassing that of the corresponding human parts. (2) The length and awkward shape of the hands and fingers preclude their being employed with as much efficiency as human hands and fingers,

84

as, for example, in making the fine thumb-and-finger pincer movement. (3) In the beginning, when primates can walk only on all
fours, it is much easier for them to carry objects in their mouths than
in their hands. This in itself predisposes toward a greater use of the
lips.

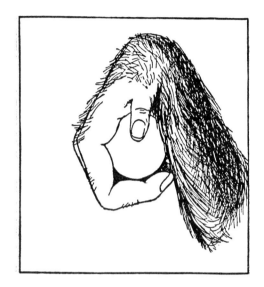

FIG. 14.—The chimpanzee
grasps a bulky object like a
ball, by pressing it against
the volar surface of the
forearm. The wrist will allow the palm of the hand
to bend in this direction
much farther than it is possible for the hand of a
human being to do. (After
Kellogg.)

To encourage Gua in an increased use of her hands and fingers,
toys and tidbits which were held out to her were not released if she
tried to take them with the lips. This method seemed to be generally effective, and its use was soon followed by a change in behavior
in which the hands came to be employed with greater frequency and
proficiency.

That Gua's *coarse* hand movements were relatively clumsy may
be accounted for in part by the backward limitations in the angles of
movement of the wrist and finger joints. The gross grasping response
for her involved not only the closing of the fingers but usually the
movement of the wrist toward the arm as well. It consisted of a sort
of rolling up on the object in a manner which sometimes suggested
the curling movement made by the end of an elephant's trunk (see
Figure 14). The thumb was seldom used in such reactions. Her
ability to bend the wrist and fingers backward often in addition made

it difficult for her to release objects from her grasp. Thus in her efforts at building with blocks she could put one block upon another readily enough, but she did not seem able to get her long curved fingers away from the second block without upsetting the whole tower, even though it might consist of no more than two blocks.

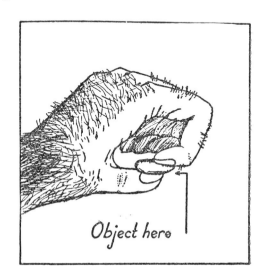

FIG. 15.—In a few instances Gua picked up small round objects like beans between the nails of the thumb and index finger. This movement was as near as she ever came to the more accurate thumb-forefinger opposition of the child. (After Kellogg.)

Object here

What shall be our criterion in the separation of those responses of the ape which show the particular effect of the human environment from those which seem not to do so? As a test upon each act we shall ask the following question: *Could the chimpanzee possibly have developed this behavior had she been reared without the pertinent stimuli of the civilized surroundings?* If the answer is "yes" or "doubtful," we shall classify the response as probably independent of the special influence of the human situation. If the answer is "no," then we shall feel justified in classifying the act as dependent upon the civilized environment.

Behavior that would have developed without human surroundings. That Gua's mouth was more mobile as an organ of prehension is independent of the civilized environment. The same was true of her more consistent avoidance of bright lights, her (apparently) keener hearing, and her many distinctive emotional reactions. Similarly we should place her greater propensity to bite and chew, her inability to pick up small objects with the fingers, and her deficiency in articulation in this category. Her further deficiencies in exploration and manipulation, her attention to stimuli for only a relatively short time, and her inferiority in imitation seem also to us to belong under this heading. She was superior in muscular co-ordination and faster in her involuntary movements, stronger, and remembered better than the child.

These characteristics we think are independent of the specific humanizing features of the environment in which Gua lived. Certainly this need not mean that the influence of some sort of environment cannot be proven in every one of them. But it does mean that *they would probably have developed much as they did in almost any environment which permits healthy and regular growth.*

Since Donald's performance was about average for his age, the respects in which the ape surpassed him are the respects in which she was generally more advanced than the average child approximately as old as herself. They cast no necessary reflection upon the child, but are rather points of special credit for the ape. She may thus be said to have become "more humanized" than the human subject.

Behavior dependent on the human environment. Here we would place her skipping, her greater cooperation and obedience, her tendency to kiss for forgiveness, her skillful opening of doors. Her more frequent sly behavior suggested the mischievousness of a lively boy, while her superior anticipation of bladder and bowel reactions were an obvious mark of progress. Her striking ability to eat with a spoon and to drink from a glass compare with corresponding abilities of children much older than she.

We conclude, therefore, that *it is possible to list a group of behavior items which depend principally on the bodily structure of the ape that would occur in any environment.* But at the same time, *Gua became surprisingly humanlike and, in the respects that we have mentioned, was actually superior to Donald.* These items we infer are dependent on the human environment in which she lived for nine months.

Summary of the chapter. There are two opposing views relating to the efficacy of heredity as an explanation for differences in human ability and attainment. Which of these views, if either, is correct cannot be discovered by direct experimentation with people for various practical reasons. We have to depend on experiments with animals. One of these, Tryon's, shows that the biological basis or bases for maze learning can be manipulated genetically. "Bright" and "dull" rats can be developed by selective breeding. But "bright" and "dull" as they refer to a particular maze may not be significant designations for other learning situations.

The experiment with Donald and Gua is a record of observations on two animals entirely different from the genetic standpoint who were reared in like cultural environments. In those acts in which the structural anatomical features are extremely important, the ape remained an ape, but in many ways she became humanlike in her reactions and in some instances actually exceeded the performance of average human youngsters her own age. Cultural modification and molding ordinarily begin with birth and progress in an integrated way with the anatomical development of the organism. These anatomical structures are inherited. No amount of environmental similarity ever makes them more alike.

CHAPTER SIX

MATURATION AND GROWTH

Aside from the general questions of the relative influences of heredity and environment that we have considered in Chapter Four, there is another important determinant of behavior generally called *maturation,* or more simply, *growth.*[1] *The factor of growth itself without any cooperation from the environment except that involved in sustenance of the organism can account for some limited types of behavior.* This hypothesis has been subjected to experimental test in several different ways and with several different kinds of animals as subjects. We will take up the simpler cases first.

1. EXPERIMENTS WITH FROGS AND SALAMANDERS

The psychologist Carmichael selected frogs and salamanders as his experimental animals. In both of these species there is considerable development in the larval stages that in mammals is accomplished in the uterus of the mother, and is therefore hidden to the inquisitive eye of the scientific investigator. Another important reason why these species are used is that the behavior of these animals is relatively very simple. It is always best to try out an idea in the simplest possible manner. When explanations are possible in the simple organisms, then it is time to progress to those forms that are higher in the evolutionary scale and more complex.

At the beginning of this century it was discovered that the drug chloretone could be used to anesthetize small animals like tadpoles so that they would continue to grow normally but would be entirely unresponsive to any kind of stimulus. Under the proper concentration of chloretone in water the larval growth is somewhat slowed down, but it continues in its essential respects while the animal

---

1 Although the terms *growth* and *maturation* are frequently used interchangeably, they are, strictly speaking, not synonymous. Growth implies chiefly an increase in body size. Maturation implies an increase in the complexity of the bodily tissue, or differentiation. Both usually occur together, although not necessarily. It should be clearly understood, therefore, that the development of behavior depends on the increased differentiation of the body tissues, or maturation, even though the word *growth* is occasionally substituted.

remains absolutely inert. If the concentration is made too strong, the animal will be killed or will develop in abnormal ways. Therefore it is absolutely necessary to maintain the concentration at just that point where the skeletal muscles will not respond, but where the vital maturation processes will not be interfered with. This condition exists when a concentration of approximately four parts chloretone to every ten thousand parts water is used. For almost a quarter of a century this discovery was only an interesting scientific fact. No one had taken advantage of it until Carmichael set to work to make use of it in answering this riddle about the relative influence of growth and experience in animal development.

Method. He collected frogs' eggs, and the eggs of a salamander, not so well known but almost as numerous as the frog in certain parts of the country. At times these eggs can be found in ponds where frogs and salamanders live. They come in clusters known as clutches and are imbedded in a jellylike substance from which they have to be removed one at a time and transferred to small laboratory dishes, one to each dish and with the dish properly labeled with the specimen number.

After a few days, the embryro can be observed directly through the transparent egg. At this stage it does not move at all. It has no eyes, ears, or limbs—these are all supplied in the next few days. In the normal course of events the animal soon becomes free-swimming and at this point we come face to face with a very important question: Does the animal learn to swim, or does it simply grow up to a certain stage of adulthood at which it begins to swim regardless of the opportunity to learn? Do the stimuli that play on the maturing animal from the outside have anything at all to do with the swimming response, or would it occur irrespective of these outside influences?

This general question had been tried out experimentally before. In one widely quoted[2] experiment, birds had been confined in small cages where they could not have possibly flown and where the experimenter thought that exercise of the wing muscles was not possible. Confined birds, when released, flew as well as those that not been con-

2 D. A. Spaulding, "Instinct, with Original Observations on Young Animals," *Macmillan's Magazine*, 1873, 27, 282-293.

fined. These results do not impress us today because it is easy to see that it would have to be a very close-fitting cage that would absolutely remove the possibility of wing exercise. The wings could be moved even if they could not be used in typical flying movements. There was not complete control over the effect of practice. *Even a little practice may be very effective.* In Carmichael's experiment, however, there is an opportunity to prevent all muscle movement by anesthetizing the animal. Indeed, the two experiments, even though they are aimed at answering the same question, are not at all comparable because the young bird, after hatching, is a much more mature animal than the Amblystoma larva.

Results. At a stage well in advance of the normal appearance of the swimming response, Carmichael[3] removed half of his developing frogs and salamanders to the anesthetic solution. The other half were allowed to develop normally. The latter group constituted a normal series with which the responses of the experimentally anesthetized animals could be compared. When the unanesthetized controls had been swimming freely for some time, the experimental animals were placed in tap water, one at a time, and their responses to a slight touch on the side of the head with a slender glass rod were noted. On the average, for the first twelve minutes there was not any response at all. Then, in response to the touch, they bent, some toward and some away from the side upon which they were stimulated. The responses continued more promptly, more precisely, more vigorously, until by the end of thirty minutes, on the average, they were swimming freely—swimming so well, as a matter of fact, that it was very difficult to distinguish them from the normal animals that had not been anesthetized and by this time had been swimming for five days.

Interpretation of the results. If it were possible to release the experimental animals from the anesthetic instantaneously, it would be possible to infer that the whole half hour was just a period of very rapid learning in which enough was learned to make up for

3 Leonard Carmichael, "The Development of Behavior in Vertebrates Experimentally Removed from the Influence of External Stimulation," *Psychological Review,* 1926, 33, 51-58.

the five days' practice on the part of the control animals. But no such inference is possible because we know that the usual effects of drugging dissipate slowly, not instantaneously. Or we could infer that the whole half hour was the period required for total recovery from the chloretone and that no learning at all took place. But this would not be a reasonable inference because it entirely neglects the possibility that learning may take place. We are left, then, with the only other reasonable interpretation, namely, the half hour is partly a period of recovery, partly a period of rapid learning.

If we are really scientifically inquisitive, a "maybe yes," "maybe no" conclusion of this kind will not satisfy us. Like Carmichael, we will seek a method of evaluating the period of recovery from the anesthetic. He reasoned this way: If it took animals who had already been swimming as much time to recover as it did those who had never swum before, then the whole half hour would be a recovery period, the learning time would be zero. If it took practiced animals only half as long to recover, then we could reasonably infer that fifteen minutes were required to eliminate the effects of the drug. The other fifteen minutes would be devoted to rapid learning.

Further experimentation to test this hypothesis. In order to find out which condition was true, the whole experiment was repeated, this time with the salamanders alone.[4] The members of a group were kept anesthetized as before until their control mates had been swimming for some time. They were then released from the anesthetic and their recovery watched as before. But this time after being allowed to swim freely for thirty-six hours, they were reanesthetized and for twenty-four hours they were held as inert as they had been before their thirty-six-hour period of free-swimming.

Results. At the end of their twenty-four-hour period of inactivity, Carmichael again transferred them to tap water. Carefully he timed the interval of recovery and again, as it had been before, 12 minutes were required to obtain a first movement and a half hour was required for complete recovery. Since there was no difference in

4 Leonard Carmichael, "A Further Study on the Development of Behavior in Vertebrates Experimentally Removed from the Influence of External Stimulation," *Psychological Review*, 1927, 34, 34-47.

the recovery time, whether for the first or second experience, the whole thirty-minute period must have been consumed in removing the effects of the chloretone; consequently, the learning time was zero, or in other words, learning did not take place.

Interpretation. Growth processes in the animal determine whether or not the swimming response occurs. When a certain maturational age is attained, regardless of whether or not the animal has been anesthetized, the response occurs; therefore one may not truly say that a larval frog or salamander learns to swim. Rather than this, one should say that *when a given level in maturation has been attained, swimming is the natural outcome of the relations which exist between the organism and its environment.*

But where is this growth? Is it in the muscles themselves, in the sense organs, or in the nervous system of the organism in question? It took the anatomist Coghill just about a quarter of a century to answer this question, but he did finally find an answer.[5]

Significance of Coghill's work. Students, in general, are not likely to appreciate the tremendous drive that would keep an investigator at a task for so long a period of time, particularly when that task involves the inconsequential end that this one seems to have. Who cares what element in a salamander's anatomy is responsible for his ability to swim? Most people would not spend a week or a day or even an hour to find out. Of what value is it to know this fact? It is not likely that Coghill himself had any final interest in Amblystoma, but he did have a nagging curiosity about human behavior. He got it in a first course in psychology when he was an undergraduate. He saw clearly that there were numerous riddles in human psychology that could not be solved until somebody had adequate explanations for kinds of behavior that are much simpler than human nature. Sometimes this simple behavior appears to be so far removed from human nature that there does not seem to be the remotest connection between them. Coghill's discovery, taken by itself, is comparatively slight. Seen in its proper perspective, it is of the utmost

[5] C. E. Coghill, *Anatomy and the Problem of Behavior,* The Macmillan Company, New York, 1929.

significance. What this significance is we will try to make clear, but first let us see why the problem was so difficult of solution.

The proposed experiment. In the first place, one has to know a great deal about the behavior of Amblystoma. The general plan of the experiment requires us to find some behavior items (swimming, simple as it seems, is much too complicated) that occur regularly in all Amblystoma and at approximately the same time in all specimens. In its early embryonic stages Amblystoma is inert. Then, as development proceeds, it will turn its head away from the side which is stimulated. Now there must be some difference between an inert animal and one that will turn its head. Taking several of each kind, we kill them, fix them, and make cross sections of them, slicing very thin sections from the tail to the head. Each section is only a few thousandths of a millimeter thick. As many as two thousand sections, each one about $\frac{1}{100}$ of a millimeter thick, are mounted separately for a single animal and each is observed by means of a microscope in order to find some difference between those specimens that do and those that do not bend the head. (The specimen shown in Figure 16 is about $\frac{2}{3}$ of an inch long.) The skill required to make the sections alone is no mean accomplishment, as some students of biology can tell you. But aside from that, additional skill in being able to detect microscopic differences between the specimens is a further preparation that demands thorough training and endless patience. If you remember having looked through a microscope for the first time, you are aware of what has been called in another connection "a blooming, buzzing confusion."

By careful scrutiny of the behavior of the salamander, Coghill detected five stages in its development, all being accomplished normally before hatching:

Incorrect explanations. So much for the behavior which is observed. Now to proceed to an *explanation* of this observed behavior. We could say that Amblystoma bends away from a slight touch near the head because it "does not like the stimulus" or because the "stimulus is painful." Such explanations, however, are not really explanations at all. They endow the animal with human character-

1. The inert, or nonmotile stage. The embryo is perfectly impervious to stimulation of any kind.

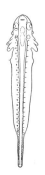

FIG. 16.—Nonmotile stage.

2. The early flexure stage. A light touch produces a movement away from the side stimulated. The movement is slow and is performed by the serial contraction of the muscle segments. As the embryo advances in age, the muscular action extends farther down the side until the entire trunk is involved.

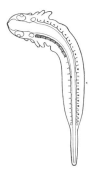

FIG. 17.—Early flecture.

3. The coil stage. The extension of the bending reaction promptly down the entire side of the embryo causes it to assume a tight coil form. Stage 3 grows directly out of Stage 2.

FIG. 18.—Coil.

95

istics. A man might *say* that he has bent his head away from an *unpleasant* stimulus, but we must remember that this embryo is not a tiny human being. It is a small bundle of developing tissues, principally muscles and nerves from the standpoint of our interest; therefore our descriptions must involve muscles and nerves and the relations between them and the external surroundings—and nothing else.

4. The S-stage. A wave of contraction starts as if the animal were going to execute a coil, but before the wave has passed the entire length of the one side, a new contraction starts at the head on the opposite side. This causes the embryo to assume an S-shape. An instant later the reverse S (ʔ) takes its place.

Fig. 19.—S-stage.

5. Swimming. When the S-reactions are sufficiently strong and fast, the embryo is propelled through the water. Stage 5 involves nothing new; it is merely an improvement in coordination over Stage 4.

Scientific explanation

STAGE 1. A living embryo that will not respond to stimuli. What could the possible reasons be? There might be something wrong with the muscles, the sense organs, the sensory pathways, the motor pathways, or the central connecting fibers. Which is it? The muscles, even during the nonmotile state, are capable of contraction. This fact was shown by stimulating them directly by means of a sharp needle. When the needle was inserted through the skin directly into a muscle cell, that cell contracted. The effects were confined to the one cell, however: there was no effect on the surrounding cells. So the difficulty is not with the muscles.

STAGE 2. There did not appear to be any difference in the sensory or motor pathways between those animals that did and those that did not respond. But there was a difference in the cells that connected the sensory to the motor paths. In the nonmotile stage these connecting cells were undeveloped, but in the bending stage they had extended themselves so that they bridged the gap between the sensory and the motor processes, a fact established by direct observation under the microscope. When the final connecting link had completed its growth, there was movement now where before there was none. *There can be no doubt that the difference between behavior and no behavior is entirely explained by the growth of a single neuron in the central nervous system through a distance of less than* $\frac{1}{100}$ *of a millimeter.*

STAGE 3. But why the coil stage? Unlike the bending stage, which is either present or not present, the coil stage is an outgrowth of bending. The bending merely progresses farther and farther down one side of the larva. This is explained by the fact that growth starts at the head end of the larva and proceeds in the tailward direction so that the same growth processes which explain the bending reaction occur successively at lower and lower levels and constitute an explanation of the coil stage.

STAGE 4. In the S-stage there are two additional growth processes on the part of the nervous system. One of these processes

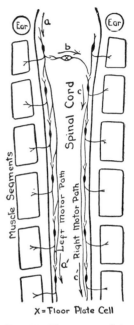

X = Floor Plate Cell

FIG. 20.—Figure to explain bending.

involves the axons of the motor pathway and is simply an extension of Stage 3. But a curious new process is also under way: in each muscle cell there appears a sensory fiber. These fibers grow as collaterals of the sensory neurons which supply the skin. Therefore the contraction of a muscle cell has the same stimulational effect as contact in Stage 2. If the animal is then stimulated near the head on the outer skin, a contraction results on the opposite side, as we have seen. But instead of the process stopping here, as it has in previous stages, the contraction of the muscle produces a further stimulation which is transmitted to the muscles of the other side. These two wavelike contractions, progressing down each side of the animal, produce the S-shaped form that we have described.

97

STAGE 5. There is nothing new in the swimming stage. When the growth processes that we have described progress farther down the sides and when these S-stages become rapid enough, propulsion through the water results.

Entirely aside from the factual information regarding growth and maturation that they provide, these experiments of Coghill's and Carmichael's will give to the reflective student further insight into the scientific method as it applies to problems of behavior. You will observe that scientific explanation is really a series of descriptions. First we need accurate and detailed descriptions of the behavior under consideration. In obtaining these descriptions we almost always need to employ various instruments of precision such as microscopes and stop watches and measuring devices of other kinds. Explanation of this carefully described behavior is then made in terms of other descriptions, this time of the relationships that obtain between sense organs, nervous system, and muscles and glands. A curious person might still want to know how the sense organs, muscles and glands ever came into being. If he pursues his objective far enough he will find another series of descriptions in embryology relating to the origin of these structures. If he still asks "why?" the embryologist will refer him to the geneticist, who in turn will give him another set of descriptions. This process constitutes scientific explanation. We never actually get to "why." "Why" questions are answered by substituting "how" answers. Some scientists doubt that anyone is ever able to answer a "why" question whether in the field of science or not.

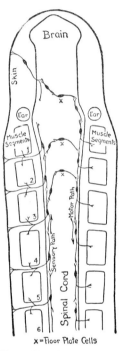

FIG. 21.—Showing the growth of proprioceptive collaterals in the motor pathway.

2. GRASPING AND CREEPING

Is growth as powerful in determining the behavior of children as it is for the laboratory animals that we have just seen? At least three lines of evidence indicate that before the school age, at least, it is. One of these lines stems from careful observations that have been made on the development of creeping[6] and of grasping.[7]

These studies involve only a description of the behavior, as we shall see, and are not explanations in neural and anatomical terms, but they reveal fairly definite patterns of response which follow on each other according to an invariable sequence, and consequently are strongly suggestive of explanation in the same terms as Coghill has used for Amblystoma. The other two lines derive from attempted modification of this sequence by allowing special opportunity or imposing special restriction on either (a) a group of children, or (b) a single child. In order to obtain controls for these experiments, in (a) another group of children has to be used; in (b) the most fruitful control has been the identical twin of the child whose environment has been experimentally modified.

Grasping. In the development of both creeping and grasping the Clinic of Child Development at Yale University has made intensive studies over a period of years. The method used in these studies is strikingly like that we have seen in the previous section on Amblystoma. Of course human infants are not sacrificed to find out just which neurons are responsible for a movement of the arms or legs, but the behavior descriptions are attempted in about the same terms that Coghill employed, and it turns out that the various stages of development in both creeping and grasping follow upon each other in a way that forces us to infer that maturational processes play a dominant role in this behavior development. Instead of attempting to make all of their observations directly, these experimenters have made extensive use of motion-picture sequences which are taken at specified intervals and provide a permanent record of the infant's behavior. These records can then be studied at leisure so that we are certain that nothing observable has been overlooked.

---

[6] Louise B. Ames, "The Sequential Patterning of Prone Progression in the Human Infant," *Genetic Psychology Monographs,* 1937, 19, 409-460.

Arnold Gesell and Louise B. Ames, "Ontogenetic Organization of Prone Behavior in Human Infancy," *Journal of Genetic Psychology,* 1940, 56, 247-263.

[7] H. M. Halverson, "An Experimental Study of Prehension in Infants by Means of Systematic Cinema Records," *Genetic Psychology Monographs,* 1931, 10, 108-285.

Newborn infants do not reach for and manipulate objects. When they do commence to make contact with objects it is found that larger objects are first reacted to by squirming and twisting the whole body and by random flailing of the arms. This reaction is definite enough so that it can be said to constitute a *stage* in development. A second stage involves raking and corralling movements with both hands. The hands themselves seem to be under the dominance of the arms, the wrists have very little independent action, and the elbows do not take part in adjusting the movements to the extent that they do in the adult. Most of the activity seems to be under the nervous and muscular control of the large muscles involved in making movements of the whole arm from the shoulder. Among the other stages are backhand approaches, where the back of the hand is directed toward the object; circuitous approaches, where the hand describes a wide arc in approaching the object; direct plane approaches, where the surface of the hand is parallel to the top of the table; palm grasps, in which the object is held against the palm by all five fingers; thumb-forefinger oppositions, where the object is grasped between those two digits alone. These responses follow one another in approximately the sequence enumerated here. They seem to be different from the development of the behavior of simpler organisms like the larval Amblystoma in that the stages are not quite so well defined. As a result one can find several of them present at one period of observation. Then, too, an infant frequently will have progressed to one of the more advanced stages and, for some reason, will then revert, for several days, to a more primitive way of behaving. Not all infants develop at the same rate, of course.

One principle is evident here which Coghill also demonstrated with Amblystoma (his experiments justifying this principle are not related here) : *The direction of maturation is from the shoulder toward the finger tips,* or, more technically, in the proximo-distal direction.

Creeping.   The same kind of patterning has also been observed in creeping. To begin with, when an infant is placed prone at an early age the head is barely lifted from the supporting surface, if at all, but by sixteen weeks most infants will use their arms first and then the hands to raise the chest as well as the head from the surface. At about thirty-two weeks, on the average, they will thrust the knees forward so that the entire torso is off the floor. After that time some six or eight weeks longer are required before creeping develops as a well-executed response. One investigator has distinguished fourteen stages in this process. One frequently hears of children who suddenly one day walk unaided. In these cases it is extremely doubtful that they have been afforded the opportunity to exhibit the stages that normally would precede this relatively mature response. It is true that some infants seem to skip a given stage, but not many of them do. It is also true that certain infants develop highly individual ways of executing parts of the whole pattern, but here again, when we try to see the essential features of a long-time development, we are struck with the similarity in the way in which infant after infant develops. One reason why this pattern is not perfectly obvious is that the development extends over so long a time. Other animals develop so quickly that we can remember from the terminal stage what the first stages looked like; not so with the human infant. Without the use of motion pictures taken at weekly or biweekly intervals, it is likely that we would not even now be able to stage this behavior so precisely. These motion-picture views may be seen over and over again until the observer has exhausted all they have to offer.

As was the case with grasping, it is felt that the way one phase leads into another is better explained by some sort of fundamental growth process. The other alternative—that learning is principally responsible—throws too much weight on the uniformity of the environment. Environments are not usually uniform enough to account for the sameness with which specific kinds of behavior is exhibited. Moreover, when special attempts are made either to enrich or to restrict the environment, at least some behavior is practically unaffected by these changes. It seems more accurate to say that an infant *grows* to *grasp* or to *creep* than to say that he *learns* to do these things.

3. NURSERY-SCHOOL CHILDREN

In a study of the permanence of certain skills when an unusual opportunity to practice was afforded, Jersild used the entire enrollment of a New York City day nursery. There were twenty-three children between the ages of four and six who were tested for their strength of grip by an instrument called a *dynamometer,* which is simply a divided hand piece that the children tried to pull together against the resistance of a spring. Connected to the hand piece was a dial, calibrated in kilograms so that the strength of each child's righthand grasp could be measured directly.

Each subject was given practice on the instrument on each Monday, Wednesday, and Friday while school was in session for a three-month period, or a total of forty-three practice periods consisting of four separate trials for every child. One might think that during so long a period of time the interest of the children would definitely lag; that they might not work at a maximum level of performance; and that the results would then be inaccurate in expressing the child's full capacity. The experimenter himself was somewhat concerned about this factor before the experiment was under way. But let us see what really happened.

Immediately following the initial tests, there appeared to be a decline in the interest shown by some of the children, but this condition quickly gave way to what seemed to be whole-hearted enthusiasm for the project. The experimenters entered into the project with appropriate abandon; cheerleader tactics while the child was squeezing the instrument, congratulations, handshakes, and applause when a past record was broken, a red-penciled entry of the score when a new high was attained, and other devices gave the project much of the flavor of an athletic event. Soon after the experiment was begun the experimenters were enthusiastically welcomed by a cluster of children whenever they were seen to enter the day nursery. The children asked to be given their turn, requests for additional trials were frequent. The subjects further expressed good will by means of Christmas cards, Valentines, etc., to the experimenters. If only one experimenter appeared, inquiries were made concerning the other, and if a new record was established by a given child requests were made that the tidings be brought to the absentee experimenter.[8]

Results on just twenty-three children would be useless unless we had something with which to compare them. Forty other children in different nursery schools in the city were examined in order to find twenty-three other children that were in age, height, weight,

[8] Arthur T. Jersild, "Training and Growth in the Development of Children," *Child Development Monograph,* No. 10, 1932, p. 26.

and strength of grip the equivalent of the experimental group. When these were selected, they were kept as controls and the practice which the experimental group had was denied them. After the three-month period, the control group was tested again, with the results shown in the following table.

AVERAGE DYNAMOMETER SCORES
(Kilograms)

	NUMBER	Av. AGE (Mos.)	WEIGHT (Lbs.)	INITIAL Nov. 1930	AFTER PRACTICE		
					Feb. 1931	June 1931	Oct. 1931
Experimental Group.......	13	63.9	43.2	9.9	15.1	17.0	17.2
Control Group ..	13	63.3	43.3	9.5	12.3	13.6	16.0
Differences......	..	0.6	—0.1	0.4	2.8	3.4	1.2

The records of ten of the twenty-three subjects over this period of eleven months were incomplete in some respects, a troublesome factor in all extensive experiments. Children become ill at the critical time of testing. Some move to other localities and some cannot be reached for other reasons. The original groups must always contain about twice as many children as the number on which the experimenter hopes to have complete records.

These factors reduced the original twenty-three in each group to thirteen. There was a difference of only 0.6 of a month in the average age of the two groups and a difference of only 0.1 of a pound in their weights. There was on the average a difference of only 0.4 of a kilogram in their initial strength of grip. Three months later, after forty-three practice periods, the experimental group had gained on the average of 5.2 kilograms, *but not as a result of practice alone.* During these three months they were also growing. *What this group would have gained without practice in this period we can never know.* The closest we can come to knowing is to observe that thirteen other children just like them, at the end of the same three months, had made an average score of 12.3 kilograms. If we compare the 15.1 made by the experimental group to the 12.3 made by the control group,

103

we see that only about one-half of the gain of the experimental group can be attributed to practice.

Permanence of practice effects.   Is this superiority of the practice group a permanent gain? If it is not permanent, then we need not be so concerned practically if a child fails to have an opportunity for early practice.

Five months after the end of the practice period, and with no further practice having been given to either group, we find a greater difference than that which existed immediately after the close of the practice session. Apparently the advantage is not only maintained but increased. However, at seven months after the end of the training, the advantage had almost disappeared. We would be forced to conclude, then, that *in this function training can produce a temporary advantage, but that shortly after the close of the practice period the comparative advantage is lost.* On the other hand, the trend of the data indicates that if practice were continued indefinitely, the practice group would widen its lead indefinitely.

Interpretation.   Of course it is obvious that the effect of practice is not completely eliminated from the control group. Everyday experiences in which the hands are used involve practice. It is only for the added formal practice which was afforded the experimental group that the conclusions hold. It might very well be that the formal practice in this instance constitutes only a very small increment to the incidental practice involved in the performance of daily tasks and that the impermanence of the advantage is due to the fact that "practice effect" in this experiment is really very small. If a function that is not so commonplace as strength of grip were subjected to the same experimental procedure, more permanent effects might be observed.

Production of tones and intervals.   A function of this kind can be found in the production of tones and intervals not included in the vocal range of the child. Eighteen three-year-old children were given tests on their ability to reproduce the eleven pitches, middle C, D, E, F, G, A, B, C, D', E', F', and twelve intervals within the

octave. The experimenter judged whether or not the child was singing the note sounded. Some of the children were soon making a
perfect score by reproducing each of the eleven pitches each time
so that the series had to be extended by adding G, A, B below middle
C, and G', A', B', C'' above the previous range, or a total of eighteen
notes. The intervals were increased to twenty-two. There were fourteen pairs of children in the pitch series and thirteen pairs upon
whom there were complete data in the interval series. The results
are shown best in a table.

	No.	Age in Mos.	Initial Test 11 Notes Jan. 1931	After 40 10-Min. Practice Periods May 1931 Initial	Ex- tended Test 18	After No Training Oct. 1931	
						Initial 11	Ex- tended
Experimental .	14	39.1	4.7	10.8	16.0	10.9	16.8
Control.......	14	40.1	4.5	6.2	7.9	7.0	10.2
		12 Intervals		22 Intervals			
Experimental .	13	39.5	4.4	11.8	19.0	11.3	18.7
Control.......	13	42.0	4.5	7.6	9.0	7.4	9.8

Comparison between the groups. Here the two groups started
with about the same initial accuracy of 4.7 and 4.5 on the average
out of eleven notes. After forty ten-minute practice periods, the
experimental group averaged 10.8 with the eleven-note series while
the control group, which had had no practice, managed to average
only 6.2. Four months later, without any additional practice for
either group, the practice group was still ahead and the gain in the
reproduction of intervals was maintained. This can only mean that
*as far as vocal ability is concerned, early practice gives a permanent
advantage.*

Interpretation of the two experiments. Taking these two experiments together, it would seem at first that we have two distinctly

divergent sets of results. The strength-of-grip experiment demonstrates that practice is ineffective in increasing performance except for the duration of the formal exercise. On the other hand, the vocal experiment indicates a positive permanent value of practice. In the first function, improvement comes through an increase in strength, which has a pretty definite physiological basis. In vocal training the physiological basis is present, but the experiment is set up in such a way that an increase in score is made by adding new items to the repertoire. Training which prompts the child to make full use of his entire repertory of achievements may produce substantial results. In the latter function, therefore, *a child who receives training may achieve a range of skill that, if left to develop at his own pace, he would not normally acquire, if at all, until a later time.*

4. IDENTICAL TWINS

This last principle is illustrated in an experiment in delayed vocabulary training conducted by Strayer on one of a pair of identical twins.[9] The method is similar to the control-group technique in that one of the twins is given special training while the other is given none. This experimental device is called "the method of co-twin control." *Since identical twins have identical genetic backgrounds, differences that appear cannot be attributed to differences in innate capacity: they must be due wholly to the opportunities provided.*

Method. The general plan of the experiment was to train formally Twin T and to keep Twin C as a control in a nonverbal environment during the training of T. Twin T was given an hour and a quarter of formal training each morning. This training consisted in presenting some object to the subject, naming it, and attempting to secure some repetition from the child. There was an attempt to keep the training in the nature of a game. The objects used—a ball, wooden duck, shoe, red paper cap, stuffed cat on wheels, and so on—were selected with the play requirement in view. After some progress had been made, instead of saying "What is it?" the experimenter commissioned the child to carry out simple commands,

9 L. C. Strayer, "Language and Growth, the Relative and Deferred Language Training, Studied by the Method of Co-Twin Control," *Genetic Psychology Monographs,* 1930, 8.

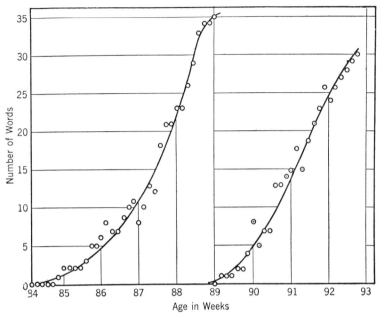

Fig. 22.—Results in delayed vocabulary experiment. Twin T was trained from the 84th week; Twin C's training did not begin until the 89th week.

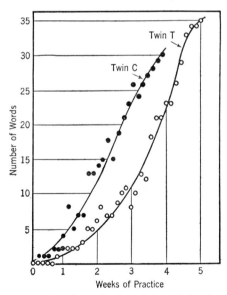

Fig. 23.—The same results, but the beginning of the training for each child is taken at the origin. This procedure shows more clearly how C learned faster than T.

107

such as "Bring the *duck* to me," "Put the *ball* on the chair." At the end of a week, a picture book was brought to the child and she was asked to "Put your finger on the *baby*," "Show me the *doll*," "Where is the *wheel?*"

Daily records were kept of the number of times a given word was repeated by the experimenter, the number of responses by the child, her errors and her successes. A dictaphone record was also made.

While Twin T was being trained, C was by no means neglected. The experimenter spent about half as much time with her as with T. Many of the same games were played, but they were silent. Expressive gestures—nodding, smiling, pointing, beckoning, and head shaking—were not accompanied by words as they ordinarily would have been. Music was not eliminated and in many situations where the nurse or experimenter would ordinarily have talked with the child they now hummed.

Results of delayed training. The principal results of the experiment are shown in two figures. Figure 22 shows the number of words that each child could say, plotted against age. Twin T's curve shows the kind of a growth curve that we have come to expect in experiments of this kind. The characteristics are a slow beginning followed by a more and more rapid rise. The flattening of the curve on the thirty-second, thirty-third, and thirty-fourth days does not mean that the word-acquisition process was slowing up. The inference would be that this relatively flat place showing little improvement on these days would be followed by a sharp rise as it was on the twenty-ninth day. Twin C's word curve starts at zero words as did T's. There is no question but that after thirty-five days of practice, there is a marked difference between the two twins, who had been almost identical in language development up to the time that they were separated. When the same practice is instituted with Twin C that had previously been used with T, C improved markedly.

The learning curve is steeper from the beginning. A given amount of practice, when it was delayed five weeks, resulted in greater accomplishment for the more mature child. This is shown more adequately in Figure 23, which is simply Figure 22 replotted to show the effect of practice. Weeks of practice rather than age are

108

plotted horizontally. It becomes immediately evident from these curves that when the training is delayed, improvement is more prompt. In four weeks Twin C accomplished almost as much as Twin T did in five. It would have been instructive to continue the experiment so that both twins would have had the same amount of practice, but unfortunately Twin C developed a kidney infection which made the precise completion of the experiment impossible. The beginning of the infection *may* have accounted for the slowing up of the learning rate in the few days before the end of the experiment.

Summary. In summary, these data show two things: First, when one of a pair of twins is kept in a nonlanguage environment while the other is instructed in vocabulary, the differences between the respective vocabularies of the two twins become increasingly apparent. *Training is effective in producing an apparent psychological difference between two organisms of identical genetic background.* Second, *when training is instituted later in the life of the control twin,* the progress made is more pronounced since *a smaller number of practice periods produces the same result in terms of accomplishment.* Presumably maturational factors are responsible for the progessively greater value of succeeding practice acts.[10]

5. JOHNNY AND JIMMY

A study by McGraw[11] followed the same pattern as the experiment previously described, except that McGraw's experiment was considerably more extensive. She investigated many more activities than speech and the program was continued for over a year.

Method. One of the twins, Johnny, was given intensive training in a number of different kinds of activities from infancy until about two years of age. His brother, Jimmy, served as a control. Jimmy's environment was not lacking in stimulation, however. Both children

[10] This conclusion is of extreme importance to the elementary school where present practices require that children learn skills that, in the light of their maturational level, had better be delayed. It is doubtful that it is ever wise to require a practice if no progress occurs for trial after trial.

[11] McGraw, M. B., Growth: A Study of Johnny and Jimmy, D. Appleton-Century Company, New York, 1935.

lived a more or less normal life with their parents. Both came to the nursery-laboratory five days a week. Here Johnny was given specific training each day in certain activities. Jimmy received no such training, but remained in a rather restricted laboratory environment. At regular intervals both children were tested to determine how well they could perform the various acts.

The activities which were not affected by training. A number of activities were affected little or none by the extensive training which was given to Johnny. The grasping response, for example, which begins as a reflex and then wanes to be replaced by voluntary grasping was not altered by evoking and practicing Johnny's grasping reflex many times. The pattern of growth of this reflex followed about the same temporal course in Jimmy as it did in the trained Johnny. This same result was found for a number of other basic reflexive types of activity—creeping and crawling, rolling over, walking, and several others.

Activities which were affected by training. The real drama of the experiment lies in the fact that training *did* profit Johnny and that he perfected some skills at a remarkably early age. When Johnny was about nine months old he was placed in a shallow tank and swimming lessons were begun. By the time he was a year old he was consistently swimming without aid. And also at an early age he could dive, roller-skate, climb and descend steep inclines, and jump from high places into the arm of the experimenter. The untrained Jimmy completely failed to develop these skills until he, too, was given special practice at a later age. It was characteristic of him that he almost never attained the same degree of facility as did his early-trained brother. A very important difference between the two children was in their attitudes toward the activities. Throughout all the performances Johnny showed greater confidence and ease, whereas Jimmy was more timid and fearful. There is every reason to believe that this attitude was learned and was one of the reasons why Johnny excelled.

A comparison of the children in later years.[12] The experiment

12 M. B. McGraw, "Later Development of Children Specially Trained in Infancy," *Child Development,* 10, 1939, 1-19.

was terminated when the children were about two years old, and Johnny and Jimmy returned to the nonexperimental routine of their home to live the usual life of growing children in a large city. After four years the experimenter brought the two children back to the laboratory to discover how they had fared during this period. Basically, what McGraw wished to learn was whether or not Johnny still maintained his superiority over Jimmy, and whether or not the children still retained some of the special skills which they learned at so early an age.

Johnny still climbed off high pedestals with easy confidence, and was still superior to Jimmy. Much the same was true of jumping from heights into the arms of the experimenter. Neither of the children had lost the ability to ride a tricycle, although they had received little practice during the four-year period.

In the climbing of steep inclines Johnny had clearly lost some of his skill, although he still excelled his brother. A marked amount of forgetting or loss of skill in roller skating had occurred for both of the boys, and Johnny did just as poorly as Jimmy. Swimming, which had been practiced only very little, had also deteriorated.

McGraw felt that there was some rhyme and reason for the fact that some habits showed no loss, others partial loss, and still others nearly complete loss over the four years. The degree of fixity of the habit at the time training ceased was one determining factor, with the better fixed habits showing less forgetting. Changes in the structure which came with maturing was another factor. The increased lengths of the children's legs made climbing more difficult, and skating as well, for it raised their centers of gravity. A third factor, McGraw felt, was a change in the children's attitude in the direction of a loss of confidence, which made them more hesitant and less facile in the execution of the different activities.

Summary of the experiment. McGraw concluded that reflexive types of activities which are controlled for the most part by lower centers of the brain are more or less unaffected by special training. Changes in these activities wait upon the structural changes in the nervous system which occur because of physiological growth and not because of practice.

These activities are common to all normal members of our species. In contrast with these activities are others which are not of necessity common to all of us—roller skating, swimming, and others. These are the skills which profit most from special training. But the student should be warned that the extent to which these acts can be accelerated in their time of occurrence is limited. Johnny was trained for many months on tricycle riding before he made any progress. Training can begin too early to be fruitful.

The ability to perform these activities after a period of time with no special training varies. Changes in the structure of the individual account for some of the forgetting; the degree of stability of the habit when training ceased accounts for some; and shifts in attitudes with increasing maturity contribute to the loss. It would be fallacious, though, to conclude that such early training is time wasted. Had Jimmy been given continuous opportunity to practice these early-learned skills, he might very well have continued superior in almost every one of the activities.

6. PERMANENCE OF ADVANTAGE

We still have to settle the question of just what kinds of responses are permanently susceptible to the influence of practice and what kinds exhibit only a temporary advantage which may not be even very appreciable. Jersild's experiments on strength of grip and on vocal ability indicated that these two functions were different in this respect. Strayer's experiment shows that training has a marked effect on vocabulary. But from these data we can certainly deduce no general principle.

In an experiment conducted at the Institute of Child Welfare at the University of Minnesota we have a distinguished contribution to this problem.

The effect of difficulty. A task was set for preschool children which involved the same *kind* of manipulation but of three different degrees of difficulty. The child holds a square boxlike affair in his hands. There is a glass top to the box and a steel ball can be seen inside. By tilting the box, the ball can be caused to roll. But it will roll only in predetermined directions. A series of carefully

FIG. 24.—The child rolls the steel ball through a pathway between posts by tilting the platform towards herself, away from herself, to her right, or to her left. There is only one way for the ball to go. The child has to discover which way this is. She cannot tell by looking at the apparatus because the difference between the true pathway and all the blind alleys is not visually discernible. (Courtesy of the Institute of Child Welfare, University of Minnesota, John Anderson, Director.)

adjusted machine-screw heads will allow only one pathway to be followed. The child cannot tell by looking at the apparatus which way the ball will go. It is also clear that the pathways can be as simple or as complex as desired. The three used are shown here. Again, it should be understood that the child could not see these patterns. They had to be discovered by tilting the platform. The time required and the number of tilts made was a measure of the success of the learner in mastering this problem.

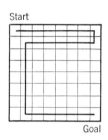 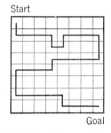 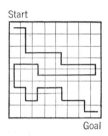

FIG. 25.—The three pathways.

Figure 26 shows the time required for the children to master the hardest and the easiest tasks. The intermediately difficult task is omitted from the figure because it merely complicates the picture. The curves showing the number of errors made are also eliminated for the same reason.

Equating the groups. One group of children who worked on the easy problem, was divided into two subgroups shown at the bottom of the graph as dotted and solid lines. These two subgroups were not selected until after four practice periods so that the experimenter would have some actual basis for asserting that the groups were equivalent. That they are *not* identical is shown by the fact that the dotted and solid lines are not *exactly* superimposed, but they are close enough together in performance so that one could say they were, for all practical purposes, groups of equal performance. The same is true in all these respects for the two subgroups, control and experimental, that worked on the hardest task.

Training the experimental group. After the fourth day, the control groups in each case rested. For the experimental groups the

114

day of practice marked "1" is really the fifth day. For twenty-six days the experimental groups continued to work, those on the hardest maze reducing their average time from about seventy to thirty seconds. Those on the easiest problem reduced their time only about four seconds in the same interval.

Test after practice. In the period marked "Test" the control groups again go to work on their respective problems. For the experimental groups there is no distinction between the test period and the previous practice periods.

Results. The appearance of the curves in the "Test" period shows that the difference between the control and the experimental groups is much greater for the hardest problem. For the easiest problem, although there is a difference, it is not marked. A further retest conducted two months later shows that the difference between the practice and the nonpractice groups on the easiest problem has practically disappeared, while for the more difficult task there is still a pronounced difference in favor of the trained group.

This result enables us to conclude that the difficulty of the task is an important factor in determining whether or not a relatively permanent advantage is gained by formal training. The complexity of the vocal responses which showed a superiority even after a period of no training is probably accounted for on this basis. Those experiments which show that the effects of training are ephemeral and confined to the period of practice and shortly thereafter have been made with simple tasks.

Summary of the chapter. The ramifications of this chapter are somewhat extended in that instances involving frogs and salamanders, nursery school groups, and twins have been cited. The specific reactions studied in this variety of forms involved swimming, grasping, creeping, walking, language, roller skating, and other motor skills both simple and complex. All of this detail should not be allowed to obscure the fact that all these instances are directed at understanding how the behavior that we observe in adult organisms ever comes to be in the first place. In all these instances it is clear

115

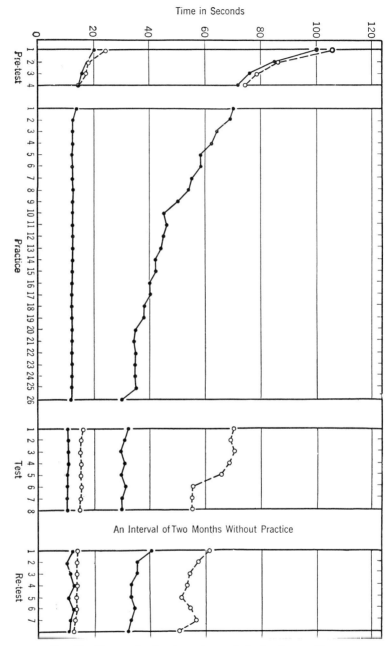

FIG. 26.—The results for the easiest and the hardest problem.

116

that structure is important, but at the same time it should be obvious that structure (inheritance) alone cannot account for behavior and that the really important determinant is the interaction between structure and environment.

CHAPTER SEVEN

INTELLIGENCE

At the beginning of this century, the Paris school directors were faced with the problem of the continuing increase in the enrollment in the elementary schools. A large part of the crowding was due to the fact that there was a large number of failing students. The directors appointed a special committee to find out which ones of these retarded students were capable and which were incapable of learning the ordinary classroom skills. The notion that some pupils were innately incapable and that others just weren't interested was then relatively new. The educational philosophy which charged school authorities with the responsibility of providing special facilities for the misfits in a system designed for the capable was just beginning to develop.

1. BINET'S CONTRIBUTION

The problem of finding a method for predicting the school achievement of children before their routine schooling had progressed very far was an intensely practical as well as a puzzling one. There was little to start with. One of the members of the commission, Alfred Binet, had for some twenty years been interested in the problem of reasoning, and it was due to an earlier publication on this topic that he was appointed to the commission on special classes.

In America, Cattell had examined and recorded the breadth of skulls, the hair and eye color, and the strength of grip and speed of movement of Columbia University students, but the newly developed correlation methods had shown as early as 1901 that there was no relation between any of these things and the marks that Columbia University students were receiving in their courses.[1]

[1] Clark Wissler's *The Correlation of Mental and Physical Tests* (1901) which examined the Columbia University data can be held responsible for retarding for almost ten years any further work in this country on the problem of intelligence. He showed that class standing correlated with reaction time to the extent of −.02; with association time +.08; with logical memory +.19; and with auditory memory +.16. He demonstrated that the correlation technique, itself, was adequate

Method of demonstrating the validity of the tests. In a previous study[2] that he had made himself, Binet had developed a method of testing out some of the things that were held by other psychologists at the time to differentiate between the dull and the clever students. Briefly the method consisted of this: Out of a class of thirty-two students, he selected two groups. One group consisted of the five best students in the class, and the other was made up of the six poorest. Binet reasoned that if the good students excelled the poor ones in his tests, the tests could then be made to serve the purpose of separating new students of unknown ability into two groups. One group would include those who, in the course of the educational process, would eventually prove to be good students. The other group would be found to contain the duller members of the class. In his preliminary tests, Binet measured the ability of these two contrasting groups of students to make tactual discriminations, to count small points placed close together, to count the beats of a metronome, to copy printed material, to reproduce a design which they had seen for a brief period of time, and to make reactions quickly. When the tests had been given and the results recorded, it turned out that some of the tests did not differentiate between the two groups at all. In some cases, the duller group actually exceeded the superior. In other cases, there was no difference at all between the groups, but in some tests, particularly the copy test, the metronome test, and the design test, the bright children were clearly superior to the dull. We see, therefore, that Binet had succeeded in isolating, by means of a scientifically controlled experimental procedure, tests of certain factors which were obviously involved in the process which differentiated good students from poor ones. Some of these tests, in improved form, are still in use today. Today we would be dissatisfied with Binet's procedure. For instance, we would not be content to take just one class of students as a fair sample of all pupils; we would demand larger groups for the two extremes.

---

to find a relationship where one did exist. The correlation between the marks in the various subject matter fields was uniformly high. The study demonstrated that with the tools then available, psychologists could not detect beforehand which people would be successful in college.

2 Alfred Binet, "Attention et adaptation," *L'Année Psychologique,* 1899, 6, 248-405.

Nevertheless this technique was a beginning in the right direction and is followed in principle today.

The age scale. Binet's major contribution to the field of testing, aside from demonstrating the kinds of items that would have to be included in an intelligence test, consisted of his development of an age scale. This notion was not completely developed until 1908, and in that year he published, with his coworker Simon, the first instrument that could really be called an "intelligence test." The new notion that was elaborated in this test was that of scaling the items in difficulty and classifying them according to the average age of the pupils who could pass the respective test items. The scale started at the age of three years and, at this level, enumerated five things that a normal three-year-old child could be expected to do. They were the ability

1. To show his nose, eyes, and mouth when asked by the examiner.
2. To numerate certain objects in a picture.
3. To repeat two figures.
4. To repeat after the examiner a sentence of six syllables.
5. To be able to give his surname.

These items were not the product of Binet's imagining of what youngsters ought to be able to accomplish. They were based on actual observation of three-year-olds. Items placed at other age levels in the scale were selected on a similar basis.

At four the child was expected

1. To name a key, a penny, and a knife.
2. To repeat three figures.
3. To differentiate between the length of two lines.

The scale continued through five, six, seven, eight, and nine years, with the items becoming increasingly difficult. At nine years, for example, the child was expected to be able

1. To give the date completely—that is, the day of the week, the month, and the year.
2. To give the names of the days of the week.
3. To give definitions of common objects that involved more understanding of definition than simply to say a chair "is to sit on."

120

4. To be able to retain six different ideas that he could get from a passage which he read.
5. To arrange five blocks in order of their weight when the difference between them was rather small.
6. To be able to make change in certain denominations.

The scale continued with more difficult items on to the ages of ten, eleven, twelve, and thirteen.

A comparison of Binet's early scale with a modern intelligence test would show this scale to be rather crude. For one thing, his methods of scoring were not precise, and for another his age scales were not arranged in completely accurate levels of difficulty. His test descriptions were all qualitative. He did not say how much the child was advanced or retarded in any precise quantitative manner.

2. THE I.Q.

It is only since 1916 that we have started to arrange the tests more precisely in the order of difficulty and have been able to specify with considerable accuracy how much a child is either accelerated or retarded in his development. As we have seen, Binet spoke of acceleration in qualitative terms, merely saying that the child was either superior or inferior to others of his same chronological age. Now, thanks to the American psychologist Terman, we see that a developmental age can be related to a chronological age by means of a ratio between them. Thus, if a three-year-old child accomplishes what average four-year-old children accomplish, his development with reference to other children of his same age can be expressed by the ratio $4/3$, or 1.33. If he is four and accomplishes only as much as three-year-olds are expected to do on the basis of three-year-old tests, then his ratio is $3/4$ or .75. In his revision of the Binet scale in 1916, Terman employed the term "intelligence quotient" [3] for the ratio and multiplied this quotient by 100 in order to get rid of the decimals. Thus the intelligence quotients, or I.Q.'s, in the above examples would be 133 and 75. It is obvious that in such a scheme normality is expressed conveniently by an I.Q. of 100. Terman also

[3] William Stern had suggested the use of "mental quotient" to express this notion as early as 1904.

named what we have called the development age the "mental age" of the child, in contrast to the "chronological age." Terman revised the 1911 Binet scale[4] on the basis of new measurements on item difficulty made in this country principally with California children. This test has come to be known as the Stanford Revision of the Binet-Simon Test from Terman's position as professor of psychology at Leland Stanford University.

A word of warning. The concept of intelligence quotient is frequently misapplied. Thus students talk about their "I.Q. Test" or ask their instructor or some college official for their "I.Q.'s" when they have in mind some college classification test which was given to them as freshmen. It should be perfectly clear that the notion of I.Q. applies directly to the rate of development in childhood and can be applied to adults only by extrapolation beyond the ages at which year-to-year increases in accomplishment (mental age) are evident. *One can truly speak of the I.Q. of an adult only by estimating what his I.Q. would have been had it been determined when he was in the elementary grades,* for even after he is twelve years old it becomes more and more difficult to separate one age group from another.

Even in childhood the concept of I.Q. is not absolutely essential in dealing with test scores. It has certain advantages, some of which we have pointed out—but the concept remains a limited one and there were many psychologists who were keenly disappointed when it was used in the 1937 revision.

It turned out as a result of wholesale testing of conscripted men during World War I that the average mental age of this tremendous sample of nearly two million men was in the neighborhood of twelve years. In the succeeding twenty years we had newspaper editorials deploring the "intelligence" of the "average American adult." There was no point to all this wasted pessimism because the editorials could, on the basis of the findings, have just as well been pointed toward an appreciation of the accomplishments of children. There are obvious differences between mature men and

[4] L. M. Terman, *The Measurement of Intelligence,* Houghton Mifflin Company, Boston, 1916.

callow youths, but they are not to be found in the stuff from which intelligence tests are constructed.[5]

What editorial writers will do with the results of "intelligence" testing in World War II it is too early yet to say, but the misinterpretations following the first World War were among the factors that led to the name "Classification Test" rather than "Intelligence Test."

3. TERMAN'S CONTRIBUTION

Terman's revision of the Binet test, in addition to introducing the concept of the I.Q. in a practical form, was superior in many other respects to the original Binet scales. In the first place, Binet was forced to work with relatively small numbers of mostly stupid children. Terman attempted to get a large number of children here who were more representative of the total population. On the other hand, Binet and some of the other workers who had used the Binet scale, notably Goddard, were principally interested in separating the subnormal from the remainder of the population, Terman succeeded in detecting brilliance among children as well as stupidity. The title of the Ph.D. thesis, "Genius and Stupidity: A Study of Some of the Intellectual Processes of Seven 'Bright' and Seven 'Stupid' Boys," which was published in the *Pedagogical Seminary* ten years before the Stanford Revision, is indicative of his early interest in the higher end of the intelligence scale. His *Genetic Studies in Genius,* published in 1925, is an account of studies of a thousand gifted children.[6]

Terman used better criteria than his predecessors for the inclusion of the items at the various age levels. The whole scale contained ninety items. Fifty-four of these were from the original Binet scales and the remaining thirty-six were entirely new. The tests were completely rearranged as determined by the results of their application

[5] There was one legitimate conclusion that could be drawn. In dealing with words or numbers directed at the great mass of the population, as newspaper or radio writing, the verbal and numerical skills of twelve-year-olds had better be kept in mind.

[6] The concept of the I.Q. permitted him to define precisely what he meant by genius, viz., any child who could score 130 I.Q. points or above. Similarly, anyone who scores below 70 is considered feeble-minded; normality, by definition, ranges from 95 to 105.

to the nine hundred California children whom we have mentioned before. There were minute directions on how to administer the tests as well as complete and detailed directions on how to score them, so that a considerable amount of close study and fairly intensive practice were required of anyone making these intelligence measurements.

Standardization. The amount of labor involved in adequately standardizing a test of this kind can be appreciated only by reviewing some of the things which it is necessary to do. If we want to determine that a given item is a satisfactory test of the six-year development, that item must be passed by a majority of children who are exactly six years old. Furthermore, it must be failed by a majority of children who are less than six years old and it must be passed by all of the children who are more than six years old. Of course, it is impossible to obtain enough children who are *exactly* six years old out of an available population; hence Terman allowed a variation of one month on either side of six years. *Majority* was defined as 75 per cent of all those of a certain age. *All* of the children means 100 per cent of them. This means that the responses of large groups of children to each one of the ninety items have to be studied in this painstaking way. The mere labor of administering the tests in the first place is also no small item in the total picture. Since this test is given to each child individually rather than to groups of children, it is often called an individual test. This does not mean that there is no group comparison, however. The standardization group determined where a given test item would fall on the final scale so that every time a child is given a test, he is being compared in effect with a group of children, even if they are not in the room with him at the time the test is given to him.

Practical results of a testing program. The results of instituting a program of mental testing in a school system are set forth in one of Terman's early studies in which he says:

> The so-called "retarded" children are in reality usually from one to three grades above where they belong by mental development; the real retardates are the underaged children who are generally found from one

to three grades below the location which their mental development would warrant. In other words, the problem of retardation is exactly the reverse of what it is popularly supposed to be.

The first grade is the most critical. It is there that retardation scores its worst record, for usually about one-third of the pupils fail of promotion by the end of the first year. Accordingly, it is especially important that in the first grade the raw material with which the school is to work should be correctly evaluated.

In one study by Dickson the mental ages found in a first-grade group ranged from three years to almost eleven years. One-third of the pupils were below a mental age of six years; 90 per cent of this group failed to win promotion. On the other hand, 15 per cent of the group were above the mental age of seven and one-half years. Doubtlessly, many of these could readily enter the second or third year.

The success of a teacher is judged largely by the absolute standard of work she is able to secure from her pupils. How unfair this may be in individual cases is illustrated by the following facts for five first-grade classes tested by Dickson. The median I.Q.'s of five first-grade classes were 87, 76, 85, 108, and 112. There was thus a difference of 36 points in the median I.Q.'s of the higher and lowest classes. The best class was fully two years above the lowest in terms of average mental age; the lack of progress in the latter room was so evident that the teacher was in despair and the superintendent doubted her efficiency. One might suppose that the teachers of these classes would have been keenly aware of the difference in the intellectual make-up of their groups. They were not, however, except in the vaguest sort of way.

It appears that the standards of work which are maintained in the first year of the average California high school cannot be satisfactorily met by pupils with a Stanford-Binet mental age below thirteen years, and that below the mental age of fourteen the chances of success are not good. It also appears that children with an I.Q. below 80 rarely succeed in entering a California high school, and that those with an I.Q. below 90 rarely graduate. A large majority of those who drop out have an I.Q. considerably below 100. The typical high school offers little work which can be mastered by pupils of much less than average intelligence. A nation falls short of the true ideals of democracy which refuses to furnish suitable training for a third of its children merely because their endowment does not enable them to complete a course of study which will satisfy the requirements for college entrance. High schools at present are in a sense "class" schools.[7]

The following table indicates the grade location of 263 eleven-

[7] L. M. Terman, "The Use of Intelligence Tests in the Grading of School Children," *Journal of Educational Research*, 1920, 1, 20-32.

year-olds and their mental ages. Four of the 263 eleven-year-olds were in the first grade. Their mental ages ranged from five to eight

GRADE LOCATION OF 263 ELEVEN-YEAR-OLDS BY
STANFORD-BINET MENTAL AGE*
(Correlation is 0.81)

MENTAL AGE	GRADE								TOTAL
	I	II	III	IV	V	VI	VII	VIII	
18							1		1
17							3	1	4
16						1	2		3
15					2	5	6	1	14
14				1	6	13	2		22
13				3	12	18	1		34
12			1	2	22	12			37
11			2	10	42	6			60
10			6	15	20	1			42
9		2	3	14	6				25
8	1	5	6	2					14
7	1	1	3						5
6	1								1
5	1								1
Total	4	8	21	47	110	56	15	2	263

* From L. M. Terman, *The Intelligence of School Children,* Houghton Mifflin Company, Boston, 1919.

years. Two of the eleven-year-olds were in the eighth grade. Their mental ages were fifteen and seventeen.

This table warrants special study because there are numerous other comparisons that will occur to the wide-awake student.

4. THE 1937 REVISION

Before progressing to a further study of the results of a testing movement, let us examine in some detail a more recent revision of the Binet scale. This revision was published in 1937, but preparations for it had been under way for several years preceding that date

The number of tests was increased from 90 to 129 and two equivalent forms of the test are provided. This made 258 items in all. More than three thousand subjects were examined in order to standardize the various items, and the full time of seven people, working as examiners in different parts of the country, was required for two years.

THE DISTRIBUTION OF EMPLOYED MALES IN THE UNITED STATES
AND THE LIVING FATHERS OF THE CHILDREN IN THE SAMPLE *

OCCUPATIONAL GROUP	PERCENTAGE OF EMPLOYED MALES	PERCENTAGE OF LIVING FATHERS
I. Professional	3.1	4.5
II. Semiprofessional and managerial	5.2	7.8
III. Clerical, skilled trades, and retail business	15.0	25.5
IV. Farmers	15.3	14.9
V. Semiskilled occupations, minor clerical positions and minor businesses	30.6	31.4
VI. Slightly skilled trades and other occupations requiring little training or ability	11.3	9.4
VII. Day laborers (urban and rural)	19.5	6.6
Total number	38,077,804	2,757

* From L. M. Terman and M. Merrill, *Measuring Intelligence,* Houghton Mifflin Company, Boston, 1937.

The Stanford-Binet test had been criticized because the nine hundred California children were not representative of all of the children in the United States. For some states, particularly, the tests were too difficult. It is also known now, but was not so well recognized in 1916, that there is a definite relation between the socioeconomic level of a child and his intelligence. It was not clear in the earlier standardization whether this factor had had an influence in making the tests too difficult for the majority of the population. In the new standardization procedure, therefore, in order to take care of the first objection, seventeen different communities in eleven different states were sampled. A special effort was made to obtain an adequate sample of the rural population. This had not been done previously and we now know that, in general, urban children do test higher than rural children. The occupational groups according to the 1930 census figures were used as a reference in selecting the standardization sample. The table shows the occupational group and the percentage of employed males in the United States in 1930 in these different occupations and the percentage of the standardization group where the occupations of the living fathers could be ascertained.

The authors note that the rural sample is still inadequate despite the fact that special precautions were taken against this very fault. This is very largely due to the extreme difficulty in moving from locality to locality in the country as compared with the ease with which large numbers of children can be obtained in the cities. The discrepancies between the lower occupational groupings and the inability to obtain children in the testing is explained by the fact that a large number of these people in the census were young men who were unskilled by reason of lack of experience and training and who had as yet not established families; Negroes included in the census were not included in the standardization groups.

It should be clear by this time, if you have followed this description, that the Binet test as developed by Terman, culminating in the 1937 revision, is based on a truly experimental approach to the problem of acceleration and retardation during the elementary-school years. The standards of performance demanded by the test are not arbitrarily assigned or imposed by adult standards or requirements. The norms are not the result of a conference on what children ought to do. They are based on careful observation of what children in our culture at this time are able to do.

5. THE EFFECTS OF PRACTICE ON TEST SCORES

Many people who use intelligence tests in practical situations are not acquainted with all of the factors which affect a person's score on a test. Many of them believe that practice, for instance, can make little difference in a test score, because in an intelligence test one is supposed to be measuring something that a person inherits. Heritable features of human make-up are not subject to practice, of course. Some tests have only one form and the directions generally state that practice effects are insignificant particularly if as much time as a year elapses between successive testings. Test manuals that make statements like this are very misleading. Thorndike found as early as 1919 that when trials were given in immediate succession, a repetition of a test raised the scores 10 per cent on the average, and

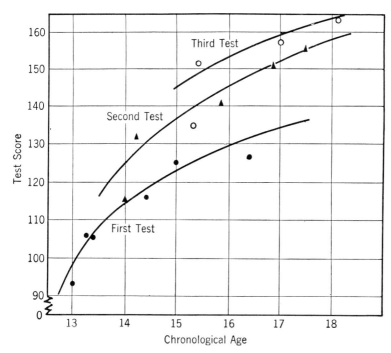

FIG. 27.—Three successive testings of the same population.

if a second repetition (a third test) followed an additional 4 per cent increment was imposed. The psychological knowledge of too many testers is entirely derived from overly optimistic test manuals.

Dorothy Adkins[8] has published a study of data collected at Mooseheart. Successive testings at approximately one-year intervals were available for several different grade levels and with several different tests.

The results for the Otis group test are in Figure 27. The solid

[8] Dorothy C. Adkins, "The Effects of Practice on Intelligence Test Scores," *Journal of Educational Psychology*, 1937, 28, 222-231.

circles represent the results of a testing program initiated in 1930. For all the children involved, this was the first time this intelligence test had been given. We have drawn a solid line, the lowest, through these data. It is drawn in a way that seems fairly to represent the trend of the small solid circles.

Approximately a year later the data shown by the small triangles were collected. The general level of the scores this time is clearly above the first administration of the test. The youngest group, now fourteen, comes very close to scoring in exactly the same place that we would have predicted it would if practice had had no effect (shown by the small ▲'s at fourteen very close to the lowermost solid line). This one point is an exception to the remainder of the data, however; hence this time we draw our solid line to represent the second testing distinctly above the first one. A third testing gave the results shown by the small open circles. Here we do not have as many experimental points to use in determining our trend so that the location of the topmost line is more arbitrary.

The conclusion is clear-cut. *Successive practices, even as much as a year apart, do affect intelligence test scores.* If we confine our attention to age sixteen, we see that a first testing gives an average score of about 130. But if that group of children had first been tested at fifteen, their average performance at sixteen would have been raised to about 145, and if two administrations had preceded the attainment of age sixteen, the average would have been raised to 152. The effect is different at the different ages and, of course, differs in amount with different tests. We cannot generalize more precisely than that there is an effect. Whether practice raises scores 1 per cent or 100 per cent depends on so many factors that to generalize is out of the question.

6. THE ARMY GENERAL CLASSIFICATION TEST[9]

Psychological selection and classification became more than an academic exercise when ten million men and women took the Army General Classification Test during the five-year period 1940–45.[10]

[9] The data in this section are from W. V. Bingham, "Inequalities in Adult Capability from Military Data," *Science*, 1946, 104, 147-152.

[10] There were four comparable forms, so that a given person could be tested and

All of the Classification Tests, some of which were designed for special purposes, pose the problem of dealing with words, as in vocabulary tests of various kinds; numbers, as with computations in simple arithmetic; and problems of visualization in space.

In all cases the problems were arranged in such a way that difficulties in writing were of small importance. A man or woman need do no more than make a simple X as far as the mechanics of "learned performance" are concerned. But they did have to "understand" in the sense that symbols on paper were designed to release responses, some appropriate and others held to be inappropriate in our "day and age." A high score could be obtained only if a person could show that he had learned to respond to certain standard and selected tasks in the way the Army,[11] or the whole of society—including the best educational institutions—said that he "ought" to respond.

The test constructors were more than ordinarily successful. An example will show how well. A standard score of at least 110 was ordinarily required for assignment to an Officers' Candidate School, but a War Department regulation permitted men to attend a school of this kind if they had had two years of Junior R.O.T.C. training. At Fort Benning thirty-five soldiers, entered because of the Junior R.O.T.C. training, scored below 110 on the test. Three of them passed the course, thirty-two failed.

Early in the war period, commanding officers were required to fill a quota for officers' training, even if they did not have enough men suitable to meet the A.G.C.T. specifications. Most of those who failed to get the required score failed the course.

An example shows how valuable the A.G.C.T. score was in military placement. In a group of 1042 in training as weather observers, the chances that a man would do average or better in the course were only 3 in 100 if his A.G.C.T. score was 80; 12 in 100 if his score

---

retested four times without having precisely the same test administered any one of four times. In addition there were two forms in Spanish used in the Caribbean Command. And as in World War I, there was a nonverbal test which could be given entirely in pantomine.

[1] The Army is emphasized here only to make the point. The Army had no special take in this instance, which is not also the stake of what we call "our society."

was 100; 35 in 100 if his score was 120; and 65 in 100 if his score was 140.

Or another example: for general clerical work the situation was:

ARMY GRADE	V	IV	III	II	I
Score..........................	60	80	100	120	140
Chances of success in 100 men......	1	5	20	47	76

Or still another: For airplane mechanics:

ARMY GRADE	V	IV	III	II	I
Score..........................	60	80	100	120	140
Chances of success in 100 men......	5	17	40	67	88

Most of the soldiers who were college graduates scored in Army Grades I and II, in fact the average was approximately 130, which is the dividing line between Grades I and II. There were 580,000 men of the 10,000,000 in Grade I, but only one fourth of them were college graduates. In Grade II the distribution was as follows:

> 184,000 college graduates
> 1,666,000 finished high school but not college
> 858,000 completed the eighth grade
> 56,000 did not complete the eighth grade

In Grades I and II together there were 3,200,000 men, all of whom would have been good college risks, but as a matter of fact, only about 23 per cent of them were actually college graduates. *More than three quarters of this group did not have the educational advantages they were capable of mastering.* For every student who has been through college, there are three, equally capable, who have not.

Summary of the chapter. We have shown how the "intelligence test" grew out of the practical necessity for predicting progress in school before it actually was accomplished. In selecting the items for the tests Binet introduced the method of comparing the tes scores of the scholastically successful and the unsuccessful. Once selected, by further experiment, these tests were modified and arranged in the form of an age scale. In order to define precisely how an individual stood he was to be compared with others his own age by means of an index known as the I.Q. When one tests "intelligence" he is not testing an inherited segment of behavior. Inherited structures probably help to determine what an intelligence test score will be, but they are not the only determiners. Successive practices, even as much as a year apart, have their effect. Just how much effect they will have depends on the nature of the test, the age of the subjects, and probably upon other factors besides. Just what some of these "other factors" are is the main topic of our next chapter. The Army General Classification Test, depending principally on skills with words, numbers and space forms, was useful in separating men who could master a wide variety of special training courses from those who could not.

CHAPTER EIGHT

THE MEANING OF INTELLIGENCE TEST SCORES

One of the studies in the previous chapter has shown that intelligence tests can be influenced by practice. This raises the question of what intelligence-test scores mean. Is the difference between Larry's and Joey's scores in the test simply due to Joey's better environment, or is it due to his superior genetic background? The answer to this question cannot be given in a simple yes or no form, but some of the experiments in the present chapter will throw light on why Larry and Joey may differ from each other.

1. CITY LIFE

In a series of studies on the effect of city life on intelligence-test scores, Klineberg[1] has presented evidence showing definite increases in scores as a result of having moved to the city. All of the subjects in this study were Southern-born Negroes who had migrated to Harlem. Selected so that they would be of the same sex and age, all were twelve-year-old girls. In the large group of children available it was possible to find a limited number who, although Southern-born, had been in the city only one year, some two, three, and so on up to twelve; the latter group, of course, were Harlem-born. In all, 619 of these twelve-year-olds were tested by means of the National Intelligence Test—one of the better tests—in February and May, 1932.

The results are shown in Figure 28. There were thirty girls who had been in the city only one year; their average score was about 63 points. There were twenty-eight who had been in the city two years; their average score was about 70 points. For a nine-year residence there were only fourteen cases and for ten years', only 15, so that the irregularity in the curve at this point is probably due to the small number of cases available. The twelve-year group was Northern-born. Since there were 359 of them, more weight should

[1] Otto Klineberg, *Negro Intelligence and Selective Migration,* Columbia University Press, New York, 1935.

134

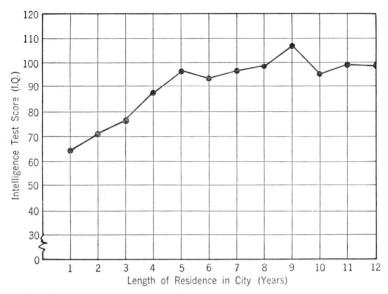

FIG. 28.—The relation between intelligence test score and length of residence in the city.

be given to this point on the graph than to the others. The trend of the averages is perfectly clear, however, and has been substantiated by eight other studies which show approximately the same thing. *It should be perfectly clear that if the more intelligent people move to the city, then there should be no dependence of intelligence-test score on length of urban residence as is shown by this study.*

2. ISOLATED LIFE

Further indication of environmental handicaps is to be found in intelligence-test measurements which have been made on people living in remote parts of the United States where the ordinary advantages of public schooling are not present to give a certain uniformity to the lives of both the urban and rural populations. In a section of Virginia within a short distance of the national capital the topography of the country has provided a natural experimental setting for studying this factor. Five "hollows" in which the penetration of civilizing influences was varied have been discovered.

(1) One hollow, Colvin, consists of a few scattered families

135

living the most primitive life without school, church, or other social organization. No one there can read or write. There is no road to the outside world.

(2) A second community, Needles Hollow, connects with the outer world by a rocky mountain trail. A few men can read and write. There is a combined church-school where meetings are held occasionally.

(3) Oakton Hollow is accessible to the skilled driver of an automobile. Agriculture is organized. There is some shipment of agricultural products to the outside world as well as the beginning of a small fruit-drying industry. There is a church-school, and two religious denominations are represented. One-room cabins have given way to three- and four-room houses. Every home has a mail-order catalog from which most of the buying is done. There is a general store with its post office.

(4) In Rigby Hollow mail can be received daily. There is a fair road connecting with the state highway system. The people generally have more money, bigger houses, better sanitation than in the other hollows. School is in session seven months a year. About three quarters of the people are literate. They read and understand the newspapers.

(5) The fifth community is a small village, Briarsville, through which a hard-surfaced road runs. It is typical of the small towns through which everybody has passed in rural districts. There is a modern school and church. Newspapers, magazines, automobiles, and radios are familiar to everyone.

The restricted environment in the four communities affected the intelligence-test scores to a very marked degree, even in the parts of the tests where the language handicap would not, at first glance, seem to be a factor. For Colvin and Needles Hollow children many of the tests were, for all practical purposes, in a foreign language.

As an example of how the environment restricts the mental test performance, we quote from Sherman and Henry's *The Hollow Folk*.[2]

2 Mandel Sherman and Thomas R. Henry, *The Hollow Folk,* The Thomas Y Crowell Company, New York, 1933. The student will find that a perusal of the entire volume will repay him. Many students have never come into contact with the complete lack of opportunity described in this book.

The road to Briarsville

The road to Needles Hollow

FIG. 29.— (From Sherman and Henry, *The Hollow Folk*. Courtesy of Thomas Y. Crowell Company, publishers.)

137

A Colvin Hollow group

A group of Briarsville children

Fig. 30.—(From Sherman and Henry, *The Hollow Folk*. Courtesy of Thomas Y. Crowell Company, publishers.)

138

The children were asked to define "postoffice." The majority of those who tried to define this word said that a postoffice was a place with baskets of apples in front of it. Some added further details, such as "and some men sitting at the door." They had seen the postoffice in Oakton Hollow which is in the general store. Not one directly associated mail with the definition of postoffice, probably because mail rarely comes into Colvin Hollow.

. . . One test item consists of a circle with an opening drawn on a sheet of paper and the child is told that it represents a closed field in which a ball has been lost. The child is instructed to trace with a pencil the path he would take to find the ball in the best way possible. The correct solution obviously is to circle the field in a systematic manner until the lost object is located. In the majority of cases this test resulted in failure. De-

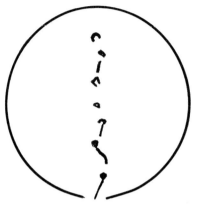

FIG. 31.—One boy's solution to the "ball and field problem."

spite patient explanations, the children did not seem able to visualize a field as a comparatively level, treeless, enclosed space. There are "fields" in the mountains planted with corn but they are more nearly vertical than horizontal. One boy made a curious effort. First he corrected the picture in accordance with his idea of what a field should be, by placing pencil marks in the enclosed space. These represented trees. Thus oriented, he proceeded to "find the ball" by hunting around the bottom of each tree.

This solution, of course, was a failure according to the standard directions for scoring the test. But this child had been presented with a problem every element of which was new to his experience. The makers of the test had not considered a child who did not know the meaning of "field." Furthermore the idea of a lost ball, so familiar to most children, was hard for these youngsters to comprehend. Playing with a ball, until very recently at least, had been foreign to their experience. They had never hunted for a lost ball. They could not understand why anyone should attach any significance to such a situation. . . .

Ability to make specific space and time differentiations also was quite undeveloped. When a boy nineteen years old was asked where the next family lived, he replied: "Over thar a piece."

He didn't know what was meant when asked whether the distance was a mile or a hundred yards. Asked where another family lived, he again replied: "Over thar a piece."

One of these families lived a mile and the other about a quarter of a mile away. He could not differentiate distance in definite terms. The nearest any child came to making such a differentiation was that one family lived "not a far piece over the hill" and that the other lived "a good piece through the woods."

The children of Briarsville, *of the same racial stocks* as those of Colvin and Needles and the intermediate communities, were not much inferior to the California children who served to standardize the test originally. The poor performance of these isolated children cannot be attributed to "poor heredity." *Environmental restriction was the only variable, and on the psychological tests the children arranged themselves in order of the opportunities and lack of them that go with the description of the way they live.*

The canal-boat children. This same retardation in relation to age has been observed in the case of a study of canal-boat children in England.[3] Throughout most of their lives these children are isolated from the contacts that ordinary children have; for instance, they go to school only one or two consecutive half days each month. As a consequence of this fact, with increasing age the retardation, which is barely evident at the earlier ages where the environment fits the needs of the maturing organism, becomes most marked as the children master their environment to the extent that no further demands are made upon them. As a matter of fact, the mental age is almost constant while, of course, the chronological age varies. This makes the younger children score between 90 and 100 I.Q. points, while the older children are definitely "feeble-minded." Gordon also reports these same findings for Gypsy children, who, like the canal-boat children, are isolated from ordinary childhood contacts.

In order to evaluate the significance of a mental test performance, it must be kept clearly in mind that *the Binet scales and others derived from them have as their criterion how well a child can progress in school.* The good students in a school system have been used as criterion groups, as we have seen (page 119). *The significance*

[3] H. Gordon, "Mental and Scholastic Tests among Retarded Children," London Board of Education, Pamphlet No. 44, 1923.

of a high or low intelligence-test score, then, is determined by the value that the cultural group places upon the classroom skills of being able to read and to write and to handle abstractions with ease and with promptness. As we have seen, *in those communities and in those social groups where these skills are not important for existence, the concept of intelligence as measured by these skills simply does not apply.*

3. PRIMITIVE PEOPLE

This latter generalization is substantiated by studies of primitive people, particularly where comparisons are to be made. A set of values, of which intelligence is an example, is entirely incommensurate with another set or system under the demands of a totally different way of living. Porteus, a psychologist who has lived among the Australian aborigines and the African Bushmen, says:

I am quite ready to admit, on the basis of my experience, that, in his own environment, under his own cultural conditions, the African native or the Australian aboriginal is not only equal, but superior, to the white man. He is a better animal—and that is saying a lot in his favor. He can endure the pains of existence with a fortitude of which I am utterly incapable. Anyone who has witnessed the victim's hardihood when suffering a circumcision or subincision operation by means of a stone knife will not doubt the stark courage of the native.

If humor be defined, not as the ability to see a subtle joke, but as the ability to keep a cheery spirit in the face of the most depressing circumstances of poverty and injustice, then the African has a decidedly superior sense of humor—and humor, after all, is the saving social grace.

If also the ability to support the rigors of a terrifying environment is everyday courage, then the Australian aboriginal is much braver than I. If the assurance that life is essentially worth living under any circumstances is more firmly set in the African native's mind than in mine, then I must give him credit for a more effective foresight and hindsight than I possess. There may be many other ways in which the black man may be considered superior and his contributions on the credit side of living should be freely acknowledged. But when it comes to his ability to cope with the white man's environment, which by reason of so-called progress, or of the turn of circumstances, has been thrust upon Negro and aboriginal alike, then I cannot but question their adaptability, especially that of the Australian. The latter, in his natural surroundings, is so far superior to the white man that if he were even equal to the white man in the latter's environment it

141

would be most surprising. If that were the case he would soon inherit the earth.[4]

Another psychologist, Margaret Wooster Curti, has had an opportunity to study the test scores of a limited group of Jamaican children.[5] She had available data collected in 1929 by geneticists, interested principally in race crossing.[6] There were only sixty-eight infants examined in all, but these three-year-old children were distributed about equally within each year of the first three. If this number appears inadequate it can be contrasted with that of the children with whom they were compared who numbered only fifty at each of these three levels.[7]

The infants were tested at the Kingston City Day Nursery, an institution which takes care of the babies of working mothers during the day. The mothers work at hard menial tasks at very low pay—about sixty-two cents a week. The homes are crowded and sanitary conditions are bad. A bed, for instance, is constructed of boards supported by empty boxes; the bedclothes consist of rags, a sheet, and a pillow stuffed with straw. Such a bed is occupied by the whole family.

The cultural background of these Jamaican children is totally different from that of the New Haven children. Manners and customs differ—children, for instance, are not taught to play; houses are built differently; different stoves and different cooking and agricultural implements are used. Pencils and paper and books are rare and play materials almost nonexistent. In tests where pencils were required they were sometimes used like spoons. A rubber ball used in some of the tests was completely new to the child and in some instances he seemed to have been afraid of it. No attention is given to counting in Jamaica, so that not one of the sixty-eight children

4 S. D. Porteus, *Primitive Intelligence and Environment,* The Macmillan Company, New York, 1937.

5 Margaret W. Curti, Francis Botkin Marshal, and Morris Steggerda, "The Gesell Schedules Applied to One-, Two-, and Three-Year-Old Negro Children of Jamaica, B.W.I.," *Journal of Comparative Psychology,* 1935, 20, 125-126.

6 C. B. Davenport and M. Steggerda, *Race Crossing in Jamaica,* Carnegie Institution of Washington, 1929, pp. 516.

7 Jamaican children were given the developmental tests described by Arnold Gesell in *The Mental Growth of the Preschool Child,* 1926, pp. 447. The New England children used to standardize these tests consequently determine the standards with which the more primitive West Indian children were compared.

was able to count four pennies. All of these factors combine to depress the test scores. As a group the children were decidedly retarded in their development, but there were certain tests in which they either more nearly approached the white norms or actually exceeded them.

No consistent effort is made in Jamaica to train the eliminative functions; even so, the native children were not markedly different from the white children in New Haven. Since no other bodily function ever receives the careful training that the eliminative functions do in America, these results raise the question of wasted labor in our culture. The suggestion is that the processes of elimination are so markedly dependent on the maturation of the controlling muscles and nerves that to try to impose training too early is a waste of time and energy.

In two other tests for the three-year-olds—"putting on shoes" and "running errands"—the Jamaican children are definitely superior as they are in the age at which they first stand and walk. This result suggests that the absence of intimate care of the young may make for self-sufficiency at earlier ages than is characteristic of American children.

4. FOSTER CHILDREN

The three previous studies leave little valid reason to doubt that environmental factors may have profound effects upon intelligence-test performance. By the very nature of their design, however, these studies could not give any information about hereditary factors and intelligence. To obtain this information we must look to another type of experiment, one in which something is known not only about the environment, but about heredity as well. Such a study was conducted by Barbara Burks.[8]

The method. The plan of this experiment grew out of the

---

[8] B. S. Burks, "The Relative Influence of Nature and Nurture upon Mental Development." A comparative study of foster parent-foster child resemblance and true parent-true child resemblance. Twenty-seventh Yearbook Nat. Soc. Stud. Educ., Part I, 1928, 219-316. A later study, A. M. Leahy, "Nature-Nurture and Intelligence," *Genetic Psychology Monographs*, 16, 1935, 1-80 is somewhat more precise than the Burks study but obtains essentially the same results.

known fact that parents and their children are similar in I.Q. Such a fact alone, however, is not very meaningful, because parents and children share not only similar genetic backgrounds but similar environment. They may be similar to each other because of the environmental similarity, the genetic similarity, or both. Nevertheless this fact can be made meaningful if we can find another group which has the same environment as its "parents" but a totally different genetic background. Such a group as this is found in the foster or adopted children, who share their foster parents' environment, but not their heredity. One group—the true child and true parent—can show how both heredity and environment operate; the other group —foster child and foster parent—shows how environment alone operates.

Burks selected for study a group of 204 children who had been adopted before they were six months of age. At the time of the study the children ranged from five to fourteen years of age. All the children and their foster parents were given intelligence tests, and, in addition to this, each home was rated for its degree of intellectual stimulation. This measure of intellectual stimulation was composed of such things as amounts of education of the parents, number of books in the library, the amount of home instruction given to the child, and other factors.

A control group consisting of 105 true child-true parent families was also selected. This group was as similar as possible to the foster group in age of the children, occupation of the parents, intelligence of the parent, and general socioeconomic level. This group was measured in the same way and on the same variables as the foster-family group.

Results. A statistical treatment of the data showed that both groups resembled their parents in intelligence, but that the degree of resemblance was greater in the true child-true parent groups than in the foster child-foster parent group. Difference in the intellectual level of the home clearly made for differences in I.Q., but differences in the genetic background also made for differences in intellectual ability.

The experiment went farther than simply pointing out that both environment and heredity operate. By means of a particular statistical method which cannot be discussed here, Burks tried to get some measure of the relative effectiveness of each of these variables. Her conclusion was that most of the differences among the children in their intelligence-test performance was due to the different hereditary background and a small portion of these differences was due to the differences in environment.

Summary of the experiment. The reasons why people differ from each other in intelligence-test performance are found in the differences both in their heredity and in their environment. The present study has indicated that, for the groups examined, most of the differences were due to heredity. One must be cautioned against generalizing broadly from this study. The range of environmental differences in the families studied, from the poorest environment to the best, was not great. If the study had included some families whose environments were like those of the Hollow children—whose environment departs markedly from the American norm—then the relative importance of environment would have been much greater. This means that if you find two individuals who differ from each other in intelligence, you cannot glibly state that most of the difference is due to the fact that they have different heredity. If on examination you discover that their environments were fairly similar, you would be justified in pointing to heredity as the major cause. If, on the other hand, their environments were greatly different, you have reason to suspect that environment is the major cause.

5. THE FEEBLE-MINDED

The question often arises as to what becomes of the children who do not get along well in school. Is there a place for them in our social scheme? What kinds of lives do they lead once they leave the school system? There have been several surveys of a limited kind which have had as their object the study of this problem, but there have been few controlled investigations made in which an equal number of children who had not been classified as subnormal have also been followed up later to find out how they turned out. A com-

145

plete study of this latter kind is available in the work of Baller.[9] The students who had been in the special classes of the public school system of Lincoln, Nebraska, and an equal number of Lincoln students who had not been in the special classes were the subjects in the study. Of the nine items especially investigated, seven concern us here:

(1) The aspects of the home background which particularly characterized these individuals.

(2) The kind and amount of schooling.

(3) The marital status.

(4) The extent to which the subjects had been successful in regulating their conduct so as to conform to the laws and social customs of the community.

(5) The occupational choice and permanence of employment.

(6) The degree of economic self-sufficiency or dependence.

(7) The respects in which mentally subnormal individuals who succeeded in making reasonably satisfactory social adjustments differ from those who failed.

The experimental and control groups. There were 206 individuals in the subnormal group, of which 126 were men and 80 were women. None of them had had I.Q.'s of more than 70 when they were tested in the elementary schools, and all of them were more than twenty-one years of age at the time this study was completed. These 206 people were paired one at a time with a normal group, on the basis of age, sex, and nationality but the I.Q.'s of the normal group were between 100 and 120 so that we have equal groups differing only in respect to I.Q. What is called normal here is actually somewhat above normal. The range was chosen in order to obtain clearly contrasting groups.

Locating the subjects. The reason why more of this work has not been done will be evident when we consider the difficulties involved in following up groups of this size after they have been out of school a few years. The first step was to look up the names of the subjects in the city directory and in the telephone book. When

9 Warren Robert Baller, "A Study of the Present Social Status of a Group of Adults, Who, When They Were in Elementary Schools, Were Classified as Mentally Deficient," *Genetic Psychology Monographs*, 1936, 28, 80.

146

the names did not appear in these places, the names of the subjects were submitted to various agencies, such as the Child Welfare Bureau, police courts, penitentiaries, reform schools, and institutions for the insane and feeble-minded. Letters to employers, ministers, lawyers, relatives, and friends were used in the hope of turning up a lead that would prove profitable. For one case fifteen separate and distinct leads had to be followed and it took 318 different leads to locate 196 of the subjects.

General description. After the subjects were located, an attempt was made to interview each one of them, to visit the home, to get acquainted with the relatives, to observe the living conditions in the neighborhood, and so forth. After a good deal of work, 196 of the 206 subnormals and 202 of the control subjects were located and complete information was obtained about them. It turned out that 7 per cent of the subnormal group and 1 per cent of the normal group were deceased. Six and one-half per cent of the subnormal group and none of the control group were in institutions for the feeble-minded. One person from each group was in a hospital for the insane. State reformatories and county jails accounted for two of the subnormal group, but for none of the control group. Fifty-nine per cent of the subnormal group were still living in Lincoln. Fifty-five per cent of the control group were still in the same town. Only 12.25 per cent of the subnormal group had moved to other states, but almost twice as many of the control subjects had moved out of Nebraska. Although the migratory tendencies of the subnormal group are thus demonstrated to be somewhat limited with respect to the states that they live in, within the town of Lincoln they change their addresses much more frequently than the control subjects do.

Family background. The family background records showed that the subnormal subjects come largely from the lower occupational levels and have practically no representation in the higher professions. In larger proportions, moreover, they have either one or both parents deceased, parents divorced, and families listed with relief agencies before the subject's twenty-first birthday, and more criminal and disorderly conduct records on the part of the parents.

147

Educational record. The educational achievement of the subnormal group is expressed in the average of four and one-half grades completed for both the boys and the girls. But what is probably more significant is the fact that twenty-three boys and ten girls completed the eight grades of work and that one boy and two girls finished high school. The work of a number of these people who got as high as junior high school was of a very special type, however. There was one pupil of the subnormal group who finally finished almost one year of college, but she was twenty-two years of age when she was graduated from the high school. The control subjects, on the other hand, on the average completed the twelve grades of school, and about half of the fifty-one boys entering college were graduated. Of these, three took M.A. degrees, one an M.D. degree, and one a Ph.D. degree. Thirty-one of the girls went to college, nine of them were graduated in four years, but none received a higher degree. As we could have predicted at the start on the basis of intelligence test scores, there is a clear-cut difference between school performance for these two groups.

Marital status. Almost 60 per cent of both the subnormal and normal women married, and about 50 per cent of the normal men were married, but a significantly smaller percentage (about 33 per cent) of the subnormal men were married. These data show that feeble-mindedness is not a preventative factor in marriage in women, but since more than 50 per cent of the normal men and only 33 per cent of the subnormal men married, feeble-mindedness is a deterrent, probably for economic reasons, among men. There are also more children among the feeble-minded than among the controls, and the feeble-minded women are married at a significantly younger age. *But notice that the great difference between the groups which was evident in the scholastic attainments no longer obtains in marital status.*

Social adjustment. There are consistent and significant differences between the conduct records as revealed by the juvenile police courts, county and city jails, reformatories, and penitentiaries for both groups of subjects. Twenty-five per cent of the subnormal subjects have appeared in juvenile court, while only 4 per cent of the control subjects have appeared there. For the police court about 18 per cent of the subnormal subjects, as compared with 6 per cent of the normal subjects, have records. About 19 per cent of the subnormal subjects have been in either the county jail, city jail, reformatory, or penitentiary, while only 3 per cent of the control subjects have been committed to these institutions. These commitments were for the comparatively serious offenses, including wife desertion, destruction of property, driving while intoxicated, and assault and battery. If violation of the traffic ordinances had been considered, then the court appearances of the normal subjects would have been doubled.

Occupational adjustment. The occupational record of the two groups shows a clear-cut superiority for the normal group with reference to both temporary and permanent employment, and the kinds of occupations represented in the two groups also indicate a higher type of adjustment. The degree of independence is shown by the fact that about 83 per cent of the subnormal subjects are either wholly or partially self-supporting, whereas 99 per cent of the control are wholly or partially self-supporting. The percentage of subjects who were aided by relief agencies is about 40 in the subnormal and about 16 in the control subjects. These figures do not tell the whole story if we consider that the per capita cost for the subnormal group was greatly in excess of that for the normal group. The fact that 83 per cent of the subnormals have been to some extent self-supporting, the amount varying from the income derived for tasks such as mowing lawns and occasional work in the homes of acquaintances to a regular income from permanent employment, is rather striking in view of their distinct abnormality on the intelligence tests. Taken together, all of these results seem to indicate that these deficient people have fared better in the task of providing a living for themselves and in getting along with their fellow men than the earlier prognoses indicated.[10]

[10] One generally thinks of commitment to a feeble-minded institution as a final disposal of the committed person: he is doomed to remain an inmate the rest of his life. But that a feeble-minded institution can be an instrument of preparation for life outside its walls is a newer notion that is just developing. Cf. E. A. Doll and S. Geraldine Longwell, "Social Competence of the Feeble-Minded under Extra-Institutional Care," *Psychiatric Quarterly*, 1937, 11, 450-464.

Baller concludes:

That it is possible for many of them [the feeble-minded] to remain law-abiding and useful citizens is suggested by the altogether satisfactory status of a considerable number of the group. *The notion that deficient mentality practically precludes social usefulness and a chance for happiness on the part of the individual is certainly not supported by the results of the present study.* That even a greater number of mentally deficient individuals may come to be well adjusted and better able to enjoy life as our program for their training in school and supervision after school is improved can hardly be doubted when their possibilities are carefully and sympathetically examined.

6. TRAINING THE FEEBLE-MINDED

Experiments at the State School for the Feeble-Minded at Letchworth Village, New York,[11] show that even the very lowest grades of the feeble-minded can be trained to be more useful than they ordinarily are. In most feeble-minded institutions the imbeciles and the idiots who can neither dress nor undress are playing around without purpose, creating all kinds of disturbance and generally making complete nuisances of themselves.

Since dressing and undressing were most troublesome, the children were given special training that finally resulted in fifty-one out of fifty-seven acquiring some considerable skill in these operations. A week of intensive training was required. They were taught to lace and to tie their shoelaces by merely giving very special attention to these processes which are picked up without special training by the normal. It required five months of practice before forty-seven of them were able to select their own names in the labels on dresses, shoes, and nightgowns. By intensive training, these very low-grade people were taught to become fairly independent and socially useful within the institution where they had previously been entirely dependent and troublesome in their conduct. Boundless patience alone is required to teach them the simple things that are learned by more competent people without special training. A rough indication of what may be expected of the various levels of mental deficiency is listed in the following pages.

[11] George J. Veith, "Training the Idiot and the Imbecile," *Proceedings* of the American Association for the Study of the Feeble-Minded, 1927, 51, 148-168.

INDUSTRIAL POSSIBILITIES OF THE FEEBLE-MINDED WITHIN AN INSTITUTION [12]

MENTAL AGE 3 OR BELOW

Boys
1. Picking up and piling stones.
2. Picking up and piling wood.
3. Putting stones in cart.
4. Using grub hoe, shovel, rake. (Rough work with no accuracy.)
5. Floor polishing with rope rubber.
6. Sandpapering. Flat surfaces.

Girls
1. Floor and table polishing.
2. Picking up and carrying to proper receptacle paper, rags, etc.
3. Carrying dirty clothes to laundry bags and clean clothes to ward.
4. Moving tables, chairs, etc., in house cleaning.
5. Carrying metal dishes from dining room to side room for washing.
6. Picking up and piling stones.

MENTAL AGE OF 5

1. Sandpapering of furniture preparatory to varnishing.
2. Harvesting vegetables not requiring judgment, such as pulling up whole field of mature beets, carrots or turnips.
3. Cutting rags with scissors into accurate strips.
4. Sorting palmetto and tampico bristles for brushes.

1. Vegetable paring.
2. Crocheting (chain stitch).
3. Knitting (simple stitch for wash cloths).
4. Bed making.
5. Dishwashing.
6. Vegetable paring.

MENTAL AGE OF 6

1. Mowing lawns.
2. All-round kitchen helper.
3. Cement mixing and mason's helper.
4. Waxing, sweeping, and all-round ward helper.
5. Weeding (coarse work).

1. Rag-rug weaving with pattern.
2. Knitting and purling.
3. Crotcheting (open mesh).
4. Embroidery (lazy-daisy and blanket stitch).
5. All-round ward helper.
6. Hanging up and taking down clothes from drying bars.

MENTAL AGE OF 7

1. Painting (farm tools, etc.) ; no fine work.
2. Shoe repairing except trimming and burnishing.
3. Harvesting garden vegetables except table corn, tomatoes, peas and other vegetables needing more mature judgment.
4. Plowing, harrowing, and cultivating.
5. Felling trees with axe.
6. Carpenter work. (Simple repairs, such as vegetable boxes, brush backs, etc.)

1. Operating household sewing machine.
2. Harvesting garden vegetables except table corn, tomatoes, peas and other vegetables requiring more mature judgment.
3. Hoeing and thinning vegetables.

[12] Adapted from C. S. Raymond, "Industrial Possibilities of the Feeble-Minded within an Institution," *Proceedings* of the American Association for the Study of the Feeble-Minded, 1926, 50, 28-39.

The occupations listed under the mental age of eight and upward represent the types of work often performed by the boys and girls who have left the school on parole and are working for wages.

MENTAL AGE OF 8

Boys

1. Operating engineer's helper: handling coal and ashes, cleaning tubes, and assisting in repairs.
2. Waiter for employees.
3. Meat cutter's helper: chopping and trimming bones; cutting meat for stews.
4. Hair cutting and shaving.
5. Carpenter's helper.
6. Cane seating.

Girls

1. Knitting (sweater, caps and neck scarfs).
2. Embroidery: French knots, buttonhole stitch and cross stitch through canvas.
3. Making hooked rugs.
4. Making dresses cut out by others.
5. Laundry: plain ironing.
6. All-round kitchen helper.

MENTAL AGE OF 9

1. Broom making.
2. High-class woodwork where accuracy in following design is necessary.
3. Furniture repairing.
4. Painting toys, games, window sashes (fine work).
5. Shoe repairing. (Whole process, including operation of burnishing machine.)
6. Harvesting all kinds of garden vegetables and fruits.
7. Gardener's helper: wheel hoe and scuffle hoe cultivating of small garden vegetables.

1. Basketry (advanced patterns).
2. Cloth toy making: stuffing and finishing.
3. Operating jig saw: picture puzzles, toys, etc. Power sewing machines
4. Pottery.
5. Cutting out and making dresses.
6. Laundry: fancy ironing, running washing machine.
7. Plain cooking or waiting table.
8. Orchestra: viola, drums.

MENTAL AGE OF 10

1. Printing: setting and sorting type.
2. Sign painting.
3. Gardener's helper.
4. Electrician's helper.
5. Steamfitter's helper: cutting and threading pipe.
6. Form making for cement walls and floors.
7. Shellacking and varnishing.
8. Band: cornet, bass.

1. Basketry: raffia and reed work with patterns.
2. Laundry: starching and polishing; sorting clean clothes for distribution.
3. Fancy cooking: frosted cakes, candy, etc.
4. Orchestra: second violin, cornet, saxophone, bass.
5. Canning plant; slicing machine.

MENTAL AGE OF 11

1. Band: trombone.
2. Janitor work: care of employees' cottage boilers with very little supervision.

1. Folding, checking from slips and bundling employees' laundry.
2. Pastry and all-round family cook.
3. Orchestra: first violin, cello, flute and clarinet.
4. Canning plant: power sealer

7. THE GENIUS

Introduction. Whether it is inspired by envy or not it is difficult to say, but it is nevertheless true that much of the world tends to view the genius as an unhappy and maladjusted person. He is considered as socially awkward and incapable of descending to the free and easy plans of social interaction which make living with other persons fun. He is pictured as being ill dressed and boorish, pale and unhealthy, and full of crotchets and conceits. If he happens to be a child prodigy, there is a lurking suspicion that he will burn himself out by early maturity.

The truth or falsity of these notions cannot be established by accepting as proof a single child prodigy who died at seventeen, by pointing to some great poet or dancer who became insane. The characteristics of the genius can be determined only by studying a group of them from childhood on and describing their characteristics, their development, and their achievements. Such a study has been conducted by Lewis M. Terman.[13]

Method. In the Autumn of 1921 Terman and his assistants went into the school system of California and discovered over a thousand children who reached an I.Q. of 135 or higher. This was his genius group.[14] Measurements of the social behavior, the physical development, the educational achievements, and the interests of these children were obtained from various sources.

Results

1. THE CHILDHOOD CHARACTERISTICS. All the racial elements in the area studied were represented in the parentage of the children. They came from the poorest as well as the best of homes, although a disproportionably large number came from parents of the professional class. In such physical measures as height, weight, strength, and general health they were superior to the average school population.

---

13 L. M. Terman and M. H. Oden, *The Gifted Child Grows Up*. Stanford University Press, 1947.

14 Notice how genius is being defined—as a score on an intelligence test and not on the basis of some other kind of achievement. One of the problems of this study will be, then, to determine whether or not persons with very high I.Q.'s do show great achievement along other lines.

They were, of course, somewhat advanced in grade placement but not to the great extent that they were advanced in their intellectual level. They read more than the average child their age, but they also engaged in sports. Actually they spent a little less time in play than the usual child, but a sports test showed that they had a better knowledge about sports than average. Teachers' ratings placed them somewhat superior to the normal child in degree of motivation, social and emotional adjustment, and in their artistic abilities.

Thus the picture of these young geniuses is not one of inferiority along every line save intelligence. Although their superiority was most marked in intellectual pursuits, they did, as an average, show superiority along almost any other line. Certainly the conclusion that the young genius is unsocial and maladjusted is not borne out by this study or by others.[15]

2. THE ADULT CHARACTERISTICS. Terman and his coworkers were able to keep in touch with most of this group over a span of more than twenty years, and in 1940 and again in 1945 he surveyed them to determine the nature of their adult status. These are his findings.

In 1940 their average age was just short of thirty years. Approximately 4 per cent of them had died, and this is 1 per cent less than would be expected for the general population. The personality adjustment of most of them seemed satisfactory, although slightly less than 1 per cent had suffered serious enough maladjustments to be classified as insane. This figure is only slightly lower than would be expected of the population at large for this age group. This finding lends no support to the somewhat popular belief that the line between the genius and the insane is a fine one which is easily crossed.

Nearly three quarters of the men and two thirds of the women had graduated from college and a very large proportion of them had returned to do graduate study in various fields. With such an educational record it is to be expected that a large proportion of them would find their lifework in one or the other of the professions. Such was the case for 45 per cent of the males, and this is in marked con-

15 Drayton W. Lewis, "Some Characteristics of Children Designated as Mentally Retarded, as Problems, and as Geniuses by Teachers." *Journal of Genetic Psychology,* 1947, 70, 29-51.

trast to the fact that only 6 per cent of the total population of California are classified as professional workers.

By the year 1945 about four fifths of the group were married, and response to a questionnaire on the degree of happiness of the marriage indicated that their marriages were no less successful than the average.

The group as a whole had succeeded well, and it had succeeded not only intellectually, but vocationally, emotionally, socially and financially. It is true that there was no indication that any single member of the group would reach the great status of Shakespeare, Goethe, Newton, da Vinci, or Pasteur, yet the achievements of many were well above that of most college graduates, and most of them excelled the general level of the population.

Summary. This study offers no support for the view that the genius is a social and emotional misfit. When genius was defined as a person with an I.Q. of 135 or higher, it was found that the child genius is healthy and adjusted—perhaps a little more so than the average child. On the whole, the group as young adults showed a level of vocational and intellectual attainment which was markedly superior to that of the population at large. In their emotional and social adjustment they were certainly as successful as the average adult.

In two other ways this study is significant. It indicates that the use of intelligence tests in childhood can be of service in predicting later intellectual achievement, for on the whole these superior children became superior adults. But contrariwise, it indicates that superior intelligence is no *sure* indication in individual instances of superior social, emotional, and economic adjustment. This is evidenced by the fact that the marriages for some of them were unhappy, some became maladjusted to the point of insanity, and some were holding down only menial laboring jobs. High intelligence is not all that is needed to make one's way in the world.

Summary of the chapter. Intelligence tests are built on the assumption that the people on whom they will be used share something of a common environment. When tests are given to people who live in a markedly different environment, the scores have little meaning. The isolated life in remote sections makes the standard intelligence test meaningless because of the extreme dearth of common experiences with those of the standardization group. The second study shows that when persons move from a "poor" environment to a more stimulating one their intelligence-test performance improves. The further dependence of intelligence upon environment is shown in the third study wherein it was found that people of a different culture excel on some items but are inferior on others. The fourth study points out that heredity is an important determiner of differences in intelligence, but that environment also operates. Children who have been classed as feeble-minded while they are in school, when compared with a normal group do not fail so miserably to make an adjustment in the world as we might expect. As we learn how to teach the feeble-minded the things they need to know, it is possible that the outlook for them will be even more favorable. The final study of the chapter on the young genius indicates that the intellectually gifted child is no social misfit, but that he is every bit, if not slightly more, adjusted than the normal child. As a group these children may look forward to a future of marked intellectual and vocational success, and with an assurance that their emotional and social lives will be as adequate as the normal in intelligence.

CHAPTER NINE

PHYSIOLOGICAL CONDITIONS

A person's physiological condition at the time an act occurs is a major determinant of the kind of behavior that will take place, but it is not the *only* determinant. That heredity and maturation are important we have seen. The cultural level of the group in which one grows up is of major importance, as the last chapter has shown. For the present we shall concern ourselves with the physiological conditions which are important in determining what a person will do when any kind of situation demands an adjustive activity on his part. These would include, among others, any new thing he has to learn; any old thing he must remember; any situation to which he has to react promptly, skillfully, without fumbling or groping; any situation requiring a discrimination between things that are very nearly alike.

Among the factors which produce identifiable physiological conditions are fatigue; stimulants like caffeine; depressants like nicotine and alcohol and a host of less well-known drugs; deprivation of food or some of the accessory food factors like the vitamins; deprivation of oxygen as that incurred in flying to great heights; toxic substances absorbed through the skin or inhaled as illustrated in some occupational hazards; toxic substances manufactured in the body as in an infected or abscessed tooth or diseased tonsils; and finally, chemical substances manufactured in the body as a result of the functioning of some gland of internal secretion, like the thyroid, the pituitary, the adrenals, or the sex glands. These chemical and toxic substances either may or may not have an observable effect on behavior.

It is clear that with all these possible factors, and this is only a partial list, it would be necessary to devote the remainder of this book to their interrelations if we examined them in detail. In order to have time for other things equally important, we will have to select from the available material that which finds more immediate application in everyday life. A person frequently comes into contact with

157

alcohol and tobacco; he infrequently meets with morphine, or heroin and hashish. We shall confine our interest in drugs to the two mentioned first and as an example of a toxic condition we shall examine the effect of tonsil infection on intelligence. Finally, because of the present interest in the results, we shall discuss the influence of a lack of oxygen on psychological events.

Psychological precautions. If one were to investigate the influence of any of the drugs on behavior, he must take special precautions to guard against two effects. First, the subjects will almost all have some preconceived bias with respect to the effect that any well-known drugs may have upon them; for instance, it is hard to convince some people that coffee won't keep them awake. Some observations have been made that indicate that a person can be slightly more influenced by the anticipation of a cocktail than he is after drinking one, i.e., he may be slightly more intoxicated before drinking a cocktail than afterward. Testimonials of the kind appearing in patent-medicine advertisements can be obtained after treatment with the most innocuous substances which can have no possible relation to recovery from colds, hay fever, or any other troublesome malady. The drug trade, in fact, supplies a variety of substances which are designed to satisfy people who demand unnecessary prescriptions from their physicians. Second, the method of administering some drugs may be more potent in influencing a person's behavior than the effects of the drug itself. Any drug that has to be administered by a hypodermic needle may produce a prompt recovery in a functional disorder because the administration is so unpleasant. One glandular substance (pituitrin), which has to be administered this way, is recommended for persistent enuresis in children. We might suppose that the same kind of painful administration of a perfectly neutral saline solution would also produce some recoveries. The rhythmical breathing required to pull on a pipe or cigarette is known to produce an effect on heart rate and possibly on blood pressure, in the entire absence of any tobacco at all. Both these effects will produce certain changes in behavior, changes which will mistakenly be attributed to the action of the drug or the toxin if controls are not used.

158

1. THE EFFECTS OF TOBACCO

Most of the work done on the influence of tobacco is perfectly useless since neither the bias of the subjects nor the incidental accompaniments of the administration were taken into account. In 1917 a committee for the study of the tobacco problem initiated an investigation finally published in 1924 in which all these factors were to be considered. The committee depended on Clark Hull,[1] then director of the psychological laboratory at the University of Wisconsin, for expert technical guidance in the problem. Hull saw clearly that the principal difficulty would be in the administration of a control dose of tobacco that would present all of the features of the actual smoking except one—the tobacco itself must not be given. He had heard that in the dark, habitual smokers frequently allowed their pipes to go out without being aware of the fact. Pipe smoking is as much, or more, a matter of watching the smoke as it is of smelling and of sensing warm air on the tongue. With this observation as a cue, he invented a pipe through which the subject could draw warm moist air but no tobacco smoke. In the dark it produced an illusory effect that satisfied even inveterate smokers. The experimenter himself smoked in the same room so that the subjects could smell the smoke, but in this way they got so little actual tobacco that the effects observed in the experiment were not made dubious.

Method. For the duration of the experiment the subjects must never be given any notion that a control pipe exists. To this end, it was necessary to mislead them as to the real nature of the procedure. They were told in two preliminary periods that the effects of tobacco smoking were to be studied by tests before and after smoking; there was never a hint that part of the time they wouldn't actually be smoking. They must, they were told, give their conscientious application to the tests throughout the entire experimental period. A solemn promise was exacted from them to keep up a maximum effort every day.

The subjects were, in this way, prepared for a rather elaborate technique. They consequently showed no surprise, either when they

---

[1] Clark Hull, "The Influence of Tobacco Smoking on Mental and Motor Efficiency," *Psychological Monographs*, 1924, 33, 161.

were blindfolded for the smoking session or when the experimenter always handled the pipe, whether it actually contained tobacco or whether it was the control. It was necessary for the experimenter to handle both pipes to keep the subject from detecting the difference between them. To the lips they felt the same, but to allow the subject to touch them would have been to give the whole thing away. To regulate the amount of tobacco, the subject was permitted three puffs every twenty seconds for twenty-five minutes.

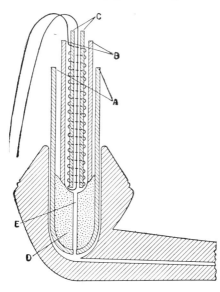

FIG. 32.—A drawing of the experimental pipe. (From Jenkins, *Psychology in Business and Industry*, p. 138. By permission of the publishers, John Wiley & Sons, Inc.)

When the subject took his usual place in the laboratory, he saw the regular pipe. The experimenter elaborately cleaned it before him. After he was blindfolded he would hear the experimenter tapping on the tin and striking the match, and he would smell the odor of the freshly lighted pipe. After the blindfold was removed he would see the burned-out ash in the pipe. The usual pauses made by the experimenter in securing the special pipe from its hiding place and preparing it for the subject were as scrupulously maintained on the days when the subject actually did smoke as on those when he did not.

The illusion provided by this method was so perfect that one man insisted on blowing smoke rings on the days when there wasn't any smoke just as realistically as he was able to do when he was really smoking. One subject's results had to be discarded because he peeped one day, saw the control pipe and couldn't be fooled again. Some of the reports of the other subjects are shown on page 166. If one examines these reports in detail he must conclude that to smoke warm air in the absence of visual cues seems, on the whole, to be as satisfactory as to smoke tobacco.

In this experiment for the first time we see the introduction of a new experimental method. There is no need for separate "control" and "experimental" groups. Each person serves as his own control in the sense that half the time he is inhaling tobacco and the other half he is inhaling moist, warm air. In the various curves shown here the results of several subjects are exhibited by their average performance on "tobacco nights" compared with "no-tobacco nights."

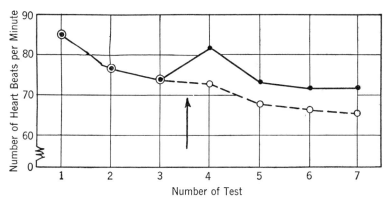

FIG. 33.—The heart rate curve.

Subjects. There were nine nonsmokers and ten habitual smokers in the group; it was one of the nonsmokers who was eliminated because he accidentally caught sight of the "fake" pipe. The routine of the habitual smokers was not disturbed except that they were not to smoke for three hours immediately preceding the experiment. We shall show only a few of the principal findings. The heart-rate curves in Figure 33 indicate a gradual reduction in the pulse rates from an average of about eighty-five to about seventy-eight in the course of sitting quietly in the laboratory for fifteen minutes. Between the third and fourth time that the pulse was taken on the "tobacco nights," as indicated in the chart, the tobacco was administered with the results shown by the solid curve, while for the "no-tobacco nights" the control dose was given with the results shown in the dotted curve. The dotted curve shows a slight disturbance in its downward trend due to the puffing and perhaps to other features of the situation, *but where all these features are the same except for the tobacco there is an unmistakable increase of almost 10 per cent in the heart rate.* This effect persists in decreasing amounts throughout the experimental period. Forty per cent of the increase

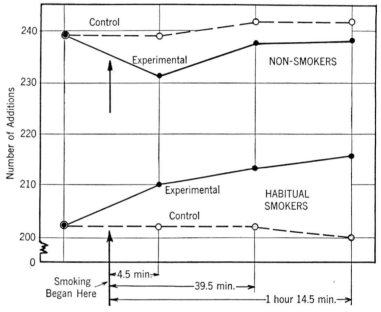

Fig. 34.—The effect of tobacco on the speed of adding.

is still present an hour and three quarters after smoking. These results were obtained with habitual smokers alone. Pulse records were not obtained on enough of the nonsmokers to warrant a conclusion for them. Hull points out that the effect of tobacco on people who don't use it presents a rather academic problem anyway.

Speed of adding. The task given to the subject was to add, as quickly as he could, a single integer starting with 6 to any two-place number the experimenter gave him. He continued to add successively 7 and 8. If the experimenter gave him 36, he would add 6 and call out 42; then he would add 7 to this total and say 49; then

THE NIGHTLY SCHEDULE OF THE NINETEEN SUBJECTS

A subject finished his evening meal at about 6:25 and reported at the laboratory at 6:50 P.M.:

6:50 Pulse taken after which subject sat quietly for about 15 minutes.

7:05 Complete series of tests given requiring 30 minutes. The tests began with counting the pulse beats. *This is the normal of the day.*

7:35 Pulse taken after which eight minutes were consumed in preparation for the smoking.

7:45 Began either smoking or taking the control dose, which lasted 25 minutes.

8:10 Experimenter puts away tobacco.

8:12 Complete series of tests repeated.

8:42 Subject rested for 5 minutes.

8:47 Complete series of tests repeated.

9:17 Subject rested for 5 minutes.

9:22 Complete series of tests repeated.

9:52 Pulse taken.

9:55 Subject excused.

8 and say 57. He then returned to 6, added it to the new total, getting 63; then 7 would make 70, and 8 would make 78. This process of adding 6, 7 and 8 was continued until the experimenter gave him a new two-place number at the end of thirty seconds. The test as a whole continued for ten minutes so that ten sets of additions were obtained. The score was the total number of correct additions in five minutes. The results are shown separately for the habitual smokers and the nonsmokers. The first postsmoking test came at

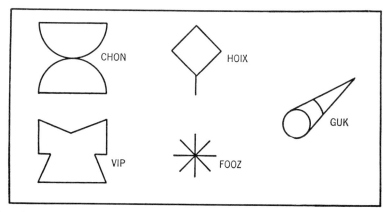

Fig. 35.—Five of the geometric characters used in the experiment. The names pronounced by the experimenter are shown to the right.

4.5 minutes after the smoking period; the second came at 39.5 minutes; the last at 1 hour 14.5 minutes after.

The effect of the tobacco is exactly reversed for the two groups.

(1) The nonsmokers show a consistent decrement lasting throughout the period of an hour and a quarter.

(2) The tobacco causes the habitual smokers to add a little quicker.

In neither case is the effect very much, about 3 per cent average decrease and 5 per cent average increase, but since every single subject in each group showed the effect, the result is highly reliable, even though small.

Rate of learning. The task which sampled the simple learning ability of the subjects was similar to that which would be involved in learning a foreign language, where five new words would con stitute each test. In order to be sure that none of the subjects started with an advantage and in order to have available a considerable body of test material of equal difficulty, none of the existing foreign languages could be used. Artificial tasks which resemble the learning of new words have been worked out in various psychological experiments. In this one, geometrical forms which had no ordinary name were given one-syllable nonsense names. Five of these are shown in Figure 35.

Details of method. The forms were presented one at a time at a small window by a machine built for the purpose. The subject never saw the one-syllable names; he heard them only when they were pronounced by the experimenter at the middle of the five-second interval that the exposure device provided. The first time through the five cards the subject would have to be prompted every time, since he wouldn't know any of the names that had been arbitrarily assigned. The second time, when the cards were presented in a different order, he might be able to anticipate a name before it was spoken by the experimenter. If he did, he got credit for a correct anticipation. If not, a minus sign was recorded by the experimenter on a prepared blank. After several presentations of the five forms, each in a different order, the subject would finally be able to anticipate the experimenter's prompting each time. The number of promptings he required before he could anticipate correctly each time would be a measure of how quickly he could learn this kind of material. The results for this experiment are presented in terms of the number of promptings required.

No single series was learned twice by the same subject. For each new test five new forms and five new syllables were used. Each point on the graph represents an average of eight to ten separate experiments for each of the nineteen people concerned (nine non-smokers and ten habitual smokers). This would make about 190 separate learning tasks if each person were tested only once each night, but since there were four tests each night the actual number of series represented is more than 750.

We go into this detail only to show how much labor can be represented in one of the graphs shown in this book. The appearance

DETAILS OF TWO SUBJECTS' REPORTS

A. M. G., one of the subjects, thinks that if he inhaled the smoke there wouldn't have been any difference in the laboratory from ordinary pipe smoking. As it was, the only way he could tell he was smoking was by the gradual increase in the strength of the smoke and the bite on his tongue. He sometimes could tell that he was smoking by the smell but he was able to tell at all times that he was smoking. There were several times that he could not tell whether the pipe was going or not. Such periods were for three or four puffs. He was always sure he was smoking most of the time on every evening. *There was never any evening when he could have been persuaded that he had not been smoking at least ninety-five per cent of the time.* He thought that some nights there was little or no stinging on the tongue. On such nights he told by the flavor. The last night of the experiment (a tobacco night) it was so strong he did not like it. It bit his tongue and it was an effort to take another pull. The night before, however (a control night), it was fairly good. It didn't bite the tongue to any great extent, not enough to bother much. *It would be an easy matter for him to break off smoking if it were always like the last night.* He enjoyed it the night before. It wasn't strong at all. It tasted fairly well and took the place of not being able to inhale. *He thinks it would be pretty hard to quit under such (control) conditions.*

G. W. M., another subject, always felt rather hungry for a smoke when he first came to the laboratory. *But after the smoke in the laboratory he was always satisfied.* He says that he did not enjoy the smoking, though, when it was going on. This, he feels, was probably because he couldn't see or handle the pipe. It was given to him more slowly than he was accustomed to taking it. He thinks it very difficult to tell while blindfolded whether he is smoking or not. He has wondered lots of times whether the pipe wasn't pretty near out. These periods were for three or four minutes. But this can't be true because he heard the experimenter light the pipe. *There was never any night when he was in doubt as to whether the pipe was lit throughout the evening as a whole.* He thinks that on one evening one might have persuaded him that the pipe was not lit. He never wondered about the matter except this one night.

These comments were taken after the experiment was finished. They show clearly that these subjects were entirely unaware that half the total number of nights they were "smoking" warm, moist air, without any tobacco at all.

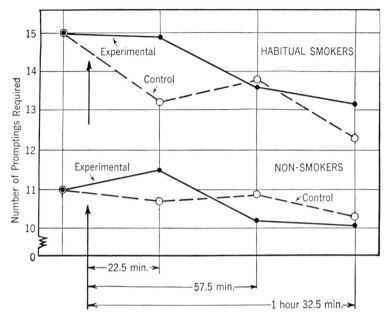

FIG. 36.—The effect of tobacco on learning names.

of the graphs is simple, but one should not be misled by the appearance of simplicity.

Results. These curves show that the habitual smokers do not learn quite as promptly as the nonsmokers at any time. Since the curves show the number of promptings, the higher the number the more inadequate the performance. A drop in the curve means a more adequate performance. Both groups show this drop on the control days. The effect of tobacco seems to be to retard this drop slightly. In any event, since the curves cross and recross, *we must conclude that there has been no definite lasting effect on either group as we have seen in the case of heart rate, and speed of adding.*

Summary. There is a small but certain increase in heart rate for both smokers and nonsmokers. For speed of adding, the effect is reversed in the two groups: nonsmokers are made slower, smokers faster, the differences being between 3 and 5 per cent. There is no consistent effect on rate of learning as measured here.

167

A practical application. If a dean of students wanted to find out whether tobacco smoking had a detrimental influence on college grades, he would probably select two groups of students, smokers and nonsmokers. After he had looked up their grades he would probably find that the nonsmokers had higher grades than the smokers, and he would be inclined to conclude that tobacco smoking *causes* lower grades. There can be no doubt but that smoking *is* associated with lower grades, but to go a step further and attribute the cause to the tobacco is not justified, either in the light of Hull's results or according to the rules of ordinary logic. The fact that low grades and smoking are related is no proof in itself that one causes the other. Both may be caused by another hidden factor. Among the hidden factors which *might* be effective is that of sociability. Those that are more active socially in college may be the smokers because smoking is essentially a social pastime. That studiousness and extreme sociability do not ordinarily go together is obvious. If this hypothesis were true, it would account for the fact that smokers, as a group, are poorer students. At present we don't know whether it is true, but *we do know that a positive statement to the effect that smoking is harmful to grades and to learning efficiency generally is not justified.*

2. THE EFFECTS OF ALCOHOL

The greatest stumbling block in finding out what effects alcohol has on human behavior lies in the lack of a control dose. Beverages which contain alcohol in even small amounts are readily detected through taste and smell from nonalcoholic mixtures. Most experimenters have made no effort at all to control this important feature of the experiment; consequently their results are of doubtful significance. The dire effect of alcohol on animals that we hear about frequently has been the result of dosing, starting with infancy, in quantities far in excess of most human inclinations or capacities.

Alcohol a depressant. Among the better known experiment with people the researches of Dodge and Benedict[2] take first rank from the technical standpoint. They did not use control doses, but th

² Raymond Dodge and F. G. Benedict, *Psychological Effects of Alcohol,* Carnegie Institution of Washington, Publication No. 232, Washington, D. C., 1915.

generalization that we can draw from their experiments does not depend upon this omission. They found that, contrary to the popular belief, *alcohol does not affect the "higher mental processes" like "judgment" and "reasoning" first and the simpler reflex acts last.* The effect of the alcohol was first detected in a change in the simpler motor coordinations and reflexes. Since this generalization involves the relative effects of alcohol on two functions, the lack of the control dose does not vitiate the conclusion. An experimenter, using instruments of precision, can detect the effects long before an observer who does not have measuring instruments available notices any change in behavior. A further generalization from these studies, and one in which all experimenters in this field concur, is that *the effect of alcohol is always depressing, never stimulating.* Again, this is contrary to the popular opinion, which has it that alcohol in small amounts, at least, is a stimulant. The popular notion is based on two kinds of observations: the subjective report, which does not often agree with objective measures of organic condition or production; and the observation of several physiological changes which superficially *appear* to mean stimulating rather than narcotizing or depressing influences. The principal physiological change so observed is that alcohol, like tobacco, increases the heart rate. To interpret an increase in heart rate as a stimulating effect is to display ignorance of the heart-rate mechanism.

Normal heart rate for a given set of conditions is dependent upon what might be considered a balance between the impulses of two sets of nerves. One nerve, the vagus, tends to slow the heart rate. Whenever impulses from this nerve are interfered with, the heart increases its rate automatically. For some unknown reason, alcohol produces more blocking in the vagus nerve than it does on the sympathetic, so that heart rate increases, not as a result of a stimulating effect but as the result of a blocking of normally inhibiting impulses.

Another observation which has been held to demonstrate the stimulating effect of alcohol is the feeling of warmth which follows alcoholic consumption. This observation is caused by the easy circulation of warm blood in the skin, but ease of circulation is accomplished by a relaxation of the walls of the blood vessels, a depressant

169

effect. The feeling of warmth is illusory, however. This mechanism allows heat to radiate from the body more easily, and hence the body temperature, carefully measured, is actually less than it is when one doesn't feel so warm.

Hollingworth's experiment. The experiments of Hollingworth[3] are among the better known ones which have principally been concerned with psychological rather than physiological effects. He used six subjects who ranged from total abstainers to moderate drinkers. Under experimental conditions, they drank 2.75 per cent beer in varying doses and a control beer of exactly the same manufacture but from which the alcohol had been removed by the brewer. Ordinary drinking water and lemonade were also used as controls in some parts of the experiment. The subjects reported that the 2.75 beer was weak; the dealcoholized beer was reported even weaker. This device, two beers of little and no alcoholic content, is the nearest approach to an experimental and a control dose that has yet been used. Even these weak beers produced measurable effects, as we shall see.

Eight different psychological tests and a count of pulse rate constituted the nine segments of behavior sampled in the experiment.

The testing schedule. The subjects reported at the laboratory at 9:00 each day where they remained until 4:00. Each experimenter stationed in a different room, gave two tests to two people. The subjects shifted from room to room until at the end of a half hour all the tests had been administered to them. Then they began all over again, continuing the routine until 12:00.

At 12:00 they ate and drank variously as the schedule (page 172) required and at 1:00 returned to the tests which were administered continuously until 4:00. There were, then, six forenoon measures on each test and six in the afternoon.

The subjects did not know the purpose of the experiment beyond that they were to be tested after drinking different amounts and different kinds of beer. They did not know that on some days they actually drank no *alcohol* when they were drinking beer.

[3] H. L. Hollingworth, "The Influence of Alcohol," *Journal of Abnormal and Social Psychology,* 1923, 18, 204-237; 311-333.

Preliminary practice. There were three days of preliminary testing to perfect the details of the routine and to make certain that the men had reached the peak of their performance uninfluenced by the special conditions which were to come later. They were also accustomed to drinking fairly large quantities of liquid—on these days either water or lemonade.

The tests included:

(1) STEADINESS. The number of contacts was counted which the subject made when he attempted to hold a stylus in a hole only slightly larger then the stylus. This is a standard test for steadiness. It was also used in the tobacco study.

(2) EYE-HAND COORDINATION. A triangular plate with a metallic contact at the bottom of a small hole served as a target for a stylus held by the subject. An electric counter kept a record of the number of hits as the subject progressed in a clockwise direction around the triangle. One minute was allowed for the test. Any disturbance of coordination showed in a reduced score as the subject fumbled, missed the target, and tried again and again to make contact.

(3) CONTROL OF SPEECH MECHANISM. The stammering, fumbling, and blocking of the speech mechanism was measured by the Woodworth-Wells Color Naming Test. Five colors occurred twenty times in random order. To name these colors as they occur at random required a high degree of speech control. Each time the subject made a mistake, the experimenter called "No," whereupon the subject had to give the correct name before proceeding. Time thus becomes a measure of the degree of speech control.

(4) ADDING. Fifty two-place numbers were presented on a card in two vertical columns. The subject was required to add seventeen to the first number, then seventeen to the next, and so on. If the answer was wrong, the experimenter said, "No," and the subject was required to correct himself before going on. The time required for fifty additions was the measure of production.

(5) LOGICAL RELATIONS. Fifty adjectives were presented on cards. The subject was instructed to speak aloud the antonym of the word he had seen. Again, if he did not give the exact opposite,

171

PLAN OF THE EXPERIMENT

Friday, June 6: First Practice day, employed in learning the method of the tests, standardizing the routine and technique. Each subject did each test six times. At lunch hour tried drinking as much water as possible, along with the three small sandwiches.

Saturday, June 7: Second Practice day, each man made ten rounds of all the tests, and at lunch hour drank three or four bottles of lemonade along with three thin slices of bread spread with peanut butter.

Monday, June 9: First Blank day, twelve rounds of all tests were made. At lunch hour each man had three thin slices of bread and one small orange, and was allowed to drink as much of one bottle of water as he cared for.

Tuesday, June 10: First Control day, each man drank five bottles, each containing 12.5 ounces, of the Control beer, no food whatever being taken this day.

Wednesday, June 11: First Beer day, each man drank, during the noon hour six 12.5 ounce bottles of the Standard beer, no food being allowed this day.

Thursday, June 12: Second Blank day, each man had the three thin slices of bread, an orange or banana, and as much of one bottle of water as he cared for.

Friday, June 13: Second Beer day, each man drank four bottles of beer, taking one bottle each fifteen-minute period, along with three thin slices of bread, spread with peanut butter.

Saturday, June 14: Second Control day, each man had two thin slices of bread spread with peanut butter, and, except for No. 2, drank six bottles of Control beer during the noon hour. No. 2 was made sick and vomited after the third bottle, and continued to vomit thereafter, so he was allowed to quit drinking after the contents of the fifth bottle had been swallowed.

Monday, June 16: Third Beer day, each man had three thin slices of bread spread with peanut butter, and drank, except for No. 2, five bottles of the Standard beer during the noon hour. No. 2, who had been uniformly made sick by more than three bottles, was again made sick, and was allowed to take only three bottles.

Tuesday, June 17: Fourth Beer day, each man had, during the noon hour four to six crackers and a bit of cheese, and three bottles of the Standard beer during the noon hour.

Wednesday, June 18: Last Beer day; after making three rounds of all the tests a halt was made for a few minutes while each man drank one bottle of the Standard beer, at 10:45 A.M. After another round of tests, each man drank a second bottle at 11:15 A.M. After another round of tests each man drank a third bottle, at 11:50 A.M. and then made another round of the tests. At 12:30, a halt was made for the regular noon hour. During the previous drinking, the six men had eaten, along with the beer, three or four crackers each. At the noon hour, each man was allowed the three thin slices of bread and peanut butter, and drank as much beer as he could during the hour, in addition to the three bottles already drunk since 10:45 A.M.

Thursday, June 19: Dinner day; instead of drinking Beer or Control, or carrying on a Blank day, this day a special six-course dinner was set, at which all the subjects ate as much as they cared for, had a small black coffee, and smoked one cigar or several cigarettes if they wished. No alcohol was included in the meal, the idea being to determine the influence of a hearty meal on the process being measured. Immediately after the meal, the tests were continued in the usual way, and as they had been also on the morning of that day.

the experimenter said "No." A satisfactory opposite was required before proceeding.

(6) LEARNING. The quickness with which the subject could substitute letters for the geometrical forms of the Woodworth-Wells substitution test constituted a measure of the learning speed.

(7) THE PULSE RECORD. The pulse was counted as physicians usually do it.

Results. Only two of the results are shown, and these graphically. The others all agree in trend with these.[4]

(1) In Figure 37 the effect of large doses of alcohol (three or four bottles of beer) can be compared with

(a) A heavy meal

(b) No alcohol, light lunch (control)

(c) Smaller doses of alcohol (one or two bottles of beer)

Although the larger amounts of alcohol definitely increase the pulse rate, a heavy meal increases it even more.

(2) The results of the adding test, similar to the test in the tobacco experiment, show conclusively that the adding performance is greatly handicapped by alcohol in relatively minute amounts.

General conclusions. Both the pulse-rate results and results from the adding test indicate that *alcohol has a definitely depressing effect on the organism.* That the heart rate is increased merely means that inhibitory effects on its rate have been removed by alcoholic blocking.

We could generalize then that *a person who drinks even minute quantities of alcohol in the face of any kind of a problem that he has to solve, is making a psychological mistake. Although he may feel more competent, and to himself may seem cleverer and quicker, actual measurement shows the opposite to be true.*

Practical application. In the same way that mere association of two factors has been confused with causal efficacy, as we have seen

Many of these same tests have been used by Hollingworth and others in studies on the effects of caffeine. All studies show that caffeine has just the opposite effect that is shown here for alcohol. There are wide individual differences in the effect, and as in the case of alcohol, a tolerance for the drug seems to develop.

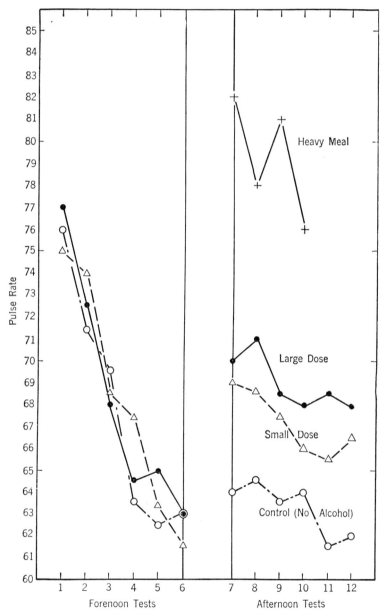

Fɪɢ. 37.—The effect of alcohol in small and large doses on afternoon pulse compared with the effect of a heavy meal. There is also a small rise in the control experiment

174

in the case of tobacco, so also has alcohol been held responsible for just about everything that can happen to a person. Insanity of a kind has been attributed to alcohol as well as inefficiencies and minor eccentricities. There is no clear-cut evidence that the various insanities and eccentricities would not have occurred without the

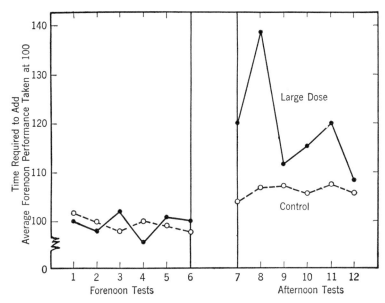

FIG. 38.—The effect of alcohol on the speed of adding. A rise in the curve means poorer performance.

alcohol. No really controlled observations have ever been made in this field. Again, in the absence of positive evidence, we must suspend judgment.

Professor Miles concludes a summary on the psychological effects of alcohol with these words:

When an individual has had the experience of promptly securing the comfort and joy of psychological escape simply by the drinking of alcoholic beverages, he readily adopts this procedure and follows it unless checked by social pressure or by an unusual degree of self-criticism. For the well-integrated individual, the moderate use of alcohol may be a habit or custom under control whose chief and perhaps only real damage is in substituting effortless escape for the learning and use of strategy and skill in meeting life's difficulties. Such an individual limits his use of alcohol, both in amount and also in frequency, by partaking only on the occasions when he desires a self-acting substitute for mental adjustment. He carries on without noticeable interference in the working-day accomplishment. If, however, tension becomes too great and he is hard pressed and fatigued, he may find it natural to drink more heavily, perhaps to the disadvantage of both work and morale. The weaker individual who is conspired against by circumstances has great difficulty in keeping himself from turning often to this ready means for personal relief. With psychological escape so accessible, the discouraged and the baffled find more and more difficulties and annoyances from which they feel justified in seeking refuge. For abnormal and unstable personalities, notwithstanding that they may have thought of it as the most divinely beneficent thing in the world, alcohol has been and still is a veritable millstone.

Miles's entire chapter in *Alcohol and Man,*[5] from which this quotation is taken, is well worth careful reading. Other sections of the book cover the effects of alcohol in its physiological, hereditary, toxicological, medical, and psychiatric aspects. They, too, are well worth reading.

The experimenters in both these studies secured positive results, i.e., *both* tobacco and alcohol showed some effect on behavior. Other experimenters working in this same general field have not enjoyed this success, and as a result their task has been much harder. Let us suppose for an instant that no effect had been demonstrable in these measurements. Would that have meant that neither alcohol nor tobacco had any effect at all on behavior? Obviously not, because of all the possible conditions that could have been investigated, only a few were used in these experiments. The tests themselves lasted only a few minutes at the most so that a subject might have been able to hold himself to a task by exerting greater energy for a short time, collapsing as soon as the experimental period was over. This has been a troublesome detail in experiments involving the use of short tests.

3. LACK OF OXYGEN

Essentially the effect of flying or mountain climbing at high altitudes is produced by a lack of oxygen. Although the proportion

[5] Haven Emerson, ed., *Alcohol and Man,* The Macmillan Company, New York, 1933.

of oxygen in rarefied air at high altitudes is the same as at sea level—21 per cent—nevertheless, the absolute amount of oxygen available in each breath becomes less with every foot of ascent. On the top of Mount Blanc at about 16,000 feet, one would have to breathe twice as often to get the same amount of oxygen as at sea level, while on Mount Everest, at about 30,000 feet, one would have to breathe three times as fast. Curiously enough there is an adaptation at high altitudes. In the Chilean Andes[6] people do live and work at altitudes as high as 19,000 feet but they do not consider their lot an easy one, and, inspite of high wages, the labor turnover is high. At 14,000 feet, however, the native Indians produced their magnificent Inca civilization.

It was previously thought that "high altitude," that is, barometric pressure itself, was the cause of the discomfort and stupor. In 1803 Robertson, a French balloonist, reported that at 22,000 feet he felt completely indifferent. "There," he said, "the scientist is no longer sensitive to the glory and the passions of his discoveries." He felt that without his "fortifying wine" he would have not been able to find even intervals of mental clarity. In 1862 Glaisher and Coxwell almost did not survive an ascent by balloon to something over 22,000 feet. Coxwell succeeded in loosening a relief valve with his teeth when he was otherwise paralyzed, Glaisher was unconscious.

It was proved[7] as long ago as 1878 that decreasing air pressure *as such* produced no untoward physiological effects. Paul Bert, a French physiologist, put men into a chamber where he was able to show that decreasing the pressure had no effect if oxygen was supplied. His method is still in use today and experiments by means of it show that subjects suffer no discomfort, at least until 30,000 feet, if they are supplied with oxygen. This situation is quite unlike that of increasing pressure, where nitrogen bubbles forming in the blood give rise to the painful "bends" experienced by divers and tunnel workers. Paul Bert's method enables experimenters working at sea level to simulate the effects of various altitudes by decreasing the concentra-

6 Ross A. McFarland, "Psycho-Physiological Studies at High Altitudes in the Andes, IV. Sensory and Circulatory Responses of the Andean Residents at 17,500 Feet," *Journal of Comparative Psychology*, 1937, 24, 189-220.
7 Paul Bert, *La Pression Barométrique*, Masson, Paris, 1878. This interesting book was recently translated by M. A. Hitchcock and F. A. Hitchcock, The College Book Company, Columbus, Ohio, 1943.

tion of oxygen available. Thus they can undertake studies that would be impractical if the apparatus and the subjects had to be taken to great heights.

In one series of investigations with pilots of the Cambridge University Air Squadron[8] simulated heights from sea level to 22,000 feet were studied. The pilots were given tests of simple reaction time, where a single stimulus had to be reacted to as quickly as possible; of choice reaction time, where four different colored lights required different reactions which had to be made promptly; of memory; of judgment; and of emotional control. The effects of the lack of oxygen (anoxia) became noticeably apparent after altitudes of 14,000–16,000 feet.

Not only was there a loss of judgment in relation to their own behavior and impairment of memory of recent events, but there was also a complete distortion of emotional control simulating many of the characteristics of certain mentally abnormal patients and of those suffering from excessive amounts of alcohol or narcotics. In the more acute experiments with 9 per cent oxygen (22,000 feet), the pilots would frequently lose the capacity for sane judgment and for self-criticism. Some of the pilots responded with great hilarity and uncontrollable laughter, while others became very angry and destructive.

Samples of handwriting and choice reaction times were secured in a number of the pilots during a period of one hour while the oxygen was gradually depleted. At a simulated altitude of 20,000 feet, for example, one subject appeared to be quite pleased with himself and became highly amused at the slightest provocation. At 23,000 feet (8.5 per cent oxygen) he began to omit letters from common words and his writing became quite illegible. He complained of his feet feeling a long way off and of his inability to orient other parts of his body. At 26,000 feet (7.4 per cent oxygen) he was greatly incapacitated and yet he appeared to be cheerful and very pleased with his performance. He became quite annoyed when he was removed from the apparatus and insisted that he could go much higher. He was convinced of his marked deterioration only after seeing his handwriting. In the choice reaction-time experiments, there was marked impairment above 20,000 feet. The mental and emotional abnormalities of the subjects in poor physical condition were very striking at simulated altitudes as low as 14,000 feet.

One subject in a low oxygen chamber containing 8.5 per cent oxygen

---

[8] Ross A. McFarland, "The Psychological Effects of Oxygen Deprivation [anoxia] on Human Behavior," *Archives of Psychology*, No. 145, 1932. Columbia University.

was unable to make the movements necessary to complete a simple form board test. His eyes were fixated on the blocks, but his movements were too jerky and his arms and fingers too rigid to put the blocks in their proper places. He knew where they should be placed, but his motor reactions were too impaired to carry out the test. These reactions tend to disappear immediately upon the administration of oxygen.

The similarity between the behavior of the subjects who suffered from anoxia and that resulting from intoxication was striking. As

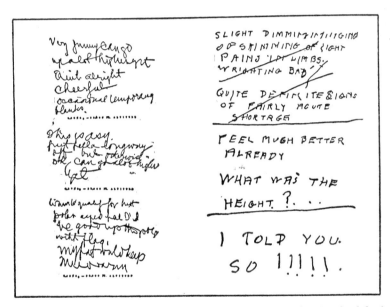

Fig. 39.—Handwriting samples under various degrees of anoxia. On the left the amount of oxygen obtained corresponded to heights of 22,000, 25,000, and 28,000 feet; on the right, recovery is shown upon administration of oxygen at 37,000 feet. Each column shows one subject's writing. (After McFarland.)

a matter of fact, it has been suggested that the effect of alcohol is to interfere with the normal use of oxygen by the individual body cells, particularly those of the nervous system.

If the ascent is abrupt, then the effects are more pronounced than if it is gradual. A scientific expedition that spent several months in the Andes collected data that indicated an impairment in all the behavior studied, but in general it was not so pronounced as in more rapid changes of altitude. They did find that the ten members of the party complained of a greater effort required to carry out tasks, of a more critical attitude toward other people, of "mental laziness," of heightened sensory irritability, of being touchy on various subjects, of disliking being told how to do things, of difficulty in concentration, of slowness in reasoning, of frequently recurring ideas, and of difficulty in remembering.[9]

In studies made of transcontinental and transpacific runs (in the latter the average altitude is 9,500, and 12,000 is not at all uncommon), the effect on the passengers, if flight is smooth, is not at all marked if they sit quietly and if the ascent has required an hour or more. The tests previously mentioned, however, indicate an impairment of from 6 to 10 per cent. The pilots and crew seem to become truly acclimated to the altitude. These altitudes are just below those in which impairment becomes acute. Planes which fly higher than this regularly make use of "pressurized cabins" where air is pumped mechanically into the ship so that the amount of oxygen available is more nearly that of sea level.

Pressurized cabins are not practicable for war planes, because any small openings made by any kind of projectile will allow the pressure to fall. This risk makes it necessary to use oxygen masks of various kinds connected to oxygen storage tanks. The important psychological fact involved in the use of this equipment is that the air crew cannot depend on direct perception of anoxia. There is no "feeling" of suffocation. The onset of the symptoms is not noted by the person himself. He may become completely incapacitated without knowing it, or he may even deny that there is anything wrong with him, whereas an observer who is supplied with oxygen can see that he is near to collapse. A great deal of attention needs to be given to the insidiousness of the effects of anoxia in training air crews, and rigid regulations concerning the use of oxygen equipment above critical heights of 10,000 to 12,000 feet have to be enforced.

Another effect of anoxia that is important to safety, in high-altitude flying, is loss of ability to understand spoken language.

[9] Ross A. McFarland, "Psycho-Physiological Studies at High Altitudes in the Andes, III. Mental and Psycho-Somatic Responses during Gradual Adaptation,' *Journal of Comparative Psychology*, 1937, 24, 147-188.

Pilots make frequent radio contact with land stations and other planes, as well as with other members of the crew, on the intercommunication system. Here again the effect of anoxia is insidious because the person believes he understands, whereas it can be shown that he cannot.

The experiment takes place in an altitude chamber. Standard lists of words, which have been worked out in the Bell Telephone Laboratories for testing the intelligibility of speech for communication equipment, are used.[10] The subjects are provided with record booklets for vowel and consonant sounds which they have to identify and check as single words which have been recorded previously and heard in earphones.

In a typical experiment[11] it was shown that intelligibility at a simulated altitude of 13,600 feet (12.5 per cent oxygen) was little different from ability to perceive sounds at sea level, but that at 16,000 feet (10.3 per cent oxygen) there was definite impairment which was even more marked at 20,100 feet (8.85 per cent oxygen). As might be expected, increased loudness helps to compensate for the loss of intelligibility so that the subjects did much better at 30 decibels than at a power level of 24 decibels. In addition there are wide variations in individuals some showing less effect at 20,100 feet than others show at 16,900.[12]

These findings are of practical importance because, even with supplementary oxygen, a pilot flying at 40,000 to 45,000 feet gets no more actual oxygen than one flying at 18,000 to 20,000 feet without the special equipment.

4. DISEASED TONSILS AND ADENOIDS

Several hundred New York City school children who had diseased tonsils were compared with an approximately equal number

[10] This and other lists used during the war can be found in M. H. Abrams, *et al.*, "Collected Informal Communications on the Basis of Audibility of English Words for Use as Oral Codes, Alphabetic Equivalents, etc.," OSRD, 1943 Publ. Bd. No. 22549, U.S. Department of Commerce, Washington, D. C., 1946, p. 166.
[11] G. M. Smith and C. P. Seitz, "Speech Intelligibility under Various Degrees of Anoxia," *Journal of Applied Psychology*, 1946, 30, 182-191.
[12] This effect is now being mentioned more and more often; cf. J. E. Birren, *et al.*, "Effects of Anoxia on Performance at Several Simulated Altitudes," *Journal of Experimental Psychology*, 1946, 36, 35-49.

who did not have infected tonsils.[13] The results are shown in Figure 40. It is perfectly obvious that there is no difference in the two distributions. The average of both is 95; they both have the same range. If there were a difference in intelligence between the children who have diseased tonsils and those who do not, the open circles would form an entirely different distribution from the solid circles, and two curves, rather than one, would be required to represent their distribution.

Twenty-eight children whose tonsils were infected were matched in intelligence with twenty-eight other children who also had bad tonsils. The first group of twenty-eight constituted an experimental group whose diseased tonsils were removed immediately after the first test was given. The other group constituted a control; their tonsils were not operated. Six months later both groups were retested and again at twelve months, but by this time, one or the other of the pairs had moved or for some other reason failed to take the test. This reduced the twenty-eight pairs to only twenty-one. The results of three administrations of a standard intelligence test are shown in the table. The units are I.Q.'s in which notation 100 is normal.

The average gain in intelligence was actually a little more for the nonoperated group than for those whose tonsils had been removed. The amounts of change are insignificant, of course. Our generalization based on these two different approaches to the problem is that *removing diseased tonsils and adenoids does not produce a change in intelligence-test score,* however important the operation may be for the preservation of health. The practical significance of this finding is obvious because tonsils have been removed in the hope of increasing the intelligence of dull children, just as infected teeth were, a few years ago, extracted wholesale in institutions for the insane in the futile hope of restoring hundreds of patients to sanity.

Summary of the chapter. Among the factors which influence a person's behavior, the physiological condition at the moment has received wide attention. This condition is modified by common de-

[13] M. C. Rogers, "Adenoids and Diseased Tonsils: Their Effect on General Intelligence," *Archives of Psychology*, 1922, No. 50, pp. 1-70.

	N-28		N-21
	First Test	*Retest 6 Mos.*	*Retest 12 Mos.*
Experimental (Tonsils removed)...................	92	94	95
Control (Tonsils not removed)...............	93	96	98
Gain................................	1	2	3

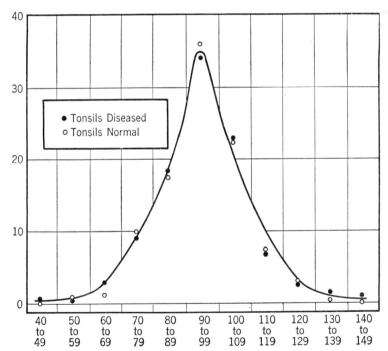

Fig. 40.—Distribution curve for intelligence of children who have diseased tonsils and those who do not.

pressants, alcohol and tobacco, as well as a host of other conditions that make up what has been called the "internal environment." Typical experiments demonstrating these effects were reviewed with special emphasis on the methods used to find out about these effects. The question of method is important in this connection because so many reformers have blamed nearly all our human ills on these two handmaidens of vice. One widespread misconception—that alcohol in small amounts is a stimulant—has also been dealt with. The effects of high altitude were shown to be due really to anoxia, and it was suggested that intoxication was also due fundamentally to lack of oxygen. Other physiological factors which do not attack the nervous system so directly do not produce the expected effects. The toxin from diseased tonsils is one of these. The intelligence test was used here only as a sample of behavior. There may be other considerations which would indicate that tonsils ought to be removed.

CHAPTER TEN

DRIVES AND MOTIVES

In addition to the physiological conditions that we have described in the preceding chapter, there is another group of a similar kind that is important enough to be dealt with separately. There are certain master tissues in the body which exert a great control over the activity of the whole body. The stomach is one of these. When food has not been taken for some time the walls of the stomach start a series of vigorous contractions which result in stimuli that give rise to activity. Any movements that a person executes at this time are definitely more vigorous. If one's strength of grip is measured before he has eaten it is found to be greater than it is after a meal; his intelligence test score is also somewhat higher. Although in most people these stomach contractions result in "hunger pangs," which are recognized for what they are, there are others who cannot report these pangs but experience only a heightened tension and a tendency to be irritable; in childhood this is typically true. Very young children do not know when they are hungry; they are aware only of discomfort and find that things do not go right with them. It has been found in nursery schools that a mid-morning lunch definitely reduces conflicts between children. Muscular tensions are generally heightened before a meal so that smaller stimuli produce larger reactions. When a person becomes older he actively seeks food, or foods of certain kinds, and is even critical of the way in which food is prepared and served, and demands certain implements with which to eat it. The particular combination of preparation and implementation which he demands depends upon the way in which he was brought up—particularly the culture to which he belongs. That the Chinese get on very well with chopsticks is a trite example.

In these cases a real change has taken place in the fundamental and mechanical process of stopping the hunger contractions. *Fundamentally,* the problem is that of getting so many calories, so much bulk, and so many vitamins and minerals into the body, but this end is accomplished under a variety of circumstances in different families within a given culture and with ever greater diversification as one proceeds from one culture to another. This fact is recognized in the literature on the subject, which uses the word "drive" when the simple mechanical facts are to be emphasized. Thus we employ the term "hunger drive" or say a person or an animal is "hunger driven" when we want to emphasize the energetic character of the response and imply that it is directed toward no special end. When we want to express the importance of the cultural, familial, or individual overlay, then we use the term "motive"; we would then speak of the "hunger motive" or say a person is "motivated by hunger." The latter expression implies that specific kinds of food and ritual are demanded, depending on individual habits, while the former term implies that any food will suffice. So many authors are careless in the use of the terms, however, that we frequently have to depend on the context for precise meanings.

More definitions. There are still other terms which are employed in this field and which demand some explanation. *Incentive* is one of these. An *incentive* and a *goal* are the same thing according to most usage—either term can be used to signify the food whether "food in general" is meant or whether some specific food is to be designated. Because most motivated activity involves a variety of preliminary adjustments, the final act by which the goal is attained is important enough to have a name of its own: it is called the *consummatory response.* This term has caused some trouble to beginning students in the past—it does not have its origin in "consume," which means "to use up" or "to destroy"; rather its roots are in another Latin word which means "to bring to completion," "carried to the utmost," "complete," or "perfect."

What has been said regarding *hunger* as an example could also be said for other tissue conditions within the body—thirst, sex, certain conditions of temperature liberation through the skin, and tensions resulting from the distention of eliminative organs. A discussion of the precise mechanisms resulting in drive behavior is a matter for the physiologist. The psychologist is more interested in the fact that *goals are generated which seem to have not the slightest connection with any of these tissue needs, but which exert just as powerful an influence on human destiny as though they themselves were biologically determined needs.* The need for companionship, or privacy; the need for recognition; and the need for social approval are common examples. Some of these will be discussed in our next chapter, but in the meantime our appreciation of the concepts of *drive, motive, incentive, frustration,* and *satiation* can be enriched by the considerations that follow here.

1. PHYSIOLOGICAL DRIVES

Scientists everywhere find they must measure whatever it is they are trying to study. In the natural sciences this requirement led to the perfection of methods of measuring weight, extent, and duration in terms of grams, centimeters, and seconds. A scientific heritage so precise impels modern psychologists to attempt to measure the strength of seemingly abstract concepts like "drive" and "motive." In the process of measurement these concepts are made less abstract because if one wants to count something he has to be very certain that he is counting.

Although there was no way of measuring drives directly, it occurred to one psychologist[1] that a barrier of some kind imposed in the path of a hungry animal on the way to food might make possible the measurement of the drive by the measurement of the height of the barrier. One such barrier could be an electric shock. If one animal could be prevented from reaching food by a weak shock and another would endure the shock or a greater one in order to perform the consummatory response, then the second animal could be said to be behaving under the influence of a stronger drive.

To a beginner this may seem a roundabout way to go after a problem, but to a laboratory scientist it is a perfectly natural way to proceed. A few years ago there was no way of measuring the light that falls on a reflecting surface except by an indirect process. The central portion of the reflecting surface was made translucent (at first by the very ordinary method of putting a spot of grease on it) . A source of illumination placed behind this surface was arranged so that it could be moved back and forth. When it was close to the

1 F. A. Moss, "A Study of Animal Drives," *Journal of Experimental Psychology,* 1924, 7, 165-185.

surface the translucent part appeared lighter than the surroundings, when it was distant from the surface the grease spot was darker. There was one point at which a balance occurred and the grease spot could not be seen; this was the point at which the light falling on the surface from the front just equaled the light transmitted through the grease spot. The transmitted light could be calculated, so that the unknown amount reflected from a source in the opposite

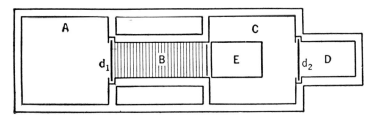

FIG. 41.—The obstruction apparatus used in measuring the relative strength of physiological drives.

The animal to be tested is placed in compartment A. The door, d_1, is raised so that the animal has access to the obstruction chamber B. The floor of B is covered by an electric grill, making it possible to give the animal a standard shock of low intensity. If the obstruction is crossed, and the animal gets to E, door d_2 is opened automatically. The incentive compartment contains food, water, or an animal of the opposite sex, depending on whether the hunger, thirst, or sex drive is being studied. It contains a newly-born litter if the maternal drive is being measured. Sometimes, however, compartment D is made much larger, contains posts and sawdust, and presents in general a "situation-to-be-explored," a device aimed at a measurement of the "exploratory" drive.

direction could also be determined. Nothing is more roundabout, and at the same time nothing is more simple.

This is only one example of the devious ways in which scientific problems are handled. In fact, some such training as this was what made Moss think of measuring the strength of the hunger drive by measuring the magnitude of an obstruction which, paradoxically enough, would keep the animal from getting food.

Moss's method. An apparatus was arranged in which a common laboratory animal, the white rat, could be put at one end. This was called the starting compartment. In the opposite end, and within sight and smell of the rat, some food could be placed. This was called the incentive compartment. In between was a narrow passageway containing an electric grill in the floor over which the rat would have to go in order to get to the incentive compartment. The voltage impressed on the grill could be varied at the will of the experimenter.

This method has since come to be known as the "variable voltage obstruction method." The strength of the drive is assumed to be proportional to the voltage which serves as a complete obstruction to the animal. Among many technical reasons why this is probably not true, one simple fact is immediately obvious. A voltage of, say, ten does not mean that every animal gets the same shock. How much shock he will get depends on the resistance of his body, and since body resistance varies over a wide range, the shock individual rats get must be different. This must mean that the actual obstruction is not what the experimenter thinks it is when he reads the voltmeter. All in all, the method is not a good one, but it is important because it was the first experiment which was ever made that attempted to measure a drive. First attempts, even if they prove to be failures, always blaze new trails.

Warden's method. A modification of Moss's variable-voltage obstruction has been worked out by Warden and his coworkers at Columbia University. They redesigned the apparatus, improving it in many ways, but the most significant change they made was in keeping the voltage constant. They used a very high voltage with a very high resistance in series with it. The reason that this is an important change is made clear in the next paragraph.

Let us suppose that one rat has a body resistance of 25,000 ohms and another a resistance of 15,000. This is a ratio of 5 : 3 and with any voltage whatsoever, these animals would be receiving shocks in this proportion. But suppose that in series with the animal's body resistance there was a high external resistance of, say, 2,000,000 ohms. Then the proportion is 2,025,000 : 2,015,000, or about 1.005 : 1.000, about ½ of one per cent difference in the two shocks, whatever the voltage.

The other change in method that they made involved counting the number of times an animal crossed the charged grill in a chosen time interval. They assumed that the strength of the drive was proportional to the activity of the animal in overcoming a *fixed* obstruction, rather than proportional to the greatest magnitude of the obstruction he would surmount as the magnitude was varied.

Typical results are shown in Figure 42 for the hunger drive.

The abscissa shows the days since the animal has eaten and the ordinates show the average number of crossings that a standard group of twenty rats made. The two curves display the results for the

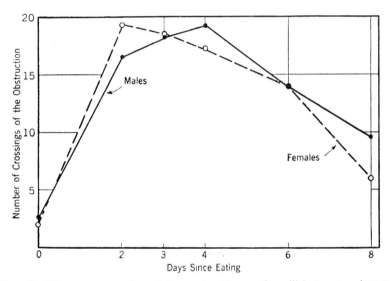

Fig. 42.—The average number of times rats will cross the grill in twenty minutes.

males and the females separately. The results are shown in this way because the maximum strength of the drive seems to come fully two days earlier for the females, although if we compare the magnitude of the maxima we find them to be the same.

These results may be somewhat contrary to what we might have expected. We might be inclined uncritically to suppose that the strength of the drive would continue to increase indefinitely. There was no way of knowing before these measurements were made that it typically increases rapidly at first and then gradually decreases. Persons who have fasted for long periods have reported that the first several days were the hardest. After this interval, the thought and odor of food may actually become distasteful. These

190

results with rats seem to substantiate the reports from human beings but by an entirely different approach.

When the rats are rendered thirsty and allowed all the dry food they will eat, the same apparatus can be used to measure the strength of the thirst drive. In this case, water is substituted for food as the incentive, but all other conditions remain the same. The total range of deprivation is less than for starvation because the rats do not live as long without water. The maximum appears on the first day and it is higher than for the hunger drive. We could conclude, then, that *comparing the maxima, the thirst drive is stronger than the hunger drive. But if the comparison is to be made later than the first day, then the hunger drive is stronger.* This conclusion is applicable only to this method of measuring these drives in these animals. It is conceivable that this relation is not universal.

In a similar way, the sex drives in both males and females have been studied. The male sex drive follows the typical pattern of rapid ascent[2] following a short period of sex deprivation; as with hunger, the drive does not build up indefinitely but rather falls off following longer periods of deprivation. The picture of the female sex drive is totally different. It does not depend upon the period of deprivation at all, but rather on the phase of the oestrous cycle under examination. The oestrous cycle is a little less than five days in the rat, so that approximately every five days we find a period of intense activity where the peak slightly exceeds that of the male at its highest point. This periodicity is completely lacking in the male unless the two are kept in adjoining cages, in which case the general activity of the male falls into the same general pattern as that of the female.

In addition to the hunger, thirst, and sex drives, the exploratory and maternal drives have been studied in the same way. By comparing the maxima in each instance we arrive at an order for the strength of these drives: (1) maternal, (2) thirst, (3) hunger, (4) sex, (5) exploratory. The incentive for the maternal drive is the new-

2 This statement assumes an intact animal. The activity pattern is completely changed by castration. Cf. R. G. Hoskins, "Studies on Vigor: II, The Effect of Castration on Voluntary Activity," *American Journal of Physiology*, 1925, 72, 324-230.

born litter of a female; for the exploratory drive a special compartment which allows for complete exploration constitutes the goal. For the other drives the incentives are obvious. It must be remembered, though, that this order is probably not universal. It depends upon the fact that groups of rats were used in each instance and upon the use of a twenty-minute test period. Even changing so simple an element as the length of the test period would probably change the order that we have given here. To argue that the order would remain the same for different species is probably unsound. What we know of the differences between individuals within a species, in the absence of any positive evidence to the contrary, would lead us to believe that the order might consistently be different for different individuals.

A further complicating feature is found in the fact that no animal ever behaves as a result of only one drive. In these experiments on the hunger drive, the effects of the sex drive were rendered as inconsequential as they could be by using males who had undergone a long period of deprivation and only females in the dioestrum, but even this leaves a host of other possible conditions which could affect hunger. As far as purely biological factors are concerned, the situation is complicated enough, but when we add the modifications that can occur as a result of learning we find a truly puzzling array of facts. When we study the behavior of human beings we find that, under certain sets of conditions, people can go on hunger strikes to the detriment of biological impulses. Hence we may hastily conclude that psychological or learned modes of behaving have definite "right of way"; but on the other hand, there are instances, and perhaps more of them, which demonstrate a clear-cut dominance of fundamental drives. Whichever is true in a given case depends upon the relative strengths of drive and motive.

2. CHANGE OF INCENTIVE

The way in which a given incentive becomes part and parcel of a habit is shown in an experiment on changing the reward during the course of learning.[3] Two groups of animals learned a standard maze pattern, one group being rewarded with sunflower seed, the

[3] M. H. Elliott, "The Effect of Change of Reward on Maze Performance In Rats," *University of California Publications in Psychology*, 1928, 4, 19-30.

other with bran mash. The group running for the bran mash made better scores consistently throughout the first few days. On the eleventh and succeeding days this group was also rewarded with sunflower seed. Figure 43 shows what happened. The errors immediately rose at first to equal the poorer performance of the sunflower-

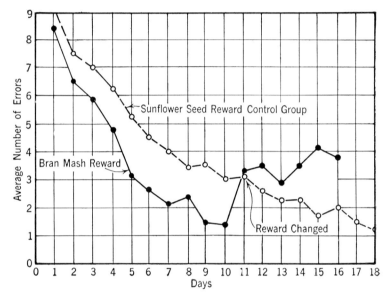

FIG. 43.—Effect of change of reward on maze performance.

seed group and later to become even greater. The effect is not temporary. This experiment shows that these rats were not just running the maze because they were hungry but because they were rewarded in a specific way. The experimental plan could have been improved by including another group of rats which would have been changed from sunflower seed to bran mash at the same time the alternative change was made.

3. APPETITES

Our environment offers us a large number of healthful foods and liquids which can be eaten or drunk. But each of these will not be accepted by the organism with the same readiness. Some objects will be received enthusiastically, others will be tolerated, and still others may be violently rejected. This pattern of the liked and disliked foods is not the same for all individuals; what is one man's drink is another man's poison.

The demand for one kind of object as opposed to another is called an "appetite," and the determination of the mechanisms which make for such specificity of demand is not only intensely interesting, but also of considerable practical value. A logical analysis of the problem points to two types of mechanisms which could be responsible. Physiological unbalances in the organism may affect gustatory sensitivity so that the taste of one food is preferred over another. Such a preference would not involve the more psychological mechanism of learning. Appetites may also have their sources in the phenomena of habit formation—a more purely psychological mechanism. Obviously these two mechanisms, the physiological and the psychological, are not mutually exclusive. One may determine the preference of one particular food, and the other the preference for another food. Nature is not simple, and seldom can we point to one factor as the single cause of any phenomenon.

An experiment was conducted by Carl Richter[4] to determine whether or not a physiological imbalance could cause an increased demand for a particular food substance. He had reason to suspect that a possibility such as this existed, for the clinical literature of medicine had reported cases of special cravings and aversions which could be interpreted in this manner. A child with rickets might show a great fondness for cod liver oil, downing it with much gusto, and cattle in areas where there is a deficiency of phosphorus (hindering bone growth) may develop strong appetites for bones.

Now each of these observations represents an instance where, because of a nutritional deficiency, there is an imbalance of the life-maintaining mechanisms. The organism arises to the occasion by *overt behavioral changes* which result in the intake of food substances readjusting the physiological processes to normal, so that life can be maintained.

The situation with which Richter worked was the reaction of white rats to the removal of part of the adrenal glands. Previous

[4] Carl P. Richter, "Salt Thresholds of Normal and Adrenalectomized Rats," *Endocronology,* 1939, 24, 367-371.

work had shown that if these glands are removed and the animal is maintained on a normal diet, death quickly ensues. If, however, considerable salt is added to the diet, life can be prolonged. What Richter wished to determine was whether or not rats whose adrenals were removed by operation would show a preference for salt.

Method. Before the operation the rats lived in a cage with two water bottles present and established habits of drinking from each bottle. During this time both bottles contained distilled water. After this, one bottle was filled with distilled water containing a very small amount of salt, and at regular intervals the concentration of salt in this bottle was increased. At first these normal rats showed no preference for the salted water as opposed to the plain distilled water, as shown by the fact that they drank equally often from each bottle. When the salt concentration in the solution reached .05 of one per cent, these animals began to show a preference for the salted water. When the concentration reached .2 of one per cent, the preference was marked and the animals drank about three times as much salt water as plain distilled water.

Next the animals were operated upon and the adrenal glands were removed. Once again each bottle was filled with distilled water, and the animals once more showed no preference for one bottle over the other. Again salt was added to one of the bottles. This time, however, the animals began to show a preference for the salt solution when its concentration was only .004 of one per cent, and by the time the concentration reached .01 per cent they were consuming over twelve times as much of the salted water as of the plain water.

The results may be stated in another way. When the salt reached a concentration of 1 part in 2,000 parts water the normal animals began to show a preference for the salt water. When the salt reached a concentration of 1 part salt to 33,000 parts water the adrenalecto-mized rats began to exhibit the preference.

Summary of the experiment. This experiment has clearly shown that the direction of one's appetite can be markedly influenced by the physiological needs of the organism. The animals with their adrenal glands removed required extra amounts of salt to maintain

195

life, and the food preference readily shifts in accordance with this physiological demand. The results, Richter says, cannot be accounted for because the animals learned that salt was good for them and made them feel better, for the preference for salt exhibited itself when the quantity of salt in the water was too slight to be of any real value. The shift in preferences more likely is related to an increased sensitivity in the taste for salt, an increase which is somehow tied up with the bodily demands.

It would be grossly in error to reason from this experiment that all our appetites are reflections of specific physiological needs. There is, on the other hand, reason to believe that the factor of learning may be even more important. Some years ago, nutritional experts in this country were worried by the large number of persons who were not obtaining an adequate quantity of vitamin B in their diet. One of the reasons for the deficiency is the fact that as a nation we prefer white bread to the darker varieties; and the extra milling required to produce white flour removes the vitamin B that is in the darker flours. Our preference for white bread as opposed to dark and polished rice as opposed to unpolished contributed materially to the deficiency; but we continued to prefer this type of foodstuff. We did not develop an appetite for the foods more plentiful in vitamin B, but continued on a culturally determined group of preferences that led along the road to vitamin deficiency. Habit was stronger than biological need, and the government found it easier to meet the problem by requiring that white flour be fortified with the vitamin than by changing our eating habits. Liver, which is filled with many valuable nutritious substances, was not long ago considered food for cats and paupers, though many wealthy individuals could have profited physiologically from its use. There are many other instances in which personal eating habits produce deficiencies which are not corrected by some unlearned biological appetite mechanism.

4. SUBSTITUTE INCENTIVES

As we shall see in the next chapter, people work for prizes and ribbons or for a word of commendation. Although these things have little or no intrinsic reward value, they serve as effective substitutes for more directly satisfying rewards. In the simplest cases they have become symbols of food, water, and more truly biological incentives. How this comes about has not been demonstrated in experiments involving human beings; hence for the most part we shall have to fall back on discursive arguments to make the point.

There are two experiments in the animal field that serve as models for the kind of experiments needed with human beings. One of these involves rats; the other, chimpanzees.

Rats learned a simple association of "white" with food.[5] They were always fed in the white compartment of a simple discrimination box. Such a box allows the experimenter to change the reward and the associated stimulus from one side to the other at will. It is generally used in experiments where the sensory capacity of the animal to make fine discrimination is under investigation. In such cases the stimulus patches would be made very nearly alike, two shades of gray, for instance. But in this case one of the compartments was always white, the other always black. No food was ever given in the black compartment. In time "white" thus became the *symbol* for food in the sense that the animal commenced to make anticipatory feeding movements for "white" as well as for food. This is quite analogous to a variety of things that human beings learn. Paper money is symbolic in this way. So is a school color, a song, a flag, a word, or a gesture. People go to great lengths to accumulate money, while a lack of reverence for a school color or for a flag has been subject to great penalties.

Once learned, can the symbol "white," which seems to provoke the same anticipation that food itself does, be substituted for food at the end of the maze? In this case no food at all would be offered; only the sight of the color white would reward the animal. That is the problem which K. A. Williams studied. The experimental plan involved the use of a control group that learned the maze in the usual way with a food reward. The comparison group was at first put into the maze without either food or the symbol for it. Even under these conditions some learning took place, presumably because being taken out at the end of the maze, though otherwise

5 K. A. Williams, "The Reward Value of a Conditioned Stimulus," *University of California Publications in Psychology,* 1929, 4, 31-55.

unrewarded, constituted an incentive. On the ninth day, however, the symbol white was introduced to the experimental group. Immediately the errors dropped to the level of the "food-rewarded" animals. *Hence we can conclude that even for a white rat a symbol is effective as an incentive.*[6]

It did not remain effective for long, however. By the fifteenth day from the beginning, or the sixth "synthetic day," there was a definite trend away from the comparison performance of the "food-rewarded" animals and by the twentieth day from the beginning, the performance of the experimental rats was no better than it would have been had no symbol been used. This latter fact was demonstrated by the use of another control group which from the very beginning had had neither food nor the symbol for food presented to it in the maze.

The decay of the incentive value of the symbol seen in this experiment is quite commonly observed in learning experiments. In the basic conditioned response experiment, for instance, a dog can be caused to salivate at the signal of the bell. This is accomplished by presenting food and the bell together a great number of times. The salivary response to the sight and the smell of food becomes conditioned to the sound of the bell, so that now the bell alone, which was formerly indifferent as a stimulus, causes almost as much saliva to flow as the food did originally; but not indefinitely. If the bell stimulus is not occasionally *reinforced* with food given at the same time, it becomes as ineffective in producing salivation as it was originally. This phenomenon is known technically as *experimental extinction*. Something analogous to experimental extinction is involved in the lapse in efficacy of the white symbol in Williams's experiment. Another example occurs in classical mythology where a shepherd boy called "wolf" too often.

Another experiment involving symbols or secondary reinforcement but with chimpanzees as subjects, was made by another investigator.[7] He first taught the chimpanzees that poker chips could be

---

[6] We refer to such a stimulus as the box as *secondary reinforcement* to distinguish it from food or water which can directly satisfy a biological tissue need. Food, water and the like are called *primary reinforcement*.

[7] J. B. Wolfe, "Effectiveness of Token-Rewards for Chimpanzees," *Psychological Monographs*, 1936, 12, 72.

used to operate a "vending machine" which could be made to supply either food or water. This corresponds to the simple discrimination problem for the rats and at this stage "chip" or "token" could not be considered a substitute incentive. Presumably, the placing of a token in the slot of the machine is no more symbolic of the final incentive than the pulling of the lever which delivered the food. However, when the chip was used as the only reward which the animal got for the performance of some other task, then it became truly a symbol of the final incentive. One of these tasks which was thus rewarded involved pulling a heavy weight. In this experiment the bars of an experimental cage kept the animal from getting the reward directly. Within his reach, however, was a rope attached to a box. The ape could see the experimenter place the reward in the box. He could then pull the box toward himself and obtain the reward. The measure of the strength of his motive, or what is the same thing—the attractiveness of the reward—is the weight in pounds which he will pull. In these preliminary studies it was shown that several chimpanzees would pull heavier weights for actual food than for a poker chip which could be used indirectly to obtain food. This is a reasonable state of affairs—the food itself has slightly more incentive value than the token. Other tokens—brass disks—had no value; i.e., the animal could not use them for anything. They elecited even less pulling.

In a more extended study[8] it was shown that the chips would even be collected, several at successive trials, saved or hoarded and at a later time and in a different place used for food rewards from vending machines. This latter finding makes it even more certain that the token was a real substitute incentive, and suggests that something analogous to this takes place when human beings learn the value of symbolic rewards. On the animal level these symbols are definitely limited in significance because animals lack language. Among human beings the elaboration of substitute on substitute produces situations difficult to untangle.

[8] John T. Cowles, "Food-Tokens as Incentives for Learning by Chimpanzees," *Comparative Psychology Monographs*, 1937-38, 14, 96.

5. HOARDING

The miser, living alone and sensitive to no other aim in life than adding to his hoard of gold or greenbacks or paper bags, has long held a fascination for his more normal fellow men. He is bizarre because one sees in him a normal kind of motivation which has grown cancerous, and has destroyed the wide variety of other motives which, to most of the world, seem socially and biologically more intelligible. What to most of us is a means of satisfying other ends has become the end for him.

It is this fact, that the means becomes the end, which demands explanation. As long as a goal object is used to satisfy some basic motive, the striving for that goal object is not greatly to be wondered at. When, however, a goal object is collected for its own sake, and is not used to quiet some other need in the organism, one speculates as to the psychological mechanism which produces it. The miser is, of course, merely an extreme case. Undoubtedly all of us show tendencies to collect more than we need at present, or will ever use, of many different kinds of goal objects. The statement often made of the no longer hungry child that "his eyes were bigger than his stomach" refers to such a situation.

In many of the lower animals this hoarding phenomenon has been noted. Squirrels collect nuts, and dogs bury bones. So common is it, that many of the early biological scientists called it a universal instinct and thought they had explained the problem. They said that their instinct explained the behavior of squirrels collecting nuts, boys collecting campaign buttons, philatelists collecting stamps, and misers hoarding gold. Such a catchall explanation is hardly adequate. There are too many individuals in any species who do not show the behavior that the instinct is supposed to explain, and which is supposed to be universal. A more acceptable hypothesis is that one is here dealing with a phenomenon which has been learned in the early childhood of the organism.

Many laboratory workers have noticed that some adult white rats will carry pellets of food from the food bin to a corner of the cage. Some of these pellets may be eaten, but many of them will lie undisturbed while the rat hops off to some other location. This is a kind of hoarding behavior, and since the white rat is a convenient subject whose environment can be readily controlled, it is possible to investigate the hypothesis that this behavior is affected by learning. Such an experiment was undertaken by Hunt, Schlosberg, Solomon, and Stellar.[9]

Methods. These workers reasoned that the tendency for hoarding developed from a past experience which contained a period of prolonged hunger, a period when the drive for food was continually frustrated. They designed their experiment to incorporate this feature.

(1) THE EXPERIMENTAL GROUP. (a) *Early history.* The rats were weaned and separated from their mothers when they were twenty days of age. For the next fifteen days of their lives they were subjected to periods of food deprivations. They were without food for two stretches of thirty-six hours and for several stretches of twenty-four hours. Even when food was given them, they had an opportunity to eat for only a short period of time. At the end of this period they were placed on a normal and unlimited diet.

(b) *Adult tests.* At a time varying from ninety-one to one hundred and ninety days after the termination of the feeding frustration (the animals would be mature by ninety days) they were placed in the apparatus and tested for hoarding behavior.

(2) THE CONTROL GROUP. (a) *Early history.* These animals were brothers and sisters of the animals of the experimental group, and thus hereditary differences between the two groups were reduced. They were weaned at the same age as the experimentals but were immediately placed on an unlimited diet.

(b) *Adult tests.* These animals were tested in the same way that the experimentals were tested and at the same ages.

THE APPARATUS. The apparatus used in testing for hoarding consisted of an alley a little over a yard long. At one end of this there was a bin filled with pellets of food, and at the other end the animals' living quarters were situated. These alleys could be attached at will to the living quarters. The typical behavior of the hoarding animal

J. McV. Hunt, H. Schlosberg, R. L. Solomon, and E. Stellar, "Study of the Effects of Infantile Experience on Adult Behavior in Rats I. Effects of Infantile Feeding Frustration on Adult Hoarding," *Journal of Comparative and Physiological Psychology,* 1947, 40, 291-304.

was to run back and forth along the runway, carrying food from the bin to his living quarters. After depositing the food in this quarter he would scurry back for another load. He could eat at any place in the apparatus, but *the hoarding animal carried far more food than he ever ate.*

The testing procedure

(1) TESTS WHILE SATIATED. For three successive days hoarding tests were conducted at a time when the animals were well fed. Each test lasted for thirty minutes, at the end of which time the hoarding alleys were detached from the living cages.

(2) PERIOD OF ADULT FOOD FRUSTRATION. For three days immediately before the crucial tests the animals were fed only once daily for a period of thirty minutes.

(3) FINAL HOARDING TESTS. Once again the animals were given the thirty-minute hoarding test. One test a day was given for four consecutive days. The animals were allowed to keep an ample supply of pellets after each hoarding test.

Results

(1) TESTS WHILE SATIATED. Neither the experimental nor the control group showed much tendency to hoard during this period when the hunger drive was satiated. The amount of hoarding averaged about one and a half pellets. It is as if they absent-mindedly walked off from the table with a bit of food in their mouths.

(2) TESTS FOLLOWING ADULT FOOD FRUSTRATION. On these test both the experimental and the control animals showed the hoarding phenomenon, but it was more marked in the experimental animal than in the controls. The mean number of pellets which was hoarded by the controls was fourteen; whereas the experimentals hoarded a mean number of twenty-seven pellets.

Summary of the experiment. This experiment, and others as well,[10] have shown that the phenomenon of hoarding need not be considered an unmodifiable instinct, but, in part at least, as a learned

10 J. B. Wolfe, "An Exploratory Study in Food-Storing in Rats," *Journal of Comparative Psychology,* 1943, 28, 97-108.

C. T. Morgan, E. Stellar, and O. Johnson, "Food-Deprivation and Hoarding in Rats," *Journal of Comparitive Psychology,* 1943, 35, 275-295.

reaction on the part of the animal. One basic prerequisite of this learning seems to be that the history of the animal includes a period of prolonged frustration of the hunger drive.

There are still, of course, many problems to solve, and we do not know, for example, whether frustration of the hunger drive will result in a general tendency to hoard or whether it is specific to food. The experiment, however, does get at a very important field of inquiry—the effect of early childhood experiences on adult behavior, or, if you wish, personality traits.

Certainly in terms of the actual behavior involved it is a far cry from the gold-hoarding miser to the food-hoarding rat. But it does not follow that there is an equally great difference in the basic psychological mechanisms which operate in each case. The solution to this question can be given us only by the results of future research.

Summary of the chapter. In this chapter we have traced the elaboration of a relatively simple drive into a more complex motive, and, because there are no experiments on human beings which enable us to accomplish this end, we have had to refer to the experiments on animal subjects to illustrate the mechanism involved. The first experiment showed how it is possible to measure a physiological drive by counting the number of times a hungry rat will surmount a barrier which is placed in the direct avenue to food. This fact makes the concept of drive less mystical than it appeared before measurements were made. Measurements have also been made on a variety of drives resulting in data which permit comparisons to be made between the strengths of various drives. The hierarchy thus established should be limited to the particular animals, apparatus, and method used in the experiments. There are observations which we have not examined that lead us to conclude that these results can not be generalized beyond the precise conditions under which they were obtained. The second experiment, indicates that the specific nature of the reward is inextricably bound up with the performance—change the reward and performance is profoundly modified. The third experiment identifies one of the conditions which result in specificity of our motivational demands. The fourth section shows how the incidental features which are uniformly present when an animal is fed can themselves serve as substitute rewards and how certain objects (tokens) can serve as symbols of distinctive reward values. The fifth experiment serves to give some clue as to what one of the psychological variables may be which gives rise to the overwhelming demand for objects for their own sake rather than for their physiological value to the organism.

CHAPTER ELEVEN

MOTIVES AND INCENTIVES

In this chapter we shall show how human beings react to a great variety of rewards which have little intrinsic value. As a result of having grown up in our culture, many people learn to respond to symbols which serve as incentives so that behavior can be motivated by the use of a symbol almost as effectively as though more direct means were used to satisfy physiological drive conditions.

1. MOTIVATION IN SCHOOL

Thirty years ago, thirty-two pupils of the 5B grade in a Cleveland public school[1] acted as subjects for an experiment by Western Reserve professors to test the efficacy of certain incentives of a different type from what we have seen before. By the time children are in the fifth grade there are all kinds of social conditions which serve as incentives. It is no longer necessary to reward with food—social approval is as effective.

Method. On the basis of preliminary tests, two groups of sixteen students each were selected for the experiment. The experimental plan here, as before, would require the use of two groups, one of which is especially motivated, the other being provided with no special motivating devices. The tests were of simple addition, geared to fifth-grade ability, and a substitution test in which geometrical figures were to be substituted for numerals given. The better a key had been learned, the less frequently a pupil would have to refer to it, and consequently the more substitutions he could make in the time allowed. The time limits were ten minutes for the addition and five minutes for the substitution.

Both groups were motivated, of course; both knew what scores they were making. As we shall see, knowledge of how we are progressing is a powerful incentive. But in addition to this ordinary moti-

[1] J. C. Chapman and R. B. Feder, "The Effect of External Incentives on Improvement," *Journal of Educational Psychology,* 1917, 8, 469-474.

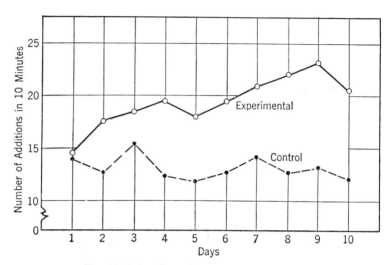

FIG. 44.—The effect of motivation on addition.

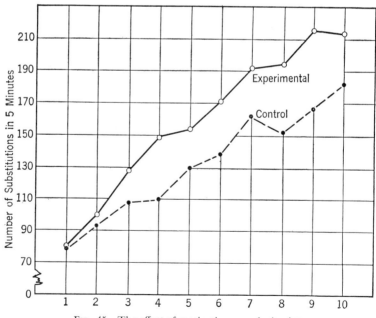

FIG. 45.—The effect of motivation on substitution.

vation there were four other ways in which the experimental group was especially motivated:

(1) Each individual's results were posted.

(2) The point that the subject had reached on the previous day was marked with a blue pencil on the fresh sheets for each day's work.

(3) The general improvement of the whole group was presented in a graph each day.

(4) Stars were given to those in the top half of the group each day. It was understood that those having the most stars at the end of ten days would receive a prize.

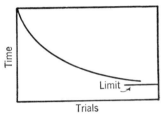 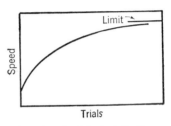

Fig. 46.—Theoretical learning curves showing the physiological limit.

Results. The results are shown in two figures. In arithmetic addition, the control group actually goes downhill. In substitution both groups improve, but the experimental group as a whole improves more than the control group. It is to be understood that these are average results. There were some *individuals* in the control group who were better than some *individuals* in the experimental group, but the group trends are, in all likelihood, real. *Additional motivation in the form of prizes, knowledge of results, and competition with oneself improves performance in learning over what it would have been had these incentives not been operating.*

If we refer to the curves shown in Figures 13, 23, 44, and 45, we see that the typical pattern of these curves is something like that of the generalized forms shown in Figure 46. A theoretical limiting performance seems to exist which the actual performance appears to be ever approaching but never reaching, however long practice is continued. This limit has been called the "physiological

207

limit" because it is supposed that there is an ultimate limit imposed by the anatomical structures themselves upon whatever behavior is under consideration. The speed with which a nervous impulse can pass from sense organ to muscle and the time required for the selection of the proper response is certainly not zero. *A person's structure, then, limits his performance.* But has this ultimate limit actually been closely approached in the experiments that we have seen heretofore? There is no way of knowing because they have all been accomplished under constant motivating circumstances. If we could increase motivation beyond the levels ordinarily employed in psychological experiments, would the physiological limits change correspondingly?

2. BONUSES

A partial answer to the question of physiological limits is found in the records of forty hand compositors[2] in a Chicago printing establishment. These men had had ten years' experience before entering this particular plant, but even so, for the first twenty weeks their production showed, on the average, a decided increase even after all these years as supposed masters of their trade. The secret of their heightened production rate *probably* lies in the way that they were paid. The output of expert compositors as determined in a preliminary study was called 100. Seventy-five per cent of this amount was called a fair day's work, and every worker was paid a flat rate based on this amount whether he actually accomplished it or not. But for every point on the scale in excess of 75, he was paid $2/3$ of 1 per cent of his base rate. This means that if he attained 100—the output of the expert—he would earn a bonus of 16.5 per cent in excess of his flat rate. The average results for the forty compositors are shown in Figure 47.

In several respects these records fail to meet the criteria of a planned experiment and as a consequence leave us somewhat uncertain as to the true explanation of the results. The observations were put together from the records the company kept. The forty men did not constitute a newly formed squad who entered the employment of the company at the same time for the purpose of

2 H. D. Kitson, "A Study of the Output of Workers under a Particular Wage Incentive," *University Journal of Business*, 1922, 1, 54-68.

making this experiment. They entered upon employment at different times and during the first twenty weeks improved their production perhaps partly because of the arrangement of the materials, the illumination, the stimulus of new surroundings, and so on. After twenty weeks their production leveled off, and later spot checks at the dates given indicate that the level was maintained.

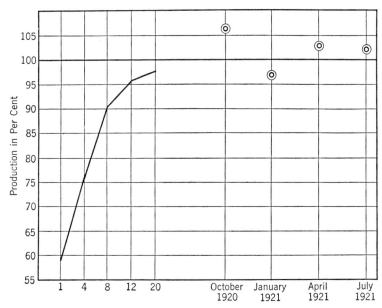

Fig. 47.—Increase in production under a bonus system.

But why did the new level assert itself? Why didn't production keep on climbing? There are several possibilities: men who earn too much are not popular with their fellow workers; men usually fear that the base rate will be changed if they produce too much; there are probably many other factors which tend to depress production, so that we cannot conclude that the new level is determined by structural limitation. The generalization still remains, however, that *even after long experience, production can be markedly improved.* It is interesting to surmise what would have happened had it been possible to increase the incentive somewhat once this new level had been reached. What are the final limits of human improvability?

209

Production cannot increase indefinitely because of the structural limits imposed by nerve and muscle.

3. INCREASING THE INCENTIVE

An experiment made in England by Flügel[3] contributes to this problem but does not finally answer it. As a matter of fact, Flügel was mainly interested in an entirely different set of facts, but he did use an increasing money reward which operated in this wise: The task involved adding numbers from a sheet provided and the work was done each school day under carefully controlled conditions. Each subject received a small flat rate as long as the experiment continued. In addition to the flat rate, the experimenter also provided a system of special prizes and bonuses. At the beginning of the first day's work, it was understood that there would be three prizes of 1s., 9d., and 6d. (24 cents; 18 cents; 12 cents), respectively, for the best performances on that day. Then the subjects were told that every time they exceeded their previous record, they would receive a special bonus. This bonus was to be gradually increased as the experiment progressed. During the first week each person who exceeded his previous record was to get 2 cents every time. The second week every time the previous record was broken, the reward for excellence was to be 3 cents. The third week the bonus was to be 4 cents, and so on, increasing at the rate of 1 cent a week through the ten weeks the experiment was to run. In the last week, the bonus would be 11 cents a day, or 55 cents a week. This would be a considerable money reward for the nine- to thirteen-year-old school-girls who served as subjects, particularly when we consider that the purchasing power of the British money, of which we have given the United States equivalents, was almost twice as great as ours. Also it would have been quite expensive to the experimenter if all of the forty-six girls who made up the group received bonuses on each of the forty-six days that the experiment lasted. This, by the way, is the principal reason why experiments like this one have not been made more frequently. An incidental result supplies another reason why such experiments are not made more often:

3 J. C. Flügel, "Practice, Fatigue and Oscillation," *British Journal Psychology Monograph Supplement,* 1928, No. 13.

The forty-six girls working furiously for a total of fifteen and one half hours in the whole experiment produced more than two million combinations. The labor involved in checking each one of these additions for accuracy is tremendous. If one clerk could check one combination per second, 3,600 every hour for eight long hours a day, about seventy consecutive days would be required to complete the job.

The money-reward system was not the only way in which the girls were motivated. They kept individual progress records; they had complete knowledge of their results and those of others; they worked in a group, a fact which in itself is known to have motivating power. When the school physician thought he detected signs of an infectious disease in two subjects and was sending them home, they rebelled because they were "test girls," set apart, they thought, from the other students, and not subject to trivial rules of quarantine. When public health measures prevailed, they left the school in tears.

The incentive, then, in this case was a complicated one, consisting of no one knows how many factors. All of them had been used before with the exception of the gradually increasing money reward with no particularly striking results. Flügel therefore attributes the unique results in this experiment to the unusual nature of his bonus system. He observes that *a reward once attained is not as attractive as it is before having been experienced, and the only way to keep motivation at a high level throughout an experiment like this is to increase the bonus constantly,* as he did.

Results. The results of this system are shown in the graph. The total number of additions in each twenty-minute work period for the forty-six girls is plotted against the forty-six experimental days. The striking thing about the graph is the fact that there is absolutely no indication of any flattening off—any physiological limit.

This experiment is weak at one point: there is no control group with which to compare the highly motivated group. But the weakness is a result of our particular point of view. All Flügel needed for his problem was a highly motivated group. He was not interested in comparing the relative merits of several different kinds of motivation. From other experiments that are similar to his—that seem to differ principally in the fact that the money reward was *not* increased—Flügel infers that there would have been little increase in score after the first ten or twelve days had he not used the increasing-bonus system.

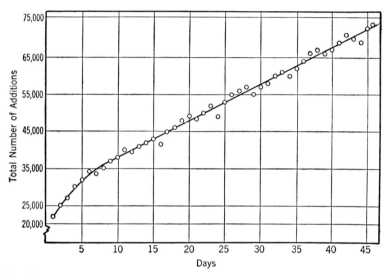

FIG. 48.—Production under a constantly increasing incentive. Notice the complete lack of any limit. Mondays are always the low points in the week with two exceptions. One of them occurs at the beginning of the learning. The other with Tuesday was a holiday. Wednesday of that week is the low point.

We can conclude, then, that a *gradually increasing reward for performance that becomes more and more difficult is effective in producing performances that greatly exceed ordinary everyday accomplishments.* Just how broadly this generalization applies in *all* cases we cannot say until more experimenters have examined the multiple relations that must be important here.

4. PUNISHMENT AND KNOWLEDGE OF RESULTS

Reward for relatively complicated learning performances is not the only way that responses can be modified. Punishment is an effective motivating agent. The relative effect of punishment and incentive in the form of knowledge of results on the time required to make a simple finger movement to an auditory signal has been

212

studied by Johanson, who employed three different conditions under which the reactions were obtained:

(1) A normal series in which each reaction was obtained in the usual fashion, i.e., without any knowledge of whether a response was fast or slow and without any encouragement or punishment. The subject was instructed to react by pressing a key as quickly as he could after an auditory signal. This stimulus was preceded by a ready signal which could come from one to several seconds before the auditory stimulus. The subject never knew whether the interval after the ready signal was going to be long or short; if he had known, or if the interval had been constant, he would soon have commenced to "jump the gun" by anticipating the auditory stimulus.

(2) An incentive series in which the subjects were told what their last reaction time had been. This procedure is known to have an effect on more complex learning processes, but it had never been studied in connection with reaction time before Johanson's experiment.

(3) A punishment series in which the subjects were automatically given a slight shock to the fingers if they started to slow down. This, again, was new. It had been supposed that since the subjects were instructed to react as quickly as they could, they were doing the best they could do anyhow.

The different series were rotated in the usual way, so that all the measurements were not made in the order stated here. Obviously, had this control not been instituted, it would have been impossible to determine whether the effects that were observed were due to the incentive and the punishment, or whether they were due to practice, or fatigue, or ennui.

Results. The results for the three conditions are shown in the graph. There are about 3,600 individual reactions for each one of the curves. These are the total responses for three different individuals. We cannot tell from the curves which response belongs to which person, but we are more interested in a comparison of the three

4 A. M. Johanson, "The Influence of Incentive and Punishment upon Reaction Time," *Archives of Psychology,* 1922, No. 54, pp. 53.

different conditions. The average of the normal series is 143.9 milliseconds; for the incentive, 135.0; for the punishment, 122.3. This is a reduction of about 6 per cent for the incentive and about 15 per cent for the punishment series.

So here we find that a little punishment is more effective than a knowledge of results. But of course *we are not justified in generalizing that punishment always gives the best results.* As a matter of fact, it may not. It is even questionable whether the use of the

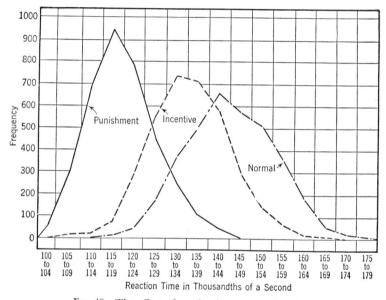

Fig. 49.—The effect of motivation on reaction time.

word "punishment" is appropriate to this situation. The small electric shock that was used may have served primarily as a very effective informant. In any event it is worth while to point out that the shock came as an outcome of the situation, precisely, inevitably, and automatically.

The word "punishment" ordinarily refers to situations in which some human being detects an infringement of some rule and since he is not present at all times to judge, or his standards differ at different times, a defection is not uniformly followed by a painful stimulus. Situations of this kind have been shown to produce neuroses. Then, too, "punishment" seldom follows *immediately* upon the mode of behavior which the "punisher" seeks to control; as a consequence its value in influencing behavior is small. All of these considerations lead to the conclusion that punishment is a poor mode of behavior control in everyday life, even though on the surface this experiment seems to show that it is effective in the laboratory. This does not mean that the laboratory experiment is useless, but only that laboratory conditions seldom obtain in our everyday relations with other people.

5. HABITS OF WORK AS MOTIVATORS

The story is told of a newspaperman who became a syndicated columnist of some note and successful enough financially to have a study in his home. He confessed to his most intimate friends that he had a study only because people expected him to have it. It was all front. His years of experience in newspaper work had so habituated him to noise and to confusion that he couldn't work where it was quiet. Reversing the commonplace, he retreated from his quiet study and sought a nice, noisy newspaper editorial room when he had a bit of heavy thinking to do.

Everybody has some notion of whether he can do his best work in the presence of a hubbub or in a peaceful quiet. Some feel that excitement surrounding them stimulates them to more accomplishment; others are just as certain that noise makes good work impossible. It may well be that the kind of task determines which condition will be true, but if it does, psychological experiments have not yet succeeded in demonstrating this truth. As a matter of fact, experiments have been peculiarly contradictory in this field. Now when experiments present contradictory evidence—when one experimenter gets one result and another one a different one, or when there is no clear-cut difference in result between what appear to be entirely different procedures—one possible explanation is that the experimenters have had more factors affecting the results of their experiments than they were aware of.

After reading all the published literature on the question of the effect of noise on the speed and accuracy with which a person could work, and making some preliminary experiments of his own, Baker[5] conceived the notion that the attitude of the subject was a probable factor which had been overlooked when the experimenters had said that "all the factors were constant except the noise." An answer to this question is of tremendous practical importance, because if noise does have a deleterious effect on production, then we should make more use of soundproofing materials than we do now and our efforts at the reduction of city noises, elevateds, automobile horns, garbage pails, and traffic noises generally, should be more consistent programs than the spasmodic noise-abatement drives that we have seen heretofore.

In a typical experiment in which production under noise was to be compared with production in the same kind of task when no noise was used, Baker proposed to examine the extent to which an attitude that was imposed upon a subject could influence the results.

Method. The problem was a simple one that has been used in numerous psychological experiments. The subject was given a two-place number and he was to add successively 6, 7, 8, 9, calling each subtotal. That is, he was given 27, he added 6 and called 33; then 7 and said 40; then 8 and said 48; then 9 and said 57; then 6 again, repeating the series until stopped by the experimenter at the end of thirty seconds; whereupon he was given a new two-place number. He did not use pencil or paper. A record of his sums was kept by the experimenter so that the time required to solve the number of correct combinations he made might be computed. This is the same method that Hull used in his study on the psychological effects of tobacco (cf. page 162).

The noise or music was supplied from a transcribed source by means of a loud-speaker. Each day was divided into two parts, a noise period and a quiet period. There were ten experimental days in all, and for half these days the noise or music came first and in the other half the quiet period came first. If the noise is called condition A and the quiet condition B, then what is known to experimenters as the A B B A order was used. This control is necessary

[5] Kenneth H. Baker, "Pre-Experimental Set in Distraction Experiments," *Journal of General Psychology*, 1937, 16, 471-488.

because if the noise always came first, then whatever results were obtained might be due to the fact that the task was performed first, and not to the fact that it was performed in the presence of noise.

The subjects were divided into groups of ten men.

Group A was called a control group because there was no attempt made to institute a special set or attitude in its members. This statement does not mean that they did not have any notion of whether they could do better under the one condition than under the other, but the experimenter at least did not try to change their attitude as he did in the experimental group. The subject was told each day what his *total* performance was, but was not told whether he did better under one condition than another.

In *Group B* each person was told that he was going to serve as a subject in an experiment to determine the effects of distraction. Other work, he was told, had been done and this experiment was to be a check on the previous work. What purported to be the results of a previous experiment were shown in a graph which contained two curves, one red and one black. The red curve was labeled "with distraction." It showed that in this imaginary experiment which all the subjects believed was a real one, noise had facilitated the performance so that there was a clear difference between the red and black curves. The curves remained in the experimental room posted in full view of the subject throughout the experiment.

Group C was composed of other men who were shown a curve in which the red and black lines were interchanged so that their inevitable interpretation was that noise interfered with this kind of performance.

Group D was shown a curve in which the red and black lines crossed in such a way that they interpreted the graph to mean that for the first few days noise had an inhibiting or distracting effect, but became less and less a distracter and finally clearly facilitated performance.

All the subjects accepted the charts as representing bona fide experiments and did not question the results.

Results. For Group A the performance curves cross and recross so that we conclude there is no consistent difference in production when no effort is made to impose an attitude either favorable or unfavorable to either one of the conditions. This conclusion is opposed to that of some other studies in that consistent differences have been found. A possible explanation for this difference in results becomes apparent when we examine the results for the other groups.

Each of the other groups reproduced the condition which had been suggested to it by word and by chart. This is even true of the last group which was told that there would be interference at first, facilitation later. There were *individuals* in all groups who resisted the suggestion, but they were not numerous enough to change the group response from the imposed set.

Summary. The general inference from this experiment is that experimenters who have obtained results showing how music or noise facilitates—together with their fellow experimenters who obtained just the opposite results—are really guilty of inadvertently communicating to the subjects the results they hoped to get. This does not necessarily mean that these experimenters were dishonest; they may merely have been enthusiastic and perhaps careless. Many undergraduates will be certain that they were not dishonest because the issues here are not significant enough for people to misrepresent them. But consider for a moment the position of a manufacturer of sound-deadening materials, whose sales will depend in theory on the outcome of an experiment like this. Or think of an educational expert whose reputation will depend upon children's learning more under one set of conditions than another. A teacher might be so convinced that one educational method was superior to another that his enthusiasm for the method would so influence the subjects that they would actually do much better under it than under its competitor. But another educator could easily be so sincerely convinced of the superiority of the rival method that he in turn could prove his method to be the better one. Now which really is the better method?

The relation of the process of motivation to Baker's experiment may not be perfectly obvious. The point in introducing it here is to show that the *production of a subject does not depend entirely on the circumstances which surround him.* He can either convince himself through observing or reading that a certain condition ought to produce a certain result, or be convinced by others so that he will produce in amounts consistent with his conviction. From a practical standpoint, where production is the only consideration, as in comparing one method of instruction with another, it makes little difference whether the increase is due to one factor or to another. But if we are really interested in understanding human behavior, we will not overlook the potency of a personal conviction in explaining the results in experiments of this kind.

6. PERSONAL MOTIVATION IN LEARNING AND FORGETTING

Almost every student has had the experience of being required to take a course for which he had no liking. The subject matter of the course may have been absolutely boring, or, worse still, it may have aroused in him feelings of antagonism. Unless he was a very conscientious student, willing to put in all the study time that was necessary to obtain a high grade, he probably breathed a sigh of relief when he came out of the course with a C or a D. More often than that—your professors hope—were the times when the student found the subject matter exciting and interesting. When this happened study was not so burdensome, and the grade was a good one.

This close tie between strength of motivation and level of performance in the learning situation has long been noted. Many experiments conducted with lower animals as subjects have shown this to be the case. In the instance of the student's grade in a course which he did not like, the exact reason for the poor performance is not completely clear. Is it due to the fact that he studied for this course less than for others, or is it somehow more difficult for us to learn material which we do not like than that which we do like? We can unravel this ambiguous situation by requiring equal amounts of practice for material to which the subject is favorable and to which he is antagonistic. Now if a difference still exists it cannot be accounted for by inequality of practice.

This necessary type of controlled condition was used in an experiment performed by Levine and Murphy.[6] They used two groups of subjects, with five persons in each group. The members composing each group were carefully selected upon the basis of their attitude toward Soviet Russia. One of the groups was procommunist and the other anticommunist. The subjects of both groups learned a passage of material which favored communism and one which opposed it.

Method. The subject was given the paragraph of material with directions to read it twice at his normal reading speed. Then the experimenter engaged the subject in conversation about topics which were not related to the paragraph he had just read. After fifteen minutes he was told to reproduce the material as accurately as he could. After a few minutes the same procedure was repeated with the other paragraph of material. Three of the subjects of each group were given the procommunism material first, and the other two were given the anticommunism material first.

This procedure was repeated at weekly intervals four more times. This constituted a *learning series.* Then for five more weekly periods the subjects came to the laboratory and tried to reproduce the material without rereading the paragraph. This is a *forgetting series.*

The experimenter scored each recitation for the number of ideas which were correctly reproduced.

Results. The achievements of the two groups with the two kinds of materials are shown in Figures 50 and 51. The graphs in Figure 50 represent the learning and forgetting for the procommunism paragraph, and Figure 51 is a representation of the performance on the anticommunism material.

In the learning of the procommunism material, the procommunists excelled, while the reverse was true regarding the anticommunism material. One cannot say that one group consisted of better learners in general than did the other group. It all depended upon what kind of material was to be learned. When a group was learning subject matter which was consonant with its own biases,

[6] J. M. Levine and Gardner Murphy, "The Learning and Forgetting of Controversial Material," *Journal of Abnormal and Social Psychology,* 1943, 38, 507-517.

then that group excelled. When a group was required to learn subject matter which ran counter to its own personalized motivation, the learning progressed at a slower rate.

Now let us consider the forgetting portion of the curves. Throughout the entire series of tests the trend is consistently the

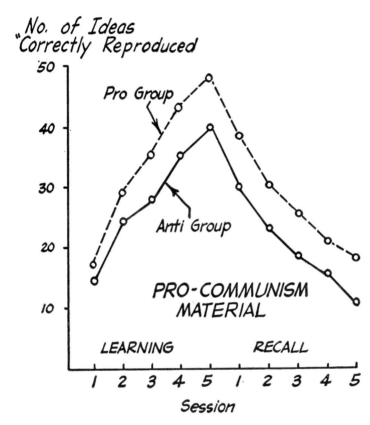

FIG. 50.—The learning and forgetting of procommunism material. (After Levine and Murphy.)

same. The level of recall was always lower for material which was counter to the groups' personal feelings than for the material which agreed with their biases. It is interesting to note that by the fifth recall periods the anticommunists recall less procommunist material than they knew at the termination of the first learning period. The procommunists, however, recall a little more than they knew at the end of the first session. Precisely the reverse is true when the material was procommunist.

Summary of the experiment. This experiment has demonstrated a close relationship between the motivational aspects of the individual and his ability to learn certain kinds of material. By controlling the number of times the material to be learned was presented—the

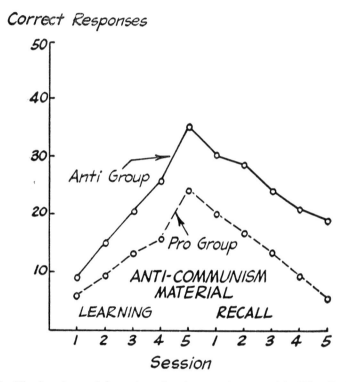

FIG. 51.—The learning and forgetting of anticommunism material. (After Levine and Murphy.)

amount of study time—the experiment indicates that poor learning of material to which we are antagonistic is not due to reduced study time.

One of the mechanisms which probably make for the difference in the learning of the two kinds of material is that biases affect the way the material is read or understood in the first place. A recent experiment[7] has shown that one's ability to interpret words which are exposed for very short time periods is closely related to the person's biases. Our motivation serves to distort what is seen. This would make us suspect that the initial understanding of the different material for the two groups would not be the same. Fewer correct ideas would be the result. Such a mechanism would affect the pro-communist group on the anticommunist material and the anti-communistic group on the procommunist material. This distortional action of our biases is one of the factors that could account for the type of results the experiment obtained. There must be other important factors as well, and this experiment serves to raise a number of questions which can be answered only with further research.

7. LEVEL OF ASPIRATION

Almost inevitably when we go to work upon some task, we set a goal for ourselves. The golfer who has never shot the course in less than 105 expects to break 100 on the next round; the consistent C student plans to make B's and A's next year; and the businessman looks forward to more profitable dealings this year than he enjoyed last year. This setting of goals for ourselves, which is so characteristic of our motivated behavior, is called our *level of aspiration*.

The previous examples imply, and the reader's own past experience will tell him, that there is a difference between the goal to which we aspire and the level of performance which is reached. More often than not our reach exceeds our grasp, and we set up levels of future performance to which we cannot quite attain. When we estimate our levels of performance we are not functioning as cold and keen evaluators of our own ability. We are on the other hand, participating humans who usually err on the side of optimism.

Various investigations have indicated that the difference between the level of aspiration and the level of achievement is not static, but that it varies with a number of conditions. The following experi-

J. S. Bruner, L. Postman, and E. McGinnies, "Personal Values as Determinants f Perceptual Selection," *American Psychologist*, 1947, 2, 285-286.

ment by Chapman and Valkmann[8] was designed to investigate one of the conditions which affect the level of aspiration.

The Problem. To understand the significance of this work, the reader should recall that behavior takes place and is evaluated within certain frames of reference. You might state that a particular drawing is very good for a six-year-old child. When you make this judgment, you are not judging the picture in an absolute sense, but within the frame of reference of what six-year-old children can do. Constantly you relate behavior to some frame of reference. You say it is a good broad jump for a high-school freshman, a poor letter to have been written by a college senior, or a crude way of behaving for a person who comes from a particular social background. You are evaluating the behavior of these persons with reference to some norm of age, or education, or social status. The individuals are above or below the norm of the group with which they are identified.

Just as we place others in particular groups, so do we also identify ourselves with one group or another. By identifying ourselves in this manner, we may obtain a norm from which to evaluate and predict our own behavior. It was the purpose of the present experiment to investigate the relationship between level of aspiration and frame of reference.

Method. Eighty-six students of psychology were given a test of literary information. On the instruction sheets which were passed out to them, the statement was made that the maximum score on the test was 50 and the chance score was 17. The following four different sets of directions were used:

1. Set A simply had the above information upon it.
2. Set B contained this additional statement: "This test has been tried on a group of authors and literary critics, who made an average score of 37.2."
3. Set C contained this additional statement: "This test has been tried on a group of students in psychology, who made an average score of 37.2."

[8] Dwight W. Chapman and John Valkmann, "A Social Determinant of the Level of Aspiration," *Journal of Abnormal and Social Psychology*, 34, 1939, 225-238.

4. Set D contained this additional statement: "This test has been tried on a group of unselected WPA workers, who made an average score of 37.2."

The final sentence on the direction sheet was the same for all groups. It simply asked them to indicate on the line below the score they expected to make on the test. This estimate was used to determine the level of aspiration for each of the groups.

All four groups of subjects worked on the test at the same time. They were not informed that four slightly different sets of directions had been passed out.

Results. The experimenters were not concerned with the actual score which was made by each group, but with the score that each group predicted for itself. These are given in the table below.

Group	Estimated Score
Group A (Neutral)	26.95
Group B (Authors and Critics)	23.09
Group C (Psychology Students)	31.09
Group D (WPA workers)	33.05

Obviously the frame of reference which is given to each group does something to determine the level of aspiration.

Discussion. The interpretation of the results must be made not only with reference to the supposed score made by authors, other students, and WPA workers, but also with reference to the group with which the subject identifies himself. Presumably he classifies himself in the student group. Such a group would be expected to stand below authors and critics in literary knowledge and above unselected WPA workers. The trend is in this direction. The level of aspiration is highest for Group D and lowest for Group B with Group C in between.

It will be recalled, however, that the level of performance for the fictional groups was 37.2, and none of the mean estimates reached this level. This result might arise from a tendency to choose a middle score of 25 as an anchoring point and for estimates to be pulled in this direction. Thus the tendency to estimate that they would do better than the WPA workers would be counteracted by a tendency to choose a middle score. (It should be noted that Group A which was given no fictional information, approximates a score of 25.)

Summary. The present experiment has shown that the level of aspiration is not constant. Even in a task in which the individual has had no previous experience, he will establish an aspiration level. He seems to do it on the basis of the most plausible frame of reference. If "knowledge" about the behavior of other groups is given him, he will use this as a frame of reference. If this is lacking, he may rely upon some such mathematical expectation as being 50 per cent correct.

8. INDUSTRIAL MOTIVATION

We have shown previously how printers of ten years' experience raised their production rate during the first twenty weeks in a new shop and how they maintained it after that time at a new high level (page 209). Some doubt was expressed as to whether the bonus system alone brought about this result—a doubt which is increased by a study[9] conducted at the Hawthorne plant of the Western Electric Company in Chicago. This study, which has since become a minor classic, started out as a continuation of studies made during World War I in England and in the United States. They were devoted to finding out more about fatigue and monotony. It had been observed that production was heightened in munitions factories and in other industries if rest periods were allowed and if hours of work were shortened.

At the Hawthorne plant five girls who assembled small electrical relays were transferred from their usual locations in the factory to an experimental room where it would be possible to vary certain surroundings. Records of their production were carefully kept and the effects of different degrees of illumination, ventilation, rest periods, midmorning lunches, and so on were observed. They generally worked under a given set of conditions for two weeks, sometimes even

[9] Elton Mayo, *Human Problems of an Industrial Civilization,* The Macmillan Company, New York, 1934.

226

In this department, anyone who exceeded the group's standard (which was low) was looked upon with disfavor, and various tactics were used to bring such people into line. In the following account, W6 was one of the faster workers and W8 one of the slower ones:

W8 (to W6) : "Why don't you quit work? Let's see, this is your thirty-fifth row today. What are you going to do with them all?"

W6: "What do you care? It's to your advantage if I work, isn't it?"

W8: "Yeah, but the way you're working you'll get stuck with them." (Meaning that W6 would have to refrain from reporting all the work he did.)

W6: "Don't worry about that. I'll take care of it. You're getting paid by the sets I turn out. That's all you should worry about."

W8: "If you don't quit work I'll bing you." W8 struck W6 and finally chased him around the room.

Observer (a few minutes later) : "What's the matter, W6, won't he let you work?"

W6: "No. I'm all through, though. I've got enough done."

W6 then went over and helped another wireman. This practice was sanctioned by the group.

longer, and since thirteen different conditions of work were examined, the experiment extended over several years. The result was that in spite of several supposedly adverse working conditions which were introduced, *their production records throughout the whole period kept climbing to entirely new levels.*

This curious outcome which was as surprising to the girls as it was to the officers in charge of the experiment, can be accounted for by the social background in which the experiment took place. *Social conditions were, then, more important in determining the outcome of this experiment than the experimental surroundings, which were varied.*

The key to the whole situation seems to lie in the transfer of these girls to a special room and the treatment accorded them there. We have already noted incidentally that in Flügel's experiment the British schoolgirls considered that participation in his experiment was a definite social distinction (page 212). This same recognition plus the further fact that the girls were interviewed frequently and that they were consulted before changes were instituted in the experiment all had the effect of imposing a sense of responsibility on them. They did not feel that they were lost in a big impersonal machine. Their attitude toward their supervisor changed, they ceased to think of him as a taskmaster. They gained confidence in him and expressed themselves freely. They reported that they felt "happier" and "freer"; that they felt no restraint. The work, they thought, was easier; they had no sense of working faster, although the production record showed that they were.

Since the relationship between the superior and the employee changed so much in this experiment it was decided to put special emphasis on problems of personnel in training the supervisors for the plant as a whole. Supervisors are the link between management and labor through whom the policies of management are explained to the employees and through whom the grievances of labor find their way to management. A survey showed that actually there was great variation in relationships that, on paper in the offices of the executives, appeared to be the same. In some instances the supervisor sided with the men and, although his control of them became more certain, he found that he had to conceal certain information from his superiors. In other cases the supervisor was essentially an outsider who imposed conditions upon the men and who as a consequence was cordially disliked. To describe this condition further would take us too far afield; the student will find the published report on the experiment interesting reading.[10]

All this work extends over a period of twelve years and consists of several experiments, aside from the one mentioned, as well as of personal interviews with twenty thousand employees. Yet a generalization on it may be made somewhat as follows: Management can not arbitrarily impose new work conditions upon workers and expect them to be accepted, even though they may ultimately benefit the employee. Men are not simply selling their services to employers. They continue to live during the time they are employed, and when groups of them work together in a single department social organizations spring up. These organizations really control production, usually by slowing it up. They are more effective in regulating production than are physical surroundings. They can be made effective agents in greater production if as much time and energy is put into studying and understanding them as is spent in studying and testing the raw materials of the industry.

Summary of the chapter. The first experiment in this chapter shows how school children react in providing learning curves that are analogous to those obtained when rats are used as subjects. With children of this age it is no longer necessary to use food as an incentive, a knowledge of results serving as an incentive for human beings, just as do bonuses, gold stars, and ribbons which express recognition. The third experiment shows how by increasing the incentive throughout the period of learning the point ordinarily thought of as the physiological limit is greatly exceeded. That behavior can also be controlled by what is called punishment is shown in the fourth experiment; but in the discussion of this experiment it is important to remember that the word "punishment" can mean several different things. The fifth experiment suggests that the conditions under which a person learns to work and the attitude he has toward these con-

[10] F. J. Roethlesberger and W. J. Dickson, *Management and the Worker,* Harvard University Press, Cambridge, Mass., 1939.

ditions serve as incentives for the accomplishment of the work, whatever it is. The sixth experiment shows how one's personal motivation can influence learning and retention. The seventh experiment introduced the concept of level of aspiration, and showed how it varied as a function of the frame of reference. The last section shows that social organization is much more important than the physical surroundings in controlling the production in an industrial organization.

CHAPTER TWELVE

THE DEVELOPMENT OF EMOTIONAL BEHAVIOR

By the time most of us are adults, our fear reactions to snakes, and sometimes to frogs and fish and worms and spiders, are so definitely fixed that it is hard to believe that there ever was a time when we didn't have them. It seems impossible that this paralyzing effect is really a learned thing. It is so intense, and so uncontrollable, that we feel there must be some basis in the notion that the fear of snakes, anyway, must be inherited.

1. FEAR OF SNAKES

Harold Ellis Jones and his wife, Mary Cover Jones, put this hypothesis to actual test by confronting infants, adolescents, and adults with harmless but vigorous snakes.[1] The idea had been tested before, but not with the care nor with the number of subjects that these investigators employed.

Method. A pen, eight by ten feet by six inches high, was built in the nursery floor. Within the pen, a number of blocks and toys were scattered. There were also two black suitcases. One contained a mechanical toy and the other a six-foot snake (*spilotes carais*). The snake was a vigorous active specimen. A mechanical arrangement allowed the concealed observer to open the suitcase containing the snake if the child himself did not do so after a reasonable time.

Results. The results are in the form of protocols, five of which are reproduced on page 234.

Of fifteen children aged between fourteen months and six and one half years, seven showed absolutely no fear that could be detected. The other eight showed various degrees of withdrawal; among them were two cases that could be definitely interpreted as

[1] H. E. Jones and M. C. Jones, "Fear," *Childhood Education,* 1928, 5, 136-143.

fear reactions. One of those fear reactions was made by a twenty-six-month-old child. Since this observation was the only withdrawal observed up to three years, it leads us to believe that there is a greater frequency of fear responses in the older age groups.

Tests with older children. To test this result further, the experiment was repeated with thirty-six school children ranging from six to ten years.

The children were sitting on low chairs in a circle about twenty feet in diameter. The experimenter placed the suitcase containing the snake in the middle of the circle, asking, "Who wants to open the suitcase?" Harry, eight years of age, opened it, and took the snake out when requested. The snake glided about the floor, passing between the feet of one of the boys; no disturbance was shown. The experimenter now asked, "Who wants to touch the snake?" holding the snake's head so that children had to reach past it, and walking slowly around the inside of the circle. The first eleven children touched the snake with no hesitancy. Four boys about ten years of age hesitated, one withdrawing markedly, another falling over backward in his chair. . . . Two girls refused to touch the snake, but jumped up and ran around behind the circle, following the experimenter and watching closely. An undercurrent of reassurance was constantly heard, "He won't let it hurt you. Go ahead, touch it, it won't bite."

Result. Only nine of the twenty-six children showed definitely resistive behavior, and these were chiefly the oldest in the group.

Tests with adults. In order to make a comparison with the behavior of adults, the experiment was repeated under somewhat different conditions with about a hundred college students.

In several classes of undergraduate and graduate students, the snake was introduced as "a perfectly harmless animal; the skin of this reptile has a smooth and pleasant feeling, and we guarantee that in touching him no one runs the slightest risk." In some classes the same reptile was used as in the preceding experiment; in others the snake was a boa constrictor, somewhat smaller and of a less "dangerous" appearance than the Spilotes. Of about ninety students nearly a third refused to have the snake brought near; a third touched him, with obvious hesitation and dislike, while the remainder (including as many women as men) reached forward with apparently complete freedom from any emotional disturbance. Several of the women obviously regarded the presence of a snake in the room as an

232

almost unbearable ordeal, and several of the men solved the problem of emotional conflict by retiring to a neighboring room until the experiment was concluded.

Summary. The whole study on fifty-one children showed that up to the age of two there was no fear apparent; by three or three and a half, there was some hesitation and caution. Definite fear responses occurred more frequently after four. The adults showed more definite fear responses than the children. The girls were no more fearful than the boys; the young women no more than the young men.

These results can be explained by regarding fear as a response to a change in the total situation: *Any change which requires a sudden adjustment that the individual is not prepared to make results in a series of responses that we call "fear."* With a very young infant, the number of different kinds of changes is limited, but as he grows older, more kinds of new things are effective as stimuli. *Fear arises when we know enough to recognize the potential danger in a stimulus, but have not advanced to the point of a complete comprehension and control of the changing situation.*

2. CHILDREN'S FEARS

Jersild and Holmes[2] have reported on an extensive study of fear by an entirely different method. They did not make an experiment like the Joneses'; they merely counted the instances of fear and made a record of what the situation was in which the fear appeared.

Method. There are four distinct parts of their study in which we are now interested: data collected (1) by observing children less than two years old; (2) by observing children between four and five inclusive;[3] (3) from children five to twelve who were interviewed; and (4) from adults who wrote their recollection of childhood fears. Groups 1 and 2 comprising 105 children, were observed by

---

2 A. T. Jersild and Frances B. Holmes, "Children's Fears," *Child Development Monograph*, 1935, p. 360.

3 There was another group in the original study between two and four, but we have not considered it here.

EXPERIMENTAL FOUNDATIONS

Subject 1. Irving, age 1 year, 3 months. Irving sat in the pen, playing idly with the ball and blocks. After being released, the snake glided slowly towards Irving, shipping up his head and deflecting his course when within twelve inches of the infant. Irving watched unconcerned, fixating the snake's head or the middle of his body, and letting his gaze wander frequently to other objects in the pen. The snake furnished only a mild incentive to his attention.

Subject 3. Enid, age 1 year, 7 months. Enid sat passively in the pen, playing with blocks in an unsystematic fashion. The snake was released and moved fairly rapidly about the pen. Enid showed no interest, giving the snake only casual glances and continuing to play with her blocks when it was within two feet of her. When (later) the snake was held by the observer directly in front of her face, she snowed no changes in facial expression, but presently reached out her hand and grasped the snake tightly about the neck.

Subject 8. Sol, age 2 years, 3 months. When the snake began moving about the pen, Sol watched closely, holding his ground when the snake came near, but making no effort to touch it. He resisted when an attempt was made to have him pick up the snake (this was the same guarded reaction that he had shown previously with the rabbit and the white rat). He stood unmoved when the snake was thrust toward him, and showed no overt response, save an attempt to follow visually, when the head of the animal was swung in front and in back of him, neck writhing and tongue darting. After the snake was returned to the suitcase, he went to it again and lifted the lid, looked within and then closed it in a business-like manner.

Subject 11. Laurel, age 3 years, 8 months. Laurel opened the suitcase, picking out two blocks which were lying against the snake's body. The snake was immobile and she evidently had no differential reaction to it. The snake was taken out. Laurel: "I don't want it." Avertive reactions, moved off, then stood up and started to leave the pen, although without apparent stir or excitement. Experimenter: "Let's put him back in the box." Laurel: "I don't want it." Experimenter: "Come and help me put him back." After slight urging, she came over and assisted, using both hands in picking up the snake and dropping him quickly when she reached the suitcase.

Subject 12. Edward, age 4 years, 2 months. Edward sat down in the pen and began playing constructively with the blocks. At sight of the snake he asked: "Can it drink water?" Experimenter: "Do you know what it is?" Edward: "It's a fish." He puckered his brows and made slight avertive reactions when the snake was swung within a foot of him, but this was overcome through adaptation in three trials. When encouraged to touch the snake he did so, tentatively, but soon grasped it without hesitation at the neck and body.

adults, generally a member of the family who offered to cooperate in the study. The period of observation lasted twenty-one days and in special cases even longer. The observers for the most part were not trained, but they were given specific directions on how to write exactly what they observed and were provided with blanks.

The following instances taken from the blanks give some idea of how the records appeared when they were returned to the experimenter.

A child aged 2 years exhibited for a period of several months a marked fear of the noise of rattling window shades. However, he showed no fear of a variety of other noises, including loud claps of thunder during storms.

At the age of 20 months, a girl who had previously often ridden in elevators began to insist that she had to be careful in stepping over the crack between the elevator and the floor. Even though the open space was only an inch wide, it seemed to trouble her. She would hesitate, draw back, look at the crack, and would ask to hold her mother's hand.

A girl, aged 3 years, was very much frightened while in the cellar of her home by a colored porter who released a rat trap which snapped with a loud noise. She subsequently showed no fear of the cellar (a response we would expect), but for some time she continued to claim that she did not "like" the colored porter.

At the age of 2 years, Albert showed extreme fright when he was taken to a lake and saw several people swimming and diving. He cried and refused to go near the water. An effort was made at once to combat this fear. The visits to the lake were repeated and the swimmers cooperated by showing signs of pleasure in going into the water, laughing when they came up after a dive, throwing sticks out to him from the water, going into the water slowly after preliminary play with him. He was enticed to put his toes into the water, following a game in which he had been induced to chase a stick. After some play with the stick, the adult threw it to a place where the child could reach it only if he went into the water a few inches. After several repetitions of this technique, the child seemed unafraid of going into the water up to his waist. Traces of fear remained for a long time, however. The following year he again showed extreme fright when he saw someone swimming in rough water. It developed that the fear was due in part to his belief that his mother was among the swimmers. When he discovered that she was not in the water, his signs of fear disappeared. (But he did not then enter the water himself.)

After these records were collected, the fears had to be classified,

235

FORM USED BY PARENTS IN RECORDING FEARS

Name of Child _____ Time When Observation Began _____

Name of Observer _____ Time When Observation Ended _____

Date _____ When Recorded:

                                           (1) At time of observation? _____

                                           (2) How long afterward? _____

If no fear occurs, simply indicate with a check mark here _____

Use a new blank to describe each fear and a new blank for each period of observation, even when no fear occurred. Use back of sheet if more space is needed.

If during the day any of these or other conditions occurred outside of the child's regular routine, please underline or specify: Child taken visiting, shopping, riding in automobile, to doctor or dentist, etc. Child came in contact with strange children, adults, or animals inside or outside of home. Child missed usual daytime nap, had less than usual amount of sleep last night, had meals at irregular hours, etc.

Underline or specify as to physical condition: normal, lack of appetite, slight cold, heavy cold, fever, digestive upset, other unusual physical conditions.

Situation in which child gave signs of being afraid (place, time, what child was doing at time, persons present, apparent cause of fear, etc.) :

Behavior of Child (words spoken, cries, other vocalizations, jumping, starting, withdrawing, running away, and other physical activity, etc.) :

236

because one could not read through several hundred specific instances of this kind and arrive at any understanding of them without classification of some kind.

From these data two important tallies were made: (1) describing the situation; (2) describing the behavior of the child.

Procedure with the older children. The chidren from five to twelve were asked in an interview to "tell me about the things that scare you, things that frighten you. Tell me what makes you afraid . . . Tell me more about that . . . What else makes you afraid? . . . What else?"

There were 398 of these interviews with 398 different children. The questions on fears were preceded by others on wishes, ambitions, likes, dislikes, and so on,[4] so that the children were not suddenly confronted with the necessity of revealing an emotional episode. Had they been required to do so they might not have talked freely about their fears. The slightly less than nine hundred fears expressed by the 398 children were classified according to the situation.

Procedure with adults. The adults were asked to recall their childhood fears in answering a questionnaire which covered four specific points.

The problem of classification was no easy one. The twenty-three principal topics required to cover all of the cases did not include the numerous subtopics and were as follows:

1. Animals
2. Specific objects or events
3. Sudden movements
4. Lights and flashes
5. Sudden disappearance of persons
6. Rapidly approaching object
7. Sudden or rapid motion plus noise
8. Noises
9. Falling, danger of falling
10. Pain and painful treatment
11. Strange objects or situations
12. Strange persons
13. Danger of threat of bodily injury
14. Warnings
15. Signs of fear in others

[4] A. T. Jersild, F. V. Markey, and C. L. Jersild, "Children's Fears, Dreams, Wishes, Daydreams, Likes, Dislikes, Pleasant and Unpleasant Memories," *Child Development Monograph,* 1933, No. 12.

16. Loss of property
17. Dreams
18. Failure and ridicule
19. Robbers, kidnappers
20. Dark and being alone in dark

21. Being alone apart from darkness
22. Dark plus mention of imaginary creature
23. Imaginary and supernatural creatures

Each one of these categories was developed until a small manual of classification was required in order to arrive at a placement. We reproduce the subtopics and category 10, *Pain and Painful Treatment*, on page 242.

Results: Classification of situations. The most important results from the standpoint of our interest are shown in the table on page 239. The various categories are combined in different ways according to the description at the left of the table. The per cent that this combination is of all fears is shown separately for infants, preschool children, elementary-school children, and adults. Noises and noisy things, and pain and painful treatment account for almost 50 per cent of infants' fear responses, but as the children become older these things are reacted to in more adequate ways. Animals gain in fear-producing potency as do threats of bodily injury, illness, and death. Imaginary creatures and criminal characters of an imaginary kind introduced through stories, books, and movies become more significant. The adults' recollections of childhood fears agree fairly well with the actually reported fears of later childhood.[5] It is significant that about one third of the fears that they recollect are still persistent problems for them.

The fears of infancy are related to concrete situations of a rather transitory nature, but as a person becomes older these are replaced by fears of an anticipatory or imaginary character.

Classification of responses. It was also possible to classify the responses made by the younger children. In making this tabulation, the given response was entered only once, even if the child exhibited it several times in the twenty-one days he was under observation.

[5] This generalization is not clearly supported as it might be in the data shown here. In the original, the years eleven and twelve are separated from the five-to-twelve range with the result that the agreement between the adults' recollections and the fears of early adolescence is more marked.

THE PER CENT OF EACH GROUP FEARFUL IN VARIOUS SITUATIONS

	MONTHS 0–23	MONTHS 48–71	YEARS 5–12	ADULTS
Number of subjects	58	47	398	303
Number of fears		127	886	1,112
Animals	6.7	17.3	20.4	18.8
Sudden unexpected movements, lights, shadows, reflections, flashes	5.6	3.1	2.4	1.6
Noises and agents of noise	25.4	9.4	3.4	3.1
Falling, loss of support, danger of falling, high places	12.7	4.7	1.4	4.8
Pain, medical treatment, etc.	17.9	8.7	3.0	5.6
Strange objects and persons	24.2	7.8	2.7	4.5
Threat of bodily injury, illness, dying	0.0	14.2	11.5	17.2
Criminal characters, burglars, kidnappers	0.0	0.8	9.4	4.0
Being alone in dark	3.4	12.6	7.9	12.9
Imaginary creatures (not including mention of darkness)	1.1	6.3	11.1	5.0

If a child in a given situation dodged, stepped aside, and then ran, a single tally was placed in the category that contained all of these criteria; three tallies in three separate categories would be misleading.

From this table it appears that as children grow older, their reactions to "fearful" situations are somewhat modified. There is less crying and screaming and more whimpering and protesting; there is less clinging to adults and more active avoidance and hiding. *Children learn to deal with situations in different and generally more adequate ways as they grow older.*

Whether or not a child becomes more or less fearful is dependent upon the way he is reared. The kinds of things his associates do when the child once becomes afraid determine whether or not he will be afraid of the same thing a second and a third time.

3. ELIMINATION OF CHILDREN'S FEARS

In another study[6] the parents of forty-seven preschool children were interviewed to find out how they handled the fear reactions

6 A. T. Jersild and Frances B. Holmes, "Methods of Overcoming Children's Fears," *Journal of Psychology*, 1, 1934, 75-104.

FORM GIVEN TO INDIVIDUALS WHO WERE ASKED TO SUBMIT WRITTEN ANONYMOUS REPORTS OF FEARS RECALLED FROM CHILDHOOD

We should like to ask your help in obtaining data in a study of fears. At present we are getting material from several sources.

We should like to get descriptions of fears remembered by adults from their own childhood. We are interested in reports on the following questions:

1. What is the earliest fear you remember? (Age when it occurred; apparent cause; history of the fear; time when it was overcome; if overcome, how, etc.) Were you living in city or country?

2. What was the most intense fear of your childhood? (Age, cause, history, effect on behavior, etc.)

3. Name other fears which were also quite intense. (Origin, history, effect, how overcome, etc.)

4. What other fears occurred during your childhood? (Describe in specific detail as many as possible.)

As far as possible, give information also on such questions as: Was any fear a major source of unhappiness during childhood? At what age? What was the original occasion or cause of the fear? What were the chief causes of fear, the chief helps in overcoming fear? What fears from childhood have persisted into adult years?

The reports need not bear any signature other than Male or Female, but should give present age.

We shall be grateful for your help.

of their children. The results are certainly not typical of what the whole population does, because these people were all well educated and lived in urban localities in or near New York City. The most popular methods among these forty-seven people turned out to be:

1. Verbal reassurance and explanation.
2. Verbal explanation, and reassurance plus a demonstration.
3. Use of an example of fearlessness in others.
4. Attempt to cause the feared object or event to occur simultaneously with an interesting unfeared event.
5. Enforced contact with the feared situation.
6. Provision of opportunities for the child to become acquainted with the feared situation of his own accord.
7. Graded introduction of feared stimulus by easy degrees.
8. Specific attempt to promote skills that will allow the child to deal actively with the feared situation.
9. Refusal to take notice of the fear, especially when the child seems afraid.
10. Removal of the cause of the fear by steering the child away from the feared situation.

The best methods. According to the results in this study, the most effective single method was that which attempted to promote skill in handling the situation. The method was used with considerable success in treating the fears of imaginary creatures as well as the more tangible objects and events. This is particularly fortunate because a technique that could be used in overcoming a fear for a real rabbit (introducing the rabbit by degrees at mealtime) would hardly work with a spook. What is meant by competence in handling a particular situation is best illustrated by means of an example.

One child was much afraid of an imaginary dog. Instead of observing the more commonplace procedure of giving the child an academic explanation of the groundlessness of her fear, the mother tried to help the child to outsmart the dangerous creature. She entered into makebelieve play with the child and brought the imaginary dog into the play. Through such games the child was helped, so to speak, to acquire skill in dealing with this spectral dog, to manipulate the dog for her own purposes as a character in her own imaginative activities. According to all indications, the child's fear of the imaginary creature completely vanished through this treatment.

241

PAIN, PAINFUL TREATMENT, PAINFUL SITUATIONS

PERSONS INFLICTING PAIN, objects inflicting pain, fears arising as result of previous infliction of pain, also tactual shocks.

PERSONS INFLICTING PAIN (other than medical) or corporal punishment with actual specific blows (as distinct from harm such as threatening to shoot, throw into water, etc.) or who by specific word or gesture are immediately threatening to hit, inflict pain or corporal punishment: boy who was slapping child; boy who strikes with fist at child's eye; older boy who claws at child's face; sister who strikes at child; older child who scratches child.

PERSONS PREVIOUSLY ASSOCIATED WITH PAIN or previously inflicting pain (as above) but not at the moment active or threatening (other than medical). Person who previously spanked; fear of child who previously hit.

FEAR OF MEDICAL SITUATION, of doctor's office and its surroundings and contents, occurring when child is brought to the situation or told that he will be brought, and appearing in response to the situation as a whole before doctor or nurses begin to approach or to apply treatment or wield any instruments; immediate fear on approach to health station; fear on approach to doctor's office; nurse's office at nursery school.

FEAR IN MEDICAL SITUATION arising only when doctor or nurse begins to perform (*Note:* If child has already shown fear in response to situation as a whole, do not tally here.); presence of surgeon who previously performed tonsillectomy (*ex.:* doctor approaching father).

FEAR IN MEDICAL SITUATION apparent only when specific instrument or piece of apparatus is introduced (*Note:* If child has already shown fear in response to situation as a whole or in response to doctor or nurse, do not tally here.): sight of hypodermic needle; doctor brings out stethoscope; clinical thermometer.

PAINFUL EXPERIENCE or tactual sensory shock, not including medical situation or pain inflicted by persons (*Note:* Count response as fear only if reaction is described as containing an element of fear, including such elements as prolonged crying, clinging, running to mother, trembling, etc., distinct from immediate cry or withdrawal in response to the impact of pain as such.): sprinkle of cold water in bathing; rush of air against child's face through mouthpiece of balloon; fear persisting following a violent coughing attack; hysterical crying and trembling for more than an hour and withdrawal following slipping against hot radiator; electric shock on contact with a transformer (*ex.:* older brother pushes blade of knife across his hand; brother hits mother and mother pretends to cry; older sister hits younger sister; fear when mother approaches to touch hot objects).

OBJECT OR EVENT previously inflicting or associated with physical pain or tactual shock: towel child had previously sat on when hot; brush with stiff bristles that previously pricked; fear of plant following previous experience of being pricked by thorns of another plant and fear of leaf of raw spinach apparently for same reason; fear of potato following previous contact with hot potato; electric light bulbs after previous contact with hot bulb; radiators after previous contact with hot radiator; bathtub in which child had hurt her elbow; water basin after previous scald; steam after previous scald; hot-water bags; iron objects after a burn.

PAINFUL SITUATION other than medical and distinct from reaction limited to specific person: fear of basin and preparations to wash child's head; fear of clipping and scissors during haircut; having head washed.

SITUATIONS PREVIOUSLY ASSOCIATED with pain as in above. Barber shop where part of child's ear had previously been clipped off.

Other instances in which the promotion of skills was effective in dealing with fears that apparently had a large imaginative element include fears of the dark or of specific dark places. One mother made a dark and much-feared closet the center of games with her child, thereby leading the child to explore the closet and to incorporate it into her own activities. One mother encouraged her child's interest in doing small errands about the house, and capitalized upon the child's enthusiasm for such activities by sending her occasionally on errands into a much-feared dark bedroom. After some time the child showed no more fear of the bedroom even when no attractive errands were in progress. In both of these instances the child was not dealing directly with the imaginary features that underlay the fear, but in making actual contacts with and coping with the abode of the imagined danger; in gaining competence in dealing with tangible features of the feared situation, the child lost his fear of hidden dangers.

When one considers the multitude of similar fears that affect children, and often persist into adult years, one cannot help wondering at the number of situations in which techniques similar to those above might be effective. In daily life there are many opportunities for helping the child to face and to master the dangers that lurk in cellars and closets, old trunks and boxes, dark hallways, lonely rooms, haylofts, mysterious houses—to mention only a few of the places which the imaginative child peoples with sinister influences.

The next most successful methods are probably (1) the provision of opportunities for the child to grow acquainted with the feared situation of his own accord by making it accessible to him in his daily environment. The success of this method is probably contingent on the use of no compulsion at all. (2) The graded introduction of the feared stimulus. (3) Verbal explanation accompanied by reassurance.

The poorest method. The least successful methods are (1) steering the child away from the contacts with the feared situation, comforting and helping him when he is afraid. (2) Ignoring the fear: changing the subject when he mentions a feared situation. (3) Enforced contact with a feared situation, verbal pressure, ridicule and invidious comparison. *Following the use of any of these methods, as a general rule the child is just as fearful as he was before, and in some cases his fears increase in number and intensity.* Sometimes, however, one observes that a child overcomes a fear even where these methods—poor in principle—are used. These exceptions

FREQUENCY (IN PER CENT) OF VARIOUS FORMS OF BEHAVIOR EXHIBITED
BY PERSONS WHEN DESCRIBED AS BEING AFRAID

	0-11	60 and over
Age	0-11	60 and over
Total	69	49
I. Vocal expressions		
A. Cries, screams	28.1	22.4
B. Yells, "makes loud noise"	2.1	0.0
C. Calls or cries for help	1.0	0.0
D. Whimpers, exclaims, "fusses," makes frightened noises, protests, "voices apprehension," "catches breath audibly"	4.2	16.3
II. Avoids, withdraws, retreats, seeks help		
A. Withdraws		
1. Runs away, withdraws, retreats, dodges, shrinks	12.5	24.5
2. Stops play, "becomes very quiet," drops toys, "hesitates," stops eating, watches, inspects, paralysis	2.1	2.0
B. Avoids feared event, goes out of way, changes direction, "steers clear," hides	2.1	10.2
C. Seeks help or protection		
1. Runs to parent or other adult	0.0	4.1
2. Looks to adult, turns to adult	1.0	0.0
3. Clings to adult, clutches, reaches for adult, reaches for help	11.5	2.0
III. Aggressive protective reactions: struggles, hits, resists, kicks, pushes, guards another, scratches, etc.	3.1	2.0
IV. Other motor expressive reactions		
A. Trembles, shivers, shudders	0.0	0.0
B. Starts, jumps, "jerks"	12.5	4.1
C. Facial expression: puckers, "screws face," "scared expression," eyes widen, eyes dilate, "downcast expressions," turns pale, flushes	11.5	6.1
D. Gestures, throws out arms, waves hands, throws up hands, becomes rigid, stiffens, shakes head, "nervous movements," "fidgets," restless movements, covers face, covers head, uneasy, excited, panicky	6.3	6.1
V. Autonomic		
A. Voids self, regurgitates	1.0	0.0
B. Sneezes	1.0	0.0

to the generalization can only mean that we do not know all the factors that are operating.

4. ANGER

Goodenough[7] has studied forty-five children's anger responses in very much the same way Jersild studied the fear responses. She depended on parents' observation in the same way and furnished the parent-observer with the same kind of guidance in instructions and blanks upon which to write the observations. Both of these experimenters recognize that a better method would be to put a psychologically trained observer in each home to record any kind of emotional response, but they both point out that such a method would be so costly that it would be prohibitive.

We may doubt whether these untrained observers could distinguish between fear and anger responses in a great many instances; they also probably based their discrimination on the emotions that they themselves would have in similar situations. What shall we do with the child who kicks, screams, struggles, and finally bites the dentist's hand when he is first brought to a dentist's office? Is he angry or is he afraid? There is really no way of knowing. The important thing is to get a description of the exact behavior. What it means in terms of adult reactions, assuming that we know what they are, is another story.

The responses of kicking; stamping; jumping up and down; striking; throwing self on the floor; holding the breath; stiffening of the body; making the body limp; refusing to budge; pulling away; struggling; running for help; turning away the body, the head, or tightly closing the mouth; refusing to swallow; pouting; frowning; pulling and pushing; throwing objects; running away and running toward the offender; reaching or grabbing; pinching or biting; crying or screaming; inarticulate vocalization; verbal refusal; threatening and calling names; arguing and insisting; are all reported in varying percentages. Most of these things indicate an active dealing with the situation which is absent in the descriptions of fear. *The fear responses involve, in most cases, a withdrawal*

7 Florence Goodenough, *Anger in Young Children*, University of Minnesota Press, Minneapolis, 1931, p. 278.

by a child from an active participation in a situation. Anger responses, on the other hand, involve an active though inadequate participation in the situation.

Some of the responses assumed popularly to be part and parcel of anger are actually observed only in a few instances. Holding the breath, for instance, occurred only four times in the 1,878 emotional outbursts which were reported for the forty-five children, in periods varying from 6 to 133 days for the various children. These children were under observation 22,716 hours.

The cause of anger. The specific and immediate causes of anger, as the table shows, change with age. Outbursts during the first year are mainly associated with bathing, dressing, and handling; during the second year problems of self-help and conflict with authority become more pronounced. From the descriptions of the situations given at the left of the table, it is clear that aside from physical discomfort, the large majority of *anger responses come when a child is somehow blocked in the activity he is engaged in or is about to become engaged in.* This blocking or *frustration* may come from the physical relations in the situation, as when the child gets a toy that he is pulling by a string caught under the rocker of a chair or behind the leg of a table. The frustration may come when an adult or another child interferes by robbing him of a toy or breaking in on an interesting activity with a call to dinner or to bed. However it comes about, there is in most of these cases interference with what to the child is an absorbing activity.

Methods used in coping with anger. Goodenough provided a list of the methods commonly used by parents in controlling a child once a temper tantrum is under way. This list follows. It is intended to include all things parents do, not just what they *should* do.

Scolding	Appeal to self-esteem or humor
Reasoning	Spanking or slapping
Threatening	Other methods of corporal punishment
Frightening	Deprival of privileges
Coaxing	Putting in a chair
Bribery	Deprival of food

Praise	Isolation in separate room or closet
Soothing	Diversion of child's attention
Ridicule	Removal of source of trouble
Ignoring attitude	Social approval or disapproval
Putting to bed	

The parent was required to write the name of the method, or the successive methods, used in handling the situation and also to indicate the outcome—whether or not the child eventually had his own way. Aside from instances in which the child got his own way because the issue was yielded, we can distinguish instances in which the child yielded, either voluntarily or involuntarily; various compromises in which the issue was yielded in part; and finally, instances in which the issue remained unsettled because of some interruption which intervened before a conclusion could be reached. Unfortunately, there were so many diverse ways of handling the various situations which arose that the number of cases wasn't large enough to permit clear-cut decisions as to which method is best. It was clear, though, that the *methods used by parents had some effect in determining both the frequency and severity of the anger behavior.*

A child was undressing herself. She got into difficulties and did not want help. She threw herself on the floor, screamed, and kicked, and the mother finally undressed her by force. A somewhat similar example is the case of a girl of three years, for whom the issue is yielded or a satisfactory compromise offered in almost 50 per cent of all outbursts recorded for her. A single instance will serve as illustration. The child had been put to bed for her nap. After the mother left the room, the child moved her bed so that she could climb out of it into the bed of her sister, who slept in the same room. The mother heard her doing so, came in, and replaced the bed. The child jumped up and down, screamed, and refused to go to sleep. The mother first threatened to spank her, then did so, then "appealed to self-esteem," then ignored her for fifteen minutes, and finally allowed her to have her bed where she wanted it.

The poorest methods of dealing with anger. Soothing, coaxing, and petting seem to be ineffective in terminating anger, and these methods, together with instances where the child is allowed to have his way, were used more frequently by the parents of the children who had more than their share of the outbursts.

247

	LESS THAN 1 YEAR	1 YEAR	2 YEARS	3 YEARS	4 YEARS & OLDER
No. of children	2	9	13	10	11
No. of outbursts	144	426	490	479	339
Routine physical habits					
Going to toilet or to bed, coming to meals, objections to specific kinds of food, washing face, bathing, combing hair, brushing teeth and dressing	27.1	28.4	20.4	16.9	19.7
Changes in routine or change in some minor habit or custom	3.5	1.9	7.6	1.4	1.2
Direct conflict with authority (other than that involved in physical habits and self-help)	0.0	26.6	21.2	16.2	15.1
Self-help					
Refusal of help in some task; refusal to put away toys; unsuccessful attempt to do something alone; assistance forced when child did not invite it	4.2	7.7	11.3	4.8	12.9
Social situations					
Desire for attention; inability to make desires understood; unwillingness to share possessions, and so forth	27.1	19.7	19.9	44.2	28.4
Minor physical discomfort					
Desire for food between meals; wet, soiled, cold; medicine administration; fear or startle change to anger	23.0	3.8	5.8	9.0	4.5
Miscellaneous					
Objection to some particular article of clothing; impatience in the face of some coming event; mother's impatience at child's slowness	8.9	6.8	8.8	9.4	17.0

A two-year-old girl was taken to her grandmother's for a visit of several days. The mother notes at this time: "Unable to get the child to go to bed either at night or for daytime nap without lying down with her—a very lengthy process." On their return home, the child continued to demand company on going to bed. On the first night the record recounts that the child was willing to go to bed, but wanted mother or father to go with her. When they refused, she screamed for two hours. The parents tried coaxing and ignoring her screaming, but after two hours, the father finally lay down with her.

On the following night the behavior was repeated. This time the outburst lasted for three hours before the issue was yielded. Again the father finally went to bed with her. On the third night the same behavior recurred. This time the child was spanked, but at the end of one and a half hours she was taken into the parents' room. On the fourth night the child went to sleep at the end of nearly two hours of screaming. The following night the parents went out at the child's usual bedtime, leaving her in the care of the maid. Although the usual outburst followed, it lasted for only fifteen minutes, after which the child went to sleep.

Thereafter the issue appears to have been forced through. However, there are sporadic recurrences of the behavior on several occasions both at night and at nap time, with outbursts lasting from fifteen minutes to an hour and a half. In this child's record there are a number of other instances in which the issue is yielded at the end of a prolonged outburst most frequently caused by the child's wanting the mother instead of the maid to do something for her. If the protest is sufficiently violent and prolonged, the child usually succeeds in getting her own way about it.

Inconsistency of treatment was responsible for a large number of anger responses.

A boy of four and a half was "wandering around looking for trouble." When his mother told him to put his blocks away, he refused, called his mother names, and "was sent to bed until he changed his mind." After a few minutes he was allowed to get up, and his mother "picked up most of the blocks for him." It may be noted here that this mother makes a greater use of threats than any other parent in our group. In many instances these threats appear to be made without any intention of carrying them out. They include a number of threats to tell Santa Claus, to tell Daddy, to put his toys in the attic in case he refused to pick them up, to go visiting without him, and the like.

Picking up toys is a frequent source of controversy between a girl of four and a half and her mother. This report occurs a number of times with no essential difference in the methods employed. The child refuses to

249

pick up her toys, she is isolated, and then the mother offers to let her come out if she will help to pick them up. (Note that in the original request no mention of help is made.) The mother then reports that she picks up most of them for the child. On one occasion this child was playing with her younger brother. She kept teasing him and snatching his toys. The mother shut her in the vestibule. The child screamed and kicked the door, whereupon she was taken out, spanked, and put to bed for a time. The mother reports that upon getting up, the original behavior was resumed, but there is no indication of further punishment. On another occasion the child was in bed for her nap when her father came home. She wanted to go down to see him. The mother at first refused to let her go. The child cried and pleaded and the mother scolded her, but as the behavior continued she was finally permitted to go down.

Typical reactions to frustration can be produced if the child is reared in a general atmosphere of disapproval. If every adjustment he makes is subject to criticism, more than the usual number of outbursts will be recorded. The following case shows how a mother is continually harping on her private "Peck's Bad Boy."

One gets the impression of an overanxious and somewhat self-righteous type of mother who continually irritates the child by a sirupy type of nagging. In the records of her own methods of control, self-congratulatory adjectives continually recur: "I spoke to him *gently*"; "*I* inquired *casually* why he was so late"; "reminded him *courteously* that *lunch* would soon be ready," and so on. The following verbatim report is an example:

"The child was eating his cereal at breakfast and complained that it was too hot. He habitually complains about his food. Was told *gently* that it had not been dished up before [the food for] the rest of the family, that mother had been too busy dampening extra clothes to iron for him to make up for the ones he got muddy in puddles last week."

The child's response commands our sympathy. He kicked, snarled, and screamed at his mother, "Don't talk, don't talk!"

The margins of the sheets are written full of accounts of the child's misdemeanors that have no direct bearing on the records. These accounts describe the child's dislike of school, his unkindness to his little sister, his untidiness, his blustering and boasting, and so forth. Apparently the child is being reared in an atmosphere of constant disapproval.

The best methods of dealing with anger. Diverting the children's attention, ignoring the outbursts, and isolating or reasoning with the child when outbursts do unavoidably occur seem to result in fewer anger displays.

Perhaps the most outstanding tendency that appears in the disciplinary methods used by parents of children who have few outbursts as compared to those used by parents of children who have frequent outbursts is an attempt to avert difficulties before they actually occur or to bring them to a prompt end by diverting the child's attention or by making the original difficulty seem trivial. Although our evidence with regard to the control of anger by prevention as opposed to the attempt to handle it purely by correction is obviously incomplete, since our records as a rule show only those instances in which the preventive method proved unsuccessful and anger resulted, there is nevertheless sufficient indirect evidence in the records to make it fairly certain that such preventive methods were used to a far greater extent by certain parents than by others. In the records of the children who have few outbursts we find occasional notes such as this: "Both children seemed fretful today, but by keeping them occupied at different kinds of things was able to prevent any actual occurrences of anger." When preventive methods fail, we find these parents employing very prompt and ingenious methods of diverting the child's attention before the difficulty becomes serious. The following example will illustrate.

A child of twenty months was pouring water in the sink and getting himself very wet. In an attempt to stop the objectionable activity without raising an issue the mother suggested that he do something else in another room. However, this time the scheme did not work. The child screamed, kicked, and refused to leave the sink. The mother ignored the behavior, went into the next room, and started an activity there in which she knew he would be much interested. This brought the outburst to a close, and the child left the sink in less than a minute. On another occasion the same child was playing with a favorite toy when bedtime came. He refused to go to bed, kicked, jumped up and down, and cried. The mother first diverted his attention away from the original activity by playing the piano for him to dance and after this he went to bed cheerfully. The entire performance occupied three minutes. It may be noted that this child has very few outbursts occasioned by difficulties over the routine habits of going to bed, meals, toilet, and so on, in spite of the fact that he is at an age when training in habits of this kind usually constitutes a real problem in child management.

Summary of the chapter. Fears of specific things like snakes and the dark are not inherited, they are learned. Fear reactions do arise naturally with little of a learned nature in them when any situation is presented to which the child cannot adjust. His inability to adjust may be due to his immaturity and his consequent inability to control the situation. The number of situations of this kind for the very young is extremely limited but unpleasant experiences of many kinds with doctors, barbers, nurses, and attendants soon result in a remarkable elaboration. As these situations are reacted to more adequately, a greater frequency of imaginary and impossible or unlikely fears develops.

The best method of eliminating any fear is to allow the child an opportunity to master the situation by attaining some skill in connection with it. Presumably the same technique would be effective for older people. Without such treatment, the fears acquired in childhood are frequently the source of a good deal of unhappiness in adult life.

Anger is differentiated from fear chiefly in that it is an active attack on a situation rather than a retreat from it. The explosive outburst is directed at the destruction of the situation and is not an escape from it. Anger results when the activity of the child is interfered with.

Anger can be avoided by making substitute goals more attractive than the one which is engaging the child's attention at the time when it is necessary to interrupt him. Of course, where one succeeds in doing this, the child isn't really interrupted. In many homes children are needlessly interrupted and interfered with, corrected and curbed, nagged and restrained. In these homes and in others they are treated inconsistently. Both conditions lead to increased frequency in anger seizures. We should also remember that if a temper tantrum results in a child's getting his way, then it is not an inadequate way of dealing with a situation. Under these conditions, it may become a favorite way of meeting any problem even in adult life.[8]

[8] For an interesting account of anger reactions in college students see H. Meltzer, "Students' Adjustments in Anger," *The Journal of Social Psychology*, 1933, 4, 285-309.

CHAPTER THIRTEEN

EMOTION IN ADULTS

The director of the Scripps Institution for Oceanography was sitting alone reading a newspaper before a fireplace in the dining room of his home in La Jolla, California, on the morning of February 3, 1922. It was just before breakfast. His niece, Alice, came downstairs ahead of the rest of the family and stood with her back to the fireplace while she prattled in six-year-old conversation with her uncle. Over her night clothes she wore a dressing gown of flannelette, a soft nap-covered cotton material. Suddenly the whole back of this garment ignited from being too close to the fireplace.

Here we have a situation which contains all the essentials of a typical emotion-producing incident: it is presented suddenly and it is a situation for which one is hardly prepared.

Research on emotion has been hampered because it is ordinarily impossible to reproduce in the laboratory a situation which is as real—as demanding of adjustment—as those that occur in everyday experience. When one tries to frighten or anger subjects, they realize that "nothing really is going to happen" to them, or that "after all this is an experiment"; hence it is difficult to get them really stirred up.

1. DR. RITTER'S REPORT

The instances in which someone has recorded, on the same day, his retrospective description of his own behavior during an emotion are consequently valuable. Dr. Ritter did just that. Later on the same day he wrote the account of his actions as we give them below. Director Ritter[1] continues his observations on what he did when Alice's clothes were flaming.

Alice was within easy arm's reach of me and my first recognition of what was going on consisted in seeing the flame over her shoulder and

---

[1] Dr. Ritter's account was turned over to his friend, Stratton, who added some interpretive comment and published it under the title, "The Functions of Emotion as Shown Particularly in Excitement," *Psychological Review*, 1928, 35, 351-366.

hearing a little outcry by her. At the very instant, so far as I can tell, of my awareness of what was happening, there was before my mind the case of a terrible burning of one of my own sisters which occurred while I was an infant, and concerning which I consequently had only indirect knowledge. The burn left my sister badly scarred for life and the event was epochal for the entire family. "The summer Ella was burned" was a more or less cardinal date of reference for many of the incidents in the family history.

Along with this memory-picture stood the picture of the little B. girl. This case happened in La Jolla some six or seven years ago and, although outside my own family connections, it was within my circle of acquaintances and I had considerable knowledge about it. The little girl, considerably younger than Alice, was clothed in much the same way, at least so far as the outer garment was concerned. The fire caught, in her case, from the flame of a coal-oil stove, but the spread of it was apparently much like that which I was here witnessing. The clear proof in these two cases of the high inflammability of cotton flannel gave me a feeling of condemnation for garments of this sort for children, at least.

The B. child was horribly burned. The hands were nearly burned off, the throat and face were made almost unrecognizable, and the little patient hovered between life and death for weeks. However, she recovered, but so disfigured as to make her a distressing object to look upon, and almost helpless. The realization that dear little Alice was in imminent danger of such a calamity was a large part of my "content of consciousness" from the very first instant.

But with all the rest there was the automatic impulse to action. To throw down the paper I was reading, to spring to my feet, and to grasp the girl with both hands were acts quite independent, so far as I can tell, of thoughts directed to them. But thought as to what course to pursue came almost simultaneously with the initial perception and actions. Four main alternative possibilities presented themselves together, so far as I can tell: smother the flame within the garment itself; smother it in a blanket or something similar; pull off the garments; or flood the whole with water.

As to the choice between these four courses, smothering the flame within the garment, being the most immediate possibility, was tried at first. But an instant of effort showed its futility. No blanket or anything suitable for smothering was available without leaving the room (the possibility of using a small floor rug that was within reach did not occur to me until later, but it seems now that the stiffness and heaviness of the rug and its inadequacy in size would probably have made this alternative less effective than the one pursued). As for extinguishment with water, the chances though something, were so remote that it was given no great consideration. The only chance was a faucet in the kitchen which meant passing through a door and carrying Alice at the same time, as there was no one to open the door; and obviously the flame was doing its deadly work so rapidly that there was little promise in this direction.

Consequently, the fourth alternative, that of stripping off the flaming garment, was settled upon as offering the greatest chance of success. Alice's outcry and effort to protect her face by throwing up her arms and diving her face down on her chest and under her arms was an instantaneous reminder of the danger of inhaling the flame. Consequently to help her instinctive action in this was part and parcel of the task in hand. My whole action-system operated to the twofold end of keeping the flame from her face and getting the garment off by stripping it over her head. Such a thing as unbuttoning and removing it in the usual fashion was obviously out of the question. To strip it over the head and by main force pull it loose from the body was the only thing. This was accomplished with, however, more hard jerking and hauling than were really necessary. The flaming garment was torn off and thrown into the fireplace to prevent its setting the house on fire, with no burns on Alice except some singeing of her hair. This fortunate outcome was undoubtedly largely due to the fact that she had on a woolen union-suit under her gown. Except for this, the body would have certainly been severely burned. The immunity of the face and mouth was attributed mainly to her own instinctive protective responses, but partly to my effort to keep the front of the garment, which was less enveloped in flame, as close as possible to her face while pulling it off.

But in connection with this part of the situation, a new and terrible thought came to me. Alice's outcries largely subsided toward the end of the struggle; and the query, "Has she actually breathed in the deadly flame?" gave me an instant of dreadful suspense. But this was only momentary, for she scrambled to her feet from the floor where my hard treatment had thrown her, and was ready to run to mother and father—clearly unhurt. The sense of relief at such an issue of such an event is great indeed!

My vocalization was, I am aware, fairly vigorous but almost involuntary and aimless. Whether I uttered any definite call words I am unable to say positively. My impression is that I did not.

The thought of help certainly came into my mind—particularly help in the way of holding Alice so that I might have something to pull against in tearing off the garment. The father naturally came forward most distinctly in this connection, but the mother and Mrs. Ritter were also dimly present in my thought, as were the two members of the household in the kitchen preparing breakfast.

I am quite sure now, as I think back over the affair, that the rapid spread of the flame and the distance away of father and mother, with closed doors intervening, influenced me against spending time or effort trying to get help. Vaguely my thought was, essentially, "yourself alone or disaster."

The organization of these observations came after the incident was over. It is most unlikely that the four alternatives were considered in the order named or that they had any order at all. But for words on paper to have meaning for us we demand organization. Had this material been put down in the way the events actually took place, instead of this neatly organized account, we would have an impressionistic jumble more like a foreign movie with its quick change of camera angle and position and its piling of scene on scene simultaneously that leaves one wondering what it is all about. As it is, there is evidence of considerable disorganization in the rough handling of the child and the aimless but vigorous vocalization of Dr. Ritter.

The usual way to interpret a situation like this is to say that the emotion is valuable to the person who has it. It makes him stronger and helps him meet the situation. Had he been calm he would not have thought of so many different things to do. The more things he can think of doing, the greater the likelihood that, before it is too late, he will hit on one that solves the problem. But there is another way to look at instances like this one. We grant that a solution was accomplished here, but at what damage to Alice? Had Dr. Ritter been accustomed to saving little girls from burning every morning before breakfast, wouldn't he have gone about it more efficiently? Alice might have been less singed than she was and she might have had fewer bruises.

The physiological changes that take place in a person who is excited, angry, or afraid do make him stronger, but they fit him for survival in a rough-and-tumble, devil-take-the-hindmost kind of living.

2. A LABORATORY EXPERIMENT

A method used in the experimental laboratory to produce a sudden and unexpected stimulus causes the subject to drop backward.[2] Blatz[3] provided a chair for his subjects, the back of which

---

[2] Other investigators have had their subjects watch the experimenter decapitate live frogs with a dull knife, put their hands in a bucket containing live frogs, and so on.

[3] W. E. Blatz, "The Cardiac, Respiratory and Electrical Phenomena in the Emotion of Fear," *Journal of Experimental Psychology*, 1925, 8, 109-132.

would drop when released by a trigger mechanism. The main group of eighteen subjects had no notion concerning what would actually happen when they first agreed to take part in the experiment. The first time the chair dropped backward gave them as much of a shock as it would anyone in a similar circumstance. Their responses were compared with those of three other subjects who were told what to expect. In the second part of the experiment the chair was dropped for a second time. The subjects were in a condition of

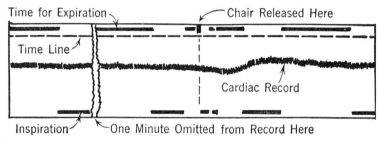

Fig. 52.—A tracing from one of Blatz's figures. Inspiration at lower edge; expiration at top. The cardiac record is in the center. (From Blatz, *Journal of Experimental Psychology*, p. 112.)

heightened expectancy during the interval between the first and second fall because they did not know the exact instant when the chair would give way.

Blatz sought to measure the changes that took place in the breathing and heart action of his disconcerted subjects. His interest in these two aspects of behavior which result from this kind of stimulation was doubtless engendered by the common observation that when a person is taken unaware—when figuratively his chair falls from under him—his heart rate increases and his breathing rate quickens.

A considerable amount of preparation is required in order to demonstrate these simple facts in the laboratory. A rather complicated setup was used to record the heart rate and breathing changes. The record finally obtained resembled that shown in Figure 52. Periods of inspiration are plainly shown at the lower edge of the plate. Alternating with these, the expiration periods are shown at the top. The cardiac record runs through the center. The change in the cardiac record at the point where the chair was released shows a change in the vigor and rate of the heart-muscle contraction, but the picture is somewhat complicated because other muscles also contracted and resulted in additional electrical effects which were also recorded.

Blatz's principal interest in this experiment was to find out whether an objective record like this could be used to find whether a person has experienced a "fear." If the subject reports that he was afraid when the chair was released, can one find any reliable indicator of the "fear" in the heart and breathing records? He concluded that it was possible. *The subjects who said they were afraid showed more profound changes than those who reported that they were not afraid.* And we must remember that Blatz was recording only a small part of the total number of internal changes that must have taken place.

When his control subjects' records were compared with the naïve subjects' records, he was able to show that the effects were less marked with those people who had an insight into what would happen to them. This observation supports a generalization that was made earlier: *An emotional response takes place when a situation is presented for which the subject is unprepared.* This experiment shows that it can be made less intense if the subject is prepared before hand for what will happen to him.

3. LIE DETECTION

If these changes in breathing and heart rate follow harsh stimuli like Blatz used could sensitive instruments record similar changes that would presumably be present when the subject wasn't treated quite so roughly? That there are internal changes of this type is evident to anyone who has ever lied to his roommate or to his girl friend. We hope that the other person won't notice these internal changes which are perfectly obvious to us even though they are principally inside us and consequently hidden to a casual observer.

The question of lie detection has intrigued criminologists since the days of Lombroso[4] (about 1880), the enthusiasts in the field

[4] A famous Italian criminologist, most of whose work has been discredited. He believed that there were "criminal types" of men who could be recognized by certain "stigmata of degeneracy" like low foreheads and eyes set too close together.

expecting to find a particular pattern in the pulse, blood-pressure, and breathing changes that would indicate whether a person was lying. But a careful study of numerous records by many competent psychologists over almost half a century has shown that *there are no special changes in a whole array of internal responses that would serve to distinguish any one emotional response from any other one.*

Lying, like being afraid, being angry, or being surprised, results in internal changes which cannot be distinguished from one another or from a whole host of other special conditions that we have names for. Precisely speaking, there is no lie detector. There is no instrument which, when attached to a person, rings a bell or lights up a red lamp when he lies. But there are instruments that have been called "lie detectors" that are simply special arrangements of standard laboratory equipment. Particular attention is given in their construction to the features of portability, compactness, and ruggedness.

One of the most popular of these instruments depends entirely upon registering breathing, pulse, and changes in blood pressure. A pneumograph is placed around the subject's chest. As he breathes, movements of his chest wall are faithfully reproduced on a moving tape by means of a writing lever. A rubber bag such as a physician uses to measure blood pressure is wound around the subject's arm just above the elbow. Unlike the physician, who inflates this bag with air so that sufficient pressure is created to stop entirely the flow of blood in the arm, the experimenter in this instance only partially inflates the bag. This technique allows a continuous registration of the pulse, and changes in level of the record give some indication of blood pressure changes, although not precisely.

Expert opinion required. Typical data may be found in **Larson's** book,[5] a record of actual police cases. It must not be assumed that such records are so clear that anyone can identify the points at which lying took place. Long experience is required, not only in identifying the significant changes but also in formulating the procedure in each new case, and few police officers have the necessary background to plan or to administer the technique.

J. A. Larson, *Lying and Its Detection,* University of Chicago Press, Chicago, 1932, p. 295.

Objections to the technique. Not all psychologists, by any means, are agreed on the usefulness of lie detection as a practical technique in criminology. Some hold that the whole procedure is in an experimental stage and that it should be withheld from the public until we are more certain of our results. Some of these objectors hope eventually, however, that the method will replace the usual "third degree." The proponents of lie detection hold that even now the method is more accurate than the usual grilling of suspects in which confessions can be wrung from innocent suspects by long hours of questions, suggestions, and accusations. Indeed, it is possible for a person to become so confused that he comes to believe he has committed a crime of which he is actually innocent.

Another objection involves more strictly technical considerations. As we have seen, *lying cannot be distinguished from a number of other conditions of which fear is one.* What would happen if an innocent person became afraid? Would he be counted guilty just because he was afraid? The proponents of the technique point out a fear of this kind is manifest throughout the record, while a guilty person shows these same changes only in response to significant questions about the crime. After the confession, as we have seen, a repetition of the same questions produces no observable disturbance. When a person meets the critical situation in which he is being questioned as a suspect of a crime actually committed by some offender and realizes the seriousness of the situation, to reply to a question which he does not wish to answer involves a conflict between telling the truth and telling a falsehood. Whether this is a stimulus which arouses an emotional response of fear, anger, confusion, or tension matters little in this instance. The important thing is not what name to apply to the response but the fact that a change in breathing, heart action, or some other organic change actually occurs at significant points.

4. GALVANIC SKIN RESPONSES

As part of a course called "psychobiology" in the medical school of Johns Hopkins University Adolph Meyer regularly requires the students to write autobiographies. These are rather frank statements

260

for the most part in which the students try seriously to write on paper a great many of their likes and dislikes, emotional responses, feelings, hopes, ambitions and wishes of a domestic, cultural, educational, and vocational kind. Some of these papers are, according to direction, marked "Personal" and are intended for the information of Dr. Meyer alone. Others, perhaps not so intimate are not so marked and as a consequence are available for other people to study.

Syz[6] has made use of some of these in a study of the galvanic skin responses. These responses are observed when a sensitive galvanometer is connected to the body, and apparently occur in response to various stimuli but more markedly perhaps to those that would be called "emotional" or affective.

Syz examined sixty-four medical students in all, administering four classes of stimuli to which reactions on the galvanometer were obtained. First, a list of fifty-five words was read at intervals of from eight to twelve seconds. Some of these related to family, sex, social standing, success, money, religion, moral standards, and self-esteem, all of which would be likely to produce emotional responses. There were included in the fifty-five, at intervals, other words like *book, green, window, basket,* which ordinarily are reported to be neutral.

After the words were read, a pinprick on the right forearm and one on the neck were administered. Then there was a threat of a pinprick on the left forearm, and after the threat—which itself could produce an emotional response—the subject actually was pricked slightly. The words were then read again.

The subject was to remain seated in a quiet semidark room, shut off from a view of the apparatus and the experimenters except when the sensory stimuli were applied. He was asked not to speak and to remain as relaxed as he could.

In addition to the galvanic response, which was registered on photographically sensitive paper, the way the subject breathed was also registered on the same tape. There was also a time line and a stimulus line. Figure 53 shows how the record looked after the sensitive paper was developed. After the stimulus word was spoken,

[3] Hans C. Syz, "Psycho-Galvanic Studies on Sixty-four Medical Students," *British Journal of Psychology*, 1926, 17, 54-69; 119-126.

there occurred typically a single deflection of the galvanometer as shown in the displacement of the GSR line. Not all of the curves look like the one shown. There are various irregularities and secondary effects which complicate the picture. There are even some curves that have no plausible relation to the stimulus at all. The number of responses that could be directly attributed to the verbal stimuli varied from seventy-one to none for the different subjects. The average frequency for the entire group was thirty-four for the one hundred and ten words.

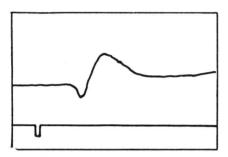

FIG. 53.—A single galvanometric deflection. This is a tracing of one of Syz's photographs.

Syz analyzed the responses aside from their frequency, in terms of their shape, their time relations to the stimulus, and their amplitude.

Relation to the autobiographies. The autobiographies enter the picture when the experimenter tried to find some distinguishing characteristics in them which would account for the wide range in the number of direct responses shown by the galvanometer. The smallest number of responses were zero, six, and eight for the one hundred and ten words. Evaluations of the autobiographies for these three subjects follow:

1. *No response.* Generally cheerful. Likes everybody; says that he never disagrees with anybody; socially well adapted; has no special problems. Describes his temperament as happy, foolish, joking, childlike. Emotions of others stir him but little.

2. *Six reactions.* Enthusiastic. Accepts things always as they are; not hard to please. Time filled with actual tasks; constant in his work and much interested in everything he does. Says he has no imagination. Conventional; no difficulties of adaptation.

3. *Eight reactions.* Interested in things. Clocklike regularity in daily activities. Says he reacts to things with calmness and composure. Ambitious, and activities well adapted in a self-confident and conventional way.

There were four people who showed an extremely high number of reactions, seventy-one, seventy, sixty-seven, and sixty-six. Summaries of their autobiographies follow:

1. *Seventy-one reactions.* Timid and overmodest. Many interests; more complex character than the average. Describes temperament as outgoing, active, happy, but oversensitive. Stirred deeply by moods of others.

2. *Seventy reactions.* Of meditating nature, musical. Difficulty in mixing; shy with girls. Easily embarrassed and influenced by slight disturbances. Overconscientious. Says he is very emotional, moody, self-centered, acting on the impulse of the moment.

3. *Sixty-seven reactions.* Cheerful. Inclination to hot temper but controlled. Uneasy with strangers. Easily homesick and "blue"; does not always get over discouragement quickly.

4. *Sixty-six reactions.* Generally in good spirits but bashful. Complains of feelings of inferiority; at times retiring. Activity in sports. Says he is influenced to a great extent by the esteem of others, that he is diffident and self-depreciating. Tendency to sarcasm.

It seems reasonable to conclude tentatively that nervous, easily worried, easily embarrassed persons give relatively large numbers of galvanic skin responses, and that, on the other hand, the emotionally stable give few. There are certain reservations to the conclusion which we will treat later.

From other observations which Syz made it appears that the *magnitude* of the response is not important in discriminating between the emotional and the nonemotional. A big deflection indicates the relative importance of a stimulus word to the subject, but that importance is specific, not general; a person who gives few responses may occasionally give big ones and still not be "emotional" as revealed by his autobiography. *There was no evidence that the different kinds of emotional responses could be identified in any characteristic of the deflections.*

This experiment is no more than a beginning in this extremely important field. The method suffers because the sixty-four casual autobiographies cannot be arranged in order like the galvanic responses, and no precise comparisons can be made. When we work with the extreme cases only we can't be certain how many of those between these extremes will violate the generalizations that we draw. When we commence to select only a few extreme cases, as this experimenter has done, it sometimes happens that we shut our eyes to all the exceptions.

The autobiographies themselves are likely to contain only the socially acceptable information about their authors. People report about themselves in stereotypic ways following conventional pat-

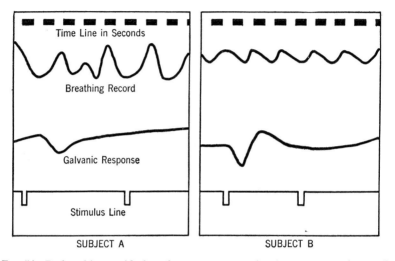

Fig. 54.—Both subjects said that there was no emotional response to the words "misspent youth," both said that there was a response to the word "Father." The objective records show just the opposite condition to obtain. "Misspent youth" was given simultaneously with the first depression of the stimulus line; "Father," at the second.

terns laid down by the novels and biographies they have read and the movies they have seen. They may not be willing to report all of the private emotional episodes that they have experienced. As a matter of fact there is some suggestion that this might be true from Syz's own work. He found that his subjects frequently reported some emotional disturbance for words like "father" when no galvanic response was present. On the other hand, a phrase like "misspent youth" actually resulted in some cases in marked deflections but the subjects denied that there was any emotional response at all. *Most of them reported fewer than one quarter of all the response that could be identified in the galvanic records.*

264

5. EMOTIONS AND GASTRIC EFFECTS

Our emotional reactions stand out in our memory not alone because a situation was pleasant or unpleasant, or because an attractive goal was attained or was withheld from us; but because of the marked physical and organic feelings we experienced during these emotional states. Some of the characteristic organic reactions which are a part of the fear response were reported by a group of Army Air Force combat veterans.[7] Their reactions during aerial combat included such things as a pounding heart, dryness of the mouth, a cold sweat, "butterflies in the stomach," nausea, and lack of bladder control. These reports attest the fact that when we respond emotionally our reaction is not limited to striped muscular activity, but it involves as well, and involves profoundly, the life-maintaining and vegetative organs of the body. The fact that emotions do result in disturbances of our visceral functioning has meant that prolonged emotional responses often result in serious physical illness.

Ordinarily it is not possible to make direct observations of some of these physiological reactions, and the fact that they have occurred can only be inferred from other behavioral measures, but occasionally an opportunity to make such measurements does happen. Such an opportunity was acquired by Wolf and Wolf.[8] An employee of their laboratory had suffered an accident in his youth that closed his throat. He was operated upon and an incision was made into his stomach so that he could be fed by putting food directly into the stomach. This event, so unfortunate for the individual, was to the gain of science; for it meant that the experimenters were able to observe directly the response of the stomach to various stimuli. They were particularly interested in the effect of emotional conditions on the secretion of hydrochloric acid. This acid is normally secreted by the stomach in response to the presence of food and is, of course, a basic part of the process of digestion. The experimental method

[7] Army Air Forces Aviation Psychology Program Research Reports. Psychological Research on Problems of Redistribution. Report No. 14, pp. 122-161. U.S. Government Printing Office, Washington, D. C., 1947.

[8] Steward Wolf and H. G. Wolf, "Evidence on the Genesis of Peptic Ulcer in Men," Journal of the American Medical Association, 120, 1942, 670-675.

was very simple and consisted of measuring the quantity of secretion in response to various emotional conditions.

Results. Reaction to depression and to fear. During one experimental period the subject was very depressed about his failure to take up an option on a house which he had long desired. After

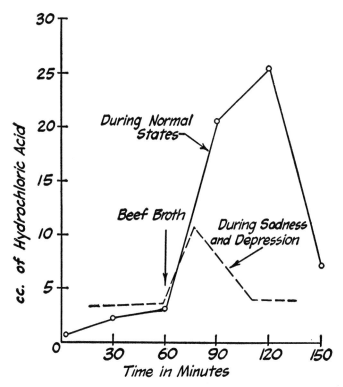

Fig. 55.—Gastric secretion following consumption of beef broth during a period of emotional depression and normal emotional feelings. (After Wolf and Wolf.)

the experimenters had established a basic level of gastric secretion, they introduced a small quantity of beef broth into the stomach and recorded the quantity of secretion following this stimulus. At another time, when the subject reported no unusual emotions, the experimenters subjected him to the same test. The results for these two conditions are shown in Figure 55. It will be seen that this emotional state acts to depress the secretion of hydrochloric acid to the stimulus of food in the stomach.

At another time, while the subject was being observed, one of the physicians on the laboratory staff entered the room muttering angrily about some important papers that were lost. Actually the subject had mislaid the papers and he feared that he had lost the record and his job as well. Immediately the normal continuous secretion of acid was reduced and it continued at this reduced state for over an hour, even though the physician soon found his papers.

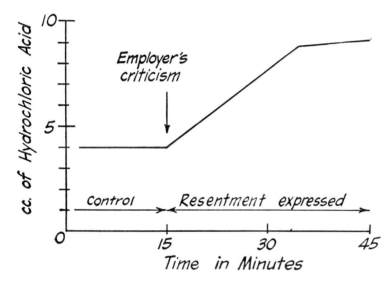

FIG. 56.—Gastric secretion during a period of emotional activity. (After Wolf and Wolf.)

Reactions to anxiety, hostility, and resentment. During another period of observation a staff member entered the laboratory and stated that some extra work which the subject had been doing for him had not been properly done. The doctor further stated that the subject need not report for more work, and that because of his inefficiency and slowness he was discharged. The subject accepted this statement quietly, but immediately thereafter an increase in gastric secretion occurred and continued for some time. These results are shown in Figure 56.

267

The reactions to resentment and anxiety were also shown at another time. The subject was not well off financially and his need forced him to accept gifts from a benefactor. The benefactor, however, was inclined to meddle in the subject's affairs and would threaten to withdraw his help if his suggestions were not followed. During a certain two-week period this situation arose to something of a crisis and the subject was in a constant state of emotional turmoil, expressing resentment about his benefactor and fear for his financial condition in the future. At the end of two weeks relief from his predicament came in the form of a raise in pay. During this two-week period of emotional stress, the quantity of gastric secretion ran nearly double its usual amount.

Summary of the experiment. The decrement in gastric functioning which accompanied reactions of fear and of depression gives an understanding of why these conditions are so often accompanied by digestive disturbances. As a result of experiencing these emotional states we are likely to find that our appetite is lost or that a recently consumed meal does not sit well on our stomachs. Some insane patients whose psychotic reactions involve a profound depression would go for days without food were they not fed, sometimes forcefully, by those responsible for their care.

The oversecretion of gastric juices during anxiety and resentment is of particular interest nowadays because of the high incidence of gastric ulcers. During the past war there were many cases of military personnel becoming incapacitated as a result of this illness. Its relation to anxiety arising from combat stress, and perhaps also from the frustrations that would result from the structure of the military hierarchy with its chain of command and social differentiation between the officer and the enlisted man, is obvious. The disorder is by no means restricted to the war situation, but is frequently found in modern civilian life where situations giving rise to frustration, anxiety, and to resentment are frequent.

A word should be said about the direct relationship between the ulcerous condition and gastric secretion. The gastric juices, as we have said before, contain hydrochloric acid. This acid is, of course, capable of destroying tissue; and, indeed, it operates that way in the normal digestive process. The acid's action is not limited to the dead tissue of consumed foods, but it will have a similar corrosive effect upon the stomach walls themselves. Ordinarily the walls are protected by a lining of mucous, but if for any reason this is removed—the simple mechanical action of food scraping it away is one—the acid can attack the stomach wall. Obviously any state which results in an oversecretion of acid increases the probability that the corroding process can be started; hence the relationship between ulcer conditions and certain other behavioral reactions.

At the present time we do not have sufficient data to generalize broadly. Many persons undergo situations which may give rise to anxiety and resentment without their developing the symptoms of ulcers. On the other hand, the personality characteristics, including their reactions to emotional situations, are not the same for all individuals who do have ulcers; and ulcers may result from other conditions. There is a relationship between emotional habits and ulcers, but it is not a perfect one.

The student with a philosophical bent probably sees in this study a case of the mind influencing the body. An analysis of the situations in these terms is not fruitful. A more accurate statement is that the emotional reaction is widespread; it is not limited to the central nervous system and the striped muscles, but also involves the autonomic nervous system and the visceral organs. All stimuli produce responses, some faster than others. Those which we call "emotional response" have the characteristic of being widespread and prolonged in their effect.

6. REDUCING EMOTIONAL TENSION

In other parts of this book we have detailed the ways in which emotional situations are ordinarily handled in children and adults. These methods boil down to: (a) recommendations that the emotion-producing situation be faced again; (b) recommendations that a person talk about the situation; (c) recommendations that the person get away from the situation by taking a vacation. All of these are competitive methods and some of them are contradictory, as, for example, the first and the last.

269

Here, as in many other cases, it is difficult to get these things into the laboratory where adequate tests of their efficacy can be made. However, Haggard[9] has developed an experiment which gives at least a partial answer.

He used the GSR as a measure of the amount of emotional response following the administration of a weak electric shock to human subjects. There were eighteen Harvard men who served as subjects. Ultimately they were divided into three groups of six each, but for the preliminary part of the experiment, called Session I, they all received the same treatment: each was shocked five times during a thirty-five minute period. During the period certain words were used as stimuli to provide a base from which the disturbing effect of the shock could be estimated. The shock itself came at a specified time after the stimulus word was spoken and always followed the name of an animal, and although only five animal names were used and five shocks given, only about half the subjects "caught on." For the half who did "catch on" the disturbance produced by the shock was much less, even though their knowledge did nothing to mitigate the shock.

This, then, is the first finding: *An understanding of a situation or a knowledge about it was definitely of value in reaction to it even when there was no possibility of escaping the unpleasantness.*

In Session II, which came later the same day for each subject, one of the three methods of dealing with emotional conflicts was tried on each person. One group simply faced the situation again without any further information about it. For them Session II was simply a repetition of Session I; another group was allowed to *rest* or "take a vacation" in the laboratory. They were not shocked nor did they actually enter the experimental room. A third group was encouraged to ask questions about the experiment talk about their reactions, tell what they thought about the experiment, etc. They also were not actually put through a repetition of the routine.

The third session was the critical part of the experiment and one which, when compared with the others, gave an opportunity

9 Ernest A. Haggard, "Some Factors Determining Adjustment during Readjustment Following Experimentally Induced Stress," *Journal of Experimental Psychology,* 1913, 33, 257 281.

to compare the efficacy of the three methods. In Session III the subjects ran through a repetition of Session I, *except that in no case was any shock given.* Even so, there were deflections following all the words in different amounts for different subjects. The subjects were not told there were to be no shocks.

A detailed analysis of these responses showed that *the rest therapy was the least effective method of reducing the responses in Session III as compared to I.*

And, on the whole, *facing the situation a second time,* as one group did in Session II, *was only a little better.*

There was a clear-cut reduction, however, in the GSR's of those who had talked about the problem in Session II. *This turned out to be the most effective of the three methods.*

Summary of the chapter. The first section gives one of the few accounts we have of a person's actions as they were recorded closely following an incident that everyone would agree is emotion-producing. The characteristic behavior seems to be a pattern of responses in which the individual is rendered less capable, albeit stronger and more vigorous. His movements are poorly coordinated and he loses his most recently acquired behavior (both ontogenetically and phylogenetically). The second section shows how conditions resembling this one are attempted in the laboratory. The principal reason for making these physiological studies of breathing and cardiac response was to find if there was a typical pattern in breathing or in any other physiological variable which would serve to differentiate fear from rage, from love, from anger, and so on. In the literally hundreds of experiments that have been made, of which this one is only a sample, no differentiae have been uniformly found. The third section discusses one of the more popular "lie detectors" and points out that the instrument is misnamed. Although there is some question about the interpretation of the results, it is concluded with some reservation that the method will prove a useful one in the hands of experts. The fourth section points out a fundamental weakness in Syz's conclusion regarding the relation between "nervousness" and the GSR, but the experimenter deserves credit for a pioneer experiment in an important field. In the fifth experiment direct observations of gastric functioning were made and correlated with emotional conditions. It clearly shows the intimate connection between the visceral processes and emotional condition. The last section shows how the GSR apparatus is used in making a comparison between three methods of handling emotional tensions.

CHAPTER FOURTEEN

SUGGESTIBILITY AND HYPNOSIS

In previous chapters we have shown how human behavior can be controlled by setting up various conditions of motivation. There was the implication that very frequently words, gestures, and symbols of other kinds were as effective in controlling behavior as the more strictly biological rewards. It is this theme which is continued in the present chapter.

When a person develops a set of symptoms for a disease after hearing them described or when he recovers from a headache after taking a harmless placebo, he is said to be suggestible. A woman recently said that when she was talking over the telephone to a particular male friend she could always smell his pipe. She was convinced that odor stimuli could be transmitted over telephone wires. We know that they cannot be, but we can accept the woman's statement as true, because the effect is easily explainable in the same terms we use for accounting for any learned effect. It could be said that this woman was suggestible to the extent that she had learned to associate the sound of a particular voice with the odor of a pipe. If that is true, then we are all suggestible, and I suspect we are, in different degrees and to sets of stimuli that are extensive in some cases and more restricted in others. Suggestibility, then, is not the unique property of a few people.

1. SUGGESTIBILITY

Suggestibility merely means that people respond to the indirection in a given situation. In the example given above, although no odor stimuli were present, the woman definitely did experience an odor of a pipe. The same result could possibly be obtained if one had commanded her to sniff and described for her the odor of burning tobacco, but in such an instance the suggestion would have bordered on a command rather and would not have fallen into a classification of suggestion.

The late E. E. Slosson,[1] a chemist, is responsible for an experiment which has been used frequently in class demonstrations of suggestibility. One day he brought to his lecture hall a bottle of what he said was a new compound having a particularly penetrating odor and he wanted to find out how quickly its odor was diffused to those in the room. Would the students please hold up their hands when they smelled the odor? Soon those in the front row were holding up their hands, then those in the second, and so forth until practically everybody was sure he had smelled something. Then it turned out that the bottle contained perfectly odorless distilled water. Many variations of this demonstration have been made. If the odor is described to be like peppermint or lemons, more people seem to smell it than if the supposed odor is not exactly specified. One experimenter made a colored grade-school pupil so sick from smelling distilled water that she had to be dismissed from school for the remainder of the day. All the experimenter did was to hold her head away from the distilled water as she poured it on a piece of cotton, all the while making a face as though the nonexistent odor were nauseous.

Another factor seems to be the prestige of the person who is doing the suggesting. We are more inclined to be impressed if one person tells us a thing than if another lesser light tells us the same thing. Slosson had more prestige than Slosson's assistant would have had. It is common to distinguish between prestige suggestion in which a person is involved and nonprestige suggestion in which the nonpersonal factors are effective in producing the effect.

Prestige suggestion.   One of the simplest examples of an experiment in which the effectiveness of prestige suggestion has been measured is contained in the pioneer investigations of the Frenchmen, Binet and Henri.[2] They had a schoolmaster show a group of his pupils a five-centimeter line and ask the students to reproduce it from memory a few minutes later. He then showed them a line only four centimeters long but told them that it was *longer* than the first

---

[1] E. E. Slosson, "A Lecture Experiment in Hallucinations," *Psychological Review,* 1899, 6, 407-408.

[2] A. Binet and V. Henri, *La Suggestibilité,* 1900.

"Place beside each name a figure indicating the order of preference you have for the following authors. Make your judgment solely on the grounds of subjective liking for the words of the writer. If you have no feeling of like or dislike for a certain author, you may omit his name. Place the figure (1) beside the name of the writer whose work you like best, (2) beside the next, and so on until you have arranged all with whom you are acquainted."

Sir James Barrie
Joseph Conrad
James Fenimore Cooper
Charles Dickens
Thomas Hardy
Nathaniel Hawthorne
Rudyard Kipling
Edgar Allan Poe

John Ruskin
Sir Walter Scott
Robert Louis Stevenson
William Makepeace Thackeray
Tolstoy
Mark Twain
Walt Whitman
Thornton Wilder

line they had seen. They were then asked to reproduce the second one from memory. Only nine of the eighty-six children were able to resist the statement of the teacher and actually reproduce the second line as it actually was—shorter. This experiment tells us nothing about the basis of prestige suggestion but merely quantifies the susceptibility of the young children to statements of a teacher when the statement is contrary to the facts. We might reasonably infer that most children go through a process of learning that most of what adults, particularly teachers, tell them is true and as a consequence any statement of an adult is likely to be accepted without questioning.

A demonstration of a more subtle kind of suggestion is found in an experiment reported by Sherif.[3] The experiment was conducted in two parts. In Part I, which was preliminary to the really important part of the experiment, the names of sixteen well-known authors were presented to the subjects in approximately the form shown on page 275. This process resulted in a series of preferences which were used in the second part of the experiment.

One month later the same subjects were given sixteen slips of paper on each of which was a short selection of three or four lines. Three judges had previously agreed that these excerpts were about equal in literary merit. Each selection was attributed to one of the sixteen authors mentioned on page 275 by placing his name under it. Actually, however, they were all from a single author—Robert Louis Stevenson. The subjects were asked to assign a number to each selection as in Part I, but this time they were to make their judgments solely on the grounds of liking or disliking the passages.

A comparison of the two orders from Parts I and II of this experiment showed that *the subjects were strongly influenced in their judgments of literary merit by the prestige of the author in question.* There were several subjects who ignored the authors' names and in these cases the relation was low. Again we find that prestige is no mysterious quality that some people carry around with them. The preference for the authors in the first place was obviously determined by an evaluation of their work arrived at either independently by

[3] Muzafer Sherif, "A Study of Some Social Factors in Perception," *Archives of Psychology,* 1935, No. 187.

each person as a result of reading, or through hearsay evidence accepted from others.

Nonprestige suggestion. In the nonprestige field we have Williams's experiment[4] which, in turn, is based on several older ones.

A coil of wire on a table was connected conspicuously to a battery through a knife switch. Closing the switch would cause the coil to become heated slightly. But current could not pass from the battery to the coil, even when the knife switch was closed, unless a button out of sight of the observer was covertly pressed by the experimenter's knee. The directions to the subject were:

The purpose of this experiment is to determine the smallest amount of heat that you can feel with your finger.

When the experimenter says "ready" you are to place your finger on the coil and hold it there until you can *just barely* feel the warmth. *At the instant* you feel any warmth whatsoever remove your finger sharply from the coil. Then wait until the experimenter tells you to replace your finger on the coil.

The experimenter simultaneously called "ready" and closed the knife switch. For the first four trials he also pressed the push button so that the coil actually did warm up. The following six trials were made by closing the knife switch alone. The subject continued to touch the coil for thirty seconds even if he did not feel the warmth. The experimenter then said, "All right, you did not feel it this time," and the subject was allowed to remove his finger. Exactly the same pause followed the last six trials as the first four, ostensibly to allow the coil to cool. Exactly the same procedure was followed whether the subject accepted the suggestion or not.

All the subjects accepted the suggestion some of the time and some accepted it every time. The average for eight subjects in twelve opportunities was approximately eight acceptances. Prestige factors are not entirely eliminated in this study, but the use of all this equipment doubtless enhanced the acceptance of the suggestions. The various pieces of apparatus helped to add verisimilitude to the

4 G. W. Williams, "Suggestibility in the Normal and Hypnotic States," *Archives of Psychology,* 1930, No. 122.

situation because of the previous experience of the subjects with like pieces of equipment.

Another older experiment is more clearly a matter of non-prestige factors and shows an additional feature of true suggestibility that is important. Daniel Starch[5] gave 106 people passages which they were told to copy in their own handwriting. There were four different samples, one typewritten and the other three written with various degrees of letter width and slant. He found that the great majority of the subjects modified their handwriting either in slant or letter width or both to conform to the model from which they were copying. *The subjects were entirely unaware of having accepted the nonprestige suggestion offered by the model.* This latter point is important because it helps to distinguish between true suggestion and conscious copying or imitation, which is a different phenomenon altogether.

The techniques of advertising and propaganda make wide use of suggestion in bringing about changes in attitude and action favorable to the particular wares of the promotional source. All of the methods employed make use of the principles of prestige and nonprestige suggestion.

2. SLEEP AND HYPNOSIS [6]

In all of the common methods of inducing hypnosis the word "sleep" is used. "Now you are going into a sound, sound sleep. You will not wake up until you are told . . ." Not only in the directions for accomplishing the trance, but also in the theory concerning it, there has been frequent mention of sleep. How alike or how different these two states are was the problem which Milton Bass[7] set out to solve.

[5] Daniel Starch, "Unconscious Imitation of Handwriting," *Psychological Review,* 1911, 18, 173-181.

[6] This chapter is written on the assumption that the student has read enough about hypnosis to know what is meant by the usual hypnotic phenomena, e.g., catalepsy, anesthesia, amnesia, posthypnotic amnesia, positive and negative hallucinations, and posthypnotic suggestion. If a demonstration is planned it should precede the reading of this chapter; if a demonstration does not appear feasible, the motion-picture film, *Hypnosis,* by Lester Beck may be used.

[7] Milton Bass, "The Differentiation of the Hypnotic Trance from Normal Sleep," *Journal of Experimental Psychology,* 1931, 5, 382-389.

Criterion of sleep. He conceived the solution to depend upon finding some bit of behavior or some reliable physiological sign of sleep which could be used to distinguish between sleeping and waking. The hypnotic trance could then be examined for the presence or absence of the sign of sleep. If the sign of sleep was present in hypnosis, then there would be some justification for asserting that there was at least some connection between the two states.

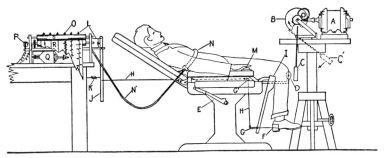

FIG. 57.—The arrangement of the apparatus and the subject in Bass's experiment.

A sign or criterion of this kind has long been known to exist in the patellar reflex. In sleep the extent of leg movement to patellar stimulation is considerably diminished or in some cases abolished altogether. Regular hammer blows to the patella which are necessary to follow the course of the decrement in the knee jerk as sleep ensues, instead of preventing a person from going to sleep, have been shown by several investigators to be actually sleep-conducive.

Method. The subject lay supine in a modified barber's chair. His legs hung freely beyond the knees so that the extent of leg movement could be recorded. An automatic device raised a hammer and let it fall through a known distance. The instant in which the hammer made contact with the leg was recorded automatically on a moving tape which also carried the record of the leg movements resulting from the striking hammer. The stimulus was given every 9.68 seconds. This much of the apparatus is all that was needed to differentiate between sleeping and waking.

279

Criterion of hypnosis. Now to differentiate between sleeping and hypnosis. It is well known that a hypnotic subject will continue to react to any intermittent stimulus if he is commanded to do so. During sleep these responses cease. They are present, of course, when the subject is awake. The choice of stimulus was a bell which was caused to sound with a single soft but clearly audible tap every ninety seconds. These stimuli were recorded on the tape together with the resultant response, which was secured by means of a button on the right chair arm to be actuated by the index finger of the subject. A breathing record was also obtained. Since it did not prove of any value in differentiating between any of the states, it will not be mentioned again.

More details of method. There were seven practiced subjects used. Each was given one hundred strokes on the patellar tendon in each of the three states, awake W, asleep S, and hypnotized T. To avoid practice or adaptation effects, the records were taken in the six possible combinations:

WST	TSW	SWT
WTS	TWS	STW

In all there were forty-three experimental periods in which about 1,300 patellar stimuli were recorded.

In the WST period, one hundred stimulations would be given when the subject was awake. This operation would require about fifteen minutes. At the end of that time the subjects would be asked to try to go to sleep. At the end of the next hundred stimulations the subject was awakened. He was then put into a trance, and again one hundred stimulations were given.

Results. The record shown in Figure 58 shows the end of a sleep period. There was no voluntary response to the bell stimuli and to the eighteen patellar stimuli shown there was not a single kick. But when the subject was awakened at the point marked W, the kicks begin as do the responses to the bell. Both of these latter continue when after about two minutes the subject is placed in a

280

trance. A practiced subject like this one can be hypnotized almost instantly.

Figure 59 shows a summary of the patellar data for all subjects and for all experimental periods. The ordinates show the amplitude of the kicks as measured in millimeters on the tape. The abscissa units show the number of kicks, or—what is the same thing—the

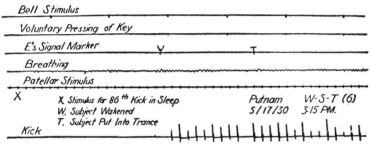

Fig. 58.—A sample of the record obtained.

time from the onset of the three states. Each five kicks are averaged for amplitude so that there are twenty abscissa units instead of one hundred.

All three curves show some tendency to fall. This can be interpreted to mean that the subjects became more and more relaxed in each of the states as time went on. The sleep curve, however, follows an entirely different course from the other two. For the first minute the amplitudes of the kicks during sleep are almost as high as for awake and trance, but this effect can be expected since it is reasonable to suppose the sleep did not ensue instantaneously. The per cent of voluntary responses to the bell can also be plotted in exactly the same way. The curves are not shown here because in appearance and interpretation they are the same as those shown for the knee jerk. The per cent of responses was clearly lower in sleep, while for hypnosis and waking there was hardly any difference at all.

Conclusion. A reasonable interpretation of the appearance of the whole graph is that in so far as the amplitude of the patellar reflex is an index of the condition of the organism, *being asleep is*

281

entirely different from both waking and hypnosis. Being hypnotized is not a physiological condition or state like being asleep, however much the behavior of a person hypnotized superficially resembles

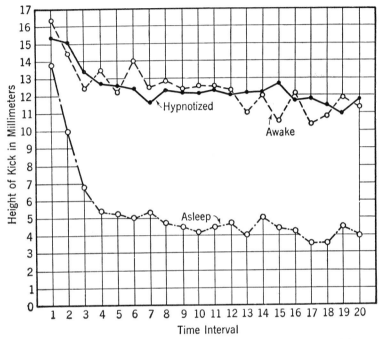

Fig. 59.—The amplitude of the patellar reflexes in sleeping, waking, and hypnosis.

his behavior asleep. If there is any difference between being awake and being hypnotized this technique does not exhibit it. Of course, there is a difference. Just what this difference is will be set forth as well as it is now understood in the following sections.

3. AMNESIA

Not only does a hypnotized subject sometimes act as if he were asleep, but very frequently he disclaims any knowledge of what has happened to him while he was hypnotized. Like the sleeping person, time passes rapidly for him and movements that he makes he does not remember. This is known as *posthypnotic amnesia.* The question that arises is: Is this effect a fundamental one involving a basic physiological process or is it simply a matter of temporary inability to recall similar to that which overtakes us all on occasions of emotional inhibition or blocking due to fatigue?

Hypothesis. If the amnesia were a complete process which involved the basic physiological processes as well as the language mechanism, then a subject who had been practicing something would show no effect of an interlude during which he practiced the same task while hypnotized. He should start, subsequent to his hypnotized practice, at the same level he left off prior to hypnosis.

Method. This hypothesis has been subjected to experimental test by Patten at Miami University.[8] He used fourteen subjects in all; seven hypnotized for a time, and seven who were never hypnotized. The task was to add successively 6, 7, 8, and 9 to a two-place number given between 10 and 99.

There was absolutely no difference between the procedures for the control and the experimental groups for the first six days. But on the seventh day, and the following ones including the twelfth, the experimental group was hypnotized and made to perform the additions in the trance. On the thirteenth day and subsequently it again practiced while awake. Uniformly the hypnotized subjects asked at the end of the hypnotic periods, "Aren't you going to have me add today?" This is the kind of evidence that is normally required to prove the existence of amnesia and it demonstrates that the subjects were satisfying the ordinarily imposed criteria for amnesia. There is no question but that they were hypnotized and that they were amnesic.

Results. The results of Patten's experiment are shown in two figures. Although the control subjects were always inferior to the experimental group in the number of additions they could accomplish in five minutes, this does not spoil the experiment. The comparison that we are interested in is that of trial six and its prede-

8 E. F. Patten, "Does Post-Hypnotic Amnesia Apply to Practice Effects?" *Journal of General Psychology,* 1932, 7, 196-201.

283

cessors with trial thirteen and its followers. Trial thirteen is not the continuation of trial six. Even if the intervening trials were not on the graph, our first inference would have to be that some practice took place in the hypnotized interval. The general appearance of the curve for the experimental and the control groups is exactly the same. Figure 61 shows this better than does Figure 60. In the former the initial performance of the control group is taken as 100 and the subsequent trials of both groups are compared to it as a base, an operation which compensates for the difference of the two groups in ability. This treatment of the data is legitimate because we are not interested in the differences in ability between the two groups. We want to be rid of it because it obscures the effects we are interested in.

Conclusion. The solid circles, showing the performance of the hypnotized group, fit into the general trend nicely. They have to be there to explain what follows. This can only mean that *the amnesia of hypnotized subjects is entirely independent of the course of learning during hypnosis.* That the subjects honestly deny remembering what happens does not mean that they are in a state of suspended animation in which ordinary experiences leave no effect.

We infer that the amnesia of a hypnotized subject is more like that of a person who knows something "as well as his own name" but is temporarily blocked when it comes to exhibiting what he knows. These results are not necessarily contradictory. It is not unusual in psychology to obtain a certain result by one method and an entirely different result by some other method. (Cf. Chapter Eighteen.)

4. RAPPORT

Hypnosis is naïvely described as the conquest of a weak-willed person by one of strong will. On the stage and in literature the hypnotist is represented as exercising an unusual degree of control over the actions of the person he has hypnotized even when the consequences of such action are clearly detrimental to the interests and well-being of the hypnotized. Scientific men have been misled by the *apparent* willingness of the subject to carry out trivial sug-

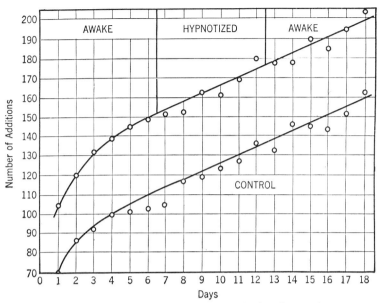

Fɪɢ. 60.—Learning curves for addition: hypnotized and control groups.

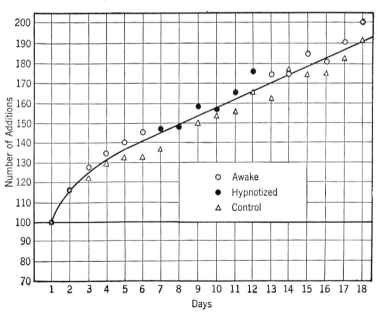

Fɪɢ. 61.—Same data as shown in Figure 60. The lower curve of Figure 60 is moved up to adjust for the difference in initial ability.

gestions until they, too, in some instances, have described hypnosis as a peculiar relationship between subject and operator which they call *rapport.*

Whether or not rapport is essential to hypnosis has been tried in a series of observations by Paul Campbell Young,[9] who asked himself several questions which he later subjected to a test.

Can a subject annul rapport? Two subjects who had previously been hypnotized several times were used. They were asked to write on a piece of paper the suggestions they would resist. A list of ten different things had been provided which would make suitable material for testing the resistance. The experimenter did not know which one of the things had been chosen, so he ran through the whole list each time the subject was hypnotized, redoubling his efforts to produce the effect if there appeared to be any resistance at all. The subjects were not told whether they would be successful in resisting or not. They were merely told that this was a point upon which some experiments would be made. The account of the sitting, as Dr. Young reports it, is shown on page 288.

Conclusion. From these two instances we can conclude that it is possible for a subject to "make up his mind" that he will not do a certain thing when the experimenter commands him to do so. *His behavior follows closely his own instruction in spite of anything the hypnotizer can do.* In these cases the subject does not necessarily "wake up." Sometimes he does wake, however, still contrary to the suggestions given him.

Emerson Hall, Cambridge, Mass., Dec. 24, 1922, Subject M. Just before sitting in the chair to be hypnotized one morning this somnambulistic subject asked the experimenter to be sure to bring the experiment to a close at 12:00. The experimenter assured the subject that he would be awakened before 12:00. At 11:55 the experimenter, noticing that the tests would be incomplete at the time agreed upon, tried to prolong the session by suggesting to the subject that his sleep would become deeper and deeper, and that he would not awake until ten minutes had passed. *In spite of the means thus employed, the subject began to toss restlessly, and at the striking of Memorial*

[9] Paul Campbell Young, "Is *Rapport* an Essential Characteristic of Hypnosis?" *Journal of Abnormal and Social Psychology,* 1927, 22, 130-139.

Hall clock awoke. As soon as he was fully conscious, and had understood the nature of the case, the subject composed himself to be hypnotized again. But in spite of his apparent co-operation and his avowed purpose, the subject, who had always been very easily inducted into the somnambulistic state, and often two or three times in one sitting, could not at this time be rehypnotized. After three vain attempts to go to sleep again, he confessed that, fearing he might be kept at this session so long as to miss a luncheon engagement at 12:30, he had before coming to the room given himself the suggestion to awaken at the sounding of twelve o'clock.

In this experiment we see that decisions made by the subject prior to hypnosis can break up the rapport of the hypnotic session and even prevent its being re-established.

These generalizations have recently been challenged by Professor Wesley Raymond Wells,[10] who has repeated Young's experiments. He used, in all, sixteen subjects who had been hypnotized from one to four times before the session in which they were to attempt to resist certain commands. These items were the same as those Young used: not being able to open the eyes; not being able to unclasp the hands; not being able to recall one's own name; not being able to hear anything except the hypnotist's voice; not being able to raise the feet from the floor; not being able to walk; not being able to feel pain (analgesia) ; having visual hallucinations; completing post-hypnotic suggestions; posthypnotic amnesia. The subjects drew by lot one of the ten items which were written on cards and, according to the experimental plan, agreed to try to resist this item when it was offered with others in the test. The subjects were required (in some instances) to write their expectation of the outcome of their attempted resistance in advance of the experiment. The experimenter did not know in any instance which of the ten commands the subject had determined to resist.

Contrary to Young's results, all sixteen of these subjects were unable to resist the commands of the hypnotist. Ten of them expected in advance to be able to resist the commands but were unsuccessful in doing so. In eleven of the cases the experimenter could not tell

---

[10] Wesley Raymond Wells, "Ability to Resist Artificially Induced Dissociation," *Journal of Abnormal and Social Psychology*, 1940, 35, 261-272. Also see W. R. Wells, "The Extent and Duration of Post-Hypnotic Amnesia," *Journal of Psychology*, 1940, 9, 137-151.

SAMPLES FROM THE EXPERIMENTER'S NOTEBOOK

April 16, 10:00 A.M.; Subject H. During the period all suggestions were carried out with the exception of those pertaining to analgesia.

When the experimenter stuck the subject as usual with a sharp skewer, the subject winced considerably. On repetition of the suggestion and renewed pricking, the painful expression became more pronounced. When challenged as usual, "Do you feel anything?" the subject said, "It hurts." After being awakened, the subject wrote the following report: "I have no definite remembrance of anything after being put in the chair. I have a vague remembrance I was told that I was not to feel it, but was fighting that order and was straining my senses to feel it. The object seemed like a pencil point, rather used and blunted. It was not painful in the least."

In this experiment it is to be noted that not only did the subject react strongly in hypnosis, contrary to the idea of rapport, but the only memory left of a long séance was the one concerning his autosuggestion, remembered despite the experimenter's orders.

The signed statement of the subject handed to the experimenter after waking was as follows: "While in a state of hypnosis I will obey all commands except that of becoming insensible to pain."

April 16, 3:30 P.M.; Subject H. As usual, the experimenter did not know what autosuggestion the subject had given himself until after the session was over, and consequently was somewhat surprised to see that every command was obeyed without any show of resistance. After the session was over, however, the operator was even more surprised to find that the subject remembered everything that had occurred during the whole time. The subject's written report after waking covered two pages and cannot be given in full here. Excerpts are as follows: "Everything in this sitting seemed clear after being wakened, whereas I can scarcely remember anything of the one just previous to it (which had taken place during the forenoon) . . . I was pricked with a pin on both hands, being ordered to move the hand touched. I could not move the 'dead' hand, although I could feel the pin-prick (it did not hurt in the least) . . . I was told that I was one-armed and that my arm had been torn off. I had a terrible sensation of pain at that time in my shoulder where it seemed that the arm had been unjointed when you 'pulled it off.' "

The subject's written instruction to himself was: "While in a hypnotic state I will obey any and all commands except that I won't forget everything or anything that goes on."

In this experiment we note that the self-suggested attitude to remember, assumed in defiance of the direct commands of the experimenter, given in this sitting as well as in all sessions, modified the kind of rapport in hypnosis and frustrated the command to forget all the events after awaking.

which item the subject was trying to resist. Professor Wells's criterion of hypnosis involves this factor of helplessness. He would simply say that those who were able to resist were not completely hypnotized. As he himself points out, if he had got these results on only one subject his argument would have been just as cogent because then these failures could have been attributed to the failure to obtain complete hypnosis in the other cases.

Neither one of these experiments is a good one, although both are valuable to us in making this point: *A good experiment would have varied the conditions leading up to the acceptance or the non-acceptance of the commands.* The variations in prior events should be of such magnitude and diversity that given such-and-such a subject with such-an-such a preconception, influenced in subtle ways by the prestige of the hypnotist, the outcome would be predictable.

Can a subject be hypnotized and then change this rapport to someone else? To test this question it is necessary that the person to be hypnotized make prearrangements with a third person present during the trance. The hypnotizer must not know what the previous arrangements between his subject and the third person have been. It was under these conditions that the following events took place in one of Young's experiments.

May 4, 4:00 P.M.; Subject R. Professor A. present. What happened in this experiment is forecast in the prior autosuggestion, which the operator at the time knew nothing about: "I will submit to hypnosis. When fully hypnotized I will not respond to suggestions from the experimenter, but will respond to A. as follows: when A. says one, relax right arm. When A. says three, I will stand. When A. says four, I will about-face. When A. says five, I will sit down. I will awake when three taps are given by A."

And so the experiment actually went, in spite of the strenuous efforts of the hypnotist to make the subject obey. There was no resistance to the experimenter's suggestions; they were simply ignored entirely.

After hypnosis, the subject remembered nothing that the experimenter had said after talking to him about relaxing, but he did remember having heard A.'s voice. He described his procedure during hypnosis in the following words: when he came into the room, he "just had the suggestion I had given myself on my mind, and kept it on my mind during the hypnosis; I did not have to think of it during the hypnosis—I was not thinking of anything. I had no difficulty in knowing what the signals meant."

289

Conclusion. Here, apparently, we have a genuine hypnosis void of rapport with the one doing the hypnotizing, but showing rapport with one who had been previously selected by the subject.

Professor Young considers the subjects whose records are given above as completely hypnotized as any he has ever worked with. If they were, then the conclusion must be: *An experimenter can hypnotize a subject who thereupon can be out of rapport with the experimenter and come back into rapport only if, as, and when he has determined to do so before being hypnotized.*

5. POSTHYPNOTIC SUGGESTION

It is well known that the hypnotist can make an appointment with a hypnotized subject during a trance. Upon waking the subject does not recall the date, but he generally turns up at the time appointed, especially if the appointment is made within the next few days. With some subjects, it is reported, private arrangements have been made in advance to have them involved in some interesting occupation or diversion; but still the appointments are almost invariably kept. The conditions under which observations of this kind have been made are uncontrolled. We are not certain how much a hypnotist has been impressed by the instances in which appointments have been kept and how many instances have been forgotten where the subject is somehow prevented from appearing. Perhaps in many instances the apparently attractive diversion was not a diversion at all. It may have irked the subject to an extent that an excuse for discontinuing the activity was a welcome escape. Our only answers to these questions must come from the laboratory where control over these factors can be exercised.

Patten[11] again has contributed to our knowledge of hypnosis here. He gave a posthypnotic suggestion to eighteen totally amnesic subjects. His testing schedule follows:

2 were tested immediately	2 were tested after 15 days
2 were tested after 1 day	2 were tested after 20 days
2 were tested after 3 days	2 were tested after 25 days
2 were tested after 5 days	1 was tested after 30 days
2 were tested after 10 days	1 was tested after 33 days

11 E. F. Patten. "The Duration of Post-Hypnotic Suggestion," *Journal of Abnormal and Social Psychology*, 1930, 25, 319-334.

This procedure leaves much to be desired in that the sampling error must be considerable, only one or two subjects being used after each interval. A better plan would have been to divide the subjects into two or three groups of six or nine subjects each. But it will remain for some other experimenter to rid this experiment of the sampling error. There are other features of Patten's experiment that make it valuable even if we are not quite certain that a repetition of it would show *precisely* the same result.

Control group. The same suggestion was given to a group of sixteen subjects who were never hypnotized at any time during the course of the experiment. They constitute the control group without which it would be impossible to interpret the findings based on the hypnotized subjects alone. These subjects were spaced like the experimental group at the various periods up to thirty-three days. None was tested immediately, since there were only sixteen in the control group.

Method. The suggestion given was most cleverly conceived. All of the subjects were shown thirty words. The words were exposed by means of an automatic device which ensured that each item in the list would be in view for the same length of time. The subject's attention was maintained during the exposure of the list by informing him, while he was awake, that one word would be repeated. He was expected to report on the word repeated at the conclusion of the experimental sitting. The repeated word was always near the end of the list, its predecessor was always near the beginning, so that for the important part of the experiment, the subject was actively looking for something in the words that were exposed.

But now the clever part. In the list, between the first and second occurrence of the word that was repeated, were the names of three animals. In the trance which preceded all of this, the experimental group was told that each time the name of an animal appeared, they would depress the index finger of the right hand without being aware that they were doing so. The finger was placed in a small loop connected by means of strings and levers to a kymograph so that its slightest movement would be recorded. The whole hand was screened from the subject. It should be remembered that the subjects were awake when they saw the list of words. The suggestion had been given in a hypnotic trance preceding the whole affair; thirty-three days previously in the case of one subject and at the intervals shown above for the others.

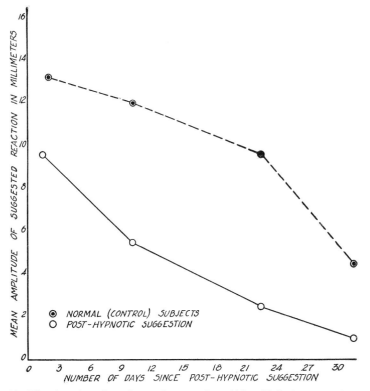

FIG. 62.—The duration of posthypnotic suggestion. (After Hull, Courtesy of Appleton-Century-Crofts, Inc.)

For the control group the procedure was the same except that this group was never hypnotized; hence the finger depression would be susceptible to the ordinary laws of forgetting.

The strength of the obedience to the suggestion was assumed to be proportional to the extent of the finger movement. This movement was measured in millimeters from the kymograph tape.

292

Results. The mean reaction in millimeters for each subject for each day was found. The means of the two subjects at each interval were averaged for the dependent variable. Because so few subjects were used, the original curves are very erratic. But Clark Hull[12] has shown how it is possible to pool the results for days 0, 1, and 3, which are plotted at day 1; days 5, 10, and 15 plotted at 10; days 20, 25 plotted at 23; and days 30 and 33 plotted at 31, into a composite for six subjects rather than two at each plotted point. This graphically reduces the data to the form suggested earlier—larger groups spaced farther apart—and it compensates in a measure for a lack of planning on the part of the experimenter.

The results show that there is a clear-cut difference between the amplitude of finger movement for the hypnotized and the control subjects, but the *posthypnotic suggestion is not as effective as ordinary waking instruction in producing a finger movement.*

Conclusion. On the basis of this experiment we are forced to conclude that the reports relating to subjects who invariably, and on the minute, keep appointments that have been made days ahead even in the face of difficult and, at times, frustrating circumstances, have been grossly exaggerated. The experiment leaves much to be desired in the way of subjects tested at each interval, but it is clear that *posthypnotic suggestion is not independent of the ordinary laws of forgetting.*

Summary. Bass's experiment showed that hypnosis and sleep were entirely different phenomena, but it did not show that there was any difference between a subject awake and hypnotized. There is a difference. Patten's experiment showed that the amnesia reported is a fact only in so far as the subject's ability to report is concerned. Measured in the effect of practice during hypnosis, there is no amnesia. Young showed that rapport was not essential to hypnosis. His observations also show that amnesia is not essential, because subjects can still be hypnotized according to other criteria and remember perfectly what has happened during the trance. Patten also

2 Clark Hull, *Hypnosis and Suggestibility,* D. Appleton-Century Company, Inc., New York, 1933, p. 163.

showed, in another experiment, that posthypnotic suggestions are forgotten as things are normally forgotten. Other experiments not cited here show that catalepsy is not essential to hypnosis. In a word, none of the usual phenomena that are said to differentiate hypnosis are actually necessary. As a result of an extended analysis of all the experimental literature on the subject, Hull concludes that *there is not a single item which is characteristic of hypnosis that cannot to some extent be produced in the waking state.* When the experimenter's suggestions and commands are accepted uncritically by the subject, he is hypnotized. People who are the most suggestible[13] while awake are not always the best hypnotic subjects, however. The subject's own preconceived notions of hypnosis enter the picture in a way that is not entirely clear at the present time.

6. REGRESSION DURING HYPNOSIS

One of the most dramatic parts of a hypnotic demonstration occurs when the hypnotist suggests to the subject that he has now become a child. If the subject is given a pencil and told to write his name, his efforts seem authentically childish. The name slants uphill or downhill and the lettering is scrawling and uncertain. He will behave childishly in other ways; he may giggle, take up the uninhibited wiggling postures of the child, ask many obvious—to an adult—questions, or otherwise behave in a most youthful manner. The observer is impressed and he feels that he is truly seeing the subject as the subject was when he was a child. The scientific question is, of course, whether or not this is an adult acting in the fashion that he thinks a child should act, or whether the subject truly regresses to a childish level of mental development. Fortunately at least a partial answer to this question can be had through the employment of standardized intelligence tests; for these tests can give us a precise mental age and hence show the level of mental development at which the subject is operating. This ingenious technique was used by Young.[14]

13 As a matter of fact, there probably is no general waking suggestibility. People who are extremely suggestible under one set of conditions may be only faintly suggestible under another.

14 Paul Campbell Young, "Hypnotic Regression—Fact or Artifact?" *Journal of Abnormal and Social Psychology*, 1940, 35, 273-278.

Method. EXPERIMENTAL GROUP. Nine subjects were hypnotized individually and were informed that they were three years old and were told that they would remain three years old until they were awakened. After the subjects had asserted that they were only three, they were given the Stanford-Binet intelligence test. Following this they were brought out of the trance and the test was administered once more to determine their normal adult intelligence-test level.

CONTROL SUBJECTS. Seven unhypnotizable subjects were treated in the same manner except, of course, that they were not hypnotized but were told to imagine they were three and to respond to the test items as they thought a three-year-old would do. Unfortunately it was not possible to obtain adult intelligence-test levels for all of these subjects.

Results. The mental ages for the hypnotized subjects during the time when they had presumably regressed to their own three-year level varied from four years and seven months to six years and nine months, with an average of five years and eleven months. Now of course it would be possible for this to have been their true mental age level when their chronological age was three. It could happen if they had been unusually bright, but it would have meant that their average I.Q. was 198. Their average I.Q. on the adult test was, however, only 102 and this fact, even allowing for discrepancies between childhood and adult test results, rather completely eliminates the possibility that the childhood I.Q. was this high. The safest conclusion that could be drawn from these data is that the hypnotized subjects did not truly return to their three-year level.

The story for the control subjects was essentially the same. Their mental ages when they pretended to be three years old varied from four years and five months to six years and nine months, with an average at five years and five months. Although these normal subjects seemed to approximate the three-year level a little more closely than the hypnotized subjects did, their results are still implausible. Their calculated I.Q. at the three-year level is 179, whereas their adult level seemed to be just a bit above 100.

Summary. The results of this experiment suggest that intellectual regression during the hypnotic trance is not a real return to the basic mental level of some earlier age. Neither the hypnotic subjects who "regressed" to the age of three nor the normals who pretended that they were three were able to act like three-year-olds. Mentally they behaved like five-and-a-half- or six-year-olds. Since the hypnotized subjects certainly did no better, and possibly did more poorly in regressing, one cannot but suspect that the regressed hypnotized subject is simply an adult acting the way he thinks he would act if he were a child.

7. ANESTHESIA

The fact that hypnotized people can be made to feel too warm or too cold at ordinary room temperatures or to writhe with pain when an imaginary cigarette is "burning" their fingers brings up a troublesome question in both waking suggestion and hypnosis. Does the subject really sense the warmth or is he just a good fellow who agrees with the experimenter because it is too much trouble to be negative? It is not beyond the bounds of probability that a verbal stimulus can actually cause an individual to sense a warmth where there is none that can be measured by a thermometer. If we instruct a subject to imagine a blue cube on the desk in front of him, there are some people who can imagine the cube so well that it has all the characteristics of a real cube and actually can be manipulated in certain ways. All the time they are wide awake, of course. It has been reported that electricians whose screw drivers slip sometimes feel a shock where no actual shock was possible; the same thing has been reported in conditioning experiments where the sound of a buzzer actually caused the subject to feel a shock even when there was no shock administered.

But how about the reverse of these phenomena? Is a tactual stimulus administered under the suggestion of anesthesia in an arm or leg actually felt, or does the subject just deny having felt it?

An old parlor trick which everyone must have seen at one time or another helps to give one answer to this question. If an individual extends his two hands in front of him with both thumbs pointing down—i.e., with the backs of the hands together—and one arm is crossed over the other at the wrist so that the palms can be made to come in contact and the fingers are intertwined, then if the arms are brought back to the body and the hands still locked together are rotated so that the thumbs are uppermost, it is extremely difficult to tell whether a given finger belongs to the right or to the left hand. If one hand were to be anesthetized by hypnotic suggestion, then it would be hard for the subject to fool either the experimenter or himself when the fingers were touched in haphazard order. If the hands were simply placed side by side, it would be easy for the subject to act as though he did not feel any touch made on the supposedly anesthetized hand. Professor Pattie[15] has made the "position of the Japanese illusion," as it is called, serve a useful scientific end in a study of the genuineness of hypnotically produced anesthesia. If he had simply touched the hypnotized subject's fingers when they were in the confusion position and then asked for a report on whether the touch had been sensed, it would have been relatively easy for the subject to have made incipient movements of the fingers, finally hitting on the one just touched and by that means arriving at a judgment of right or left; from that he could infer that he should say "felt" or nothing at all. But Professor Pattie had a method by which he could completely disconcert such too cooperative subjects. He had them count the number of stimulations they sensed. In a series of touches, which came at the rate of about two a second, he kept them so completely occupied that they didn't have time to cheat. If the "anesthesia" were genuine then they would be able to count only the contacts on the unanesthetized hands; but if they simply failed to report on what they thought was the anesthetized hand, the confusion position would ensure their making an appreciable number of errors.

An anesthesia of the right hand and arm was suggested, and the sensitivity was tested by pinching, pressing, and pricking the subject's hand. If he declared that he sensed nothing, he was then blindfolded by tying a thick newspaper around his head. The subject's hands were then put into the position of the Japanese illusion, and the following instructions were given:

15 Frank A. Pattie, Jr., "The Genuineness of Hypnotically Produced Anaesthesia of the Skin," *American Journal of Psychology*, 1937, 59, 435-443.

You can feel nothing with your right hand. You will now receive a number of touches, and since you can feel nothing with your right hand, they will be felt only on the fingers of the left hand. Count the touches received by the fingers of your left and report the number as soon as they cease. No finger will be touched twice in succession. Do not estimate, but count as well as you can.

The touches were delivered by the experimenter, who touched the fingers of the left hand, and an assistant, who touched the fingers of the right hand. The stimulators were pieces of rubber taken from ordinary large rubber erasers and with dimensions of 1.5 × 0.5 (the surface applied to the skin) × 2 cm. They were attached to thin strips of brass (11 × 1.5 × 0.03 cm.), which in turn were fastened to wooden sticks of a size convenient for the hand. The brass strips projected over the end of the wooden stick 3.5 cm. A wire fixed above the brass strip marked the amount of bending of the strip necessary to produce a pressure of 75 grams. Care was taken to insure that the experimenter's and the assistant's touches were equally intense. The experimenter's touches were applied at a variable rate, which did not exceed 2 a second. A stop watch was used to time the touches so that the maximum rate might not be exceeded. . . .

Ten series of touches were applied to each subject. Each series consisted of 20 sets of stimulations ranging in number from 11 to 30 applications on the critical hand. The order of these 20 stimulations was determined by chance (numbered cards were used and shuffled before each series was made up). Five series were given in the first hour of experimenting, and five in the second hour, which came after two or three days. To be sure that the subject knew what he was to do, he was first given 11 or 12 touches on the left hand, while the assistant also was touching him. His report on this first stimulation was not recorded.

Subjects were scored thus. The errors made in each of the 20 reports in a series were added without regard to sign (e.g., the error was 4 if the subject called 11 touches either 7 or 15). If the subject said that he lost count, the particular number on which he lost count was repeated at the end of the series. Losing count was infrequent.

There were five hypnotized subjects and in the first series they made forty-four errors on the average. Their results are shown by the solid curve in Figure 62. Of course these data are useless unless we have a comparison group; hence the whole experiment was repeated with fifteen subjects who were awake, but in other respects comparable to the hypnotized group. Their results are shown by the broken curve in Figure 63. It is perfectly obvious that, taken as a whole, there is no basis for the conclusion that the suggestion actually made the one hand as anesthetized as some drug would have done. In contrast, Pattie found that when the hands were clearly separated the subjects made practically no errors. As a matter of fact, the hand which had been anesthetized by the suggestion employed could

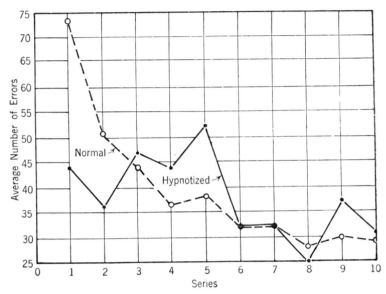

Fig. 63.—Comparison between number of errors of identification made by hypnotized and nonhypnotized subjects when the hands are in the confusion position.

be pricked or slapped or pinched and still the subject gave no overt evidence of having sensed the stimulus. But are the various implicit signs of painful stimulation, such as heart rate and galvanic skin response, inhibited?

Sears[16] has made an experiment which answers these specific questions.

On numerous occasions he produced anesthesia in one leg of seven different subjects. There were 101 experimental sessions with the seven subjects. The other leg of the subject was stimulated without suggestion of anesthesia and constituted a control. The painful stimulus was the prick of a needle administered in a special way so

16 R. R. Sears, "An Experimental Study of Hypnotic Anesthesia," *Journal of Experimental Psychology*, 1932, 15, 1-22.

that the exact time and vigor of the stimulations could be recorded pneumatically on a kymograph tape. (See Chapter Thirteen.)

The facial grimace of the subject in the region of the eyes was recorded if it occurred. This operation was accomplished by attaching a lever by means of adhesive tape to the left cheek, just below the eye. The lever actuated a Marey tambour, another tambour re-

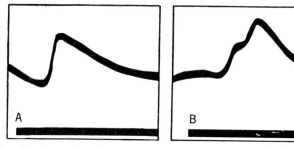

Fig. 64.—A tracing of one of Levine's galvanic records. In the figure to the left there was no suggestion of anesthesia as the skin was punctured with a needle at A. In the record to the right with suggested anesthesia, there is still a response when the same stimulus is applied at B. (After Levine, *Bulletin* of Johns Hopkins Hospital, 1930, 46, 333.)

converted the resulting air pressure variations to mechanical movements which were recorded by means of a stylus. Breathing records and records of the galvanic skin response and pulse were also recorded. (See Chapter Thirteen.)

We have, then, the verbal response of the subject and, correlated with this record, the automatically recorded grimace, breathing, pulse and galvanic skin reflex, including some items under voluntary control and some which are not, although they differ in the degree to which they can be kept under control.

Results. In general, considerably more reduction was observed in the voluntary than in the involuntary segments of behavior examined (verbal reports of pain and facial grimace were practically eliminated), but even in the galvanic skin reflex there was a suppression of the effect in about 20 per cent of the stimulations. In waking, none of these things could be modified to any extent. There is evidence, then, that the reactions to painful stimuli are not only modified verbally but are also changed somewhat in other segments as well.

Summary of the chapter. The intent of this chapter has been to show that behavior can be controlled by the use of verbal stimuli and other forms of communication involving gesturing. Totally aside from the specific words which are used in various situations, the person who gives the suggestion is important in determining the outcome. A schoolteacher, for instance, has greater prestige with school children than another child or even a stranger. In all social situations these prestige factors seem to operate, as, for example, in the field of literature, where we showed there was a relationship between the prestige of an author and the rating of a literary passage which was falsely attributed to him. It is also important to distinguish between prestige suggestion of the kind we have been talking about and nonprestige suggestion in which another person is not involved but where a situation indirectly leads to a certain result as was demonstrated in Williams's experiment. The ultimate effectiveness of suggestion is found in the phenomenon known as hypnosis. As Bass's experiment shows, the states of being hypnotized and being asleep are totally different from each other as both are different from being awake. The next experiment shows that, although it is possible to produce amnesia in a hypnotized subject, one does not actually at that time eliminate what he has learned from wherever it happens to be located deep in his organism. Post-hypnotic amnesia is a blocking phenomenon. The next section on rapport shows that there is nothing mysterious at all about the peculiar relationship that exists between the hypnotizer and the one hypnotized, and in connection with the work of other authors who have obtained different results we conclude that additional information is needed in this field. One puzzling phenomenon has to do with the production of anesthesia under hypnosis. The question has always been: How is it possible to burn or to lacerate tissue while a person is hypnotized and still have him report that he feels no pain? Sears's experiment shows that physiological effects over which the subject has no voluntary control actually do take place although they are suppressed, and that hypnotic anesthesia is therefore not the same thing as an anesthesia produced by drugs, where it is actually a blocking of the nervous impulses.

Thus we are left with the generalization that hypnosis is a special kind of suggestion phenomenon. Nonprestige suggestion is probably not related to hypnosis at all, and prestige suggestion is not related to it in any *precise* way that has yet been discovered.[17] The subject's own preconceived notions regarding hypnosis profoundly influence his reactions. Persons are not equally susceptible to different kinds of suggestion. It is not possible, therefore, to speak of a general suggestibility nor of a general hypnotizability, and the relation between them. Hypnosis is different from waking only in the heightened susceptibility to prestige suggestion, but no point can be undisputably located on one side of which we could say that a person is hypnotized and on the other that he was awake. In this respect hypnosis is not unique among psychological phenomena.

[17] Waking suggestions to the effect that the subject will fall in a certain direction may be an exception to this generalization. Hull reports that practically all subjects who exhibit an acceptance of a suggestion to fall are good hypnotics.

CHAPTER FIFTEEN

PERCEPTION

Perceiving is a process of reacting to the physical changes of our environment as signs or signals of events which have adjustmental significance for us. We do not react to noise as a simple noise; we react to it as a noise of *some thing* coming from *some place*. It is the ringing of a telephone; not just an auditory sensation; or it is an auto horn sounding a warning, and not a noise of a certain pitch. The changing patterns of lights that stimulate us on the highway are not merely reds and blues and greens and yellows. They are configurations informing us that we are approaching a gas station, a restaurant, or a traffic light. We react to the stimuli, not in and of themselves, but as indicators of something more.

We make these perceptual reactions not only because we have sense organs which are responsive to different kinds of physical energy, but because we are capable of learning. As infants we react to physical stimuli only as physical stimuli, but as we come into contact with the stimulus objects they become defined in terms of their significance for us in the act of getting along in the world. The stimulus acquires meaning and begins to serve as a guide for our behavior.

The act of perceiving is a very complex phenomenon, often determined by the interaction of many stimuli about which the perceiver can report very little. It is the purpose of the present chapter to describe some experiments which point up the basic nature of perceptual reaction, and which, by isolating various aspects of the ordinarily complex stimulating situation, show how some of our perceptual responses are determined.

1. PERCEPTUAL CONSTANCY

If you are walking in the sunlight with a companion and pass into the shadow cast by a tree, a very marked reduction in the physical energy of the illumination occurs. Your partner's white shirt which reflected a large amount of light in the sunlight now reflects much less light, and the energy of the stimulus falling upon your retina is far less than it was a moment before. Yet even though there is a great change in the intensity of the physical stimulus, there is no corresponding change in how you see or perceive the shirt. It does not seem to change from a fleecy white color to a dull gray; it remains the same white shirt. Again, the grass within the shadow of the tree does not appear to be a dark green while that in the sunlight is a bright green; it is the same grass and of the same shade of green. The fact that the actual energy of the shadowed and unshadowed grass is different is illustrated by what you would do if you were painting the scene. You would mix in some black or dark blue to make your shadowed green.

Thus the psychological fact is that, though the stimulus may change in physical value, the object is perceived as remaining the same. To the type of phenomenon described above, the name *color constancy*[1] has been given.

The precise manner in which color constancy operates was investigated in the laboratory by Katz.[2]

Method. The plan of the experiment was essentially simple. One color, a gray, was placed in a shadow and another was overshadowed. The subject was asked to adjust the brightness of one of these until it looked exactly like the other. This was done twice. During the first part of the experiment the subject looked through a screen which permitted him to see only the color patches and none of the background. He could not even see that one was in a shadow and the other was not. This type of matching would force the subject to match the physical energy of the two stimuli. During the second part of the experiment the screen was removed while the matching was done. The subject could see that one color was shadowed and the other was not. During this situation the psychological factors which make for color constancy are brought into play.

The color stimuli were produced by color wheels. A color wheel is a circular metal plate attached to the rotating shaft of a motor.

[1] The word "color" is used to refer to blacks, grays, and whites as well as those colors which possess hues such as red, green, blue, or yellow.

[2] David Katz, *The World of Color* (Translated by R. B. McLeod and C. W. Fox), Kegan Paul, Trench, Trubner and Co. Ltd. London, 1935, XVI + 300.

A disk of white paper and one of black paper, each of which has a cut from the center to the outside, can then be interlocked and placed upon the wheel. When the wheel is revolved rapidly the separate black and white colors disappear and one sees only a homogenous gray, just as one does not see the blades of a fan when it

Fig. 65.—The arrangement of color wheels in Katz's experiment.

revolves. The proportion of black to white can be easily changed, and obviously the more black there is, the darker the mixture becomes. Katz used two of these color wheels, with a screen between so that one was illuminated fully by the light coming in from the window, and the other was in the shadow cast by the screen. An approximation of Katz's experimental setup is shown in Figure 65.

Part I. Matching when only the two disks were seen. In the first part of the experiment the subject looked through two small peepholes and could see only the color wheels. None of the background was visible and the subject could not tell that one wheel was in a shadow and the other was not. The shadowed disk was then made completely white and the subject was asked to adjust the unshadowed disk until it looked like the shadowed one. Since the unshadowed one was in a brighter light, a large amount of black had to be added to it in order to obtain a match. Actually the subject was satisfied that the brightness of the two stimuli was alike when almost 99 per cent of unshadowed wheel surface was black. This means that the *physical energy* coming from the two wheels and falling upon the retina of the eye was the same, or nearly so, when one wheel was completely white and the other was almost completely black.

Part II. Matching when the disks and background were visible. The same procedure was repeated with the peephole screen removed, so that the subject could readily see each wheel against its background. Under these circumstances he put only about 70 per cent black in the unshadowed wheel to match the 100 per cent white of the shadowed wheels.

This is the constancy effect. The matching has not been done for physical brightness; for if it had been, then the observer would have placed approximately the same amount of black on the wheels under both conditions. Instead the observer has partially compensated for the fact that one of the wheels stands in a shadow and the other is under full illumination. This compensation was made possible by the fact that the respective backgrounds were visible.

The observer is equating the things *out there* so that they will be alike regardless of the illumination in which they may be placed; he is not equating for physical intensity.

His equating is not, of course, perfect. He does not make the two objects out there exactly alike; for if he did he would have placed 100 per cent of white on the unshadowed wheel. The reader may have noted similar tendencies in another field in which constancy operates, and that is in the size of objects. Distant objects subtend smaller angles on the retina of the eye than do the same objects close to us, but size constancy operates and they do not seem to diminish in size when they are far away. Yet occasionally when we view the world from some height, from a plane, a mountaintop, or a tall building, it may look like a doll's world.

Summary of the experiment. Katz's experiment is a simple demonstration of the fact that we react to things as we think they should be rather than in the precise way they stimulate our sense organs. When his subjects could see the color wheels and the backgrounds, and when they could see only two wheels, their matching was different. Psychological equality was not the same as physical equality.

This process of reacting to objects according to their structural characteristics and not according to the precise way they stimulate our sense organs is a basic characteristic of perception. We do it unthinkingly. The objects of the world about us are perceived as remaining relatively unchanged under a variety of conditions, and they remain that way without conscious effort on our part.

2. LEARNING TO ESTIMATE RANGE

An efficient antiaircraft gunner must not only be able to aim his gun with accuracy but, if his fire is not to be wasted, he must have some knowledge of the distance of the target from him. During the past war the physicists developed many effective instruments for giving correct range, but data from such instruments could not readily be made available to each gunner. In most instances men operating machine guns were required to make judgments about the range of approaching aircraft without the aid of range-finding equipment. The decision as to when to open fire was an important one, for if it was made too early, the ammunition in the magazine might be expended before the plane was within effective range of the gun. If the gunner waited too long, the plane's bomb might have been released, perhaps with disastrous accuracy, before hits could be scored on the plane.

It is not a very difficult matter to estimate the distance of an object from oneself if the object is within a few hundred yards of our location. Within this distance we have available for our use an extremely valuable cue, the fact that the object will produce an image on the retina of one eye slightly different from that produced upon the retina of the other. This difference in the characteristic of the two images is caused by the fact that the position of one eye with respect to the object is slightly different from that of the other eye. It is called *retinal disparity*. However, when the object is beyond four or five hundred yards from the observer, these differences become too slight to serve as a cue for depth perception. One is forced to rely upon the type of cues that the painter uses to create the illusion of depth in his pictures; such cues as size of the object, its height in the visual field, and its degree of clarity. Since the efficient gunner was expected to open fire when the plane was nearly a mile away, he was, of course, working at ranges well beyond the point where retinal disparity is a cue for depth. For this reason errors in determining when to open fire were great, and psychologists, as experts in the field of learning and perception, were requested to aid in training gunners to become more proficient in this job.[3]

Method. Gunners with no previous sea duty who were assigned to the twenty-millimeter machine gun were instructed in using the circular reticle of their gun sight as an aid in determining when a plane was at an open-fire range—actually a distance of 1,700 yards from them. The instructor pointed out that as a plane approached it would seem to grow larger, and when it occupied a certain proportion of the reticle it would be 1,700 yards from the gunner. One of the planes the gunners might see would occupy one third of the reticle and another, because it was larger, two fifths of the diameter. They were also shown a chart which illustrated the size relationship of each of the planes to the gun-sight reticle when the planes were 1,700 yards away.

On the following day the men were taken to a gunnery range and given a test to determine how well they could estimate when a plane was at opening range. Each man took his place at a gun and tracked or followed the target plane in the reticle of his sight, keeping it centered in the circle. On the test trials the plane flew in over

[3] M. H. Rogers, J. J. Sprol, M. S. Viteles, H. A. Voss, and D. D. Wickens, Memorandum on evaluation of methods of training in estimating a fixed opening range. OSRD Report No. 5765.

the sea directly toward the men, and during the trial the men were required to estimate when the plane was at opening range.

Their estimations were made in the following manner: As the plane flew toward the men, letters of the alphabet were called out over the range loud-speaker. Since a range finder was directed at the plane at all times, the experimenters knew the exact range of the plane when each letter was called. The gunners noted the letter which was being called when they thought the plane was 1,700 yards away and wrote it down on a card. Afterward the cards were collected and by noting the letter which was written down the amount of error made by each man on each trial could be determined.

Six test runs were conducted. During three of these the plane flew a simulated torpedo attack run, coming in from 50 to 100 feet above the water. During the other three runs it flew in at an altitude of approximately 2,000 feet.

Following these tests the training procedure was begun. The procedure consisted simply of requiring the subjects to track the plane in their gun-sight reticle as it flew toward them and they were told when the plane was at the ranges of 5,000, 4,000, 2,500, 1,700 and 1,000 yards. Three such trials were given.

On the following day a number of these trained men were returned to the same range and were tested on three low-level and three high-level runs of the plane. On this day the letters called out were different from those used on the first day, so that the letters which were correct during the first days' pretest were not correct on this post-test.

There were eighty-two men who were used as subjects on the first day, and forty-seven of them were given the post-test on the second day. Actually not all of the eighty-two or forty-seven men were tested on the same day; they were taken in groups of about seven each on a number of different days.

Results. The basic data which indicate the performance of the men before and after training are shown in Figure 66. The statistic employed is called the Mean Point of Estimation (MPE). It is, in other words, the average actual range of the plane when the men considered it to be 1,700 yards away. During the pretraining test there was a very marked tendency for the men to *underestimate* the range of the plane, that is, they thought it was at 1,700 yards when it was considerably farther away. They made an error of nearly 500 yards in the torpedo runs and of 800 yards on the medium-altitude runs. This tendency to underestimate can be translated in combat terminology into a tendency to open fire too soon, and this action was generally characteristic of inexperienced gunners. These results indicate that this kind of behavior in combat was not due solely to overanxiousness, but was partly a result of perceptual errors.

On the tests given the day following training the performance of the men was markedly superior to the pretraining performance. The mean error for the torpedo runs was reduced to nearly zero and the median altitude error declined to a little over 200 yards. In other words, this simple training procedure was very effective in reducing the perceptual errors of these untrained gunners.

There are certain other data from this experiment which throw light on the stimuli which determine the perceptual reactions of the individual. It will be recalled that the data were collected over a number of days, with about seven subjects performing each day. As one might expect, the degree of visibility varied somewhat from day to day, the weather being clear, bright, and sunny on some days, and somewhat hazy on other days. Presumably this variation in visibility should not affect the estimation, for the men were directed to pay attention to the relation of the size of the plane to the gunsight reticle, and visibility should not affect this relationship. Actually weather conditions had a marked effect on the extent of errors. On days when the visibility was excellent the tendency to underestimate (to "open fire" too soon) was far greater than on the days of poor visibility.

Another condition which produced variation in the judgmental error was the length of run the plane made as it came toward the gunners. On some of the test trials the experimenters would begin calling letters when the plane was 5,000 yards from the observer, on others when it was 4,400 yards, and on still others when it was 3,200 yards away. Obviously, again, the range at which the letter calling was started could not have influenced the appropriate size relations at 1,700 yards, but the effect upon judgments was marked.

310

The farther away the plane when the calling of letters started, the greater was the magnitude of error.

One last factor that should be mentioned is the difference in the magnitude of error in the high-level runs as compared with the low-level runs. These differences are shown in Figure 66. Plane size from wing tip to wing tip would be unaltered by the altitude of the plane, but the error in one case is greater than in the other.

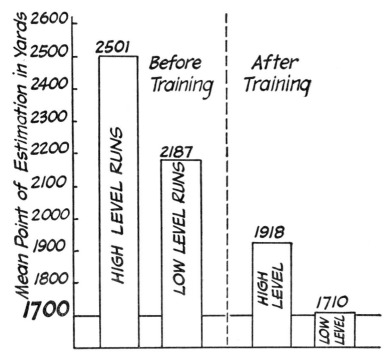

FIG. 66.—The average point of estimation before training and after training. The men were attempting to judge when the plane was 1,700 yards away.

Summary. The data of this experiment have served to indicate the interdependence of stimulating conditions in their effect upon our perceptual reactions. The subjects were presumably reacting to a single cue—the apparent size of the object—but clarity of the image, the duration of the time it was reacted to, and the postural position of the subject (looking up at the plane in the high-level runs, or looking straight ahead in the torpedo runs) were stimuli to which the subjects unwittingly reacted. This is ordinarily the case in our perceptual reaction; we respond not to a single stimulus but to the interrelationships of a number of them. Consider, for example, how the taste of lukewarm coffee differs from that of hot coffee, or crisp celery differs from the wilted variety. Taste we consider as being determined by our taste receptors, but our perceptional reactions are made not only to chemical stimulation but to temperature and muscular feel as well.

The experiment has also demonstrated the ability of the individual to learn to make new spatial discriminations. The experiment is, of course, limited; the retention period is short—only over a period of twenty-four hours—and the person may not be said to have learned to estimate range in general, but only to recognize when a plane is at one particular range.

3. AUDITORY LOCALIZATION

When someone calls us unexpectedly or when the horn of an auto is sounded, we can locate the source of the sound with ease. Unless we are in a location where confusing echoes are apt to arise, we seldom hesitate because of an inability to determine the position from which the sound arose; we turn our heads to the right or left as the occasion demands. Though we have been doing this sort of thing for many years, and doing it with remarkable accuracy, most people cannot describe how they are able to do so. What is the difference between the sound we localize to the right of us and the one we localize to our left? About all we can say is that one sound seems to come from the right and the other from the left. This explains nothing. The identification of the cues which we use in locating sounds can be discovered only through laboratory experimentation.

It has been shown in many experiments that subjects have considerable difficulty in locating sounds which are in a plane vertical to the ground and bisect the subject's body, a plane called the sagittal plane. Sounds at ear level in a plane parallel to the ground are, however, easily located. This fact can serve as a first clue to the solution of the problem.

The geometry of these situations is illustrated in Figure 67. A sound source is equidistant from each ear, when it is in the sagittal plane, but of unequal distance from the two ears when it is in the horizontal plane. This means that the characteristics of the sounds would be the same for each ear in the sagittal plane, but not in the horizontal. These differences which are present in the horizontal

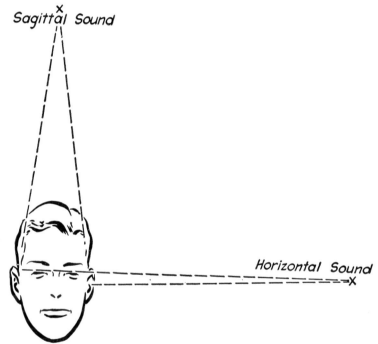

FIG. 67.—The distance relation to the two ears when the sound is in the sagittal and horizontal planes.

plane must be the factors that make localization accurate in that plane, and the lack of such differences makes localization poor in the saggittal plane.

One manner in which the sound characteristics would differ in the horizontal plane is in the fact that the sound must reach one ear slightly before it reaches the other. Because the speed of sound is great, and the width of the head small, this time difference must be of very short duration and the question can be raised as to whether or not the human organism is able to discriminate such small time differences. This question was investigated by Trimble.[4]

Method. The first technical problem that must be solved before the experiment can be conducted is to find a way of having the sound reach one ear before it reaches the other without varying any other factor such as a difference in intensity with which it will reach the two ears. This can be done if the experimenter employs two identical sound sources, each with the same intensity, and each the same distance from its respective ear. By doing this it can be arranged to have a sound reach one ear before the other by any amount of time the experimenter desires, while all other factors will remain constant. When this is done in the laboratory and both sounds occur simultaneously, the subject will report that he hears only one sound.

Trimble employed a restraining device which kept the subject's head absolutely motionless. Exactly 72 centimeters from each ear an ordinary commercial spark plug was located, and the sound which he used in the experiment was the slight noise the spark made as it jumped the gap between the two poles of the spark plug. Each spark plug was connected to a different electrical circuit in another room so that each one could be activated independently of the other. In this other room the experimenter also located his timing device. This device was a pendulum which, as it fell, would trip two switches, one of which sent the current into the spark plug at the left ear, while the other sent current into the spark plug at the right ear. By changing the distance separating the two switches along the arc of fall of the pendulum it was possible to have both spark plugs fire simultaneously or for one to precede the other by any desired time interval. The time intervals used were, of course, extremely small, so small that instead of using a second as his time unit Trimble used a millisecond. A millisecond is one thousandth of a second.

During the experiment the seven subjects were seated in the apparatus with the room darkened and told to listen for the sound

4 O. C. Trimble, "Some Temporal Aspects of Sound Localization," *Psychological Monograph*, 1928, 28, 172-231.

and then to report the location from which it seemed to come. The experimenter then systematically varied the time relation between the firing of the two spark plugs. Sometimes they would fire together, at other times the right one would lead, and again the left one would lead. The time by which one led the other varied from zero milliseconds to 2.76 milliseconds.

Results. When the sounds to the two ears were given simultaneously or nearly simultaneously, the subjects reported that a single sound was heard which seemed to come from in front of them. As the time differential increased they showed more and more of a tendency to locate the sound as coming from the side which fired first. When the point was reached where the separation in time between the two stimuli was .16 milliseconds, there was a consistent tendency for the sound to be heard on the side of the lead noise. As the separations in the time became greater and greater, the sound source seemed to travel back toward the ear. By 2.76 milliseconds the sound was located as coming from a point opposite one ear or another by all but two subjects. When the separation time was increased beyond this point, the illusion of a single sound was lost and the subjects heard two separate sounds.

Summary. This experiment has clearly indicated that time differences between the moment a sound strikes one ear and the moment it strikes the other can be used as a cue for the location of a sound source. By the technique of eliminating every other possible difference in the sound other than time, and varying time systematically, the experiment has arrived at its result. It does not follow, of course, that this is the only cue which is used in sound localization. Actually there are other experiments somewhat along this same line which indicate that the differences in intensity between the sounds which strike the two ears are also a factor. There are others as well, but they are too complicated to be considered here.

Perhaps the most remarkable aspect of the experiment is the fact that the human organism can react to time differences as small as .16 millisecond. Expressed in terms of a second this gives a figure of .00016 second, an amazingly small figure. It is on such minor physical differences as these that many of our very adaptive perceptual reactions to the environment depend.

4. AUDITORY REVERSAL

"Suppose," writes Paul Thomas Young, "a master surgeon could transplant the right inner ear to the left side of the head." Suppose that the auditory nerve could be stretched so that none of the neural connections would be disturbed. And suppose that at the same time the left ear were in the same manner transferred to the right side. Now an operation of this kind is entirely out of question, so Young proposed to reverse the auditory field by means of an instrument called a *reversing pseudophone*. Two trumpets for the hard of hearing were modified in such a way that they constituted a soundproof extension of the auditory canal from one side of the head to the other.

The following quotation is an excerpt from Dr. Young's notes made while wearing the pseudophone for the first time.

While writing in my notebook the creaking of a door was heard directly behind and then a laboratory assistant was seen entering the door immediately in front (180° reversal). A few minutes later this same assistant stood beside his desk on my left and dictated a letter. His voice seemed louder than normal and it had an unfamiliar timbre. When I looked at him the localization of his voice was entirely normal. The same door opened a second time. At first the creaking sounds were heard in the rear but when I looked at the man entering the room the localization of these sounds changed to front.

The noise of rain pattering on the windowpane across the room at my left was distinctly localized off to the right and at the same time a watch seen on a table on my right was heard ticking at the left (double simultaneous reversal). The assistant who stood in front of the window spoke and his voice was normally localized but at the same time the rain pattering on the window was heard on the opposite side (simultaneous normal and reversed localization).[5]

Two days later the account continues:

On May 14 I stood before an open window of the Institute[6] and listened to the street sounds in front and a few feet below. The tread of horses

[5] Paul Thomas Young, "Auditory Localization with Acoustical Transposition of the Ears," *Journal of Experimental Psychology*, 11, 1928, 399.
[6] The Psychological Institute in Berlin

PLAN OF THE EXPERIMENT

During the experiment the pseudophone was worn for a period of eighteen consecutive days. For the first nine days the pseudophone was worn an hour daily (11 to 12 A.M., June 10-18). For the following six days the period was lengthened to two hours (10 to 12 A.M., June 19-24). Most of this time was spent upon the streets of Berlin in the region of the *Kurfürstendamm,* observing the localization of various street sounds. Finally the pseudophone was worn continuously for three complete days. At night during the latter period the pseudophone was removed and the ears were plugged with *Ohropax* (a commercial product) and vaseline. The time (June 25-27) was spent on the street, in the house under everyday conditions, and in the psychological laboratory. During the main experiment the pseudophone was worn for a total of fifty-eight hours. From first to last in the present investigation the writer observed with the pseudophone approximately eighty-five hours.

EXCERPT FROM NOTEBOOK ON EIGHTH DAY

"I have learned that when I hear a sound on the left it is necessary to look to the right in order to see the source, and vice versa. Consequently I sometimes look deliberately in the *wrong* direction and this generally brings the expected source into view. The most natural thing to do is to look towards the place where the sound is heard. Sometimes I follow the auditory cue and sometimes I reinterpret the cue and deliberately look in the opposite direction. I do not mean to imply that I always look or start to look when I localize; this is not the case. In most cases the localization is immediate; it is made before there is any observed bodily movement; the sound is initially heard *there;* movements may be absent or unobserved."

on the pavement, auto horns, streetcar bells, the hum of motors, etc., seemed to be normally localized. Once a horse came from the left to the median plane. The sound of the tread was normal in localization. When the horse reached the median plane I closed my eyes. Then the horse was distinctly heard to recede in the direction from which he came. A moment later the eyes were opened and when the horse was again seen the localization of the tread quickly became normal.

While walking along the sidewalk I heard the voices of two ladies and their steps approaching and overtaking me from behind on the right. Quite automatically I stepped to the left, making more room for them to pass. I looked back and found that I had stepped directly in front of them. My automatic reaction as well as the localization was reversed.

There were repeated cases in which I would expect a truck, horse, streetcar or something else to appear in the left (or right) portion of the visual field but, contrary to expectation, the object would appear on the opposite side. In some of these cases I noticed a gross bodily adjustment towards the position of the expected source.

I found myself deliberately correcting known reversals. I heard a pedestrian overtaking me from behind on the right. Knowing that the person was actually on the left, I stepped aside to the right to let him pass. Once I heard a team of horses drawing near on a side street to my right. Deliberately I looked to the left and saw the team there, and at the same time the localization of the sound shifted.

I heard a pedestrian overtaking me on the left. As the sounds came nearer I expected the person to pass on the right but the sounds were still heard left. For a moment there was an interplay between sensory expectation (left) and intellectual expectation (right). Then I *heard* the pedestrian on the right at the moment he appeared there in indirect vision.

The effect of habituation. Throughout the main experiment, when a sound came suddenly, unexpectedly or from an unknown position, the localization was reversed. When, in other words, localization was made on a purely auditory basis, reversal was the usual thing at the close of the habituation period.

The case is different when the influence of vision is considered. At the very start of the experiment localizations were occasionally normal when the source was seen or when its position was attentively fixated. This was reported by every one of the nine control subjects, who, incidentally, gave reversed localization when tested with closed eyes.

As the experiment progressed a casual glance at an object was sufficient to check up the fact that its sound was normally localized. With habituation, all of the sounds in a complex situation were normally localized without any thought about the matter. On a busy street, for example, with streetcar *here* and a man talking *there* and an auto passing *yonder,* etc., all

318

sounds were normally localized and the total visual-auditory experience was as it is in everyday life without the pseudophone. And not only this! When a source passed out of view its localization remained normal when I paid any attention to the matter. In other words, at the start vision sometimes determined the localization, and with habituation there was increasing dominance of vision until finally a stage was reached indistinguishable from normal. There was increasing and finally complete visual dominance in determining sound localizations but, as noted above, this did not extend to auditory localizations lacking a visual cue.

In everyday life one does not have to search far to find situations in which vision dominates in determining sound localization. The ventriloquist speaks consistently in one voice when he moves puppet A and in another voice when he moves puppet B. The onlooker becomes gradually adjusted to the situation and then gets the well-known ventriloquist's illusion. The talking motion pictures gives a further illustration of the same principle. The voice of a speaker in an auditorium may be indefinitely localized but fixation upon the speaker makes the localization more definite. Here are cases of visual-auditory localization!

Conclusion. The present experiment has made it clear *that sound localization is not merely a function of the ear. It is an accomplishment of the organism as a whole involving muscle systems common to both eye and ear.* The process of localizing is a process of learning to react appropriately to the environment, guided by the kinds of stimulus differences and configurations which are illustrated by Trimble's experiment.

5. VERBALIZATION AND PERCEPTION

If a certain event or object is viewed by several individuals and they are asked afterward to describe what they have seen, there will, in all probability, be as many different descriptions as there were witnesses. Some of the descriptions would conform closely to the event but others would differ markedly; and there might even be instances where observers report contradictory occurrences. Here we are dealing with the perceptual reactions of individuals, and the psychologist is concerned with the determination of why, in the process of perceiving, one person's report of the stimulating situation may differ, not only from the real nature of the objective situation, but also from the reports of another person. There are many reasons for these divergencies and the identification of one of them is described in an experiment by Carmichael, Hogan, and Walters.[7]

These authors were concerned with the manner in which verbal stimuli—words—heard at the time of perceiving—affect the perception of simple figures.

Method. They constructed first a series of twelve relatively ambiguous figures like those shown in the central column of Figure 68. The names were then assigned to each figure, and these names appear in the columns to the right and left of the center column. The figures were presented to the subjects by means of a device which timed the period of exposure so that it was the same for each figure. Preceding each figure there was a pause during which no figure appeared in the opening of the exposure device.

Three groups of subjects were employed. They were all told that they were to be shown a list of twelve figures, and after the list was shown they were to attempt to reproduce each of them. If they failed to do so, the list would be repeated until they succeeded.

This was all that was told the control group, but groups one and two were given additional information. Before each figure was presented the experimenter would state, "The next figure resembles . . ." For group one the words of list I were given, and group two were given the words of list II.

Results. After all the data were collected, the experimenters sorted the drawings into categories based on the degree of resemblance to the stimulus figure. They then took a group of 905 drawings which departed most markedly from the visual stimuli and found the number of these which could be classified as visual representations of the figures named.

In group one, 74 per cent of these drawings were like the names given in list I, in group two 73 per cent were like the names given in list II, and only 45 per cent of the control group's drawings could be classified as similar to the words of either list.

[7] L. Carmichael, H. P. Hogan, and A. A. Walters, "An Experimental study of the Effect of Language on the Reproduction of Visually Perceived Form," *Journal of Experimental Psychology*, 1932, 15, 73-86.

Representative distorted reproductions for groups one and two are illustrated in the outside columns of Figure 68. The percentage

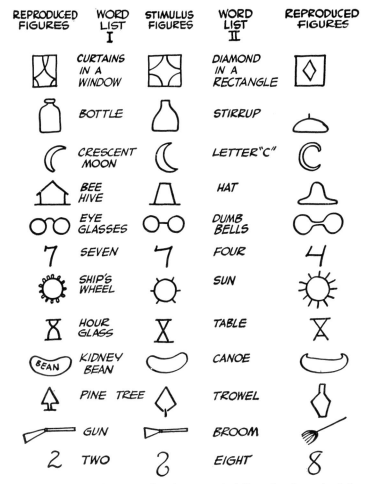

REPRODUCED FIGURES	WORD LIST I	STIMULUS FIGURES	WORD LIST II	REPRODUCED FIGURES
	CURTAINS IN A WINDOW		DIAMOND IN A RECTANGLE	
	BOTTLE		STIRRUP	
	CRESCENT MOON		LETTER "C"	
	BEE HIVE		HAT	
	EYE GLASSES		DUMB BELLS	
	SEVEN		FOUR	
	SHIP'S WHEEL		SUN	
	HOUR GLASS		TABLE	
	KIDNEY BEAN		CANOE	
	PINE TREE		TROWEL	
	GUN		BROOM	
	TWO		EIGHT	

Fig. 68.—The stimulus figures used and some typical distortion for each of the two experimental groups. (After Carmichael, Hogan and Walters.)

of drawings for groups one and two approximating a representation of the verbal stimulus is given in the table.

Summary. This experiment has very nicely demonstrated that our visual perceptions can be distorted by verbal stimuli which are concurrent with the visual stimuli. A question it does not answer, however, is why some of the stimuli are so readily distorted while others show considerable resistance to distortion. The answer to this question could be achieved only by experiments in which both the figures and the names are systematically varied.

Figure	List I	List II
1	47	78
2	100	69
3	65	48
4	69	75
5	45	81
6	87	94
7	54	47
8	83	100
9	90	63
10	86	100
11	76	85
12	87	40

One may generalize and see more meaning in these data than the mere distortion of nonsense figures by words in a laboratory experiment. It is reminiscent of the name-calling technique of the propagandist, and it should make us wary of the description we and others give of any event; for in the process of describing we may distort the event. Once we have distorted it, we will remember it in this incorrect form.

6. SOCIAL FACTORS IN PERCEIVING

From the previous experiment we have learned that our perception of an object could be modified by the particular verbal tag which we happen to apply to the object. This is not the only type of condition which can distort our way of seeing things. The strength and the direction of our personal motives can have a similar effect. We are not so likely to observe infringement of the rules by a player on our own side as by an opposing player. The writer can recall several instances of disputed plays which were crucial to the outcome of the game. Even movies of the game failed to settle the disputes.

the supporters of each team continued to disagree, and continued to rule in favor of their own side. These are cases where the direction of motivation served to bias the perception.

Two hypotheses which were tested by Bruner and Goodman[8] dealt with the operation of socially developed motivational forces in the perception of physical size. These are the hypotheses:

Hypothesis 1. The greater the social value of an object, the greater will be the tendency to overestimate its size.

Hypothesis 2. The greater the individual need for the object, the greater will be the tendency to overestimate its size.

Specifically, the experimenters predicted that the amount of overestimation of the size of a coin of high value would be greater than that of the size of a coin of low value. They predicted also that children of poor families would overestimate coin size more than would children of well-to-do families.

Subject. The subjects employed in the experiment were thirty ten-year-old children of normal intelligence. Ten of these children were the sons and daughters of prosperous business and professional people, and ten came from a settlement house in the slums. Unfortunately the socioeconomic level of the other ten is not specified by the experimenters.

Method. The children were seated at a table on which a small box was placed, and on the end of the box, facing the subject, there was a five-inch square ground-glass screen. A nearly circular patch of light was cast on the center of the screen by a bulb within the box. A knob in front of the box was geared to a diaphragm in the box and the size of the patch could be varied from one-eighth inch to two inches in diameter by turning this knob.

The subjects in the control group sat at the table and were given an opportunity to vary the diaphragm from one extreme in size to the other. After this introduction was completed they were asked to match the size of the light with five disks that the experimenter held, one at a time, in his hand. These objects were medium

J. S. Bruner and C. G. Goodman, "Need and value as Organizing Factors in Perception," *Journal of Abnormal and Social Psychology,* 1947, 42, 33-44.

gray cardboard disks identical in size to a penny, a nickel, a dime, a quarter, and a half dollar. Four estimates were made on each object, two trials beginning with the spot larger than the object to be matched, and two with the spot smaller than the disk to be matched. In one series they began by matching from the smaller object on up to the larger, and the reverse order was employed in the second series. No mention was made of money to this group.

The twenty experimental subjects were given the same introduction and were then asked to estimate from memory the size of a penny, nickel, dime, quarter, and half dollar. Next they were shown coins in the same manner that the experimental group had been shown the paper disks, and they followed the same procedure in making their estimates.

Results. The results are shown graphically in Figure 69 and they support the hypothesis that coin value influences the perception of objective size. The control group, which worked only with paper disks, made estimates which were extremely close to the actual size of the objects they were matching. The experimental group, however, shows a consistent tendency to overestimate each coin, and with the exception of the half dollar, the extent of overestimation is directly related to the monetary value of the coin. Just why the fifty-cent piece is not overestimated more is unclear, but it is perhaps significant that the control group also shows a decline in its estimation from the quarter-sized paper disk to the half-dollar-sized disk. This suggests that there is some unidentified factor operating such as the fact that the size of the half dollar is approaching the magnitude of the maximum opening of the diaphragm.

It will be recalled that the twenty subjects who constituted the experimental group in the test of the first hypothesis consisted of ten children of well-to-do parents and ten children of poor parents. It is logical to assume that the need for money is greater for the poor than the well-to-do children. By comparing the performance of these two groups we can test the hypothesis that the degree of overestimation will vary with the degree of need.

The results confirmed the hypothesis; for with every coin the

324

error in estimation of the poor children was greater than it was for the well-to-do children.

Summary. This experiment has illustrated another characteristic of our perceptual reactions. Again, as in the previous experiment, it is seen that the organism puts something into the objective

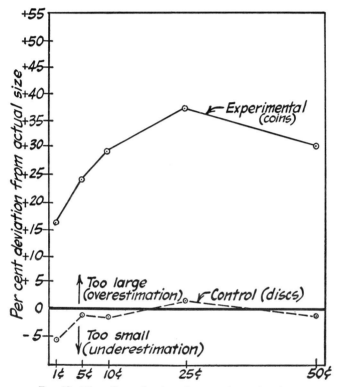

Fig. 69.—The effect of coin value on size estimation.

physical situation, and the result is a distortion of this physical objectivity. In the present instance the distorting factor is a socially acquired motivational force.

Summary of the chapter. In this chapter we have given some indication of the highly complex phenomena of perception. The first experiment demonstrated the operation of perceptual constancy and showed how organisms react to what the object itself is known to be rather than to the exact characteristics of the specific stimulus. In the second experiment we have isolated one of the cues which permit us to make correct judgments as to the source of a stimulus. The third experiment demonstrated not only that humans show a considerable capacity for learning distance discrimination, but also that our perceptual reactions can be determined by many stimuli which are presumably irrelevant to the situation. The fourth experiment has indicated that no precise relations need obtain between the various sense departments. Any relation can, after a period of readjustment, serve as satisfactorily as its predecessor. The fifth and sixth experiments have both shown how readily our visual perceptions can be distorted. The fifth has indicated that verbal processes occurring simultaneously with the visual stimulation modify what is seen. The sixth points to the importance of motivational needs of the individual as a distorting factor.

CHAPTER SIXTEEN

CONDITIONING

Early in this century an American psychologist[1] was studying the knee jerk. He had arranged an apparatus which gave uniform light hammer blows on the leg just below the patella, and was measuring the amount or extent of the reflex movement which takes the form of a rapid kick of the leg. As an entirely incidental matter this experimenter observed that when the apparatus accidentally became stuck and a blow was not delivered to the kneecap, the leg kicked anyway. In commenting about the results he attributed it to "association of ideas" and thereby missed the opportunity to become the accredited discoverer of a phenomenon which has since come to be called the *conditioned response.*

1. THE CONDITIONED RESPONSE

It remained for the Russian physiologist Ivan Pavlov to see the significance of these "conditioned reflexes." He stumbled upon the phenomenon in the course of a series of studies on the digestive processes in dogs, an endeavor which later earned for him the Nobel prize in Physiology. What he observed was very simple: If an incidental stimulating condition (noise or light) is uniformly present at the time dogs are fed, it becomes the stimulus for reactions previously associated only with food. Anybody who has called "Kitty, Kitty!" or whistled for a dog at mealtime has observed as much.

The basic type of experiment which was conducted by Pavlov was quite simple. His animals were prepared by an operation so that the duct of one of the salivary glands was led to the outside of the dog's cheek. The drops of saliva were collected in a measuring device which permitted the experimenter to make a very exact quantification of the amount of saliva that was secreted. If a stimulus which had no effect on salivation—a noise or a light—was then presented for a number of times along with food, this previously neutral stimulus would acquire the power to evoke salivation.

[1] E. B. Twitmeyer, *A Study of the Knee-Jerk,* University of Pennsylvania, Philadelphia 1902, pp. 36.

327

Pavlov and his students continued to do research on the conditioned response until his death only a few years ago. During this time through a series of imaginative and painstaking experiments they were able to sketch out the general characteristics of this phenomenon. It has remained for later experimenters to fill in the details, to make new contributions, and to verify the general outlines of the psychological picture that Pavlov began. These later experimenters have profited not only from the facts about conditioning that Pavlov discovered, but also from the development of superior recording equipment, and the fact that we know today much more about the technique of designing experiments than did Pavlov. One of the trends in this more recent research has been to employ humans rather than animals as subjects, and to record responses other than salivation.

A large number of modern experiments use the reaction of the upper eyelid to a puff of air on the cornea of the eye as the response to be conditioned. These measurements are made photographically through the use of a thin bamboo lever attached by a thread to the upper eyelid. This lever casts a shadow upon a moving strip of photographic paper, and a permanent record of the response is thus obtained. The stimulus which preceded the air puff and to which the wink response becomes attached or conditioned is usually an increase in illumination. This, too, is recorded by permitting some of the light to fall upon the photographic paper. The rush of air which stimulates the eye to produce the wink sets a small piece of paper to vibrating and the shadow of this falls upon the paper to mark the onset of this stimulus. Lastly, the blades of a motor, which move rapidly and at a constant speed, cast shadows which produce lines on the paper. The resulting record permits a precise measurement of the magnitude of the response as well as its exact occurrence in time in relation to various stimuli. A specimen set of records is shown in Figure 70.[2] These records are tracings from actual photographic records. This specimen set is a very good description of the process of becoming conditioned. The top record comes from a trial

[2] These records were obtained from some experiments conducted by Hilgard and are taken from E. R. Hilgard, and D. C. Marquis. *Conditioning and Learning,* New York, D. Appleton-Century Company, Inc., New York, 1940

before the conditioned response has developed. Note the slight response to the onset of the light and the large response to the air puff. The successive records show the development of the conditioned response. The conditioned response (CR) is first shown as a slight an-

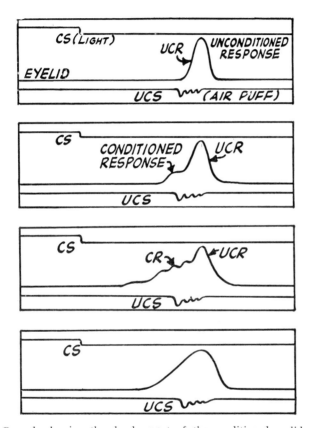

FIG. 70.—Records showing the development of the conditioned eyelid response. (After Hilgard and Marquis.)

icipation of the response to the puff (UCR) and it becomes, by the ast record, a complete closure of the lid which serves to protect the eye from the puff.

These records are, of course, samples chosen from various stages of the training series. If a complete series of records were to be shown, they would picture a gradual increase in the magnitude of the response with the increasing number of trials. The conditioned response does not occur on its first occasion full-blown and complete. Its acquisition, like that of so many other habits, is gradual.

2. TIME RELATIONS

It may have passed the reader's notice, but in the above description of the conditioning process the statement was made several times that the conditioned stimulus was *followed* by the unconditioned stimulus—the light and then the air puff, or the sound and then the food. This statement implies a temporal order of events, and it raises the question as to whether or not there is any significance to the amount of separation in time between the onset of one stimulus and that of the other. This question was investigated in a recent experiment by Reynolds.[3]

Method. His conditioning technique was essentially the same as that previously described. A click served as his conditioned stimulus and a puff of air to the eye was the unconditioned stimulus.

Four groups of subjects were employed with about ten subjects in each group. For all of these groups the click or CS preceded the UCS or air puff. The amount of time by which it did so was, however, different for each group. The time separations which were employed were 250, 450, 1,150, and 2,250 milliseconds.[4] In all other respects the four groups were treated alike. There were ninety paired presentations of click and air puff, and each response was recorded photographically in the manner described in Section 1.

Results. A word must be said about the measure of the strength of conditioning that this experimenter used. As a general rule, even after a fair amount of training, the conditioned response will not be given each time the conditioned stimulus is presented. In a series of ten trials for example, it may occur nine times, or five, or three

---

[3] Bradley Reynolds, "The Acquisition of a Trace Conditioned Response as a Function of the Magnitude of the Trace Stimulus," *Journal of Experimental Psychology*, 1945, 35, 15-30.

[4] A millisecond is one one thousandth of a second. In other words, 250 milliseconds could be written as .250 second. It is more convenient to employ the millisecond as a time unit than to use seconds and be required to work with decimal points.

or one, depending upon how strongly conditioned the subject has become. Thus the frequency of occurrence of the conditioned response in a certain number of presentations can serve as an index of the strength of the conditioned response. In the present experiment the per cent frequency of the conditioned responses in the last ten trials was the measure that the experimenter employed.

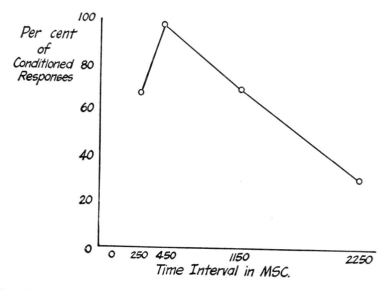

FIG. 71.—Efficiency of conditioning plotted against the time by which the conditioned stimulus precedes the unconditioned stimulus. (After Reynolds.)

The magnitude of conditioning for each of the four difficult time intervals is presented in Figure 71. It is immediately apparent that the amount of separation in time between the conditioned and the unconditioned stimuli is an important determiner of the facility with which the conditioned response can develop. The experiment seems to indicate that the most rapid conditioning occurs when the onset of the two stimuli is separated by 450 milliseconds—roughly a half second. Another recent experiment[5] has supported this conclu-

Gregory A. Kimble, "Conditioning as a Function of the Time between Conditioned and Unconditioned Stimuli," *Journal of Experimental Psychology*, 1947, 37, 1-15.

sion and has shown that the efficiency of conditioning continues to decrease as the time interval is reduced to 100 milliseconds.

In both of these experiments the conditioned stimulus preceded the unconditioned stimulus. What if it had been the other way around, with the puff first and then the click? Several experiments have investigated this relationship and there is no clear evidence that the typical conditioned response can be established in this fashion.[6]

Summary. These experiments point to one of the most fundamental conditions in the formation of stimulus-response connections, namely, the great importance of time relations. Again and again, in many different contexts, the psychologists have discovered that temporal separation is a factor which determines efficiency of learning. The significance of this time relationship has so impressed some psychologists that they feel no other principle need be advanced to understand why a particular stimulus becomes attached to a particular response. That the stimulus and the response occur together in time is thought to be enough.

If the student has been tempted to explain conditioning by saying that the person expects the puff after the click, and therefore he blinks, this experiment should give him pause. Why should the expectation be stronger or greater if the two stimuli are separated by 450 milliseconds than by any other time interval? His explanation is inadequate. It would appear that we are here operating with some basic timing or pacing mechanism which is an essential part of the biological structure of organisms.

3. STIMULUS GENERALIZATION

It may be said of the conditioning situation that it results in a new stimulus response connection. A response which was formerly given to one stimulus now becomes attached to a new stimulus as well. Thus Pavlov's dogs may salivate to the sound of a bell, or the college students may wink in response to a change in illumination

[6] W. F. Grether, "Pseudo-Conditioning without Paired Stimulation Encountered in Attempted Backward Conditioning," *Journal of Comparative Psychology*, 1938, 25, 91-96. A. Spooner and W. N. Kellog, "The Backward Conditioning Curve," *American Journal of Psychology*, 1947, 40, 321-334.

A question of considerable importance is whether the response becomes attached only to the particular stimulus used in the training or to other similar stimuli as well. An experiment by Hovland[7] attacks this problem.

Method. The response which Hovland decided to condition was the galvanic skin response, hereafter called the GSR. This response has been mentioned in the chapter on emotions, and it consists of changes in the electrical resistance of the skin. It can be measured quite readily by means of a galvanometer. When this instrument is wired into a circuit of which the subject is a part, it will swing in one direction or another as the skin resistance of the subject varies. The magnitude of the swing can easily be recorded by following the movement with a pointer. If one end of a string is attached to this pointer with the other end attached to a marker which is riding on a strip of continuously moving paper, then the magnitude of the movements of the pointer can be recorded and measured. It was in this manner that Hovland recorded the GSR of his subjects. The stimulus which he employed to produce the response was an electric shock to the wrist. The reader should not get the impression that the electrical current directly causes the movement of the galvanometer. It simply serves as a stimulus which sets off a chain of physiological reactions in the organism and these reactions produce the change in skin resistance that is recorded. At exactly 495 milliseconds (MSC) before the shock was to be given a tone began to sound and continued for 400 MSC. This tone was the conditioned stimulus. The shock lasted for 75 MSC and, of course, came on 95 MSC after the tone ceased.

Sixteen presentations of the tone and shock were given, this number being sufficient to develop a strong conditioned reaction—that is a galvanic skin response to the tone alone.

Following this, the testing was begun to determine whether the subject had become conditioned to only the one particular tone employed in the experiment or to other tones as well. Previous to

[7] C. I. Hovland, "The Generalization of Conditioned Responses: I. The Sensory Generalization of Conditioned Responses with Varying Frequencies of Tone," *Journal of General Psychology,* 1937, 17, 125-148.

the experiment the experimenter had selected four tones ranging from one which was rather low in pitch to one of medium pitch. They were selected in such a way that each tone seemed to be just as much above the previous one as the previous tone was above the one before it. This is a way of saying that the psychological differences between each adjacent tone were equal.

In the experiment half of the subjects were trained to the highest of the tones, and half to the lowest. Then, after the sixteen paired trials the shock was eliminated and the subjects were tested twice to every one of the four tones. The magnitude of the response to each tone was recorded.

Results. For the sake of ease in understanding the data we shall label the tone which was paired with the shock during the training as S_0. The tone which was just higher than that, for half the subjects, or just lower than that for the other half, will be called S_1. The tone just higher or lower than S_1 will be called S_2, and so also for S_3. In other words, *as the magnitude of the numerical subscripts increases, the degree of similarity to the original training tone decreases.* Using this method, we can determine whether or not there is a relationship between the tendency to give the conditioned response and degree of similarity to the training tone. The data of the experiment, expressed in terms of the average magnitude of reaction for all subjects to all tones, are presented in Figure 72.

There are several important facts which can be adduced from this figure. One of these is that the conditioned response is not limited to the training tone; the other tones are capable of producing it *even though those particular tones have never been paired with the shock.* This is called *stimulus generalization.* The other is the fact that the less similar these other tones are to the training tone, the less effective they are in producing the conditioned response.

Summary. The value of the phenomenon of stimulus generalization for adjusting to the world about us is very great. If each time we were presented with a slightly different stimulus we were required to learn how to react to this stimulus, so many of our hours would be spent in blundering movements and in learning rudimentary acts, that our psychological world would be as limited as that of the one-celled organisms. Instead of this the learning in one situation is carried over to another similar one, and we are immediately capable of making an appropriate response. The stop signal in one traffic light may be of a slightly different shade of red from that of another, but we react to both in the same way. The words printed in one kind

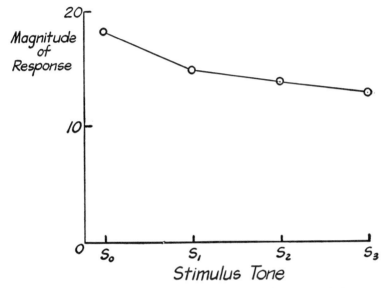

FIG. 72.—The magnitude of the conditioned response to four tones. S_0 is the tone which the subjects were conditioned. S_1 is most similar to S_0, and S_3 is least similar. S_2 stands midway between these tones in similarity. (After Hovland.)

of type carry the same meaning as those same words printed in another.

It is also appropriate that as the characteristics of the new stimulus differ more and more from the original stimulus, the strength of the learned response becomes less and less. If we reacted to any light in the same manner that we react to red of a traffic light, worldly progress would indeed be at a standstill.

4. EXTINCTION OF THE CONDITIONED RESPONSE

The value of the conditioned response to the organism as a means of adjusting to the environment is apparent. It is a means by which the organism learns to react to the stimuli as cues for later events. By doing so he may keep himself from harm's way or may prepare himself to receive beneficial stimuli. Winking to the light before the air puff came on avoided a mildly noxious stimulus; and the occurrence of salivation to the conditioned stimulus before the food is given has prepared the organism for the reception of this physiologically necessary material.[8] Our environment is not, however, completely stable, and oftentimes the later events do not follow the "cue" stimulus. If the organism continued to react to the cue or conditioned stimulus as if some particular event were to occur later, and that event did not occur, his behavior would be maladaptive in the sense that it would be at variance with the demands of the environment. In the exact terms of a conditioning experiment, this is a case where, after the conditioned response has been developed, the conditioned stimulus is repeatedly presented without being followed by the unconditioned stimulus (the food, or air puff, or electric shock). What occurs to the conditioned response under these circumstances was the subject of an experiment conducted by Humphreys.[9]

Method. Humphreys' subjects were first conditioned to give wink reactions to a light stimulus by use of a technique essentially the same as that described in Section 1. A total of forty-eight paired stimulations of light and air puff were given, with twenty-four of them being administered on the first day of the experiment and twenty-four on the following day. After the forty-eighth stimulation the air puff was eliminated and the light alone was presented twenty-four times. The response tendencies of the subjects are presented in Figure 73. The measure along the vertical coordinates of the graph is the percentage of conditioned responses that were given, not the magnitude of the response. The trials are divided into four groups of six trials each. Thus point 1 represents the frequency for trials

---

[8] Conditioning does not always work to the advantage of the organism. It may also develop habits which have no utility or have a negative utility. Phobias are an example. Like the gentle rain from heaven the mechanisms of conditioning are indiscriminate, and they develop the bad as well as the good.

[9] Lloyd G. Humphreys, "The Effect of Random Alternation of Reinforcement on the Acquisition and Extinction of Conditioned Eyelid Reactions," *Journal of Experimental Psychology*, 1939, 25, 141-158.

1 through 6, point 2 the frequency for trial 7 through 12, and so on. Point zero is a reference point which indicates the level of performance during the last twenty-four of the training trials.

This curve shows that the continued omission of the air puff or, as it is commonly called, the reinforcing stimulus, has a marked effect

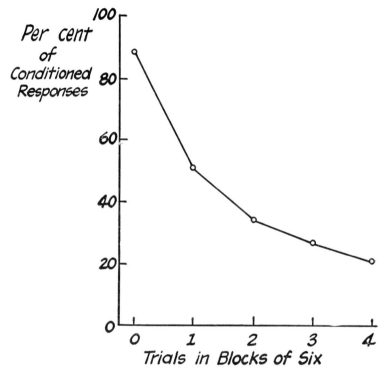

FIG. 73.—Experimental extinction of a conditioned response.

on the strength of the conditioned response. Unless reinforcement is present, the process of experimental extinction will occur and the conditioned response will become extinguished. Just as the conditioned response can be learned, so also can it be unlearned.

Summary. This experiment has demonstrated that the continued occurrence of the conditioned response is dependent upon the presence of the reinforcing stimulus. It would be false, however, to make the generalization that the conditioned response is particularly unstable, and, hence, of very little significance in everyday behavior. There are two lines of evidence which indicate that such a generalization is not true. In the first place, it has been demonstrated experimentally that extinction will not occur if an occasional reinforcement is given among many non-reinforced trials. Secondly, if after extinction has occurred and the subjects return to the laboratory, the conditioned response will once more be present, even though no additional training is given. Thus through a lapse of time alone there is a spontaneous recovery of the previously extinguished response. These two sources of evidence indicate to us that once a conditioned response has been developed, its complete and permanent elimination is not easy of attainment, but that, on the contrary, the likelihood of its continued operation is great.

5. SENSORY PRECONDITIONING

In the experiments presented thus far the fact that the conditioned response is developed can be accounted for by observing that the development takes place in the presence of either strong approach or strong avoidance reactions. The incentive value of both noxious and more attractive stimuli has already been elaborated (Chapter Ten), but there are instances in which an incentive does not seem to be a necessary factor in conditioning. In such cases the mere simultaneity of two stimuli without regard to motivation may be enough to cause a connection between them. This phenomenon is perhaps most clearly shown in an experiment by W. J. Brogden[10] involving dogs. Brogden used eight dogs who were subjected daily for ten days to a pair of stimuli—one a light the other a sound—twenty different times a day. There was no feeding or withdrawing for either of the two stimuli—they simply were presented together for two seconds, a short wait, then two seconds of sound and light together again. After ten days of this procedure the eight animals were divided equally into two groups. One of these groups was conditioned in the ordinary manner to withdraw the foot when a bell was rung,

10 W. J. Brogden, "Sensory Pre-Conditioning," *Journal of Experimental Psychology*, 1939, 25, 323-332.

the unconditioned stimulus in this case being a slight shock to the left foreleg. Twenty times each day the bell would be sounded to be followed a short time later by a shock which could be avoided if the animal raised its left forepaw. The second subgroup was conditioned to a light stimulus in the same manner. The results of this conditioning are shown in the table. The numbers in the column on the extreme left are those of the experimental days. On each of these days twenty combinations of either bell and electric shock (BE) or light and electric shock (LE) were given. Since dog 1 avoided the shock twice in the twenty opportunities on the first day, a score of 10 per cent conditioning was entered for him. In the next two days, however, he failed to avoid the shock at any time and as a consequence got two scores of zero. After that the percentage of correct responses gradually increased until by the tenth day he was completely conditioned. The other dogs show about the same picture in the acquisition of the conditioned response, but in some instances more time was required to reach the criterion of always anticipating the shock.

The third part of the experiment consisted in giving only the light to the subgroup that had previously been conditioned to the bell and vice versa. These results are shown at the bottom of page 341. Dog 1, for instance, *reacted to the light as though it were the signal for an impending shock in 55 per cent of the cases on the first day.* It was as though this dog had been conditioned before to the light. In the preliminary experiment he had experienced two hundred combinations of the light and bell, but it could not be said that he was conditioned to either one because neither had been reinforced. Two of the eight dogs showed no influence of the preliminary association, but the others reacted to either the light or the bell in varying percentages from 10 to 40.

Control. In order to show that the preliminary association is the effective agent in determining these results, the whole experiment must be repeated with a different group of dogs in which the preliminary training is omitted. Brogden made this control experiment. Had he not done so he could never have been certain that the preliminary training was at all effective, for, as other experiments have shown, the phenomenon *stimulus generalization* could have accounted for his findings.

The results of Brogden's control experiment will not be given in detail. Suffice it to say that seven of eight dogs gave zero withdrawals when the preliminary training was omitted. The other dog gave 20 per cent withdrawals the first day, but none the second.

We may conclude, then, that *the simple association of two stimuli when neither is reinforced can result in the establishment of some connection between them.* It cannot be said that these stimuli are completely interchangeable because in the critical experiment the highest percentage of responses was 55 and in two instances there was no sensory preconditioning.

This finding is important because it has been asserted that all learning has to be motivated in some way. On the basis of this and other experiments, a better generalization would be that *although learning can take place without identifiable incentives, it is uniformly more prompt and more complete when some incentive condition is present.*

6. CLASSICAL AND INSTRUMENTAL CONDITIONING

In the particular conditioning situation employed by Pavlov the occurrence of the conditioned and the unconditioned stimuli is completely in the hands of the experimenter. The subject cannot by his action force the occurrence of the unconditioned stimulus. The food or the shock are administered by the mechanical device that the experimenter sets in motion by a flip of the switch. The subject himself is merely the recipient of these environmental changes. Now, although such situations as these do occur in our everyday life, there are other situations in which the person himself determines whether or not the food or its counterpart will occur. It is valid to raise the question as to whether or not the principles of behavior which operate in the Pavlovian type of conditioning (it is often called *classical conditioning*) are also operative in other situations. A research study which was conducted by Youtz[11] was designed to determine whether or not the phenomena of experimental extinc-

11 R. E. P. Youtz "Reinforcement, Extinction, and Spontaneous Recovery in a Non-Pavlovian Reaction," *Journal of Experimental Psychology*, 1938, 22, 305-318

RESULTS OBTAINED FROM THE EXPERIMENTAL ANIMALS

The scores in the table represent *in percentages* the number of times conditioned flexion occurred to the conditioned stimulus. Twenty stimulus-presentations were given during each test period.

Bell and light given in combination for 2 seconds, 20 times per day for 10 days.

EXPERIMENTAL DAY	GROUP BE				GROUP LE			
	Bell and Shock to Left Forepaw				Light and Shock to Left Forepaw			
	No. 1 Score	No. 2 Score	No. 3 Score	No. 4 Score	No. 5 Score	No. 6 Score	No. 7 Score	No. 8 Score
1	10	0	0	15	0	0	10	0
2	0	0	0	20	0	0	0	15
3	0	50	0	20	20	35	15	10
4	35	85	50	30	20	25	0	0
5	90	85	75	40	75	15	0	0
6	95	95	90	75	50	20	35	0
7	95	95	95	85	55	30	70	15
8	90	95	75	75	65	10	55	10
9	90	95	95	70	95	55	75	40
10	100	95	95	80	100	60	90	60
11		100	90	95		30	90	75
12			95	90		65	85	90
13			100	95		70	100	85
14				100		95		90
15						90		90
16						85		100
17						90		
18						100		

CRITICAL TESTS

EXPERIMENTAL DAY	LIGHT ALONE				BELL ALONE			
1	55	0	15	0	40	25	10	20
2	30		10		5	0	0	20
3	10		10		5			45
4	5		0		0			20
5	0							30
6								25
7								10
8								0

341

tion and spontaneous recovery, which are so clearly apparent in classical conditioning, will also be present in another learning situation.

Apparatus. The apparatus he used is called the Skinner box. This consisted of a box whose interior dimensions measured approximately one foot each way. At one end of the box there was a food trough and a lever. This lever operated a hidden mechanism. When it was pressed by the white rats, who served as subjects in the experiment, a pellet of food dropped into the food trough. The box was ventilated and sound-proofed so that extraneous noises were reduced to a minimum.

So much for the box. Now consider the type of situation which confronts the hungry rat. There is no single external stimulus which is turned off and on as is the conditioned stimulus (the tone or light) in the classical conditioning situation. Even more important than this is the fact that the reinforcing stimulus—the food pellet—is given only as a result of the action of the animal himself. He must press the lever to obtain food; he cannot wait passively as did Pavlov's animal until the food slid into the tray in front of him.

This type of learning situation wherein the response of the animal determines whether or not he will receive reinforcement (food in this experiment) is called *instrumental conditioning* to differentiate it from Pavlov's *classical conditioning.* Clearly this situation differs from Pavlov's; the real question is whether or not the same principles of behavior operate in each situation.

Procedure

(1) HABITUATION AND TRAINING. The nine white rats who served as subjects in the experiment were first placed singly in the apparatus where they found five pellets of food in the food trough. Later the experimenter himself operated the food-vending mechanism from outside so that pellets of food would drop into the trough. As they were delivered from the vending tube a sharp click occurred, and the animals soon learned to run to the food trough when the click sounded. During these two steps the bar which was to be pressed in order to deliver food was not present. On the following day it

was placed in the apparatus and a small amount of food was placed upon it. The hungry rats were, of course, attracted by the sight and odor of the food, and in the process of obtaining it they pressed the bar. This pressing activated the food-vending mechanism and a pellet of food dropped with a click into the food trough. Thus the rats learned to press the bar in order to obtain the food pellets. They were permitted to work for ten pellets of food on this day. For the next three days they were given ten more trials a day so that they received forty trials in all. Such a trial as this, wherein the pressing of the bar is followed by the delivery of food, is usually referred to as a *reinforcement*.

(2) EXPERIMENTAL EXTINCTION. In the Pavlovian situation extinction occurs when the conditioned stimulus is not followed by the unconditioned stimulus. The comparable design in the Skinner box is to throw a switch which prevents the food from being delivered even though the bar is pressed. In the present experiment Youtz began his extinction series immediately after the fortieth trial, and he considered that extinction had occurred when the animals went for twenty minutes without pressing the bar.

(3) SPONTANEOUS RECOVERY. Spontaneous recovery of the classical conditioned response was briefly mentioned in the fourth section of this chapter. It is the phenomenon which may occur when, after the conditioned response has been extinguished, the subject is tested to the conditioned stimulus alone some time later. During the time between the last extinction trial and the next test to the conditioned stimulus no reinforcements are given. If now the subjects give a conditioned response, it is said that spontaneous recovery has occurred. This phenomenon is found very commonly in classical conditioning.

Youtz tested for spontaneous recovery in the Skinner box in the following manner: On the day following the extinction series the rats were once more placed in the box. They were given no reinforcements, and again the switch was pulled so that the pressing of the bar would not deliver food. They remained in the box until twenty minutes passed without a response to the bar. Precisely this same procedure was employed fifty-five days later.

343

Results

(1) LEARNING THE BAR-PRESSING RESPONSE. The animals readily learned the relationship between pressing the bar and receiving food, and they became more proficient at it each day. This proficiency was shown by the decrease in the total amount of time required to earn and to get the daily ten pellets of food. On the four successive days of the experiment these times were 5.00, 3.3, 2.2, and 2.6 minutes.

(2) EXTINCTION. When, following the fortieth trial, the switch was thrown and no food resulted from pressing the bar, the animals continued to respond for some time. In fact, they averaged forty-eight responses before the reaction was extinguished.

(3) SPONTANEOUS RECOVERY. On the following day, without any additional training the animals pressed the bar twenty-eight times before complete extinction. Of course, none of these responses was followed by food. Fifty-five days later spontaneous recovery was again evidenced by an average of twenty-two responses.

Summary. This experiment serves to bridge the gap between the relatively simple environmental situation characteristic of the classical conditioning situation and the more complicated types of learning situations. The difference between the classical conditioning situation and the Skinner box instrumental conditioning situation has already been noted. In the former the reinforcements occur independently of the animal's action, but in the latter the animal actively determines his nutritional fate. Despite these differences, the same principles of behavior which operate in the one situation operate also in the other. In each of these situations the tendency to give the learned response, whether it is pressing a bar or salivating to the sound of a tone, decreases if the occurrence of the response is not followed by some reinforcing stimulus. Also in each of these situations the response will be restored by the passage of time even though no additional training has been given during this time.

This experiment is one of a number which has indicated to the psychologist that there is a wide generality of the principles of learning. The principles or phenomena which operate in one situation can frequently be detected in another even though the complexities of the other situation may be great enough to obscure them from immediate recognition. It is because of this generality that the psychologist often uses very simple situations to investigate the phenomena of learning; for the nature of the phenomena can often be more clearly identified if studied in the setting of a simple situation than in that of a complex situation.

Summary of the chapter. This chapter has illustrated several important aspects of behavior as they are shown in the conditioning situation. The first experiment served as an introduction to some of the technical aspects of modern conditioning experimentation. The second one pointed to the extreme importance of time relations in the learning of organisms. The third has identified a certain economy of behavior—stimulus generalization—which causes the results of learning in one situation to be carried over into new and partially different situations. The fourth experiment indicated the manner in which previously established stimulus response connections can be abolished. The fifth experiment revealed that associations can be made without the occurrence of obvious responses. The sixth experiment serves as a bridge between the simple *classical conditioning* situation and more complex environmental conditions. The experiment shows that many of the basic principles of behavior in the simpler situation hold true in the complex situation.

CHAPTER SEVENTEEN

LEARNING

One of the central problems in psychology today concerns the manner in which a person learns something. Considerable progress has been made in the direction of solving the problem, but scientific explanations frequently do not satisfy people who are looking for final causes. We find people impressed with the fact that "scientists can't tell us what electricity is," for instance. Much is made, in their thinking and talking, of the inability of the scientist to tell them what electricity is so that they can understand it. They grant that physicists and engineers and, for that matter, housewives and power station attendants, can control electricity, but they regard as a fundamental failure the incomplete understanding of the nature of the phenomenon. Exactly the same kind of criticism, if it is a criticism, can be leveled against the psychologist's explanation of learning. It consists of descriptions of the way learning rates vary under different conditions. Situations can be set in which no modification of behavior at all will result; there are others in which the modification comes about with varying degress of promptness and permanence. The relation between the individuals who are to learn and the innumerable factors of the situation which can change the extent and nature of the modification of the learner's behavior is the problem of learning. A *description* of these relations is a scientific *explanation* of learning.

1. KNOWLEDGE OF RESULTS

We have already pointed out (Chapter Eleven) that a knowledge of results is one factor which modifies the rate of learning. To emphasize this important point we look to another experiment on the same topic. It is an experiment conducted by the Army Air Forces psychologists on the learning of flexible gunnery, that is, learning to operate machine guns in the waist, tail, and turret of the larger bombers.[1]

[1] Army Air Forces Aviation Psychology Program Research Reports, "Psychological Research on Flexible Gunnery Training," Report No. 11. Nicholas Hobbs (ed.) U.S. Government Printing Office, Washington, D. C. 1947.

The trainer. For a variety of reasons it was not possible to give gunners in training much experience in firing live ammunition at targets, and, as a substitute, the Armed Forces developed a number of synthetic trainers. These trainers embodied the essential characteristics of the real task, but were freed from the necessity of using ammunition. One of these trainers which was used extensively by the Army was the Waller trainer.

The trainer consisted of a large, spherical movie screen extending 170 degrees in the horizontal direction and 55 degrees in the vertical. It corresponded to the segment of the sky from which a gunner might expect an attack by an enemy plane. Upon this screen moving pictures of attacking planes were projected, and what the gunner saw was a series of "attacks" upon his plane by these enemy fighters.

The gunner was equipped with a mock gun which vibrated realistically when it was fired and, to give further realism to the situation, noises typical of combat were heard through earphones which the gunner wore. When the man pressed the trigger of his gun an electrical circuit was activated which recorded the number of rounds fired. In addition to this, an ingenious device made it possible to determine whether or not the aiming of the gun was correct. If the gunner was firing in such a way that he would hit the attacking plane, another counter was activated. Thus the scoring system could tell for each gunner the number of rounds he fired and the number of hits he made. Connected to this scoring system was an auditory signal—a beep tone which could be sounded when hits were being made. This circuit was controlled by the instructor, and he could cut it in or out at will. When it was cut in the gunner could tell immediately when he was firing correctly by the fact that the beep would be heard; when it was cut out the gunner obtained no knowledge of his results during his firing period.

The method. The subjects of the experiment were sixty-four men awaiting assignment to gunnery training. They were divided into two groups, each of which was given eight training sessions on the trainer. For Group A the beep was on for the first three trials, and off for the last five. The reverse of this procedure was followed for Group B—that is, they ran three trials without knowledge of results and then were given knowledge during the last five trials. Thus the experiment was designed to test the value of the beep as a training device; to measure, in other words, the effect of knowledge of results upon the rate of learning.

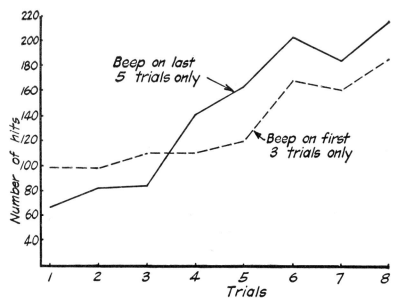

FIG. 74.—The effect of immediate knowledge of results on gunnery performance.

Results. The results of this experiment are shown in Figure 74, and the facilitating influence of the beep on the men's performance is clearly in evidence. As long as Group A received the beep signal—that is for the first three trials—it excelled Group B. When the procedure was reversed, Group B took the lead and remained superior until the end of the experiment. The knowledge of how he was performing, a type of information which was supplied by hearing the beep tone when he was on target, was obviously advantageous to the gunner.

The curves show that learning occurred even when the beep signal was not employed. There are probably several reasons for this. For one thing, the men would have been learning the motor

348

skill of handling the gun and of using its sight. Also, since the same film was used on each trial the men could learn from what sector of the sky the attacks originated as well as the path of the attacking plane. This would result in their picking up the target earlier in each attack and staying on it better.

Summary of the experiment. The opportunity to obtain knowledge of the correctness or incorrectness of an act, and to obtain this within close temporal proximity to the act, is a prerequisite of efficient learning. Without such knowledge no sign can be given to the subject as to which of the many responses he makes should be selected and fixed. This fact is one of the reasons why synthetic gunnery trainers were used by the Armed Forces. With such trainers the men could be given knowledge of how they were performing as they performed; but when they were firing live ammunition at a target, it was frequently impossible to determine whether or not hits were being made. Course examinations serve the same function; if they are properly constructed, they not only give a grade for the student but will inform him of his strong and weak points. In many other situations, of course, such devices as beeps and examination scores are not necessary, and knowledge of the results of the act is inherent in the very performance of the act. We do not need an umpire to call out a score against us when we hit a tennis ball into the net, and we can readily tell when we are steering the car in a wobbly fashion.

2. PRACTICE IN ERROR

Dunlap has pointed out[2] that there are three logical possibilities in connection with the relations between practice and learning, of which "practice makes perfect" is only one. As he states them, practice may facilitate learning (this is the most common notion, but we have been demonstrating its falsity); practice may have no effect on learning at all; practice may inhibit learning. The first and most common of these statements he calls the alpha hypothesis, the second the beta, and the third the gamma. The most useful

2 Knight Dunlap, "A Revision of the Fundamental Law of Habit Formation," *Science*, 1928, 67, 360-362.

thing about an array of hypotheses of this kind is that they cause one to plan experiments to test them that would never even have been thought of in the absence of the hypothesis.

Dunlap's beta hypothesis, has for instance, resulted in several experiments in which the subjects practice their errors instead of practicing the correct ways of doing things.

If practice in itself has no effect on learning, its main function must be that of allowing other causal factors an opportunity to operate. Patently, one *does* have to practice, even if it should turn out that actually the *mere* repetition of an act does not account for what and how much is learned. One could never learn to operate a typewriter without actually manipulating a keyboard. But the point of the beta hypothesis is that, if practice allows favorable factors to function, it also allows an equal, or more than equal, opportunity for factors unfavorable to a certain performance to operate, whatever they might turn out to be.

In one experiment to test this hypothesis[3] forty night-school students who studied shorthand acted as subjects. Dictation was given to them which contained an unusual number of words frequently misspelled. From their papers which contained no erasures or corrections of any kind, a study of errors was made. If any error in spelling was found four times, and if the student could spell it correctly orally, the error was classed as a constant automatic error in typing. There were two students who made eight such errors apiece, and nine more who made four each. These words were then divided into two equal groups. Group one was to be practiced in error and group two practiced correctly. The student's attention was called to the fact that he was making automatic errors and he was instructed to write the words of group one incorrectly, i.e., as he had been making the error. These instructions were uniformly considered unusual, funny, mysterious. The practice in error was supervised to assure that the students would, as directed, type eight full lines of each error. The words of the other group were assigned for the same amount of ordinary drill, i.e., typed correctly.

In an examination of the subsequently typed papers *not a single*

[3] J. Q. Holsopple and V. A. Vanouse, "A Note on the Beta Hypothesis of Learning," *School and Society*, 1929, 29, 15-16.

*one of the eleven students made an error in the words which were
practiced in error while all except one continued to make the errors
which were supposed to have been drilled out of them* by practicing
the correct responses.

3. MOTIVATION AND LEARNING

The connection between the problems of motivation and learning can best be perceived by recalling the experimental situations in
which motivation is studied in animals. We have shown how
Warden and others (page 189) put an obstruction between a hungry rat and a dish of food. This arrangement permitted them to
study the drive or "energy" with which an animal went about obtaining the food. The process of crossing a charged grill was very
simple. In the maze experiments with animals there is also an obstruction interposed between the hungry animal and the food box.
But this obstruction is of an entirely different nature from the
electrically charged grill. It is a long, and in some instances a complicated, pathway which, to be mastered effectively, does not require
so much brute force as cleverness on the part of the animals.

So long as the maze remains constant and the degree of hunger
or the amount and kind of reward is varied in different experiments, the maze technique can be used to measure the strength of
different drive conditions (page 193). But the fundamental assumption in these experiments is that the cleverness—or, more technically, the maze-learning ability—of the different groups of animals
is the same. The assumption is probably warranted because large
enough groups are used to iron out individual differences.

There is another possibility. If we are interested in the effect of
alleys of different lengths or of turns in different directions or maze
floors of different composition, these things can be varied and the
motivating conditions kept constant. Then we are studying learning.[4]

Kuo's[5] apparatus allowed his animals to get to food by four alter-

[4] There is still another possibility. When the maze is constant and when the
motivating conditions are constant, some animals still learn more quickly than
others. We have already discussed an experiment of this kind.
[5] Zing Yang Kuo, "The Nature of Unsuccessful Acts and Their Order of Elimination in Animal Learning," *Journal of Comparative Psychology*, 1922, 2, 1-27.

native routes. One of them had an electric grill in the floor; as far as this one alley was concerned, the situation duplicated Warden's (cf. page 189), but the other three alleys presented possibilities of selection that Warden's setup did not offer. One of these three was arranged so that if the animal chose it he was confined for a short time. Another alley led to a long pathway with several turns in it before food was available; the last led directly to the food. In actual practice the position of the compartments was changed so that the easily learned position habits would not be confused with the effect of the different kinds of alleys.

We will not go into detail in examining the behavior of the thirteen rats Kuo studied, although their responses are interesting. It is sufficient for our purpose to observe that on the whole the electric shock compartment was eliminated first, the confinement compartment second, and then the long path. The short path compartment for most rats was the one eventually used exclusively. This result shows that *the consequences of an act are powerful determiners of whether or not it will be repeated.* A shock causes an actual withdrawal from the point where food is. As a consequence behavior for a time is variable and some other method of solution is tried. The confinement causes an interruption in the goal-directed activity and the consequent variability in performance is the same. Least interference with motivated activity comes about as a result of the latter two paths. They survive the elimination process. We can infer from this that any condition which intercepts or deflects the activity of a goal-directed animal will finally be eliminated in favor of an alternative possibility in which the consummatory act can take place more promptly or more completely.

Human subjects have been shocked for taking the right pathway in ordinary finger mazes and some modifications of them. The promptness of their learning has been compared with a shock administered for going into the blind alleys. Under these conditions it sometimes happens that the correct path for which the subject is shocked—punished, if you will—is learned more promptly than the reverse condition, where he is punished for making the errors. The interpretation of these experiments is still being argued, some holding that they show that punishment cannot explain why errors are eliminated. But there is little agreement on this point; a final interpretation will have to wait for more experimental evidence.

4. LEARNING ABILITY AND DELAY OF REWARD

We usually learn for a reason, and more often than not, that reason is some reward which is given to us for a correct performance. It may take any form—an approving word, a high examination grade, or a material gain in the form of food or money. The nature of this reward—its quantity or quality—is significantly related to the manner in which we perform in the task we are learning. A matter of further significance is the degree of separation in time between the moment a response is made and the moment that the rewarding for that response occurs. The importance of this temporal separation was investigated by Riesen[6] in an experiment with chimpanzees as subjects.

The problem. The task which Riesen set for his two chimpanzees was to learn to find food behind one of two doors. The doors were colored red or green, and the animal was required to discover which color concealed the reward—a small section of orange.

The apparatus. The chimpanzees were confronted with a box in which there were two doors made of milk glass. Lights from behind shone on the glass, coloring one of the doors red and one green. Above each of the doors there was a button which, when held down continuously, caused the doors to move backward. If the correct button was pressed, food would be delivered in ten seconds by a vending machine that was tripped by the door movement. In addition to these buttons there was a lever between the doors which also had to be depressed for food to be obtained. The apparatus was constructed so that either color could light either the right or left door.

Preliminary training. The animals were first trained in the use of the buttons as a way of obtaining food. In the beginning, the period of delay between the time the button was first pressed and the food was delivered was only a second or two. After the animals

6 A. H. Riesen, Delayed Reward in Discrimination Learning," *Comparative Psychology Monographs,* 15, 1940, p. 54.

had learned this, the delay was increased to ten seconds. Next the chimpanzees were trained to press the central lever, this being demonstrated to them by the experimenter. During all of this period the doors were not colored but remained a neutral gray. In other words, this preliminary training simply taught the animal that he could get food by pressing down one or the other of the buttons. It also taught him that he would have to wait ten seconds for the food to come after the button was first pressed.

The experiment. After the animals had become proficient in manipulating the apparatus, one door was lighted red and the other green. Food was given only behind the red doors. In order that color alone would serve as a cue for the correct response, the colors were shifted from one side to the other in a random sequence. Thus sometimes the food would be behind the right door and sometimes the left, but always it was behind the door that was lighted red. Training was continued until the criterion of eighteen correct trials out of twenty was reached. After this the food was placed behind the green door for a series of trials and the chimpanzees were required to learn to avoid the red and approach the green. Success in reaching the same criterion in this habit was then followed by another series of trials with red once more becoming the signal for the correct door.

You will recall that the food was not delivered until ten seconds after the lever was pressed. Now if the light remains on until the food is delivered, there is no time separation between the termination of the cue stimulus, the color, and the occurrence of the reward. That is the situation just described. A temporal separation can be introduced by causing the light stimulus to terminate before the food is presented. This is what was done during the remaining parts of the experiment.

When the colored stimulus light was turned off one second before the food was delivered, the number of trials required to learn the act was increased 148 per cent over what it had been with no temporal separation. With a two-second separation the increase was 240 per cent. At four seconds one animal failed completely and the other showed a 527 per cent increase. Neither of the animals could solve the problem when the separation was as long as eight seconds.

354

Summary of the experiment. The result of this experiment seems at first glance to be either contradictory of common experience or simply an indication of the stupidity of chimpanzees. All of us can cite instances from our past when we have learned connections which have been separated in time by more than a few seconds. Actually in a later part of the above experiment Riesen did discover that the chimpanzees could learn with delays if certain very special conditions were employed. When the apparatus was arranged so that the animal was required to make a kind of response when reacting to one door different from that when reacting to the other, learning at long delays did occur. This gives us a cue as to the wherefore of the apparent contradiction between the experiment and personal experience. Humans are equipped with language mechanisms by means of which we can make a differential response which can carry over the stimulus in time. We can say "It's behind the red one," or "behind the green." We use the symbols of language to bring the stimulus forward in time so that it coincides with the reinforcement.

Infants, since they do not possess language facility, or have only a meager number of verbal responses, would be limited in their performance in the same way as chimpanzees are. Even in older children the temporal factor is an important one, and a wise parent does not set up goals for his child that lie in the distant future. The present experiment, and many others, have attested to the great significance of time relations for efficient learning. A matter of seconds, or perhaps a fraction of a second, may make the difference between good and poor learning. It is a basic principle of learning that *the closer in time the consequences of acts are to the stimuli which guide the acts, the better will be the learning.*

5. GUIDANCE

If a typical human subject who is trying to learn a maze is told, "Now here is a difficult problem. I am going to help you by telling you that the correct turn at the first chaise point is to the right," we might expect that many of the total number of errors would be eliminated. Whether this reduction would actually result from instructions of this kind in this problem we have no way of knowing in the absence of an actual demonstration of its verity. But one frequently hears a teacher say, "Now you take my word that such-and-such is so. Then try to find out the answer to this, and this, and this on your own." The usual teaching techniques involve guidance and direction and limits as to the final outcome of a problem, particularly in the earlier stages of solution. After that wise teachers gradually withdraw their directional influence while foolish ones solve problems completely for their pupils and, as a consequence, develop a group of intellectually ineffectual dependents.

Carr and his students[7] have tried to find out whether a subject, either animal or human, can master a problem more quickly when his reactions to that problem are guided and directed than when he is compelled to solve the problem on his own initiative. The guidance that they used was mechanical in some instances, i.e., a maze, for example, had all of the blind alleys plugged so that no errors could be made in certain guided trials. In other cases the guidance was manual, in which case a person who knew the way through a maze actually led a person who didn't know by the hand. This technique may have been suggested by the etymology of *educate,* which comes indirectly from the Latin *educere,* "to lead out of." In still other cases the guidance consisted merely of information about errors, a function fulfilled by the professional teacher who marks errors on papers. In still other cases the guidance was given by verbal direction, a technique frequently used as a practical timesaving device in laboratory courses.

In all of the experiments which Carr reports, whether made with rats or human beings, the device used to measure the effectiveness of the learning was related to this timesaving feature of teaching. If a group of subjects required, on the average, thirty trials to learn a maze, and another group, after five guided trials, had to have twenty more to reach the same criterion of mastery, then it is clear that five guided trials are equal to ten unguided ones. Each guided trial is equal in learning effectiveness to two unguided ones. On the other hand, it might turn out that after five guided runs, an additional twenty-five trials would be required to meet the criterion. In

7 Harvey Carr, "Teaching and Learning," *Journal of Genetic Psychology,* 1930, 37, 189-219. This is a summary of several experimental studies.

that case since the total is thirty, there would be no advantage at all in the guided trials. Each guided run is equal to one unguided.

There is also the possibility that a group of subjects might be somewhat worse off after having had guidance. This would be true if they required more trials to learn than a comparison group which had not been guided.

Table A shows results of this kind for several different experiments with human subjects on mazes. The table is to be read as follows: When 2 guided trials are numbers 1 and 2, each guided run is equivalent to 3.7 unguided. When trials 1 and 2 are undirected and 3 and 4 are guided, then each unguided trial is equal to —3.0 directed trials. The minus sign indicates that more trials were required by the guided group.

Note that guidance is never detrimental when instituted late in the practice, but neither is it very effective. On the other hand, *it may be positively detrimental, as shown by the minus sign, if instituted early in the practice.* This statement is truer for the longer periods of guidance than it is for the shorter.

In another set of experiments the alleys in the mazes were not blocked, but a person who knew the maze pattern manually directed the subject. The results for this kind of guidance are shown in Table B.

Manual guidance was never detrimental, but in all those cases where the numbers in the table are less than one, guided trials are not so effective as the unguided. The larger the numbers, the more effective is guidance. These large numbers occur first, *where the amount of guidance is small,* and second, *where guidance comes early, but not at the very beginning of the learning process.*

Summary. On the basis of far more data than we have given here, Carr concludes,

For the most part, the efficacy of the tuition [guidance] tended to decrease with the amount given and the later in the learning stage in which it was instituted. The most effective results are secured generally by giving a small amount of tuition [guidance] relatively early in the process. Detrimental results were generally secured when too much tuition [guidance] was given or when it was inserted at an inopportune time.

TABLE A

MECHANICAL GUIDANCE

NUMBER OF GUIDED TRIALS	NUMBER OF UNDIRECTED RUNS THAT ARE EQUIVALENT TO ONE DIRECTED RUN					
2	3.7 (1–2)	−3.0 (3–4)	0.6 (5–6)	1.6 (7–8)	4.3 (9–10)	3.0 (11–12)
4	1.8 (1–4)		0.15 (5–8)		1.7 (9–12)	
6	0.1 (1–6)			1.2 (7–12)		
8	−1.6 (1–8)				0.9 (9–16)	
12	−0.12 (1–12)					

TABLE B

MANUAL GUIDANCE

NUMBER OF GUIDED TRIALS	NUMBER OF UNDIRECTED RUNS THAT ARE EQUIVALENT TO ONE GUIDED RUN			
2	3.8 (1–2)	5.9 (3–4)	3.2 (7–8)	0.4 (11–12)
4	0.9 (1–4)	2.0 (5–8)	1.0 (9–12)	
8	1.2 (1–8)			
12	0.9 (1–12)			
16	0.2 (1–16)			

6. RECITATION

If you read anything over twenty times you will not learn it by heart so easily as if you were to read it only ten, trying to repeat it between whiles, and when memory failed looking at the book.[8]

Gates's experiment was designed to answer the extremely prac-

[8] Francis Bacon, *Novum Organum*, 1620, Trans. James Spedding, 1863, 229; cited by Gates, *op. cit.*

358

'ical question, "What are the relative values of learning by reading as compared to learning by recitation in the case of school children working under school conditions and with the ordinary schoolroom methods of attack?"

To satisfy the practical nature of his problem, Gates[9] secured his subjects from a grammar school in Oakland, California. All the grades from the first through the eighth, comprising somewhat more than three hundred individuals, took part in various parts of the study.

Some preliminary experiments indicated that material similar to the sample shown on page 360 could be used and at the same time was nearly enough like the kinds of things that children have to do in the classroom to form a reasonable task.

It was planned to provide for six different combinations of reading and recitation:

	1	2	3	4	5	6
Per cent of time reading	100	80	60	40	20	10
Per cent of time reciting	0	20	40	60	80	90

It is perfectly obvious that if a single group of subjects using a single text used method 1 and was compared with a different group of subjects using method 2, there would be no assurance that whatever differences were found would not be due to a difference in the groups. The problem of *equalizing* the groups and the materials, the time of day and the amount of previous practice was solved according to the following plan: At 9.00 A.M. of the first day, a group was given its first sitting under method 1, using text 1. A second group then studied the same text according to method 2; then group 3 worked according to method 3. The complete details of the plan are shown in the table on page 362. The personnel of each group—seven or eight individuals—remained constant for the duration of the experiment.

Method of studying. A single squad was seated at the table in the experimental room, a copy of the material was passed out face

9 Arthur I. Gates, "Recitation as a Factor in Memorizing," *Archives of Psychology,* 1917, No. 40.

downward before each pupil, and the following instructions were given:

> On each of these cards is a biography (show a sample). Now the object of the test today is to see how many of these things you can learn in a certain short time.
>
> We will proceed like this. I will give you two signals to start. At "Ready" you take the card at the corner like this and at "Go" you turn the card over and begin to study.
>
> Now you are going to study for a while in one way and then later you are going to study in a very different way. To begin with you are to study by reading this material over and over from beginning to end [illustrate]. Remember you are to read only. You should never look away from the paper; never close your eyes to see if you can say the words; in fact never say a single word unless you are actually looking at it, actually reading it. Remember you are to read through from the first to the last every time.
>
> After you have read the material through and through in this way for a while, I am going to give you a signal "Recite." When I say "Recite" you are to hold your paper in front of you so that when you are looking straight ahead, you look over the top of it and you can see it by glancing downward a little like this. Now you are to try to say to yourselves as much of the material as you can without looking at the card. When you cannot remember the next word look down at your card and then go on saying as many of them as possible without looking. Glance at the card again whenever you cannot remember. Go through the list from the first word to the last in this way and continue until the word "Time" is given. Remember you are not to look at the words unless you absolutely have to.
>
> When the learning period is over I am going to ask you to write as much of this material as you can.

Method of scoring. The sense material was scored by dividing the original texts into details, ideas, or facts that were mentioned, to serve as a guide. One credit was given for the correct reproduction of each of these "details" when they fell under the proper name. When a detail, such as a birthplace, was correctly reproduced but applied to the wrong person, one half a unit was given. In some cases the credits of one half or three fourths were given to details or facts partly correct, depending upon the judgment of the grader.

Part of the sense material was scored by one individual and part by another, neither of whom was acquainted with the experiments in general. To test the reliability of the judgments, forty papers were scored independently by each grader. Variations of

Sample of Material Used in Grades 5, 6, 7, and 8

James Church, born in Michigan, February 15, 1869. Studied in Munich, and later studied forestry and agriculture. Director of Mt. Rose Weather Observatory in 1906. Studied evaporation of snow, water content, and frost.

John Clark, born in Indiana, June 4, 1867. Studied surgery and became a doctor in Philadelphia. Taught at Johns Hopkins. Has visited Italy and Russia. Has a brother in Vancouver.

Morton Clover, born in Ohio, April 25, 1875. Studied chemistry at Michigan. Worked in Manila for eight years. Wrote articles on the content of dogwood, of sugar, and acids. Now lives in Detroit.

Clarence Cory, born in Indiana, September 4, 1872. Studied in Purdue and Cornell Universities. Now he lives in Berkeley. Is Professor of Engineering and Dean of Mechanics. Since 1901 has been Consulting Engineer of San Francisco. Is a member of the British Institute.

George Curtis, born in Massachusetts, July 10, 1872. Studied geography at Harvard. Won gold medals at Paris in 1900. Member of Boston Scientific Society. Went on the Dixie Expedition in 1902.

The eighth grade used five biographies; the fifth and sixth used four. There were six texts of equal difficulty in all.

Sample of Material Used in Grades 3 and 4

Harry is fourteen years old. His father is a farmer. Around the farm are red stones, blackberry bushes, red clay, green clover, and small trees. Harry is in the eighth grade and is tall and slender. He likes dancing and singing.

James was born in June, 1905. He is going to be a carpenter. He can make a chair, a stool, a box, a gate, and a window. His mother has white hair and wears a black dress. His father is fifty-five years old.

Harold was born in New York. He came to California when six years old. He is now fifteen years old and has a gun, a bicycle, a kite, a pair of skates, and a baseball suit. He is going to be a lawyer and live in Seattle.

Fred was born in March, 1898. He lives on 31st and Parker streets. He goes to business college. He is tall, has black hair and blue eyes, wears a gray suit and brown necktie. His home is made of brick and granite.

The fourth grade used four biographies; the third grade used three. In all here were six texts of equal difficulty.

PLAN OF THE EXPERIMENT

Day 1	Day 2	Day 3	Day 4	Day 5	Day 6	Total
Method 1						
Group 1	Group 2	Group 3	Group 4	Group 5	Group 6	All groups
Trial 1	Trial 2	Trial 3	Trial 4	Trial 5	Trial 6	All trials
Hour A	Hour F	Hour E	Hour D	Hour C	Hour B	All hours
Text 1	Text 2	Text 3	Text 4	Text 5	Text 6	All texts
Method 2						
Group 2	Group 3	Group 4	Group 5	Group 6	Group 1	All groups
Trial 1	Trial 2	Trial 3	Trial 4	Trial 5	Trial 6	All trials
Hour B	Hour A	Hour F	Hour E	Hour D	Hour C	All hours
Text 1	Text 2	Text 3	Text 4	Text 5	Text 6	All texts
Method 3						
Group 3	Group 4	Group 5	Group 6	Group 1	Group 2	All groups
Trial 1	Trial 2	Trial 3	Trial 4	Trial 5	Trial 6	All trials
Hour C	Hour B	Hour A	Hour F	Hour E	Hour D	All hours
Text 1	Text 2	Text 3	Text 4	Text 5	Text 6	All texts
Method 4						
Group 4	Group 5	Group 6	Group 1	Group 2	Group 3	All groups
Trial 1	Trial 2	Trial 3	Trial 4	Trial 5	Trial 6	All trials
Hour D	Hour C	Hour B	Hour A	Hour F	Hour E	All hours
Text 1	Text 2	Text 3	Text 4	Text 5	Text 6	All texts
Method 5						
Group 5	Group 6	Group 1	Group 2	Group 3	Group 4	All groups
Trial 1	Trial 2	Trial 3	Trial 4	Trial 5	Trial 6	All trials
Hour E	Hour D	Hour C	Hour B	Hour A	Hour F	All hours
Text 1	Text 2	Text 3	Text 4	Text 5	Text 6	All texts
Method 6						
Group 6	Group 1	Group 2	Group 3	Group 4	Group 5	All group
Trial 1	Trial 2	Trial 3	Trial 4	Trial 5	Trial 6	All trials
Hour F	Hour E	Hour D	Hour C	Hour B	Hour A	All hours
Text 1	Text 2	Text 3	Text 4	Text 5	Text 6	All texts

small magnitude were found, but these were due to variable errors that compensated each other in the long run, producing, on an average, forty scores with very slight differences.

Results. The results for the eighth grade and the third grade are shown here and are typical of the results from all the grades and from a few adults who also served as subjects.

	1	*2*	*3*	*4*	*5*	*6*
Grade 8.	20.8	22.4	24.8	25.0	25.3	23.8
Relative score.	87.8	94.6	105.0	105.5	106.8	100.0
Grade 3.	8.7	10.3	11.2	14.2	13.1	12.1
Relative score.	74.8	89.3	96.5	121.9	113.1	104.4

The relative score was computed by taking the average raw score of all methods and all grades as 100. Proportionally as the results from individual methods are above or below this average, they either exceed or fall short of 100.

We may conclude:

(1) The best results are obtained by introducing recitation after having devoted not more than 40 per cent of the time to reading.

(2) The *best* method for the various groups (condition 4) is from 17 to 47 per cent better than straight reading.

(3) Reading alone without recitation always gives the poorest performance.

(4) The lower grades benefit most from recitation.

Practical application. Many students know no better method of studying than to read over and over again the material they are trying to study. According to the results of this experiment, this is the worst possible method to use. Frequent reviews, thinking the matter over by oneself, writing briefs of the main points, conversation with other students, and the like, are valuable because they throw into relief the portions that are hazy, inexact, and confused and because they fix more clearly in mind the material that is rehearsed.

Various opinions have been expressed with regard to methods

of taking notes during lectures. Doubtless the method must be varied somewhat to suit the material that is presented, but the findings in the present study suggest a method which, although seldom employed, should bring good results. Instead of making oneself a mechanism for transferring spoken words to paper with but little heed to their meaning, the student could devote his attention to a thorough understanding of the material presented, selecting the important points, organizing them into a systematic whole as the lecture progresses, and, for the most part, delaying until a later hour the writing of the notes. Later in the day or evening, the lecture could be rehearsed and an outline written down for future reference. While some disadvantages or, more likely, inconveniences of such a method may appear, certain advantages of an important nature are obvious. First of all, the student may develop better habits of attention during the lecture. He forces himself to pick out the essentials, to grasp the relations of ideas, and to unify and to organize the material presented.

7. THE TRANSFER OF TRAINING

In an article in a nontechnical magazine which describes the kinds of things a boy should learn in order to become an effective adult in outlook and action, the notion is expressed that fencing is a valuable art. It is believed that the speed and dexterity necessary as part of this art will make the boy quick and accurate in his later intellectual accomplishments. The same idea motivates football coaches who are more interested in training for teamwork and cooperation than in winning games. Whatever we may think privately about the sincerity of most coaches, there must be some who are firmly convinced that teamwork learned now on the gridiron is to be useful later when the player sells bonds. The same idea is expressed when it is more romantically said that "the Battle of Waterloo was won on the playing fields of Eton." The technical term used by psychologists to cover phenomena of this kind is *transfer of training*.

Originally the concept of transfer of training was based on the notion that psychological functioning is like muscle functioning It makes no difference how an individual muscle cell is stimulated. It grows stronger with use whether that use comes in connection with rowing, hoeing, raking, sawing, or routine gymnastic exercise. The doctrine of formal discipline attempted to apply this same idea to reasoning, honesty, memory, attention, and the like. Experiments finally showed that this notion was false. They failed to show that transfer from one activity to another was always on the side of advantage for the later task and always complete in the sense that nothing was wasted or lost. We now know that one thing learned can aid, hinder, or have no effect on the learning of some subsequent performance. The aiding and the hindering can appear in different amounts. Whether it will aid or hinder subsequent learning depends on a number of factors.

We have touched on this general topic in our first chapter where we showed that the superiority of Latin students over their fellows who are not taking Latin is due to selection rather than to any direct contribution to scholarship from the Latin course itself.

In this section we reopen the problem with the description of an experiment by Bruce[10] which makes an analysis of some of the factors involved in the transfer of training. This experiment accomplished the analysis by breaking down the two tasks learned into the particular stimuli and the particular responses involved. The problem it investigated was whether or not similarity between the stimuli in the first and second tasks, and similarity between the responses in the first and second tasks had any effect upon the amount and direction (whether helpful or harmful) of transference.

The general plan of the experiment required the subjects to learn one list of nonsense syllables and then to learn another list. The first and the second lists were related to each other in various ways. In some lists the stimulus words of each list were alike, in others the response terms being alike, while in still others neither of these terms were alike. By making a comparison of the rate of learning of these lists it became possible to determine what conditions produce transfer.

Subjects. The subjects in the experiment were eighty-one college students.

[10] Robert W. Bruce, "Conditions for Transfer of Training," *Journal of Experimental Psychology*, 16, 1933, 343-361.

Methods. Each list consisted of pairs of syllables, one of the syllables being the stimulus term and the other the response term. There were from five to seven of these pairs in each list. The subjects were seated before an exposure device consisting of a shield in which a small window was cut. The various syllables were printed on a strip of paper, and when this paper was moved behind the shield the syllables could be exposed one after another. The stimulus term of a pair was first presented for a period of two seconds, then the strip was moved and both the stimulus and response terms appeared in the window. After two seconds the stimulus word of the next pair was exposed, and so on through the list. The subjects' task was, of course, to give the correct response word when its stimulus word was shown. The two-second interval between the time a stimulus word was exposed and the time the response term appeared gave the subject an opportunity to anticipate the correct response to each stimulus word.

The experimental conditions. The specific questions that the experimenter was attempting to answer were these:

(1) How is the learning of the second list affected when it involves making *a new response to an old stimulus?*

(2) How is the learning of the second list affected when it involves making *an old response to a new stimulus?*

(3) How is the learning of the second list affected when *the stimulus and the response terms of both lists are unlike each other?*

The answers to these questions could be obtained by requiring the subject to learn pairs of lists in which the stimulus and response terms of the pairs bear a certain relationship to each other. This relationship is dependent upon the question to be answered. In the table an example is given of the kind of relationship of the stimulus and response terms for each of the three conditions.

In order to determine what effect learning the first list had upon learning the second it was necessary to run a control condition in which only the second list was learned. By comparing the performance of these control groups with the groups who learned both lists, the effect of the first list upon the second could be readily evaluated. For the experimental groups who learned both lists, the

First List Learned		Second List Learned		Nature of the Condition
Stimulus	Response	Stimulus	Response	
Reg	Kiv	*Reg*	Zam	Stimuli the same—responses different
Lan	*Gip*	Fis	*Gip*	Stimuli different—responses the same
Xal	Pom	Bef	Yor	Stimuli different—responses different

first list was always presented twelve times. The second list was repeated until the subject was able to recite it once correctly. The number of times that the list was presented until this criterion of one perfect recitation was reached was the subjects' learning score.

Nature of the Condition	Trials to Learn for Experimental Group	Trials to Learn for Control Group	Per Cent Experimental of Control
Stimuli same—response different	11.2	10.3	109
Stimuli different—response same	9.0	14.4	63
Stimuli different—response different	8.3	9.9	84

Results. The results of the experiment are presented in the table. These results are averages of the number of trials in presenting the second list before the criterion of learning was reached. The results are given for the control group, which learned only the second list, and for the experimental group, which learned another list before the second one.

From an examination of the scores for the three conditions of

367

the control groups it is apparent that the three lists are not of equal difficulty. This does not matter, however, for the experimental group learned the same list that its respective control group learned. The answer to the three questions that were asked may be obtained by looking at the percentage column and finding out how well the experimental group did in comparison with its control.

1. The results under condition one show that when the task involves attaching a new response to an old stimulus the transfer is negative or detrimental. The previous learning, far from developing some general ability called "memory," actually interferes with the new task to be learned. This is called "negative transfer," and it is not uncommon. The reader who has learned two foreign languages has probably noticed this phenomenon when he tries to think of the foreign equivalent of an English word in one language and comes up with the proper word in the other language. Years ago the various automobile manufacturers used different positions of the gear shift for the different gear speeds. What was the location of low gear for one make of car might be reversed for another. To the stimulus "put it in high" one response had to be made in one car and, to the same stimulus, a different response was required in another car. The negative transfer which drivers encountered when driving different cars produced so much confusion that the manufacturers were forced to adopt a standard gear shift.

2. Condition two reverses this trend. The experimental group took only 63 per cent as many trials to learn as did the control group. Obviously a great deal of gain accrues when we attach an old response to a new stimulus. A famous right-handed tennis player was noted for the great strength of his backhand stroke. One of the reasons for his excellence lay in the fact that he had batted left-handed in baseball and the general form of this batting swing could be carried over to the new stimulus situation of a backhand and stroke in tennis. The student who has taken objective examinations in one course finds it easier to take similar examinations in another. He has learned techniques of evaluating and weighing the choices, of looking for possible pitfalls, of reading the items carefully, and these techniques aid him in handling the new material in the new course. In social situations it operates as well. The child who learns the response of

throwing a temper tantrum in one situation will more probably use it in another. Many of the learning situations which the adult meets permit him to draw from his past repertoire of responses and thus to facilitate his learning.

3. Condition three stands, in efficiency, between one and two. At first glance it might appear that we are dealing here with a training of the general ability of memory; for neither stimulus or response terms of the first and second learning are the same. Actually if we analyze the situation we will recognize that there is something in common between learning the first and second lists. True, the nonsense syllables used are different, but some responses that the subject has learned in the first situation can be used in the second. He may have learned some system of recalling the syllables, he probably has become adjusted to the two-second pauses between the stimulus and response words, and he may have learned to disregard irrelevant stimuli in the room. All of these general responses, and probably others as well, could be carried over to the learning of the second list.

Summary of the experiment. One clear implication of the results of this study is that the transfer of training cannot be accounted for by the development of some very general psychological function such as memory. If this had been the case, then each of the three groups would have shown the same amount of transfer. The amount and the direction of the transfer can be best understood on the basis of the types of stimuli and the types of response involved in the two situations. If two situations require similar responses, then the learning of one of these situations will aid in the learning of the other. Contrariwise, if two situations have similar stimuli but require different responses to be made to these stimuli, then the learning of one will interfere with the other. We do not train for memory in general; we learn stimulus-response relationships.

8. AGE AND ABILITY TO LEARN

There is an adage which says that you cannot teach an old dog new tricks. None of us are quite willing to accept this statement as completely true; for older people, we know, can learn. Yet it does seem to be true that persons of middle age and beyond have more difficulty in mastering certain materials than do young adults. An experiment by Ruch gives some precise information on the ability of the young and old, and, in addition, throws some light upon the reason for age differences in learning ability.[11]

Subjects. One of the most difficult tasks in making comparative studies of the young and the old is to obtain groups at each level who would have been comparable in ability at birth. If the young are drawn from college classes and the old come from a county home, it is fairly certain that the two groups differ not only in age, but also in the socioeconomic level from which they come. Almost certainly, then, the two groups would also differ in their original genetically determined level of ability. Ruch avoided this pitfall by a very clever technique. He offered to give a certain sum of money to a girl scout troop for each scout who would agree to be tested in his experiment, and would bring her parent and her parent's parent to the laboratory. This gave him three different age groups—the child, the mother, and the grandmother. The resultant groups were thus unusually comparable not only culturally, but also genetically. There were forty subjects in each group, and the age range for the young group was twelve to eighteen, the middle was thirty-four to fifty-nine, and the old was sixty to eighty-four.

Method. Five different learning tasks were employed:

(1) DIRECT VISION PURSUIT METER LEARNING. The pursuit meter consists of a phonograph disk made of some insulating material such as hard rubber or Bakelite. A small metal plate about the size of a dime is imbedded in this disk, its surface being flush with the surface of the insulating disk. All of this is mounted on a phonograph motor. The subject is given a stylus and is directed to keep the end of the stylus in contact with the small plate as it revolves. The task is made difficult not only because the disk revolves, but also because the stylus is hinged between the handle and the end. This means that the subject is unable to hold the stylus on the metal disk by

[11] F. C. Ruch, "The Differential Effects of Age upon Human Learning," *Journal of General Psychology*, 11, 1934, 261-286.

sheer pressure, but can keep it on only by making the proper following or pursuit movements. An electric clock operates all the time that the stylus is in contact with the metal plate, and when the stylus slips off this onto the insulating disk, the electrical circuit is broken and the clock stops. Performance is measured in terms of the number of seconds on the plate during each trial. In the present experiment each trial lasted thirty seconds, and twenty-five such trials were given. The subject's score consisted of the total amount of time the stylus was on the spot for all twenty-five trials.

(2) MIRROR VISION PURSUIT METER LEARNING. The procedure here was the same as in procedure one except that a screen was superimposed between the subject's eyes and the turntable, and the disk could be seen only by looking in a mirror.

(3) PAIRED ASSOCIATES LEARNING. The materials for this test were presented in a memory drum which automatically exposed the stimuli for controlled periods of time. These materials consisted of a list of paired words, composed in such a way that those in each pair were meaningfully related to each other. Such pairs as man—boy; soft—chair; walk—car were used. The first word of each of these pairs was presented for five seconds, then the second word appeared in the aperture of the memory drum for one second. The drum then moved on to the next pair on the list, and so on for each of the ten pairs of words. The subjects memorized as many of these pairs as they could. As in the previous experiment the subject was expected to give the correct response word before it appeared in the window. His score was the number of correct anticipations made during fifteen presentations of the list. The test is one which obviously measures the subjects' ability to memorize somewhat meaningful verbal material.

(4) The procedure of this test was the same as that of the test in step three, but the type of material differed. In this instance the materials were arbitrary and nonsensical pairs. Some examples are: $E \times Z = G$; $A \times M = B$; $N \times M = C$.

(5) This step was the same as the two above save that the subjects were required to learn materials which were contrary to their past experience. They were required to learn such pairs as $3 \times 5 = 25$; $3 \times 1 = 1$; $3 \times 4 = 2$.

Before the results of the experiment are considered it would be wise to glance back at the tests employed and consider their rationale. Of the two manual tasks, one is consistent with our past habits, and the other—the mirror pursuit test—requires the learning of eye-hand coordinations that are contrary to our accustomed habits. Of the verbal tasks, one is consonant with past experience, one is neutral, and the other is contrary. The question is whether or not the age effects will show up equally on each of the tasks.

Results. On each of these tests the younger group excelled the older groups, but the extent to which it was superior varied with the task. The relative performance on each of the tasks can be discovered from an examination of the following table. For all tasks the level of performance of the youngest group is given as 100 per cent, and each of the other groups is shown as being a certain percentage of this younger group. Perhaps the first thing to be noted in these results

TASK	PERCENTAGE SCORE		
	Young	Middle	Old
Direct Vision Pursuit	100	98.17	83.72
Mirror Vision Pursuit	100	95.85	52.59
Meaningful Associations	100	91.85	82.96
Nonsense Associations	100	80.00	48.28
Contrary Associations	100	71.72	46.56

Comparison of performance of the three age groups on the different task: The level of performance of the young group is always set at 100 per cent.

is the gradual decline in learning ability with age; for not only is the oldest group inferior to the middle group, but the middle group is, in turn, inferior to the young group. But the inferiority of the older groups differs in amount from task to task. It is least if the task to be learned is consonant with their previous experiences; it is greatest if the task is antagonistic to their previous experiences. The most marked inferiority of the older groups is shown in the minor pursuit task and in the contrary associations; the least in direct vision pursuit and in meaningful associations.

Summary. This experiment has demonstrated that there is a decline in learning ability with increasing age beyond the teens.[12] It has shown also that this decline is greater in some areas of performance than in others. These results could be predicted from our knowledge of the existence of positive and negative transfer. In the instance of the mirror pursuit task and incorrect multiplication the subjects were required to attach new responses to old stimuli. Transfer effects would be negative and the group that had lived the longest would be expected to suffer most. When, as in the meaningful tasks, transfer effects would be mainly positive, the older group did not show such marked inferiority. Age effects in learning are not merely a matter of difficulty in forming stimulus—response connections because of some lack of plasticity of the nervous tissue that aging produces; the effect age will have upon learning will vary with the nature of the new task and the nature of the person's past history. This explains something that many of us may have noted—the ease with which an older person may learn new materials in the field of his life speciality, as contrasted with an apparent denseness of understanding in some new or radically different field.

Summary of the chapter. Modification of behavior is secured more promptly—other conditions remaining constant—when the learners are aware of their progress. Our second experiment shows that if the errors rather than the correct responses are practiced, modification is more permanent in correcting certain kinds of errors in spelling. The third experiment indicates the importance of the consequences of the act in the elimination and fixation of the acts. As the fourth experiment shows, time relation between the consequences of the act and the termination of the stimulus which serves as a guide to the correct choice is an important determiner of the ability to learn.

[12] Actually the ability to learn most tasks increases until somewhere in the middle twenties, and the decline begins very gradually after that.

Teaching involves an active attempt on the part of one person to modify the course of learning in another. One can generalize that guidance should come early in the learning process and that there should be only small amounts of it for the most positive facilitating effect. Making errors is not to be avoided; for from errors some of the most instructive experiences come. The sixth experiment demonstrates that learning is an active process. One must participate; he cannot learn effectively when he passively reads material over and over.

The seventh experiment deals with one of the most important topics in the field of learning—the transference of training. It demonstrates that earlier learning may either facilitate or inhibit later learning, and whether or not it does so can be partly understood on the basis of the stimuli and responses in the two situations. The last experiment compares learning in the young and old and shows how a part of the inferiority of the older people can be understood in the light of the principles of transfer of training.

CHAPTER EIGHTEEN

REMEMBERING

One of the simplest questions that one can ask a person is, "How much of some poem, some course, some mathematical operation, or some remote childhood experience do you remember?" Nevertheless these simple questions have no simple answers. How much of a given experience is retained depends, among other things, upon the way in which retention is to be measured. If one requires a perfect reproduction immediately, with no aids of any kind and with no stumbling around, it is perfectly clear that a high standard is being set; the amount of forgetting a person does, measured in this way, would far exceed the amount he retains.

On the other hand, if a person is required to select only the items he has learned from those that he has not experienced before, the task becomes simpler and the amount that he could be said to have retained would be more.

1. RELATIVITY OF REMEMBERING

The exact relationship between five different methods of measuring retention has been studied by C. W. Luh,[1] who, at the time he made these experiments, was a graduate student at the University of Chicago.

Method. In order to make experiments like this it is necessary to use large amounts of material of equal difficulty. If the memory for a task has been tested twenty minutes after it has first been learned, then that task cannot be used again when the experimenter wants to compare the amount remembered at one hour with that of the twenty-minute period. Another equally difficult task must be used, not the same one. If five different ways of measuring retention are to be compared, as in this experiment, then it would appear that five times as much material must be on hand as would be required for a single measurement. In this experiment there were five periods

[1] C. W. Luh, "The Conditions of Retention," *Psychological Monographs,* 1922, 31, No. 142, 87

of delay after the original learning, twenty minutes, one hour, four hours, twenty-four hours and forty-eight hours. This would mean twenty-five tasks of equal difficulty. As will be explained later, Luh cleverly cut this number down to ten by combining the various retention measures. But even ten different and equally difficult tasks are not easy to provide.

The nearest approximation to this ideal is to be found in nonsense syllables. A series of twelve syllables was learned for each task. The syllables were presented one every two seconds by means of an automatic device. All series were learned to a criterion of one perfect reproduction at one sitting. Then the experiment proper started.

Twenty minutes after the learning, the subject was again seated in front of the exposure apparatus.

(1) He was required to anticipate each exposure of the twelve syllables. Since the rate of exposure was one every two seconds, he had two seconds in which to recall and spell each syllable. The number of times he was correct was recorded. Later the per cent of twelve was determined. The same procedure with a change in lists was repeated twenty-eight times with eight different subjects, the average per cent retained turning out to be about 68, as shown in Figure 75.

(2) The drum was started again and continued to run until the subjects could again anticipate correctly every syllable. Of course, fewer repetitions were required to relearn than to learn, so a comparison of the number of trials for relearning with the number for original learning always shows some retention. In this experiment nine different subjects gave on the average about 75 per cent retention after twenty minutes. For the other time intervals the results closely approximate the curve labeled "Relearning."

The possibilities from this list of syllables were then exhausted so that it had to be discarded. All the subjects then learned another list. This list gave three measures of retention:

(1) The subject was given a piece of paper with twelve lines on it and instructed to write the syllables that he had learned twenty minutes previously. On the average this gave 88 per cent retention. For the other intervals the results follow the curve labeled "Written Reproduction."

376

(2) Immediately following the subject's attempt at written reproduction, he was given a list of twenty-four syllables and required to check the twelve he had learned. There was a time limit of ninety seconds on this task. It revealed on the average a retention of about 98 per cent after the twenty-minute interval, and it consistently gave the highest retention over the whole range of delays, as is shown by its topmost position.

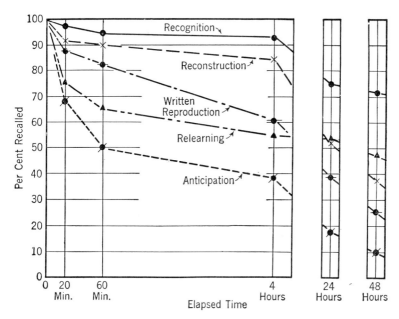

FIG. 75.—Percentage retained measured in five different ways.

(3) Finally the subject was furnished with the twelve syllables he had learned and required to reconstruct the order of the original presentation. This reconstruction method resulted in about 92 per cent accuracy at first. It was second place of all the methods for the first twenty-four hours, after which time it took third position.

If one asks what per cent of a list of nonsense syllables is retained four hours after learning, the answer depends on the method used to measure retention. It can be read from the graph. The same methods of measuring, however, give different results after forty-eight hours. The only generalization that can be made is that the anticipation method invariably shows the least retention; the recognition method, the most. The order of the other methods depends on how soon after the learning retention is tested. These results may not be true for other kinds of material or for other criteria of mastery. Obviously this is not a simple question.

2. REMINISCENCE

Retention curves do not always show a continuous drop; some show an actual increase in the amount recalled as time progresses. In order to distinguish between the two types, those that show decrement have been called *curves of obliviscence,* and those that show increments have been called *curves of reminiscence.* Reminiscence can be observed only in partly learned materials. If material is perfectly learned, there can obviously be no more than 100 per cent recall.

Although the phenomenon of reminiscence has been found in the learning of verbal material,[2] it is most marked in certain motor skills. An experiment conducted by Buxton[3] not only demonstrates the existence of reminiscence, but also shows how its magnitude is related to the degree of mastery of the task at the time that the rest pause occurs.

The task. The motor skill which was measured in this experiment was pursuit meter learning. The apparatus was essentially similar to that employed in the Ruch experiment, which is described in the previous chapter. In the present experiment each trial lasts for fifteen seconds, and the score for each subject was the amount of time the stylus was on the metal plate. The time units used were 1/120 of a second. Between each of the regular trials there was a thirty-second pause. A perfect score on a trial would be 15 times 120, or 1800.

The procedure. Four groups of subjects were used, and they differed from each other only in the time at which a "forgetting"

[2] L. B. Ward, "Reminiscence and Rote Learning," *Psychological Monographs* 1937, 49.
[3] C. E. Buxton, "Level of Mastery and Reminiscence in Pursuit Learning," *Journal of Experimental Psychology,* 1943, 32, 176-180.

interval of ten and one-half minutes was introduced during the learning series. For group one this pause was introduced immediately after the trial on which the subjects had obtained a score which was 7 per cent of the maximum. The pause for group two came following the trial of 26 per cent level of mastery, and the group three received its rest after the 40 per cent trial.[4]

The Control Group. Now in order to know what any one of these groups would have done if the pause had not been introduced, it was necessary to complete the experimental plan by including a control group. The procedure was the same for this group as for the others except that no pause was introduced after any of the trials. They followed throughout the standard procedure of fifteen seconds work, a thirty-second interval, then fifteen seconds work, thirty seconds interval, and so on. This was exactly what group one did until its 7 per cent trial, what two did until its 26 per cent trial, and what three did until its 40 per cent trial. If the original ability of this group was the same as for the control—and there is reason to believe it was—one can compare their trial immediately following their 7, 26, or 40 per cent trial to determine how the ten-and-one-half minute pauses of the experimental groups affected their performance.

It may at first be confusing to notice that there was only one control group for all three experimental groups. Actually no more than one group was required. A control group was required to discover what would have happened if the training had been continuous, and the ten-and-one-half minute pause had not been introduced. By running the control group straight through, the experimenter could notice what their score was on the trial following the 7, 26, and 40 per cent level of mastery and use this for a comparison with the appropriate experimental group. In this way this single group would serve as a control for all of the experimental groups.

The results. The comparative performance of the controls

---

[4] Actually the experimenter had planned to measure at levels of mastery of 5, 20, and 35 per cent, but it was not possible to stop at precisely these points. Because the learning of any subject is not absolutely regular, the subject at one trial might be at 4 per cent of maximum level, and on the next he would jump to 8 per cent of the maximum. All the experimenter could expect to do was to choose the trial on which the score was close to his arbitrarily chosen figures.

and each of the experimental groups is shown in the table. These scores are the mean scores for all the subjects of the particular group. The first column of numbers gives the score of the different groups

Groups	Criterion Trial	Trial After Criterion	Per Cent Increase Over Criterion Trial
7% Experimental..............	151.0	241.7	60
7% Control..................	144.5	171.3	19
26% Experimental.............	438.8	523.4	19
26% Control..................	446.2	417.8	—6
40% Experimental	713.2	714.6	0
40% Control	717.4	637.9	—11

on the trial when the level of mastery of 7, 26, or 40 per cent was reached. It can be seen by examining these scores that the assumption that the control and experimental groups were fairly much alike was warranted. In all cases the differences between the paired groups are very slight.

But although the groups are alike on this trial, they differ quite markedly from each other on the following trial. In each instance the experimental group excels its control on this trial. The difference in procedure between the two groups is that the experimental has had a pause for ten-and-one-half minutes between the criterion trial and its next trial, and the control has simply had the standard thirty seconds wait. Ordinarily when a longer than usual period of time passes between the last learning trial and the next trial, there is a decrease in efficiency and we say that forgetting has occurred. In the present instance there has been an improvement. The psychologists call this *reminiscence*.

Interpretation. At first one is likely to interpret this as recovery from fatigue, but there are several lines of evidence against this view. For one thing, the task is hardly an arduous one. The stylus is light; the subjects worked only fifteen seconds and then had thirty seconds of rest; and the number of trials required to reach even the top level of mastery would sum up to only a few minutes of actual work. Another very significant fact is that the percentage of reminiscence is greatest for the 7 per cent group, the one which would be the least fatigued. This and other studies indicate that reminiscence cannot be accounted for merely by recovery from muscular fatigue. Reminiscence is the product of more complicated psychological processes.

Summary of the experiment. This experiment demonstrates clearly the phenomenon of reminiscence. It goes a step further by showing that the amount of the reminiscences will be related to the degree of learning of the task at the time the pause in practice occurs. It does not, however, explain the phenomenon by isolating all of the various conditions which are necessary for its occurrence. This is a complicated problem which as yet is by no means completely solved. We are as yet unable to say just when we will obtain reminiscence rather than forgetting.

3. BURTT'S EXPERIMENT

We have pointed out in previous experiments that even when there is no overt evidence that a person has ever learned a thing, it is possible to show that previous experience is still effective because he can relearn the same task in much less time. That even very early childhood experiences can be effective was shown by Burtt.[5]

Burtt read passages to his young son from Sophocles' *Oedipus Tyrannus* in the original Greek. At the time of the original reading the boy was between fifteen months and three years of age, a mere infant, so that there was no assurance that he actually learned the material. In the experimental situation he was kept entirely free from toys or playthings.

Beginning at fifteen months, three passages of twenty lines—240 syllables—were read daily for ninety days, i.e., there were ninety repetitions. At the age of eighteen months these three passages were dropped and three more were substituted. This procedure was continued until the child was three years old, whereupon the whole matter was dropped until he was eight and one half years old.

5 H. E. Burtt, "An Experimental Study of Early Childhood Memory," *Journal of Genetic Psychology*, 1932, 40, 287-295.

Selection	Age at Original Learning	Repetitions Required at 8	Average
1	15-18 months	382	
2	18-21 months	253	
3	21-24 months	385	340
4	24-27 months	379	
5	27-30 months	328	
6	30-33 months ·	226	
7	33-36 months	265	299

Average for seven selections.....317

A	8½ years	409	
B	8½ years	451	
C	8½ years	455	

Average for three selections.....435

In the twenty-one months between fifteen and thirty-six there were seven passages read. These seven and three others were learned at age eight and one half years. The three new ones (A, B, C) were presumably of equal difficulty to that of the previously learned selections. The nature of the experiment was explained to the subject, but he was not told which selections had been learned previously and which had not been. For the first seventeen trials the experimenter merely read the selections in the same fashion that they had been read in the beginning. But with the eighteenth trial the subject anticipated wherever he could as the selection was read very slowly. As the experiment progressed he was supplying more and more words and phrases. This procedure, with minor changes, was continued until every word except the cue words at the beginning of each selection was anticipated. It required about eleven months for the first selection to be learned. It was then dropped from the schedule. In sixteen months all the selections had been learned.

The averages to be compared are, in the first place, 435 repetitions required for the new passages (A, B, C) and 317 for the ones heard previously—a saving of 27 per cent.

382

If we compare the repetitions required for material heard at less than two years of age and for new material, we find a 21 per cent saving. But during the latter half of the period, when 299 trials were required, we observe that the saving is 32 per cent. This finding is astounding. One would not be surprised perhaps at 5 per cent saving. But at eight and one half years, to find that almost one third fewer trials are required to learn material *only heard* in the years before three, indicates an influence exerted by the experiences of the early years that could hardly have been foreseen.

SELECTION	AGE AT ORIGINAL LEARNING	REPETITIONS REQUIRED AT 14 YEARS	AVERAGE
1a	15-18 months	142	
2a	18-21 months	139	
3a	21-24 months	169	150
4a	24-27 months	151	
5a	27-30 months	145	
6a	30-33 months	169	
7a	33-36 months	127	148
D	14 years	169	
E	14 years	151	
F	14 years	166	162

Burtt had not used all of his material in this experiment at eight and one half years. When his young son was fourteen, he produced enough material to repeat the whole experiment. The procedure was the same as at eight and one half. For the first eighteen trials, the material was simply read to the subject. Beginning with the nineteenth, every third trial made use of the prompting method in which the subject tried to anticipate as many words and syllables as he could while the passages were slowly read.

The results are shown in a new table (on page 183) which corresponds in significance to the table on page 182.

D, E, and F were new selections which correspond in significance to A, B, and C. The principal comparison is between the average of 162 trials for this new material and 149 for the material experienced between fifteen months and three years of age. This is a saving of thirteen trials or about 8 per cent. Since this saving is to be compared with the 30 per cent that was observed six years previously, it is apparent that there has been a real loss in retention during the interval. It is likely that by the time the boy is of age, there will be no saving at all in favor of the infantile experiences.

4. RETROACTIVE INHIBITION

Forgetting is inevitably tied up with the passage of time. We learn something, we cease to use or practice it, and when we return to the material after this interval of no practice, we usually discover that our skill is less than it was at the end of the learning period. We say that we have forgotten, and we "explain" the act of forgetting by the time that has passed since the last practice period and the period of recall. Superficially this explanation appears satisfactory; lapse of time and forgetting always seem to go hand in hand.

Many years ago a psychologist observed that equal amounts of time did not produce equal forgetting. He noted that the amount of forgetting will be very greatly influenced by *what we do after the original learning.* If the time following the learning was spent in a quiet relaxing activity, the amount of the learned material that was forgotten was far less than if the time were spent in the learning of some other material. To this fact, that material learned at a later date may work back and inhibit the recall of previously learned material, he applied the name *retroactive inhibition.*

Now not all materials are equally productive of retroactive inhibition; some kinds of materials produce more of it than do others. A problem which McGeoch and McDonald[6] investigated was how different degrees of similarity between the first material learned and the second would affect the retention of earlier learned material.

The method. The general plan which was used in this experiment, and in most experiments on retroactive inhibition, is illustrated in the diagram below. From this diagram it can be seen

[6] J. A. McGeoch and W. T. McDonald, "Meaningful Relation and Retractive Inhibition," *American Journal of Psychology*, 1931, 43, 579-588

384

that the two conditions are alike except for what occurs in step two. Now if the two groups are different from each other in the

THE PLAN OF A RETROACTIVE INHIBITION EXPERIMENT

GROUPS	STEP 1 ORIGINAL LEARNING	STEP 2 INTERPOLATED ACTIVITY	STEP 3 RETENTION TEST
Control.........	Learn material A	Rest or relax	Recall material A
Experimental....	Learn material A	Learn material B	Recall material A

amount of material recalled in step three, it must be due to the activities performed in step two. The present experiment is complicated by the fact that there is not one experimental condition, but several. They differed only in the kinds of materials learned in step two.

Six different conditions were used, five experimental and one control. The procedure in step one was the same for all of them. It consisted of five presentations of a list of eleven adjectives. During step two each of the five experimental conditions required the learning of another list of materials. These materials were lists of eleven units and they were presented ten times. The kinds of materials which were presented were:

> Experimental Group I —Synonyms of first list
> Experimental Group II —Antonyms of first list
> Experimental Group III—Unrelated adjective
> Experimental Group IV—Nonsense Syllables
> Experimental Group V —3 place numbers
> Control group—Reading *College Humor*

The control group were not required to memorize anything in the magazine, but were told to relax and read it for enjoyment. It is fairly obvious that these six conditions represent a descending order of similarity from the nature of the first-learned material. It goes from high similarity in the case of the synonyms to very low similarity in the case of the relaxing reading of *College Humor*. The amount of time spent in each of these activities was the same—ten minutes.

Immediately following this the subjects were asked to recall as many words of list one (the list of adjectives learned in step one) as they could.

There were twelve subjects who were used in the experiment. Every subject learned under each of the six conditions. This list was learned in a counterbalanced order, that is, two subjects would first learn under condition one, then under condition 2, and so on. Another pair would start under condition two, then go to condition three, and on through the remainder of the series. This meant that no single condition was favored over another.

Results. The mean number of syllables which were recalled under each condition is shown below. The scores range from one and a quarter syllables in group one to four and a half in group six.

1. Synonyms 1.25
2. Antonyms 1.83
3. Unrelated adjectives............................. 2.17
4. Nonsense Syllables............................... 2.58
5. Three place numbers............................. 3.68
6. College Humor................................... 4.50

There is an unmistakable and undeviating relationship between the degree of similarity of the second list to the first and the amount of retroactive inhibition produced. The fact that these other conditions gave increasing retention scores makes it difficult to account for the superior score in the light-reading situation by maintaining that the subjects were rehearsing what they had just learned instead of reading. The conditions two through five gave no opportunity for rehearsal.

Summary of the experiment. This experiment is one of a number in the literature of psychology which points to the inadequacy of sheer lapse of time as an explanation of forgetting. It, together with others, indicates that most of what is forgotten may arise from the development of conflicting response tendencies following the original learning. The learning of synonyms, which, of course, is very similar to the original material, gave only about 25 per cent as much retention as did the control condition of light reading. It could be predicted from this that if it were somehow possible to suspend all psychological activity after the learning, then when activity was once again resumed, the retention would be perfect or near perfect. This, of course, is impossible, but a close approach to it was made by some experimenters[7] who compared retention when the subjects went to sleep soon after learning with retention when they continued on their normal daily activities. There was a very marked difference in the amount of material retained favoring the condition of sleeping after the learning. This should not, however, be considered justification for dozing off in class.

There is one complication which should be mentioned before this topic is finished. A very important fact is how soon the intermediate activity is begun after the original learning. Experimental work has shown that retroactive inhibition is most marked when it occurs shortly after the learning. This finding would point to the wisdom of a rest pause after the student has finished the study of one assignment and before he begins another.

Summary of the chapter. The first experiment shows how five different answers can be obtained for the simple question of "How much of a given thing do you remember?" The second introduces the concept of reminiscence and indicates that pauses during learning may produce increases in performance rather than losses. The third experiment indicates that retention of verbal material may persist for years even though the material is not meaningful to the subject. The fourth experiment demonstrates one of the most important principles in the field of forgetting; the principle of retroactive inhibition. The amount of forgetting is closely tied up with what we do immediately after the learning. Forgetting does not come about simply because of the lapse of time between learning and recall.

[7] J. G. Jenkins and K. M. Dallenbach, "Oblivescence during Sleep and Waking," *American Journal of Psychology,* 1924, 35, 605-612.

CHAPTER NINETEEN

REASONING

For many centuries it was held that one of the distinguishing characteristics of man was his ability to reason. Reasoning was held to be entirely impossible in animals, whereas it was the most excellent accomplishment of man. Men who didn't act in a manner that others thought they should were frequently described as "bereft of reason." It was as though reason were something that could be put on and taken off like a coat. This was the position of the scholars and the churchmen, who grasped at any suggestion that man and animal formed two entirely different and unrelated systems of life.

Bergen Evans in his *Natural History of Nonsense* makes the point that for hundreds of years "animals were studied not to observe their actual characteristics but to find moral examples in their nature of behavior." Some scholars such as Sir Thomas Browne held that even though most of these stories were "impossible falsities," their "wholesome morality" expiates "the trespass of their absurdities." If a story teaches a wholesome moral, thought Browne, it makes no difference if it is a true story or not.

The common people, while for the most part accepting this dogma, held an ambiguous position. They observed their household pets and their farm animals doing certain things which gave the appearance of their having perceived certain relations. Their dogs and cats were, in many instances, endowed with an ability to reason and to understand that we now know is entirely beyond their capacities. This process of interpreting the behavior of animals in terms of one's own reactions is called "anthropomorphism."

As zoology became less the handmaiden of a doubtful ethics, some students spent a great deal of time emphasizing the random and undirected character of animal behavior. Many books were written which "proved" that animals were incapable of reasoning.

As is true so often in these extreme views, modern findings have shown both camps to be wrong, although there need no longer be ambiguity in a view which allows animals a limited ability to see relations and combine experiences in new ways.

388

The year 1910 marked the appearance of two small volumes which were to have a tremendous influence on all later studies of reasoning, or problem solving, which really mean the same thing. In this year Ruger's study of puzzle solving, published under the misleading title of "The Psychology of Efficiency," [1] and Dewey's *How We Think* made their appearance. Dewey's[2] revised edition should be read by every student who has any interest in the problems of thinking or reasoning.

1. RUGER'S STUDY

Ruger's volume was the report of an experimental study which he made of adult subjects who solved the kinds of puzzles that all of us have amused ourselves with at one time or another. A familiar example of the kind of task he used is to be found in the "twisted nail" puzzle. Two common nails are twisted together in such a way that they have to be turned just right with respect to each other before they can be got apart. If you will recall your own fumbling with the nails and how, after a great deal of twisting which got you nowhere, suddenly the nails seemed to fall apart without your being able to observe in what relation they were to each other when they came apart, you will have some notion of the problem which confronted Ruger's subjects. He found that the highly touted reasoning ability of adult human beings is a gross misstatement of fact. His subjects made as many random undirected movements as any lower animal ever did. Many subjects arrived at solutions that took them entirely by surprise and that they could not repeat. Ruger concluded that *there was no sharp line of demarcation between the human being who could reason and the infra human who could not.*[3] But aside from this generalization, important though it is, his experiments showed how problem solving, or reasoning, could be experimentally

---

[1] *Archives of Psychology*, 1910, No. 15.

[2] John Dewey, *How We Think*, 1910, D. C. Heath and Company, Boston, Rev. Ed., 1933.

[3] This generalization would not have been justified if based on Ruger's data alone. He worked only with human subjects but he had available in the work of others fairly complete descriptions of animal behavior. For an extensive treatment of the data and generalizations in the field of reasoning animals see N. R. F. Maier and T. C. Schneirla, *Principles of Animal Psychology*, McGraw-Hill Book Company, Inc., New York, 1935, especially pages 444-479.

manipulated. This was an important methodological step, because the so-called "mental processes" had previously resisted the methods that had been used to study them.

2. DEWEY'S CONTRIBUTION

Dewey's principal contributions were his analysis of the conditions under which reasoning occurs and his outline of a typical reasoning process. In the first decade of the twentieth century, before his book appeared, most psychologists had been interested in a rather futile argument about whether or not there could be any thinking without images of concrete objects and events. But Dewey's little book exerted a marked influence in turning the interest away from sterile controversies of this kind.[4] There is nothing experimental in his book, but it shows how the environment and the human organism together in interrelation must be considered if one is to set up experiments to answer questions about problem solving. It suggested that good reasoning was not wholly a matter of being born capable. It held that normal people can be trained to be more effective reasoners than they now are. Aside from its effect on psychology, it has had a tremendous influence on the course of education, particularly in the elementary school where there has been a complete revision of the curriculum because of the principles set forth in it.

Dewey showed that as long as the previously learned reactions were adequate for situations, no problem-solving activity occurred. But when none of these old patterns of response results in a consummatory activity, then the stage is set for a rather definite process which he outlines. It consists essentially of formulating a hypothesis and testing it out, generally, but not always, through the process of talking to oneself. If the hypothesis is substantiated by further observation, it is held to be true. He illustrates by pointing to an experience of his own in trying to find out for himself the function of a white pole that extends horizontally from the upper deck of a ferryboat. His first hypothesis was that "it might be a flagpole," but the further

---

[4] The controversy was not uninfluenced by others who held similar views, especially William James, James R. Angell, and Harvey Carr. Cf. Fred S. Keller, *The Definition of Psychology, 1937,* D. Appleton-Century Company, Inc., New York, pp. 40-53. and Edna Heidbreder, *Seven Psychologies,* D. Appleton-Century Company, Inc., 1933.

observation that there is no rope or any other kind of gear attached to the pole, added to its horizontal position, an unusual one for the flagpoles, leads him to discard this hypothesis. That it might be part of a radio apparatus is discarded because he recalled that ferryboats do not carry such equipment. That it is ornamental, a third hypothesis, is discarded because tugboats, usually not heavily ornamented, also have it. That it is useful in guiding the boat, a necessity in fact because the pilothouse is so far forward, is a fourth hypothesis which is finally satisfactory to him. Inquiry at the pilothouse verifies the latter hypothesis.

Substitutes for reasoning. Now it is perfectly clear that a situation of this kind does not always result in the process just outlined. It has been observed many times that people, particularly the dull and stupid, quit working on the problem assigned to them by the experimenter and satisfy themselves with the solution to some other problem.[5]

In the example above, Professor Dewey could have appealed to the authority of the pilothouse in the first place and saved himself a great deal of trouble—a device not uncommonly practiced, by the way. An appeal to the untested authority of laymen results in numerous hypotheses which are accepted as true but which are really misconceptions. But the value of problem-solving activity becomes apparent when we consider problems for which there is no authority, problems like those which confronted the nuclear physicists in 1941. The procedures which have been used in several scientific fields in solving problems of this kind are set forth in a small volume called *A Guide to Thinking.*[6]

Frustration and reasoning. The problem-solving situation comes very close to being identical with the kind of stimulating conditions of a frustrating situation. As a matter of fact, emotional reactions,

---

[5] Cf. Gertrude Hildreth, "The Difficulty Reduction Tendency in Perception and Problem Solving," *Journal of Educational Psychology*, 32, 1941, 305-313.

[6] Olin Templin and Anna McCracken, *A Guide to Thinking*, Doubleday, Doran & Company, Inc., Garden City, 1927.

See also P. M. Symonds, *The Education and Psychology of Thinking*, McGraw-Hill Book Company, Inc., New York, 1936, especially pages 125-143.

grading from mild annoyance to serious displays of temper, are commonly employed in situations that demand analysis, hypothesizing, and testing. The reason is perfectly obvious. In the past we have met our problems in this manner. Solutions of an inadequate kind, generally avoidances and evasions, have removed the necessity of the rigorous observing, defining, calculating, and testing demanded in reasoned solutions. Because we have evaded responsibility in the past in this way, we continue to employ the method—it seems to result in a satisfactory arrangement.

From the stimulational point of view, whether a situation will result in unbridled emotional discharge or strictly harnessed problem-solving procedures, depends on the threat the situation holds for us, either to our actual existence or to our prestige. If a situation is really important to us, biologically or socially, we may not react in a precise and reasoned manner with respect to it—we may explode in the face of it. Reasoning can take place only when we succeed in gaining enough detachment not to be completely adrift in a situation but have some firmly anchored security outside its present confines.

Unclear reasoning, reasoning that is termed "muddy" or "foggy" thinking is generally a matter of failing in the close observation required or in telescoping and reversing the various steps in the reasoning process. What is termed clear, logical thinking is a matter of fine discrimination in perceiving the factual elements, the suitability of the hypothesis, the adequacy of the tests, and the arrangement of the various steps in a manner calculated to convince others.

One essential tool in laying the foundation for precise reasoning is the acquisition of accurate language habits, because most problem solving is done with language symbols rather than with real objects and events. Even where actual objects are to be manipulated later, the preliminary planning is done in terms of words and diagrams.

Language. We have previously pointed out (page 106) the manner in which vocabulary is acquired by an infant. In releasing appropriate responses words become the equivalent of objects. If one says the word "candy" in the presence of a two-year-old, the child commences to make the responses that he would make were he actually about to receive candy. That is why it is sometimes found expedient to spell words in family conversation when youngsters are present. Later, spelled and written words become as effective as the auditory stimulus alone. This elaboration continues until foreign words and phrases or mathematical and technical symbols have significances in terms of the objects and operations they designate. As Watson[7] has said, "After words are once formed, the human ever has two worlds—a world of objects and a world of words which are substitutable for the world of objects."[8]

Direction. Aside from a lack of accurate language habits, another principal difference between good reasoners and poor ones is that the former group goes from one mode of attack to another in its attempted solutions, while the latter persists sometimes for hours in a narrow attack that fruitlessly attempts to overcome the impossible. Many of these unsuccessful attacks are the result of habitual sets or attitudes.

Valuable suggestions for the solution of problems are frequently made by people who know very little about the problems at hand. Their very ignorance of conventional ways to do things in the problem under consideration is an aid to them in seeing new attacks that are completely overlooked by persons already intimate with the conventional methods. Previously learned patterns can never be appealed to for original solutions. That there are not more instances of originality by people without experience is probably due to the fact that information of a factual kind has to be available to the reasoners. Experience ordinarily provides these facts, but it also provides solutions which blind one to better ways of doing things.

[7] John B. Watson, *The Ways of Behaviorism,* Harper & Brothers, New York, 1928, pp. 80ff.
[8] A symbolic process once started can continue of its own momentum. Consider: a^1 represents the length of a line, a^2 represents a square of dimensions a; a^3 represents a cube of dimensions a; a^4, a^5, a^6, . . . , a^n, can all be written and manipulated according to the same rules that apply to the lesser superscripts; still they represent nothing tangible like a line, a square, or a cube. Where the referents are not clear, as in the case of some of the abstractions in the social sciences, words get us into trouble, as Stuart Chase points out in his *Tyranny of Words,* Harcourt, Brace & Company, Inc., New York, 1938. Every student of the social sciences should put this book on his must list.

Billings,[9] in subjecting the question as to whether the good reasoners in a given field are also the good ones in other fields, finds that they are, provided the necessary data for the solution of the problem are supplied.

Experiments[10] with normal and feeble-minded children have shown that the feeble-minded lacked the flexibility in mode of attack that characterized the normal. If rats are deprived of a part of their cerebral cortex, the same invariability and stereotypy is observed.[11] Both these experiments suggest that an inability to reason effectively may be actually due to the lack of gray matter —an inference so often made by our friendly critics, as well as by some who are not so friendly. But cerebral cortex is not the only factor in reasoning. There are numerous habits of thinking and attitudes that have nothing at all to do with gray matter but which still exercise a noticeable effect on reasoning and problem solving.

3. MAIER'S EXPERIMENT

Maier[12] has designed an experiment which was aimed at finding out how much rather general instruction in the breaking down of directional habits would be effective in reasoning problems. He used 384 students in elementary psychology at the University of Michigan as his subjects, dividing them into two groups. The experimental group received a twenty-minute lecture followed by a three-point program of "How to Reason." The program was merely a summary of the lecture. The control group went to work on the problems without any of the tuition that the experimental group had.

Individual work was required of all students. Their solutions to the problems were written out on paper. When a solution had been formed, it was presented to the instructor. He either accepted

9 M. L. Billings, "Problem Solving in Different Fields of Endeavor," *American Journal of Psychology*, 1934, 46, 259-272.

10 K. Gottschaldt, "Zur Methodik psychologischer Untersuchungen an Schwachsinnigen und Psychopathen." *Bericht über den V Kongress für Heilpädagogik*, 1931, cited by Maier.

11 N. R. F. Maier, "The Effect of Cerebral Destruction on Reasoning and Learning in Rats." *Journal of Comparative Neurology*, 1932, 43, 45-75.

12 N. R. F. Maier, "An Aspect of Human Reasoning, *British Journal of Psychology* (Gen. Sec.), 1933, 24, 144-155.

it, rejected it as impractical, or asked for a different solution. This work was all done as a part of a regular three-hour laboratory period, thus assuring whatever motivation is involved in a three-hour course where the student is more or less at the mercy of an instructor.

The lecture on the nature of reasoning with the specific hints on how to reason was part of the regular course. This is an outline of the lecture.

(1) The solution of a problem, when it is the product of reasoning, consists of a pattern which is made up of parts of different past experiences.

(2) The pattern forms suddenly as does the hidden face in a puzzle picture.

(3) Meanings of elements depend on the pattern of which they are a part. The sudden formation of a pattern therefore results in sudden changes of meaning.

(4) The solution-pattern overcomes a difficulty.

(5) The difficulty is what one sees it to be. It is not in the problem. (Illustrations were given which show how the same problem can be solved in different ways, each solution being the conquering of a different difficulty.)

(6) The particular difficulty one sees determines what one will do about it, i.e., what direction one will take (e.g., one doctor will seek a serum to immunize man to certain germs, another will seek a means for preventing the germ from traveling).

(7) All difficulties cannot be overcome. Hence one must find a difficulty which can be overcome.

(8) Most people see the same difficulty.

(9) The difficulties we see are often determined by our past contact with problems (e.g., other diseases have been conquered by the discovery of serums). Such difficulties are habitual difficulties and give rise to habitual directions.

(10) Habitual directions do not solve difficult problems. Problems are difficult when a successful direction is not obvious.

The hints on how to reason were as follows:

(1) Locate a difficulty and try to overcome it. If you fail, get it completely out of your mind and seek an entirely different difficulty.

(2) Do not be a creature of habit and stay in a rut. Keep your mind open for new meanings.

(3) The solution-pattern appears suddenly. You cannot force it. Keep your mind open for new combinations and do not waste time on unsuccessful attempts.

Three problems were used for both the experimental and control groups as follows:

(1) THE STRING PROBLEM. One string was fastened to the ceiling and was of such length that it reached the top of a heavy stationary table. Another string was fastened to the wall about six feet above the floor and was of such length that it reached to the floor. The problem was to tie the ends of the two strings together. This operation was difficult because when either string was held by the subject, the other was completely out of his reach, however much he stretched to reach the other.

Simple solutions were demonstrated by the experimenter. These solutions are (1) hooking one string in with a pole; (2) increasing the length of one of the strings; and (3) tying one of the strings to a chair and placing the chair halfway between the cords in order to keep one string within reach while getting the other. These demonstration solutions, the subjects were warned, were not to be used even in a modified form by the subjects.

The solution desired of the students was that of converting one of the strings into a pendulum by means of a piece of equipment to be described later.

(2) THE HATRACK PROBLEM. Making use only of the material on the table, subjects were required to construct a hatrack sturdy enough to support a heavy coat. It was to be built in an empty room of ordinary size.

The only available materials which were useful were two poles (between six and seven feet in length) and a piece of standard laboratory equipment called a table clamp.

The problem could be solved by clamping the two poles together and wedging them between the floor and the ceiling. The clamp could be used as a hook. (Cotton waste was present in case a student wished to protect the ceiling.)

(3) THE CANDLE PROBLEM. Lighted candles set on a table were to be put out from a fixed distance of eight feet. No one could extinguish the candles by blowing over that distance, but there was available a supply of glass and rubber tubing ranging from six to twelve inches in length. These pieces could be fastened

together to form a long tube, but the tube was so flexible that it was useless until it was fastened by means of sturdy clamps to a long pole. The candle could then be blown out.

All problems were to be solved with the use of the materials on the table. In addition to the material which was applicable to the solutions, the table contained such things as washers, bolts, pliers and chalk. These were confusion materials. They represent objects which in life situations would be present along with the pertinent materials. They can be used as raw material out of which to formulate hypotheses regarding their use in the solution, but the material was selected by the experimenter so that these hypotheses will necessarily be wrong.

Results. In the second and third problems the experimental group showed a decided advantage over the control group. In the whole series of three problems the difference averages about 10 per

	N	PROBLEM 1	PROBLEM 2	PROBLEM 3	AVERAGE
Experimental.......	178	50.6	28.7	68.3	49.2
Control...........	206	49.0	22.3	47.8	39.7

cent. Regardless of whether this difference was 1 per cent, 10 per cent, or 100 per cent, it means very little because the equality of the groups has to be assumed to start with. If the ability of the experimental group was only slightly above the control group *at the start,* then we could easily account for the apparent 10 per cent gain of the experimental group on this basis—the lecture and the hints would have meant nothing.

Extension of the experiment. Maier planned another experiment with the idea of controlling this weak point in his evidence for the efficacy of suggestions on how to reason. This experiment involved the use of only one instead of two groups of students, so that there would be no question but that they were the same in initial ability. They solved two of three problems of a paper-and-pencil nature as follows:

(1) THE SQUARE PROBLEM. Given three quarters of a square; divide the area into four parts which are equal in shape and size.

(2) THE DOT PROBLEM. Given three rows of three dots each; pass through each of the dots with four straight lines without raising the pencil from the paper. Retracing a line is regarded as making a line.

(3) THE "T" PROBLEM. Each student was given four blocks of wood. From these he was asked to construct a perfect "T."

One of the two first problems was selected for period I of ten minutes. Some students finished the problems. They were then given others to keep them busy, but those results do not concern us here. Period I was followed by period II, also of ten minutes' duration. It involved the control problem, one of the latter two above. Period III followed II and was a return to the first problem for those who had not solved it in the first period. Period IV was preceded by the lecture on reasoning already described. The problems were the same as for period II. The results follow:

	PERIOD	N	SUCCESSES	PER CENT SUCCESS
Control Problem.............	I	169	29	17.2
	III	140	26	18.6
Experimental Problem........	II	169	30	17.8
	IV	139	52	37.4

The table shows that the control and experimental problems were of equal difficulty. The abilities of the groups were the same because they are composed of identical people. In a second ten-minute period (III) preceded by no lecture, 18.6 per cent of the 140 who failed to solve the problem in the first ten minutes, were successful. But when equally difficult problems were preceded by a lecture on "How to Reason," the per cent who were successful jumped to 37.4. We must therefore conclude that *this lecture just about doubled the successes that presumably would have occurred in the second ten-minute period without it.*

398

There were still some people who had not solved the problems. Maier concludes that *we cannot, by this method, equip a person to solve a problem, but we can aid him to clear the field so that a solution is not prevented from appearing by virtue of his persistence in previously learned modes of response.* This shows that *reasoning is in part a matter of overcoming or inhibiting habitual responses.*

4. PROBLEM SOLUTIONS BY GROUPS AND INDIVIDUALS

The parliamentary process is often slow and cumbersome. Most of us, at one time or another, have become exasperated with the apparent inefficiency of a committee, which, as it tries to solve a problem, shifts back and forth like a playful fox terrier from one scent to the next. The bright suggestions of one member seem false to another member. There are long moments of silence followed by the enthusiastic expounding of inspirations which may be rejected almost as soon as they are uttered. Then a promising lead is taken and is followed until it terminates in a blind alley, and a new beginning must be sought. Out of all this backing and filling a suitable plan or solution may develop and the committee will have fulfilled the purpose for which it was appointed.

Oftentimes one reacts to the slowness and vacillation of committee work with the thought that a single bright and strong-willed person could have accomplished all this with far less fuss and bother. One feels it is a case of too many cooks spoiling the broth. If this is truly the case, then the only justification for committees is in deference to the principle of democracy. On the other hand, the committee system may actually be superior to individual efforts, and the impressions that its products are no better than that of the best individual in the committee may actually be incorrect. The truth or falsity of these divergent opinions can be discovered only through controlled experimentation which pits the committee against the individual. A study by Shaw[13] has done this.

[13] M. E. Shaw, "A Comparison of Individuals and Small Groups in the Rational Solution of Complex Problems," *American Journal of Psychology*, 1932, 44, 491-504.

Method. The design of this experiment simply consisted of measuring the ability to solve problems of persons working individually and persons working in groups of four. The total experiment can be considered as being divided into halves. During the first half, five groups composed of four individuals each attempted to solve a set of three difficult problems. The second half of the experiment was essentially the same as the first except that the persons composing the previous groups worked as individuals, and those who had worked individually in the first half worked now as groups. Thus within the total experiment the subjects served both in the individual situation and the group situation. A different group of three problems was used in the second half of the experiment.

The problems used were of several sorts. In some of them a part of a paragraph or a part of a sonnet was given and the task was to complete it by putting together in the correct order a group of isolated words. Other problems were of the familiar cannibal-and-missionary type.

Within each group one person was designated as chairman, and he was expected to manipulate the necessary materials. Actually there were no restrictions which prevented any other person in the group from taking over these duties. A note taker was also assigned to each group, and his duties consisted of recording what suggestions were made, who made them, and whether they were accepted or rejected.

Results. There were in all sixty-three chances for the problems to be solved by individuals—that is, twenty-one individuals each worked on three problems. Only five correct solutions were obtained. In the group situation, however, there were eight correct solutions out of fifteen possibilities. The percentage of solution for the group situation was 53 as compared with 7.9 for the individual situation. Clearly persons working together were superior to persons working alone.

This is also shown in another way. In most of these problems the solution was not an all-or-none matter, but was approached through successive steps. Obviously an error at any one of these steps would result in failure. Individuals working alone tended to

400

err more frequently in the earlier steps than did groups, and thus were farther from reaching the correct solution.

This fact, together with the notes taken by the recorders, is significant, for it gives some indication of why the groups excelled the individual workers. As a general rule, when incorrect suggestions were made they were rejected by some other person than the maker. Thus the members of the group operate as checks upon each other and prevent the problem from being turned in the wrong direction. When the individual is working alone, he himself must act in this censoring capacity, and it appears that he is not likely to be so effective as is another individual.

When one considers the very nature of reasoning toward the solution of a problem, he can readily understand why group work may excel individual work. Problem solving, whether done alone or socially, is a continuous process of stimulus and response. We throw out a suggestion to ourselves, this serves as a stimulus for another response, and so on until success or failure occurs. When we work alone we have only ourselves to initiate the idea and to judge it. Inevitably our initiated ideas are determined by our sets and ways of perceiving; if these are slanted in the wrong direction we may be doomed to failure. If we work in a group, however, another individual with his sets and ways of perceiving may direct the problem in the generally correct sector and we may enter in to refine and improve it. Reasoning is a dynamic process, a give and take between stimuli and responses. When we work alone we limit the possible number of responses because each of us is limited, and we are apparently limited also in our ability to judge the soundness of our responses. Where there are others who are sharing the situation with us, the total psychologically possible number of responses is increased, and with this increase there is a greater possibility that the correct response will be forthcoming.

Summary. This experiment has indicated that persons working in groups excel individuals in their ability to solve problems. It appears that all of us are brighter than any one of us. One of the major reasons for the group superiority lies in the fact that other persons serve to check and evaluate the suggestions that are advanced.

401

Often this results in rejecting false suggestions which might otherwise be followed and would eventually lead to failure.

5. KÖHLER'S EXPERIMENTS

Strikingly enough, the principal impetus for Maier's experiments and for the experiments of others[14] on reasoning and problem solving comes not from work on humans but from a series of experiments with nine chimpanzees conducted by Wolfgang Köhler.

The story of how Köhler came to make these experiments is an absorbing one. A professor of psychology of Berlin University, he was on a vacation tour in the late summer of 1914. His itinerary included a biological research station maintained by the University on the Island of Teneriffe, one of the Canary Islands. With the outbreak of hostilities, he was interned on the island for the duration of the War. The complete story of his experiments is told in a book called *The Mentality of Apes*.[15] A clearer, simpler, more interesting account of psychological experiments has never been written, before or since. A rapid reading of the entire book will repay any thoughtful student.

Köhler found that chimpanzees could, without any special training, use sticks to pull food lying just outside their cages but beyond their reach into the latitude of their grasp. Of course, the fact that they didn't have to be especially trained to use sticks as rakes does not mean that they hadn't *learned* previously to do so. But the significance of the observation is that animals lower than the great apes—the chimpanzees, the gorillas, the orangutans and gibbons[16]—are extremely inept in the use of even so simple a tool.

Longer poles were sometimes provided to see if they would be used to dislodge food placed beyond reach overhead. Here a most instructive observation was made. Instead of using a pole as a man

[14] Augusta Alpert, "The Solving of Problem Situations by Pre-School Children: An Analysis," R. H. Wheeler (editor), *Readings in Psychology*, The Thomas Y. Crowell Company, New York, 1930, 114-144.
    Edgar A. Doll and Cecelia G. Aldrich, "Problem Solving among Idiots," *Journal of Comparative Psychology*, 1931, 12, 137-169.
[15] Wolfgang Köhler, *The Mentality of Apes*, Harcourt, Brace & Company, Inc., New York, 1925.
[16] For descriptions of these forms see R. M. Yerkes and Ada Yerkes, *The Great Apes*, Yale University Press, New Haven, 1929.

would to knock down suspended fruit, the chimpanzees set the poles up vertically under the food, and then, before they could fall over, they quickly climbed the pole and secured the food in an entirely nonhuman manner. Their natural agility prevented the animal from solving the problem in the more indirect human way. The indirection easier for a human being because of his handicap is not easier for the chimpanzee.

Nevertheless there was one humanlike response in the face of a difficult problem. When food was suspended overhead and the required solution was not immediately evident to the animal (in the case when he was required to stack several heavy boxes one on top of another so that the tower so constructed, if mounted, enabled him to reach the incentive) the keeper was led to a position under the food and by gestures and grunting the notion was conveyed that the keeper's help was wanted. On several occasions the ape climbed to his shoulders and used the keeper as a vaulting pole.

A dependence of this kind on a keeper of animals is perfectly analogous to the appeal to authority mentioned as a deterrent in human reasoning. This dependence has been observed frequently in students who, asked to tie the two strings together in Maier's experiment, literally withdrew from the field all the while "registering," in the sense of the most up-to-date movie directors, an appeal for help from the instructor.

In other experiments with the chimpanzees a short stick within reach could be used to obtain a long one out of reach. The long stick would reach to the incentive, but the short one wouldn't. In cases of this kind, which greatly increased the complexity of the problem, the apes were sometimes observed to take a box which had been previously successful for suspended food and, as if intending to use it as a rake, push it in the direction of the food on the ground beyond the bars. This is another example of the use of a previously appropriate habit in the solution of a new problem which the animal, either human or infrahuman, makes when faced with a frustrating situation. A box makes a very unsatisfactory rake at best; to get it through the bars was impossible. But here, again, we have a response perfectly analogous to responses that you have certainly seen in other people even if you have not observed it in yourself.

I am reminded of a rather dense student who finally grasped the notion of disparate images in connection with space perception. But ever after in the face of difficult problems, however remote from space perception, we were certain, in that class, to hear something about disparate images from this particular person. A response that had been successful once was used again and again because the student lacked the ability to discriminate its suitableness in exactly the same way that the ape failed to perceive that the box which had been successfully used in another connection would not go through the bars of his cage.

In all of these experiments, Köhler observed that a problem was difficult to the extent that it was impossible for the ape to survey the total situation. A stick placed in close proximity to the food was more likely to be used than one placed so that the chimpanzee could not see both the tool and the incentive at the same time. Items that are located together in space belong in Köhler's terminology to one constellation, whereas if they are more dispersed they may be grouped into different patterns. *Whatever is a part of one perceptual pattern is difficult to separate and to integrate with another.* This generalization is illustrated in another experiment that he made. Instead of the sticks used in some experiments, a small bush or sapling was planted in the cage, any branch of which would make a suitable wand or rake. But *it was a much more difficult problem to separate a branch from the plant and thereby make a stick than it was to use sticks already provided.* Things perceived in a certain setting, or belonging to a particular constellation, are so definitely a part of that setting that their utilization in some other setting is particularly difficult. This observation is as true of human problems as it is for the chimpanzee attempting to employ a stick which is not perceptually separate. Man's superiority over the chimpanzee in being able to make use of only the essential elements of a concrete situation depends in part on this ability to use words as symbols for the various parts of a specific situation. Words and symbols are more easily manipulated into new constellations than objects themselves are.

Köhler also investigated the possibilities of invention among the chimpanzees. If a chimpanzee is given two sticks, neither of which will reach the food alone but which can be jointed together so that they make a stick of sufficient length, will the chimpanzee ever succeed in manufacturing the long stick? Köhler found that only one of his animals was able to achieve the long stick. It happened this way:

... He pushes one of the sticks out as far as it will go, then takes the second, and with it pushes the first one cautiously towards the objective, pushing it carefully from the nearer end and thus slowly urging it towards the fruit. ... (In this way he actually touches the fruit with the first stick several times.) ... The proceeding is repeated; when the animal has probed the stick on the ground so far out that he cannot possibly get it back by himself, it is given back to him. But although in trying to steer it cautiously, he puts the stick in his hand exactly into the cut (the opening where they are to be joined) of the stick on the ground and although one might think that doing so would suggest the possibility of pushing one stick into the other, there is no indication whatever of such a practically valuable solution. Finally, the observer gives the animal some help by putting one finger into the opening of one stick under the animal's nose (without pointing to the other stick at all). This has no effect; Sultan, as before, pushes one stick towards the objective, and as this pseudo solution does not satisfy him any longer, he abandons his effort altogether, and does not even pick up the sticks when they are both thrown through the bars to him. The experiment has lasted over an hour and is stopped for the present, as it seems hopeless, carried out like this. As we intended to take it up again after a while, Sultan is left in possession of his stick; the keeper is left to watch him.

Keeper's report: "Sultan first of all squats indifferently on the box, which has been left standing a little back from the railings; then he gets up, picks up the two sticks, sits down again on the box and plays carelessly with them. While doing this, it happens that he finds himself holding one rod in either hand in such a way that they lie in a straight line; he pushes the thinner one a little way into the opening of the thicker, jumps up and is already on the run towards the railings, to which he has up to now half turned his back, and begins to draw a banana towards him with the double stick. I call the master; meanwhile, one of the animal's rods has fallen out of the other, as he has pushed one of them only a little way into the other; whereupon he connects them again."

All of this description shows that occasionally chimpanzees will be found who are able to fabricate very simple instruments. But since there has been no real follow-up in these studies, it is not clear how far it is possible for these animals to go. After the experiments are over the creatures revert again to a simple caged-animal existence in which care is provided by a keeper. The profound effects upon people of a protected life of an analogous kind have been observed to lead to a complete lack of accomplishment. It is probably equally true that an anticipation of every need has a deleterious effect on chimpanzees.

Aside from all this, another hindrance to more complex accomplishment on the part of chimpanzees is their complete lack of language mechanism. Although there is some use of symbolism,[17] Köhler and others have observed that there is very little value in allowing one chimpanzee who cannot accomplish a given act to observe another who can. This means that every animal has to learn all of his repertoire for himself. Cultural background is nonexistent for every generation starts *de novo*. If such a condition obtained among human beings we would still all be living in caves and hunting with clubs. Every human generation, for the most part, starts where the previous one has left off. Its accomplishments, through the symbolism of words, are built onto the accomplishments of people that it has never seen.

Further problems having to do with what are called the "higher mental processes" as well as those in which most of the data are in the animal rather than the human field are those relating to delayed response and to abstraction. The delayed response problem is simply this: If an animal, human, or infrahuman receives a stimulus now, he can apparently react to it a few seconds, a week, or a month from now, depending upon his position in the animal series. Hunter made the first experiment in this field in 1913. He found that if the experimenter expected a rat to select one of three doors that had just been lighted up in order to be rewarded there with food, the delay after the light had been turned off could be only about two seconds. He also worked with dogs and with one child and found correspondingly longer delays possible. Using a somewhat different method, Köhler found that chimpanzees could "delay" several hours. The mechanism of this response has never been identified. We know that it is not true that the stimulus is dammed up in the central nervous system somewhere and released at an appropriate time.

[17] J. B. Wolfe, "The Effectiveness of Token-Reward for Chimpanzees," *Comparative Psychology Monographs*, 1936, 12, 1-72.

Hunter thought that in rats bodily orientation was responsible for the response. If the rat remained "pointed" at the position where the stimulus had been he would choose correctly, but later work has shown that explicit bodily orientation does not have to be maintained although it helps in human beings as well as in infrahuman animals. In people the response can be seen to be related to the language mechanism, but there is no generally accepted explanation. To go into the controversy extensively would take us too far afield. Interested students will find a summary of the literature to 1935 in Maier and Schneirla, *Principles of Animal Psychology*.[18]

The problem of abstraction involves essentially what Köhler was requiring of his apes when he furnished them with a small tree from which they could manufacture sticks that would reach food. They were to abstract "stick" from a collection of "sticks" called a tree. Abstraction is the essential mechanism in the problem of classification. When a series is arranged the individual items which have numerous properties are grouped according to some abstract quality. Rocks varying in size, shape, color, and so on, can be arranged in a "hardness" series quite independent of any other quality. The problem of classifying is one of the preliminary steps in any science. The growth of a young science depends on the adequacy, for their purpose, of the particular qualities which are to be abstracted. Thus in some early zoological classifications, bats were classed with birds because they fly. But it turned out that their flying was relatively unimportant in zoology and that the qualities of their reproductive mechanisms, together with other morphological considerations, throw them definitely into the classification "mammal."

Everywhere in science superficial resemblances are not important; the most useful classifications are made on the basis of hidden, unobtrusive qualities. We have seen how sleep and hypnosis were confused (Chapter Fourteen) on the basis of a most striking resemblance in the apparent behavior in the two states. Little progress was made in understanding hypnosis until it was shown that the resemblance was entirely superficial, like the resemblance of bats to birds and whales and porpoises to fish.

18 McGraw-Hill Book Company, Inc., New York, 1936.

Because the perception of abstract qualities was so important in human activities it was deemed an indicator of higher thought processes[19] until recently, when it was shown that the lowly rat and other subhuman forms could abstract qualities like "triangularity" with sufficient accuracy to pass difficult test situations.[20] In the animal field there is a considerable literature growing up in "abstraction" or, as it is generally called, "equivalence of stimuli."[21]

Summary of the chapter. To say that reasoning or thinking differentiates man from the lower animal forms is not true in the light of experimental evidence, which shows that the only difference in the behavior of the various animal forms is in the complexity of the problems that can be solved. Man has a tremendous advantage over forms that do not have language because reasoning and reflective thinking are most efficiently accomplished by means of symbols. Symbols once invented can be handled independently of the objects they originally designated so that in effect man possesses "two worlds." Aside from language, the use of tools by human beings as extensions and improvements of manipulatory organs like the hands is of the greatest significance.

Effective use of tools cannot be accomplished without the sensory, motor, and central nervous equipment possessed by man. The hope of future experimentation in the field of problem solving should be, according to one student[22] of the field, "directed at determining what the factors are which condition the success of one individual or genus, and the absence of which limits the achievements of another." Most of the work, he feels, has been of a preliminary nature in an attempt to find out what animals can do in

---

[19] C. L. Hull, "Quantitative Aspects of the Evolution of Concepts: An Experimental Study," *Psychological Review Monographs*, 1920, 28, 85.
[20] P. E. Fields, "Form Discrimination in the White Rat," *Journal of Comparative Psychology*, 1928, 8, 143-158; "Studies in Concept Formation," *Comparative Psychology Monographs*, 1932, 9, 70.
[21] L. W. Gellerman, "Form Discrimination in Chimpanzees and Two-Year-Old Children," *Journal of Genetic Psychology*, 1933, 42, 3-50.
   J. A. Gengerelli, "Studies in Abstraction in White Rats," *Journal of Genetic Psychology*, 1930, 38, 171-202.
   H. Klüver, *Behavior Mechanisms in Monkeys*, University of Chicago Press, Chicago, 1933, 387.
[22] Kenneth W. Spence, "Experimental Studies of Learning and the Higher Mental Processes in Infra-Human Primates," *Psychological Bulletin*, 1937, 34, 806-850.

comparison to man and to one another. We do not now know how important previous habits are in comparison with structural equipment in determining the accomplishment of either man or animal. Among the many structural factors we do not know relatively which are more important. Aside from gross structural defects, as in some of the low-grade feeble-minded, we have no explanatory principles in this field.

One of the elements of habit equipment that is important in limiting reasoning has been demonstrated by Maier in what he calls "direction." He showed that if habitual ways of regarding problems could be overcome, solutions occurred in larger proportions. This observation is probably a special case of the difficulty Köhler noted in connection with his chimpanzees—an item perceived in one constellation is difficult to abstract from its concrete setting so that it becomes free for incorporation into new forms.

CHAPTER TWENTY

LEARNING, THINKING, IMAGINING, DREAMING, AND THE BRAIN

Early theorizing about the part that the brain plays in determining behavior led to the mistaken notion that the brain somewhat resembles the wax cylinder of a dictaphone. Impressions made on it by experience were thought to be recorded in much the same way that the cutting head on this instrument makes grooves of varying depth in the soft wax surface. Memory was explained by actual physical impressions which remained engraved on the surface after the experience itself was long gone. In an extreme form this theory called for an exact location in the brain for each different thing a person could recall: a different brain cell stored each item of experience. Forgetting meant that with time the precisely engraved experiences lost their detailed contours, became fragmented and badly eroded. Things that one couldn't forget were incised so deeply through the intensity of the original experience, or through the constant recurrence of experiences of lesser intensity, that they resisted the smoothing effect of time.

Anatomical evidence. Early anatomical evidence seemed to strengthen this theory. Locations were found on the exposed brains of animals that when directly stimulated resulted in fairly definite movements of individual muscle groups. From certain brain areas uniformly in different animals, movements of the digits, the hind legs, the forelegs, the head and lips could be elicited. All this was very impressive. It led to the notion that sense organs were connected with the muscles through the nervous system, like subscribers are interconnected by a telephone system. All the facts which violated this notion were unknown at the time this generalization was made.

As the nerve pathways from the eyes and the ears and the nose and the other sense organs were traced they seemed to lead uniformly to definite brain areas—from the eyes to the rear of the brain, and from the ears to the temporal region. From observations on the difference between man and animals and from clinical cases among men in which certain deficiencies were observed, other areas of the brain were supplied with theoretical properties when the anatomical evidence was not so direct. Thus there were centers isolated for reasoning in the frontal lobes because men, who could reason—compared with animals, who were not supposed to be able to reason—had a greater development of the frontal lobes. For the same reason, speech was located in the parietal lobes. There was even supposed to be a difference in the locations of written and spoken language.

All this development is quite independent of the story of phrenology (Chapter Two) which asserts that in the individual a difference can be discerned between the psychological properties and the *surface* contours of the skull. It is true, however, that Gall and Spurzheim, the founders of phrenology, made significant nonphrenological observations and thus contributed to our present understanding.

1. BEHAVIOR STUDIES WITH RATS

As we have pointed out, the sensory nerves from the retina of the eye, after a series of fairly complicated connections, finally end[1] in the outer layer of the brain on the extreme back surface. An area of this kind on the cortex is called a *projection area*. Anatomical evidence of this kind would lead one to believe that if these occipital lobes are invaded and destroyed in any way, the individual would become hopelessly blind.

Lashley has tested this hypothesis experimentally by having a group of white rats learn a problem which required a visual discrimination. A special apparatus presented two areas—one brightly lighted, the other dark. By always allowing the animals to eat after going through a passageway containing the light and by always giving them a slight shock if they entered the darkened passage, all of the animals soon learned to take the lighted alley without exception. The apparatus allowed the light to be presented first on

[1] They do not actually end here except for purposes of arbitrary classification. The occipital surface is a tremendous distributing and connecting center. Nerves can be traced from this area to motor end organs of wide distribution over the whole body.

one side and then on the other in some random order so that the experimenter could be certain that they were actually reacting to the brightness and not to the *position,* right or left, of the stimulus pattern. Since rats learn position habits very readily, a control of this kind is absolutely necessary.

After the problem had been learned, the skull of the animal was opened—under deep anesthesia, of course—and the exposed brain surface was destroyed by cautery. Ten days later, after they had recovered from the effects of the operation, the rats were tested for retention.

Animals so operated were no longer able to make brightness discriminations. The ten-day delay for the recovery from the operation did not cause the forgetting because normal animals who served as controls showed but slight decrease in their scores.

Another control experiment showed that *the same amount of brain substance destroyed in other regions produced no loss of the habit.* It would appear that the hypothesis has been substantiated. If an animal has to make brightness discriminations it would appear that he must have a complete visual projection area in the cerebral cortex.

But in an extension of this experiment it was shown[2] that animals devoid of cerebral cortex in the occipital region *could relearn brightness discriminations* which were lost as a result of the operation.

The only possible interpretation of these facts is that some other uninvaded part of the brain took over the function of the areas that were destroyed.[3] Similar studies have been made on the auditory areas with the same conclusions and interpretations.[4]

If an auditory discrimination has been learned, it is destroyed along with the destruction in the temporal lobes; invasion of the other lobes causes no loss of the habit. But if the temporal area is

[2] K. S. Lashley, "The Relation between Cerebral Mass, Learning, and Retention," *Journal of Comparative Neurology,* 1926, 41, 1-58.
[3] K. S. Lashley, "Vicarious Functions after Destruction of the Visual Areas," *American Journal of Physiology,* 1922, 59, 44-71.
[4] L. E. Wiley, "The Function of the Brain in Audition," *Journal of Comparative Neurology,* 1932, 54, 109-141, and "A Further Investigation of Auditory Cerebral Mechanisms," *Journal of Comparative Neurology,* 1937, 66, 327-331.

destroyed first, and then the animal is trained in an auditory discrimination, he learns as readily as an intact animal. As a matter of fact, there is a very slight *advantage for the operated animals in both the brightness discrimination and the auditory problem.*

When the experimenter opens the skull and touches the surface of the brain with a cautery, he cannot be certain exactly how much of the brain tissue is going to be destroyed. Considerable skill is required in order to confine the injury to the cortex. If the subcortical structures are involved, the results for that animal have to be discarded. The experimenter knows in general whether the damage will be large or small, but a precise measurement must wait until after the behavior data are collected and the animal is finally sacrificed. After the animal's death, the entire brain is removed from the skull and preserved in the proper solutions. Even yet it is impossible to tell how much cortex was destroyed. The scar can be seen on the brain surface, but it has little relation to the amount of damage that is done immediately under the external surface. The subsurface damage can be observed only by making cross sections of the entire brain.

The results of studying these cross sections by means of a microscope are transferred to greatly enlarged charts that have been prepared beforehand. Figure 76 shows an injured area in the occipital lobes (visual area) taken from one of these reconstructions of a rat's brain; Figure 77 shows an injury confined to the auditory area. The areas shown in black are measured with an engineering instrument (planimeter) designed for measuring the areas of irregular figures. Then the per cent that this magnitude is of the total brain area is computed.

When these measurements and computations are made and related to the errors made in the retention tests, it turns out that within the occipital region where, as we have just seen, an extensive lesion produces a complete loss of the brightness discrimination habit, lesser injuries produce smaller effects. The amount of interference with the habit is roughly proportional to the amount of damage that was done by the cautery. *A small lesion produces a few errors, but an extensive lesion produces a complete loss of the habit.* The same is true for the auditory habit.

Localization of the maze habit. Learning a relatively more complex function like a maze does not depend upon any single sense department as a visual discrimination depends on the eyes and

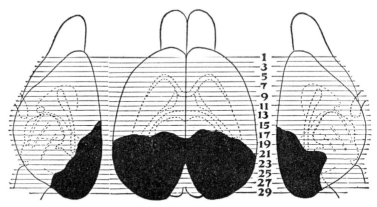

FIG. 76.—The reconstruction of an extensive injury to the occipital, or visual area. (After Lashley, courtesy of the University of Chicago Press.)

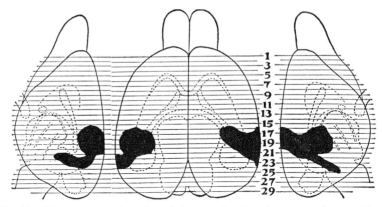

FIG. 77.—The reconstruction of an injury confined to the temporal, or auditory regions. (After Lashley, courtesy of the University of Chicago Press.)

the visual projection areas in the brain. An animal deprived of the use of one sense department through an operation or through stimulus control[5] will depend upon other cues. Lashley has studied

[5] Making the entire field uniform so that no differences exist in excitatory field which can serve as cues at critical points. Presumably a complete control of this kind over all factors including internal ones in the animal would result in an insoluble problem.

the effect of brain injury on the learning of simple mazes and has related the amount of destruction to the number of errors made in the process mastering the mazes.

Typical results showing this relation are exhibited in Figure 78. This diagram shows that *there is some relation between the number of errors made and the per cent of destruction.* The relationship is not very precise. The animal with the largest per cent of the cortex

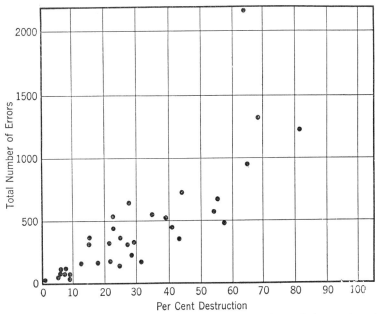

Fig. 78.—The relation between the per cent of destruction and the number of errors. (After Lashley.)

destroyed required about half the number of trials to learn the maze as did another animal with about 15 per cent less destruction. Our interpretation would be that there are other factors, aside from that under observation, that determine how many errors a rat will make. One of them might be his ability before the operation was made, another might be a lack of reliability in the maze. But in spite of these and other factors there still exists a definite trend to the data.

From a close study of the areas in which the destruction took place it was evident that, *unlike the visual and auditory habits, maze learning has no precise localization within the cortex.* It is the

415

amount of destruction, not its locus, that is the determining factor in slowing up the learning.

2. STUDIES OF BRAIN FUNCTION IN HIGHER ANIMALS

As one examines the brain of four animals, the rat, the dog, the chimpanzee, and man, he is impressed not only by the differences in the total size of the brains, but also by the differences in the various proportions of the brain. The most marked of these differences is the increasingly great development of the frontal portion of the brain as we move from rat to man. Since these neural changes are also paralleled by an increasing capacity for complex behavior, the hypothesis is inevitably suggested that higher intellectual functions were localized in this area of the brain. This hypothesis is further supported by another interesting fact. It can be shown anatomically that most of the other portions of the brain are either terminals for tracts which begin at one or another of our sense organs, or are the initiating areas for tracts which lead eventually to the muscles. This is not true of the frontal area, and for that reason it was sometimes called the great silent area. Anatomical structure suggested that this area had no specific sensory or motor functions, and this supported the hypothesis that its primary function was concerned with intellectual activity.

In the light of such a hypothesis it was rather astounding to discover that large portions of the frontal lobe could be destroyed without reducing the subject to complete intellectual incompetence. There were several lines of evidence that pointed in this direction. Occasionally accidents occurred which resulted in destruction of the nerve tissue in the frontal lobe, and occasionally a neurosurgeon was required to remove frontal lobe tissue in case of tumor of the brain. Although personality and intellectual changes were reported for some of these cases, the intellectual deterioration was by no means marked.

There have been several cases of brain tumor in human subjects that have necessitated the removal of large portions of the brain. In three such cases reported by Dandy[6] one entire half of the brain was

[6] Walter E. Dandy, "Physiological Studies Following Extirpation of the Right Cerebral Hemisphere in Man," *Bulletin*, Johns Hopkins Hospital, 1933, 53, 31-51.

removed. Because subcortical structures were removed along with the cortex, the patients were hopelessly paralyzed on one side of their bodies, but there were no signs of deterioration or disorientation. As a matter of fact, there was marked improvement in the way the patients could carry on conversation. With the tumor they were showing signs of breakdown, but with the tumorous growth removed along with half the brain, they improved. Dandy was very much surprised by these results. He had expected, in view of the current tradition in brain physiology, that the patients would show a considerable loss of ability to reason when one half of their frontal lobe complement was removed, but they did not do so.

Dandy did not administer psychological tests to his patients as a general rule, but depended on his observation of the patient's conversation, ability to solve simple problems, and general orientation. More recently[7] a patient was observed for forty days before and forty days after the removal of the right frontal lobe and standard tests were administered before and after the operation. A score of 139 I.Q. points was obtained when using the two forms of 1937 revision of the Stanford-Binet test both before and after. Another intelligence test which was repeated gave a score of 95 before and 99 after, while still a different one involving principally perceptual responses gave exactly the same score before and after. These observations merely serve to qualify Dandy's observations.

Observations on monkeys. Carlyle Jacobsen[8] has studied the effect of removing the frontal lobes in monkeys. These observations are more convincing than those on human subjects because the whole thing can be planned beforehand, and the monkey can be trained before the operation and retrained afterward. We generally know little about human subjects beforehand, and more frequently than not observations on them afterward are made by surgeons who are more adept with a scalpel than in psychological discernment.

[7] Lidz, T., "A Study of the Effect of Right Frontal Lobectomy on Intelligence and Temperament," *Journal of Neurological Psychiatry*, 1939, 2, 211-222.
[8] Carlyle Jacobsen, "Functions of Frontal Association Areas in Primates," *Archives of Neurology and Psychology*, 1935, 33, 558-569, and *Comparative Psychology Monographs*, 1936, 13.

Jacobsen[9] found a distinct difference in the effects of frontal lobes removed in infant monkeys and in adults. Effects that were enduring with adults were only temporary with infants. Thus it ap-

Fig. 79.—Apparatus used for testing the effects of frontal lobe injury on monkeys. The top two pictures show the monkey responding correctly to the right position, regardless of the object. The bottom two pictures show the monkey responding correctly to the cue of the saltcellar, regardless of its position. (Courtesy of Dr. H. F. Harlow.)

pears that after specialization has taken place, removal of certain areas produces permanent effects, but before specialization has taken place some other part of the brain takes over the function of the destroyed area.

9 Carlyle Jacobsen, F. V. Taylor, and G. M. Haslerud, "Restitution of Function after Cortical Injuries in Monkeys," *American Journal of Physiology*, 1936, 116, 85-86.

In a series of recent studies Harlow[10] and a group of coworkers have attempted to discover more about the functioning of the frontal lobes in monkeys. They set up an experiment to test the hypothesis that animals with frontal lobe destruction are peculiarly unable to shift from one kind of habit to another.

Five monkeys were operated upon and the frontal portion of both hemispheres of the brain was removed. After they had recovered from the operation and had time to adjust to the laboratory routine they served as subjects in the experiment.

The testing apparatus is illustrated in Figure 79. It consisted of a panel with two shallow depressions, serving as food wells over which test objects were placed. In testing, the animals' view of the apparatus was screened off while a food well was baited and the test object and panel were placed in position. Then, after a screen had been lowered in front of the experimenter to conceal him from the animal, the screen in front of the animals' cage was elevated to permit a choice. Food was obtained if the correct object was chosen.

There were two types of problems which were used. In one type a series of trials was conducted in which the food was always placed on one or the other side of the panel. Thus the monkey could find food by picking up the left or the right object. This is called *position discrimination*.

In the other type of test problem food was always hidden under one particular object. Sometimes this would be on the left, and at other times it would be on the right. Thus the nature of the object was the cue as to where the food was hidden. This is called *object discrimination*.

The basic plan of the experiment consisted of running the animals through a series of trials in which, let us say, the object on the right side was always correct, then to shift so that food was always under one particular object, then to shift perhaps to the left side or to another object, and so on. This meant that the animal must learn to respond to one cue for a while, then this learned response must be repressed and another connection learned, and so

[10] P. Settlage, M. Zable, and H. F. Harlow. Problem solution by monkeys following bilateral removal of the prefrontal areas. VI. Performance on tests requiring contradictory reactions to similar and to identical stimuli. *Journal of Experimental Psychology*, 1948, 38, 50-65.

forth. There was no way for the monkey to figure out in advance of the trial series whether the problem was a positional discrimination or an object discrimination. He could learn this only by making a few mistakes at the beginning of each new test group. Five normal monkeys were run on the same problem as the five operated animals.

The performance of the animals with the brain lesions was con-sistently inferior to that of the normal animals. However, in experi-ments in which operated animals are simply required to choose the object on the right, or some particular object, they do not show this marked inferiority to the normal animal. What is unique about this experiment is that the animals were forced to shift from using one kind of cue to another, and so back and forth. The authors felt that it was this characteristic of their experiment which made the task difficult for the animals with the brain destruction, and that the destruction of the frontal lobes interfered with the ability to shift from one habit to the next. The point should be emphasized that brain lesions interfered with this ability, but they did not destroy it completely. The animals with the lesions were still able to perform the habit but at a lower level of efficiency than was shown by normal monkeys.

Summary of these studies. The results of these and many other studies indicate rather clearly that the notion that particular parts of the brain are responsible for specific acts is an error. There is, however, an important principle which should be stressed. As we progress up the phylogenetic scale from the lower animals to man there seems to be an increasing specificity of function. Whereas visual habits can be easily relearned in rats following the removal of the visual projection area, this is not so in man. This increasing depend-ence in higher animals upon the higher parts of the brain is called *encephalization.* This principle leads us to expect that there will be a greater degree of localization of brain function in man than in any other animal. Yet even in man habits are not specifically and narrowly localized in a particular spot. Furthermore, when sometimes a habit or group of habits is destroyed following some brain destruc-tion, the loss may not be permanent and the habit or habits may be relearned.

420

3. THINKING

What happens when a person thinks? Is it, as an older psychology taught, totally a matter of brain activity? Is it true that thinking is a function of the cerebral cortex in the same way that contraction is the function of a muscle? Or is it true that the motor segments are an integral part of the thinking process? Even when overt movement cannot be observed, however intently we scrutinize a thinking person, is it true that muscular movement is still present but at a low level of intensity? This latter notion, that thinking is a matter of implicit bodily movements—a kind of a shorthand, low-energy-level way of dealing with things as a substitute for actually performing the movements of handling them—has been subjected to experimental test.

For many years the experimenters had to depend on mechanical devices fastened directly to various muscle-groups to magnify the tiny muscle changes (if any) that are present when we think. These devices were usually unsatisfactory because even if they showed no activity it was no proof that activity wasn't there. It was recognized that the instruments were very insensitive and that a considerable amount of activity might have been present in amplitudes too small to be recorded.

With the development of thermionic amplification—the same kind of amplifying that enables a radio set to pick up very feeble radio signals and make them audible—it became possible to amplify small potentials that come about as a result of nerve and muscle activity.[11] These potentials are very weak—sometimes in the relaxed subject they are of the order of a millionth of a volt. After they are amplified they are made strong enough to affect a very sensitive string galvanometer, whose vibration under the control of potentials is then photographed on a moving film.

The increased sensitivity of this apparatus over the old mechanical and pneumatic devices had one drawback: the instrument sometimes turned out to be too sensitive. When most people lie with eyes closed in a darkened and partially soundproof room and are instructed to relax, unless they are actually sleeping the action-

[11] Edmund Jacobson, "Electrophysiology of Mental Activities," *American Journal of Psychology,* 1932, 44, 677-694.

currents are still present to such an extent that the instructions "to *think* of something" produce no observable changes in the record. There is so much "spontaneous" activity that the increment produced by the special instructions is no more detectable in the total pattern than a thirteenth person's voice in a room where twelve are already loudly talking. But if a subject is trained to relax, the record becomes steadier and provides a stable base line against which comparisons can be made. Under these conditions the instructions to *think*—to solve a problem—result in easily observed differences in the record.

When the galvanometer is recording practically a straight line from the right biceps muscle, a signal is given to the subject to begin thinking or imagining a movement of the right arm. Within a fraction of a second the galvanometer string begins to swing and continues to do so until the signal to stop thinking is given. Control electrodes put on other parts of the body show that the action currents are confined to the regions that the subject is instructed to think about. *They do not involve the whole body.* Another control —"This time when the signal is given do not imagine a movement in the right arm, remain relaxed"—shows that the action currents are not due to the subject's hearing the signal.

In about half the cases where various subjects were required to: "Imagine writing your name"; "Imagine yourself rowing a boat"; "Imagine yourself boxing"; "Imagine scratching your chin"; and so on, it turned out that there was no great difference in the record when a comparison was attempted between the experimental period and the pre-experimental relaxed period. In some of these cases the subjects reported that they *visualized* themselves performing these acts rather than taking part in them. If the subjects were reported accurately, then potentials should be available for registration near the eyeballs. An analysis of records obtained from these points indicate that in imagining the Eiffel Tower, for instance, the eyeballs move slightly upward, somewhat as they actually would do if the tower were really seen.

In different subjects the *same muscles do not always contract during the imagination of a particular act or object.* But the results do indicate that *if these contractions are absent in one region, they*

422

(Courtesy of Edmund Jacobson)

FIG. 80.—*Record 1.* The signal to begin imagining is shown at the top of the record by a white line. A similar line indicates the end of the imagining process. During the interval, lasting a little more than a second, the subject was to "imagine lifting a ten-pound weight with the right arm." The potentials are recorded during this interval as shown.

Record 2. The subject is to imagine lifting with the left arm. The right-arm record shows no electromyographic response.

Record 3. Two distinct volleys are separated by a relaxed period when the subject is instructed to "imagine hitting a nail twice with a hammer held in the right hand."

Record 4. The record shows typical responses in the imagining of rhythmical acts like rowing a boat.

will be found in another. This principle explains why the instruction to "imagine using the right arm" is not *invariably* followed by action potentials in the right arm; in some instances the subject merely visualizes the act, and if he does, movements are made in the region of the eye.

Aside from imagining an experience kinesthetically or visually a person may think about it in terms of words.[12] If he does, we might expect that electrodes in the muscles of the tongue or under-lip would pick up potentials associated with tiny muscular movements in these regions.

Instructions to the subject which were designed to bring out lip and tongue movements include: "Imagine counting"; "Imagine telling your friend the date"; "Recall certain poems or songs"; "Multiply numbers." Almost anyone would agree that tongue movements would be associated with these acts even though they refused to agree that "mental" processes did not accompany them. But the subjects were also instructed to "Think of 'eternity' "; "Think of electrical resistance"; "The meaning of 'incongruous'; of 'everlasting.' " Most people would hold that thinking of these abstractions is a purely "mental" process. During the experimental periods there are potentials for all these instructions which disappear in the relaxed subject. The vibrations occur in patterns which evidently correspond to those present in actual speech. The kinds of instruction given above are different from those like "Imagine moving your left arm," because here there are no arm potentials. *Thinking in abstract terms is then a matter of incipient movement of the speech apparatus at so low a level that the ordinary subject overlooks it entirely.* The reverse is also true: in imagining a left-arm movement no potentials are present in the speech regions.

4. DEAF-MUTES

In deaf-mutes the principal organs of speech are the fingers and hands rather than the tongue and lips. Deaf-mutes therefore become valuable subjects because it is much easier to attach electrodes to the hands, arms, or fingers than it is to put them on the

---

[12] There are, of course, other possibilities. These are merely the most frequent ways of imagining.

tongue and lips. It was L. W. Max of New York University who first pointed out these advantages[13] and was the first to examine the action-potentials from these regions in deaf-mute subjects. The apparatus that he used was very similar to that used by Jacobson, although there were important technical differences that we cannot go into here.

Max found that he could get subjects to relax enough to provide a stable base line by allowing them time to get used to the experimental setup.[14] They were allowed to lie on a wide bed in a darkened quiet room. Under these conditions, although they were tense at first, most of the subjects learned to relax without any direct training in relaxation. In this respect his experiment is entirely different from that of Jacobson. One girl was unable to relax after a prolonged attempt before the experiment started. This preliminary general training was in the hands of an assistant. When Max himself took over the experiment in order to find out why the girl could not relax when the others could, a satisfactory record was secured in a short time. Higher responses returned when the same assistant again took charge. It turned out finally that the girl was in love with the assistant, and was therefore tense when he was around. Other subjects were tense because they thought that certain assistants were too brusque or unsympathetic. All records affected by factors like these had to be discarded.

The subjects did not know that their finger movements were the principal interest of the experimenters. The electrodes were attached to the forearm over the flexors digitorum, the muscles which control finger movement. The potentials were thus picked up some distance away from the fingers themselves. There were eighteen deaf subjects and sixteen hearing subjects who were used as controls. Five of the eighteen deaf subjects were more intensively studied because they could relax better than the other thirteen. Some of these subjects volunteered because they were interested in the problem, others were in effect paid for serving for they were drawn from the relief rolls.

Two amplifiers and two string galvanometers were used. Gen-

---

[13] Louis W. Max, "An Experimental Study of the Motor Theory of Consciousness," *Journal of General Psychology*, 1935, 12, 159-175.
[14] Louis W. Max, "An Experimental Study of the Motor Theory of Consciousness," *Journal of Comparative Psychology*, 1937, 24, 301-344.

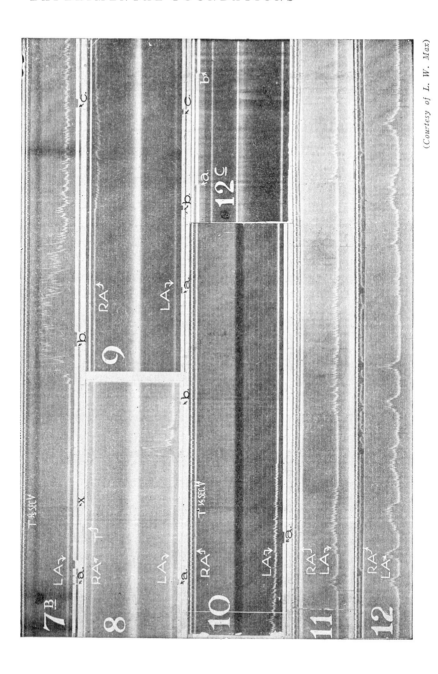

FIG. 81.—Electromyographic Responses of the Deaf.

Record 7B. Time in fifths of seconds is shown on the extreme top of the record. The electromyographic record from the left arm is marked *L A.* At signal *a* a card was illuminated in front of the subject who, although deaf, could speak. The card contained the following problem: "Is this true? If Paul is taller than Herbert and is also shorter than Robert, then Robert is taller than Herbert." At *b*, the subject said, "Yes, he is the tallest." During the solution there was no hand movement, but movement of the left hand accompanied speaking. The subject's report indicated that the absence of hand movements during the solution could be accounted for in the way the subject solved the problem. He said: "First read the card rapidly, then pictures of three boys; lined them up with tallest at right, then gave the answer . . . ."

Records 8, 9, 10 do not concern us here.

Record 11. Electromyographic responses to the problem "Think the word 'Heavy' again and again till the light goes out." In the section shown there are three signings.

Record 12. Two overt signings of the word "Heavy" photographed with the sensitivity of the instruments greatly reduced.

Record 12c. A control experiment on a hearing subject instructed to "Think the word 'Heavy' again and again till the light goes out." The light was turned on at *a*, off at *b*. There was no response in either arm.

erally the electrodes were placed on the two arms, two on each arm, so that simultaneous records could be obtained from these parts, but other segments, such as the eye and brow region and the legs, were also used as controls.

Analysis of hundreds of records from these subjects shows that *finger movements are present in deaf subjects when they are solving problems, imagining, and dreaming.* These movements are not present in hearing subjects. In hearing subjects this activity is present in the tongue and lips, could it be recorded satisfactorily. The finger movements of deaf subjects during a dream are sometimes complete enough so that someone who knows the manual language signs can infer what the dream is about in the same way that, with hearing subjects, ordinary speech sounds give enough significant information so that a listener can accurately reconstruct a dream of the sleep-talker.

The records shown in Figure 81 indicate the kinds of records that Max obtained from his subjects. We are particularly interested in records 11 and 12. Record 11 (Figure 81) shows an entirely implicit imagining response. The subject is totally unable to report any movement at all, but the instrument shows three distinct periods of activity corresponding to what the subject would call three entirely "mental" performances. The amplifiers and the galvanometers are more sensitive than the subject's own kinesthetic sense organs. Record 12 shows the electromyographic responses when the sensitivity of the instrument is greatly reduced and the same subject actually "signs" the same word that he merely "imagined" in record 11. The response in record 12 was entirely overt. It was evident to the subject and to everybody who watched him that there were two distinct responses; the word "heavy," chosen because in "signing" it calls for distinctive movements, was repeated once.

There are three comparisons that can be made from these two records. First, the two overt "signings" of the same word in record 12 do not result in exactly the same pattern of response;[15] second, there is no precise similarity between the implicit and the overt records; third, there are three *implicit* responses in the time that is required for two *overt* responses. These observations allow us to

[15] It has been said that no two responses of whatever kind are exactly identical.

428

conclude that *implicit responses are considerably more rapid than equivalent overt responses.* The same conclusion is suggested when we observe that silent reading is faster than oral reading.

It should also be emphasized that nobody can read these electrical records. One cannot tell from the record *what* a person is thinking about; he can only infer that reasoning, imagining, or dreaming is taking place. That no one ever will be able to read a person's thoughts from these records is strongly suggested by theoretical considerations that we cannot go into here, but we must also remember that at one time it was "scientifically proved" that an airplane could never fly. Action-potential researches are about in the same stage of development that airplanes were in when this discouraging prediction was made.

5. "BRAIN WAVES" [16]

Electrical potentials of the brain, popularly known as "brain waves," were first discovered in animals in 1875, but not until the beginning of the 1930's were extensive experiments made nor did widespread interest in the phenomenon develop. In 1929, Hans Berger,[17] a German investigator, first recorded electrical variations from the surface of the head of intact human subjects. In a series of well-controlled experiments he was able to show that *the electrical potentials are due to the activity of the brain itself* rather than to the activity of neighboring muscles, circulatory pulsations, eye movements, or other artifacts. He demonstrated that the electrical changes recorded from the surface of the scalp are practically identical, except for differences in magnitude, with those recorded directly from the exposed surface of the brain, a fact which has greatly facilitated the investigation of brain potentials in human subjects.

Several groups of investigators in this country and abroad have confirmed and extended many of Berger's original observations in normal and pathological cases. They have studied sleep, unconsciousness, anesthesia, hypnosis, epilepsy, mental deficiency, and other psychologic and neurologic disorders in human beings and have performed significant experiments on aimals. Students interested in

[16] This section was written by Donald B. Lindsley.
[17] Hans Berger, "Über das Elektrenkephalogramm des Menschen," *Archiv für Psychiatrie und Neurologie,* 1929, 87, 227-270.

the details of this work will find Jasper's[18] recent review of it valuable.

In Berger's original experiments potential changes were led from two needle electrodes inserted through the scalp or from two large pad electrodes attached to the surface of the scalp, usually one over the forehead, the other over the back of the head. Many recent investigations have employed small metal plate electrodes which may be placed fairly close together on the surface of the scalp over localized regions and which are held comfortably and securely in place by collodion or bandages. An electrode paste or jelly usually serves as the conducting medium between an electrode and the surface of the skin. Because of the differences in the pattern of the electrical activity over different regions of the head it is important to know the position of the electrodes.

Two main types of waves were described by Berger, alpha and beta waves. The alpha waves are large, rhythmic oscillations which may be observed best when the subject is quiet and relaxed, with sensory stimulation at a minimum. In normal adult subjects alpha waves range in frequency from eight to thirteen per second with an average of about 10 per second. The potentials are of the order of 10 to 100 millionths of a volt. The beta waves are even smaller and faster and are often superimposed on the alpha waves. Their frequency ranges from about twenty to fifty per second. Although alpha and beta waves appear in records from most regions of the head, the alpha waves are more prominent over the occipital, parietal, and temporal regions, whereas the largest beta waves are usually found in the frontal region, particularly over the motor area.

Alpha waves are diminished in amplitude or abolished entirely by visual, auditory, tactual and pain stimuli, but the beta waves do not seem to be affected. "Mental" arithmetic or problem solving often diminishes or abolishes the alpha rhythm for the duration of the problem-solving process. The reason for this seemingly paradoxical effect—amounting to a reduction in the electrical activity of the brain with increased stimulation—is not clear for the physiological basis of the alpha and beta waves is not entirely understood.

[18] H. H. Jasper, "Electrical Signs of Cortical Activity," *Psychological Bulletin*, 1937, 34, 411-481.

According to the hypothesis proposed by Adrian and Matthews,[19] individual brain cells when "at rest"—that is, in the absence of external stimulation—are continuously and "spontaneously" charging and discharging. It has been shown in simpler organisms that when groups of nerve cells are "spontaneously" active they tend to discharge in unison. Thus the extremely minute potentials from single neurones, too small to be detected through the scalp and skull, are thought to produce alpha waves when the thousands of brain cells constituting a particular region discharge synchronously. An external stimulus disrupts the synchronous discharge of the cells and destroys the summation effect, thus reducing or abolishing the alpha waves.

Rhythmic alpha waves first appear in infants at about 3 months of age at a frequency of three to four per second. The frequency of alpha and other types of waves increases with age in children according to a definite growth function and reaches the fairly stationary adult level between ten to twelve years of age. In normal adult subjects the frequency of the alpha waves varies little from day to day and even from year to year. Likewise the pattern of the waves, whether very rhythmic or very irregular, remains much the same. It has even been suggested that the pattern of the waves is correlated with certain characteristics of the personality but this finding has not as yet been substantiated.

Recent studies of brain potentials during various stages of sleep have indicated that changes in the frequency, amplitude, and pattern of the brain waves constitute an important index of the depth of sleep. Modifications of the brain potentials during unconsciousness and deep anesthesia are similar to those during sleep. Striking and characteristic changes occur in the brain potential records of epileptic patients slightly preceding and during convulsive seizures but a comparison of the records from normal and mentally deficient subjects has so far failed to reveal marked differences.

One thing is clear: "brain waves" are not even remotely related to the kind of electrical activity that is imagined to be responsible for one person's being able to read the mind of another. They are

19 E. D. Adrian and B. H. C. Matthews, "The Berger Rhythm: Potential Changes from the Occipital Lobes in Man," *Brain,* 1934, 57, 355-385.

not capable of being transmitted over the distances required and no person has the receptive equipment required to pick them up.

Summary of the chapter. The brain alone is not the organ of reasoning or learning or thinking or imagining or recalling or any other property of man. The greater elaboration of certain brain parts in comparison with other species makes it apparent that these parts are important to man, but to differentiate one person from another on the basis of microscopic differences in brain structure cannot now be done. It is even likely that it never can be done, and to expect to do it is to misunderstand the nature of psychological functioning.

The principal experiments on localization of brain function are reviewed. They show that the brain is much less specific in its function than might be expected. At the present time we are a long distance from having any even moderately complete knowledge of how and what part of the brain functions in complex psychological acts.

Experiments on the action currents present in imagery, thinking, problem solving, and so on, show that the whole organism is involved in these processes—not just the brain. There is the further indication that to have a "mental experience" of these kinds means that objects and relations are dealt with in much the same way as if we were actually handling them, except that the implicit responses are a kind of muscular shorthand.

CHAPTER TWENTY-ONE

PERSONALITY

If someone asks you what another person is like, you think back and begin to recall the many things that he has done and said. You think of the wishes he has expressed, the way he acted at a dance, how quickly he understood a difficult point, how hard he has worked to gain a goal, and whether he is usually lighthearted or somber. These and many other things you think of. Out of all these remembered events you will try to sketch a portrait of the person. If your observations have been numerous and accurate you will succeed in drawing a picture which is unique; it will not be exactly like the portrait of any other person; it will differ in one way or another.

In your description of the person, you will probably intermingle verbs of the past, the present, and the future tense. You will do so because of the inevitable feeling that the threads of behavior which you have seen in the past will carry through the present and into the future. You might even make a prediction of what the person will do in a situation in which he has never been placed before. You dare to do this because you have discovered that the habits we have learned in the past are carried with us and serve, along with the exact nature of each new situation, to determine what our reactions will be. These habits of reaction in many different areas, perception and motivation for example, are what make up our personalities.

1. PERSONALITY TESTS

If one is concerned with determining the relationship between two or more factors, it is absolutely necessary that he have some way of measuring each of the factors. If you wanted to know what effect rate of speed had upon gasoline consumption, you would need gauges or dials to measure speed, miles traveled, and gasoline consumed. If any one of these three measures were lacking, the answer to your question would not be forthcoming. Furthermore, if two of your measurements were made with accuracy, but the third was only

433

approximately correct, your answer would be correspondingly erroneous.

Because scientific progress is so completely dependent upon accuracy of measurement, much time and effort have been expended by psychologists in developing tests of personality. The aspects of behavior which have been examined are many. There are tests designed to measure honesty, social aggressiveness, emotional stability, direction and strength of motivation, and almost any other characteristic of personality that the reader can think of. Considerable ingenuity has been used in developing these tests, but despite this fact few if any of the tests can be called completely successful. The psychologists have yet to develop in the field of personality any tests which even approximate the degree of reliability and validity that most intelligence tests have.

One of the more recent trends in the field of personality testing is in the development of tests which have been labeled *projective techniques.* In their general form these tests consist of presenting the subjects with material to which a variety of appropriate reactions can be made—we call these materials unstructured—and recording the particular responses which occur. The assumption is made that each of the responses is an expression of the underlying personality traits of the individual, and that by evaluating all of the responses or types of responses one is also evaluating the subject's personality. In the section below a few of the more common of these projective tests will be described.[1]

The Rorschach test. This test is perhaps the best known of all the projective techniques, and it has been very influential in setting the direction of much of the testing in the personality toward unstructured tests. The test itself is very simple, for it consists only of a series of standardized ink blots, each on a separate card. In the administration of the test the subject looks at one card at a time, and he tells the tester everything he sees in the card. He may spend as much time as he wishes on the card, and he may turn it in any direction he wishes. The test administrator records each response

[1] A very competent review of these tests may be found in J. McV. Hunt, *Personality and the Behavior Disorders,* The Ronald Press Company, New York, 1944. Chapter 6 in Volume I, by Robert W. White, deals with the projective tests.

FIG. 82.—An ink blot of the type used in the Rorschach test.

that is made and in what part of the blot the figure was seen. A sample of the type of figures used in the Rorschach test is shown in Figure 82. The reader will notice that it is not difficult to see many objects in this blot, and he will notice, too, that it is fun and interesting to do so. Because of its intrinsic interest value few persons balk at taking a personality test of this sort.

The scoring of this test is too complicated to be described in any detail, but some of the types of responses which are particularly significant can be mentioned. In the first place the total number of responses made is considered important. Another measure of interest is whether the subject reacts primarily to the blot as a whole or to small parts of it. A ratio is also obtained between the number of pure form responses, and the responses which imply color in the imagined object—even though the blot itself is all black. The objects may be seen as objects in movement or as motionless and static things, and this, too, is considered significant.

The score on the test is not obtained simply by adding up the frequency of each of these items. This is done, but the real significance of the test result is thought to come from the tester's ability to see interrelationships between the various responses. Indeed, there are some users of the test who object strenuously to any attempt to give a numerical score for the test.

The Thematic Apperception Test. The TAT, as the Thematic Apperception Test is usually called, is another unstructured test which makes use of visual material. It consists of a series of pictures of the sort shown in Figure 83, and the subject is asked to tell a story of what he imagines might be happening in the picture. None of these pictures are structured completely enough for only one story to emerge. In all probability the reader can find several possible plots for Figure 83, and if he were to show it to his friends they might see other totally different events in it. Once again the theory holds that what will be seen is characteristic of the viewer, and a reflection of his basic needs, attitudes, and way of seeing the world. The sources of the stories may be pure imagination, something out of a book or a movie that the subject has read, or an event from his life. Regardless of the source of the story its plot is considered

436

important, for it is considered significant that this particular movie or novel is remembered and not some other, and that the subject's imagination should lead in one direction rather than another. The clinical psychologist seeks to find some constant thread of meaning recurring in the material of the various stories, and thus to obtain an insight into the personality of the subject. Thus even to a greater

Fig. 83.—The type of picture used in the TAT. (Courtesy of Dr. J. B. Rotter.)

extent than the Rorschach, the TAT fails to give a quantitative score.

There have been a variety of other unstructured tests that have been employed, but the two described above are the most common. They should serve to give the reader an understanding of the basic assumptions behind such tests, and their general nature.

The validity of the tests. The statement was made in the chapter on aptitudes that tests cannot simply be made. They must also be validated. That is, it must be demonstrated that the tests are measuring what their deviser claims they measure. A science cannot accept a dictum that something is good or poor; it must evaluate it by the methods of science.

437

In order to validate a test two kinds of data are necessary, a reliable score on the test and some independent measure of what is being tested. In the case of intelligence tests both of them can be obtained. The tests are constructed so that they give a reliable quantitative score. This fulfills one demand. A moderately satisfactory fulfillment of the other demand can be obtained through the use of such a measure as school grades, if we are willing to make the assumption that to a great extent these are a function of intelligence. Thus by comparing scores on intelligence tests with school grades we can indirectly determine whether or not a test is valid and is measuring intelligence.[2]

Validation of these personality tests is not so easy a task. In the first place, the projective tests are seldom designed to give a precise numerical score, and, as we have mentioned above, some clinical psychologists hold that the basic value of the test is destroyed if numerical scoring is sought for. In the second place there is no independent criterion for personality of the same quantitative and reliable nature that school grades are for intelligence. The measure which is ordinarily used is a cruder one, consisting of an evaluation of the subject's personality by some other individual. The other individual may be a close friend, a teacher, or a clinical psychologist or psychiatrist who has had the subject under his care.

Several special validating techniques can be employed using these two kinds of data, the general evaluative (and sometimes quantitative) score on the personality test, and the independent opinion of the teacher, friend, or clinician. One of these methods is called *blind matching*. The tests are given to a group of individuals and, in addition, short descriptions of each individual are written by someone who knows them well. Any signs which would serve to link a particular test with a particular biography are then removed and all the materials are given to some expert. He examines biographies and test results and tries to match them correctly. The extent to which he can match the biographies with the proper test is a measure of the validity of the test.

Another method of validating the tests consists of comparing

---

[2] There are other ways of validating these tests, but they are too complicated to be considered at this time.

the scores of a group of persons who as a group have certain personality characteristics with another group who differ from them. Thus one might compare a group of diagnosed neurotic individuals with a group of normals. If the test is valid the responses of one group should differ markedly from those of the other.

The number of studies dealing with the validity of the various projective tests is many. Some studies have indicated good validity of the tests, while others have been essentially negative in their findings. At this time it is still impossible to state the exact validity of these tests with any degree of confidence. There are few if any psychologists who would hold that any of the personality tests we have developed to date are the final answer to the measurement of personality. Most certainly the future years will find many research workers developing, refining, and evaluating tests in the hope that they will someday achieve a measuring stick of personality that has the precision and validity needed for accurate scientific work.

2. THE ASSESSMENT OF MEN

Another approach to the measurement of personality is shown by the work of a group of psychologists, psychiatrists, and sociologists who were requested by the United States Army to evaluate the volunteers for work with the Office of Strategic Services.[3] The billets to which these persons might be assigned were extremely variable. They might be required to lead a guerrilla group behind enemy lines, to engage in propaganda that would undermine the morale of the enemy, or to perform other tasks that often required physical daring, intelligence, social tact, leadership, and general resourceful adaptability. It was the purpose of the assessment program to weed out those applicants who might falter in a time of stress or who for any other reason might not be expected to perform their mission adequately.

The method which the OSS staff employed is radically different from the usual personality test battery. Essentially it consisted of putting the subject into a variety of situations and observing and rating his behavior in these situations. The data on which the staff made their judgments were, for the most part, on actual behavior

---

[3] OSS Assessment Staff, *Assessment of Men,* Rinehart & Company, Inc., New York, 1948.

in social, intellectual, and stress-producing situations, though some of the data were obtained from more or less typical tests and from interviews.

Several different assessment stations were established to accomplish the evaluation work. Some were located overseas, but the bulk of the work was done in two units in the Washington area. The program at Station S, which was located at an estate in Virginia a few miles from Washington, was the most ambitious.

The procedure at Station S. The recruits reported at a specified time to a house in Washington. There they were asked to remove their outer clothing and to destroy all identification marks on their underwear. Each person was issued Army fatigues and boots. He was entering a three-day period during which all signs of his rank or status, whether military or civilian, were removed. Along with this sartorial anonymity he was told also that he must choose a false name and conceal his true identity. This was his "cover story," and he was to be measured in part by his ability to stick to it during the next three days, and to keep his true identity a secret.

Late in the afternoon the men boarded Army trucks and were driven to Station S. There they were welcomed by the director and told that they were to be evaluated for their prospective jobs by a series of tests and interviews which would be administered during the following days.

It is not possible to describe all of the test situations which were employed, but the basic characteristic of the program can be illustrated by a few of the tests.

The wall. A group of four to seven men were confronted with a wall, ten feet high and fifteen feet long. Behind this wall, separated by a distance of eight feet, was another one parallel to it. In front of the wall there was a heavy log, an old board a few inches longer than the log, and a couple of two-by-fours, one two feet and the other three feet in length. The men were told that these walls were separated by a two-hundred-foot canyon, and that they must cross this canyon to escape from some Japanese soldiers. In order to fulfill their mission, they must carry a king-sized bazooka (actually a log) with them. They could cross the canyon any way they wished, except

440

Fig. 84.—The wall problem: bridging the gap.

Fig. 85.—Construction test (the helpers start to work—on the candidate).

441

walking around it, but whoever or whatever fell into the canyon would be counted lost.

The solution to the problem consisted of getting two men to the top of the wall, and they, by using the old board as a measuring device, would discover that the log was just long enough to bridge the canyon. Next they must solve the problem of how to rest the log upon the opposite wall. The orthodox solution to this was to rest the light board upon the opposite side and use it as a sort of bridge or track for pushing the log to the opposite side. Once this was done, the problem was solved. Occasionally a man would jump from one wall to another, and occasionally a team would stand the log on end on the near wall and drop it neatly onto the top of the opposite wall. Usually such an attempt failed.

The psychologists observing the men rated them for initiative, intelligence, social relations, leadership, physical ability, and energy.

Construction. Ostensibly the purpose of this test was to measure the ability of the candidate to direct two helpers in building a large wooden construction. Actually it was more of a test for emotional stability or frustration tolerance; for the two helpers were stooges who hindered more than they helped. One of the helpers, Kippy, was something of a gold-bricker. Sluggish and passive, he stood around with his hands in his pockets and would do absolutely nothing more than he was directed to do. The other helper, Buster, was aggressive and critical. He was ever ready to offer impractical solutions and to express dissatisfaction with the way the job was being done. The task of the candidate was to direct these men to build a cube out of some wooden sticks and blocks similar, except in size, to children's Tinker-Toy sets. An appreciation of the nature of the task can be obtained from an inspection of Figure 85.

The two helpers, who were actually staff members, though the candidate was led to believe that they were hired hands, tried to break the subject's cover story and to frustrate him in any way possible. The manner in which the situation could be used to assess the personalities of the candidates is illustrated by the following extract from one of the protocols:

442

STAFF MEMBER (calling toward the barn) : Can you come out here and help this man for a few minutes?

BUSTER AND KIPPY: Sure, we'll be right out.

STAFF MEMBER: O.K., Slim, these are your men. They will be your helpers. You have ten minutes.

SLIM: Do you men know anything about building this thing?

BUSTER: Well, I dunno, I've seen people working here. What is it you want done?

SLIM: Well, we have got to build a cube like this and we only have a short time in which to do it, so I'll ask you men to pay attention to what I have to say. I'll tell you what to do and you will do it. O.K.?

BUSTER: Sure, sure, anything you say, Boss.

SLIM: Fine. Now we are going to build a cube like this with five-foot poles for the uprights and seven-foot poles for the diagonals, and use the blocks for the corners. So first we must build the corners by putting a half block and a whole block together like this and clinching them with a peg. Do you see how it is done?

BUSTER: Sure, sure.

SLIM: Well, let's get going.

BUSTER: Well, what is it you want done, exactly? What do I do first?

SLIM: Well, first put some corners together—let's see, we need four on the bottom and four topside—yes, we need eight corners. You make eight of these corners and be sure that you pin them like this one.

BUSTER: You mean we both make eight corners or just one of us?

SLIM: You each make four of them.

BUSTER: Well, if we do that, we will have more than eight because you already have one made there. Do you want eight altogether or nine altogether?

SLIM: Well, it doesn't matter. You each make four of these and hurry.

BUSTER: O.K., O.K.

KIPPY: What cha in, the Navy? You look like one of them curly-headed Navy boys all the girls are after. What cha in, the Navy?

SLIM: Er—no. I am not in the Navy. I'm not in anything.

KIPPY: Well, you were just talking about "topside" so I thought maybe you were in the Navy. What's the matter with you—you look healthy enough. Are you a draft dodger?

SLIM: No, I was deferred for essential work—but that makes no difference. Let's get the work done. Now we have the corners done, let's put them together with the poles.

KIPPY: The more I think of it, the more I think you are in the Army. You run this job like the Army—you know, the right way, the wrong way, and the Army way. I'll bet you are some second lieutenant from Fort Benning.

443

SLIM: That has nothing to do with this job. Let's have less talk and more work.

KIPPY: Well, I just thought we could talk while we work—it's more pleasant.

SLIM: Well, we can work first and talk afterward. Now connect those two corners with a five-foot pole.

BUSTER: Don't you think we ought to clear a place where we can work?

SLIM: That's a good idea. Sure, go ahead.

BUSTER: What kind of work did you do before you came here? Never did any building, I bet. Jeez, I've seen a lot of guys, but no one as dumb as you.

SLIM: Well, that may be, but you don't seem to be doing much to help me.

BUSTER: What—what's that? Who are you talking to, me? Me not being helpful—why, I've done everything you have asked me, haven't I? Now, haven't I? Everything you asked me. Why, I've been about as helpful as anyone could be around here.

SLIM: Well, you haven't killed yourself working and we haven't much time, so let's get going.

BUSTER: Well, I like that. I come out here and do everything you ask me to do. You don't give very good directions. I don't think you know what you are doing anyway. No one else ever complained about me not working. Now I want an apology for what you said about me.

SLIM: O.K., O.K., let's forget it. I'll apologize. Let's get going. We haven't much time, you build a square here and you build one over there.

BUSTER: Who you talking to—him or me?

KIPPY: That's right—how do you expect us to know which one you mean? Why don't you give us a number or something—call one of us "number one" and the other "number two"?

SLIM: O.K. You are "one" and he is "two."

BUSTER: Now, wait a minute—just a minute. How do you expect to get along with people if you treat them like that? First we come out here and you don't ask us our names—you call us "you." Then we tell you about it, you give us numbers. How would you like that? How would you like to be called a number? You treat us just like another five-foot pole and then you expect us to break our necks working for you. I can see you never worked much with people.

SLIM: I'm sorry, but we do not have much time and I thought—

KIPPY: Yes, you thought. Jeez, it doesn't seem to me that you ever did much thinking about anything. First you don't ask our names as any stupid guy would who was courteous. Then you don't know what you did before you came here or whether you are in the Army, Navy, or not, and it's darn sure you don't know anything about building this thing or directing workers. Cripes, man, you stand around here like a ninny arguing when we should be working. What the hell is the matter with you, anyway?

444

SLIM: I'm sorry—what are your names?

BUSTER: I'm Buster.

KIPPY: Mine's Kippy. What is yours?

SLIM: You can call me Slim.

BUSTER: Well, is that your name or isn't it?

SLIM: Yes, that is my name.

KIPPY: It's not a very good name—Dumbhead would be better.

BUSTER: Where do you come from, Slim?

SLIM: Cincinnati.

BUSTER: That's out in Ohio, isn't it?

SLIM: Yes.

BUSTER: What's the river it's on?

SLIM: Uh-why the Ohio.

BUSTER: You don't sound very sure. I almost wonder if you do come from there. I'd think any Cincinnatian would remember the name of the river.

SLIM: I'm from Cincinnati, all right. I lived there for eight years.

In this situation the staff rated the candidates on leadership, emotional stability, energy, initiative, and social relations.

The stress interview. The subject reported at a certain time to a room where he found a paper with the following directions upon it.

The examination you are to undergo is designed to test your resourcefulness, agility of mind, and ability to think quickly, effectively, and convincingly. This is an important test and it is important that you do well. *In twelve (12) minutes report to the basement room at the foot of the stairs.*

The test will measure your ability to establish and maintain a cover story for the situation outlined below. Your cover story must be told convincingly, intelligently, and clearly. The examiners will try to trip you up on your story, to lead you into inconsistencies, and in general to confuse you.

Several students in the past have failed in this test because they forgot or did not understand the directions and requirements. We are listing below the important "rules" of this examination. If you do not remember these rules you will fail.

1. YOUR COVER STORY MUST GIVE A PLAUSIBLE AND INNOCENT REASON FOR YOUR ACTIONS.

2. YOU MUST ANSWER EVERY QUESTION ASKED. ANSWERS LIKE, "I DON'T REMEMBER," "I DON'T KNOW," "I AM NOT PERMITTED TO DISCLOSE THAT INFORMATION," ETC. ARE NOT PERMISSIBLE AND WILL COUNT AGAINST YOU IN THE FINAL RATING.

3. YOU MUST AVOID BREAKING EITHER PERSONAL OR

ORGANIZATIONAL SECURITY IN YOUR ANSWERS. NONE OF YOUR REPLIES SHOULD DISCLOSE YOUR FORMER OCCUPATION, PLACE OF RESIDENCE, ETC.

Here is the situation for which you are to construct a cover story:

A night watchman at 9:00 P.M. found you going through some papers in a file marked "SECRET" in a Government office in Washington. You are NOT an employee of the agency occupying the building in which this office is located. You had no identification papers whatsoever with you. The night watchman has brought you here for questioning.

In developing your cover story you may assume that you are clothed in any manner you wish.

After the expiration of the twelve minutes he went into another room where he was grilled by several staff members. During the grilling he was forced to face a bright light while his inquisitors remained in the background. Actually this situation, which offhand seems relatively mild, did place a considerable amount of stress on the candidates. Several of them became so emotionally disturbed that they asked to drop out of OSS training following this test.

Other measurements. In addition to other test situations, the men were interviewed on aspects of their personal history, were given some formal paper-and-pencil tests, and were observed in their daily social give-and-take with the other candidates.

After these three days of observation the staff met together to evaluate the candidate. Using all the data which they had collected, the staff rated each candidate on a number of traits and then made a recommendation as to whether or not he should be accepted for work with the OSS.

The validity of the ratings. In a wartime situation it is very difficult to obtain a good measure of the actual efficiency of a predicting device. There are a number of reasons for this, but one of the most important is the difficulty of obtaining an accurate measure of the individual's proficiency on a job. The present type of program is particularly fraught with this sort of difficulty. Ratings on such personality characteristics as level of motivation or emotional stability are hard to make even if we know the person whom we are rating very well. They will be much less meaningful if the ratings are to be made upon someone with whom we have had very little

446

contact. In this situation evaluations were obtained from the theater commander, from the comments of other OSS workers who had had some contact with the man in the field, and from an interview with the man himself. None of these methods are anywhere near satisfactory, and they most certainly give only a very crude measure of the man's real effectiveness.

Another error-producing factor in evaluation lay in the fact that the men and women were given quite different jobs to perform. The job for one man might be a relatively easy one, while another might have been assigned a very difficult task. The man who performed effectively in the simple task might well have been given a better rating than the man who performed less well on a difficult task. Nevertheless, the second man might actually have been a superior individual. It was unfortunate that the staff doing the assessment could not have been told the type of billet to which the men were to be assigned.

Despite all these difficulties, some relationship was shown between the score obtained by the men in the assessment program and the various ratings of the effectiveness of the men on the job. The relationship was not high, but it was sufficient to indicate that this method of appraising personality was getting at something basic. There is reason to believe that the relationship would have been higher if some of the previously mentioned sources of errors in the evaluation of the men's and women's effectiveness in the field could have been removed.

Another measure of the effectiveness of the assessment program can be obtained by determining the frequency of neuropsychiatric breakdowns of the men in the program. It was estimated that about 0.26 per cent of the OSS personnel developed psychotic or neuro-psychotic disabilities which were severe enough to remove them from duty. Only about a quarter of all the OSS personnel were run through the assessment program. Of this group 0.13 per cent became psycho-logically disabled. Actually the percentage is even less for the Station S alone. Two of their men became psychoneurotic. In the case of one of the men, the station had recommended that the individual be excluded from OSS duty, but the recommendation had been disre-garded by higher officials. The other man had been viewed with skepticism, and was passed with a warning that he be carefully watched during his training period.

Summary of the program. The program of the assessment group in OSS has an approach to the measurement of personality radically different from that which characterizes the projective tests or some of our paper-and-pencil tests. In the projective tests one obtains data upon how a person reacts to ambiguous figures—ink blots or pictures, for example—and on the basis of these reactions makes predictions about the behavior in many very different situations. Thus because he sees these blots in a certain way, we may predict that he will react in a certain way in a social situation or in a time of stress. The data we collect are, on the face of it at least, quite different from the nature of the data we predict.

Some of the paper-and-pencil tests do try to get at the actual behavior by asking the subject what he did in certain situations or what he might do in certain hypothetical ones. These answers are not, of course, truly indicative of what the individual did or might do; rather they reflect what the person *thinks* might be the case, and there is much evidence that there is often a great difference between what we think of ourselves and what we actually are.

The OSS assessment program went a step farther and actually observed the behavior of the individuals in certain standard situations. These particular situations were devised to include many aspects of behavior which might occur in the "real" or to-be-predicted situation. Certainly this kind of personality test measures behavior which is very similar to the nonlaboratory behavior about which predictions are to be made, but this alone does not mean that the test is perfect. For one thing, the laboratory situation is only similar to the "real" situation and sometimes slight differences in situations can make for real differences in behavior. For another, the test results cannot be scored with the objectivity of a paper-and-pencil test. The score is the over-all impression made by the person on the rater. This is certainly more subject to error than counting "yeses" or "nos" or some other such response. Much research work will need to be done in the future before we can conclude that such tests as these are or are not the final answer to the problem of the measurement of personality.

3. DISCIPLINARY METHODS AND PERSONALITY

Just what methods should be used in disciplining the child is a perplexing problem to any conscientious parent. It is uniquely perplexing because the punishing act carries a double meaning. One meaning is whether or not it will be effective in preventing the child from committing this particular misdemeanor at a later time. If this were the sole significance of the act the parents' concern would not need to be great, but unfortunately there is another meaning. Within every act of discipline there lurks this question, "What effect will this act which I commit now have upon the total personality of this child? How will it effect his behavior four years, ten years, or twenty years from now?" It is not only the present but the future that looks down on each disciplinary method used by the parent.

When the parent is concerned with this question he is, of course, assuming that the nature of the child's personality is somehow molded by the type of discipline employed. Whether such a molding effect does exist and what specific patterns of punishment lead to what personality characteristics was the problem that Radke[4] set out to investigate.

Subjects. The subjects of the investigation were forty-three kindergarten and nursery-school children at the University of Minnesota Institute of Child Welfare and their parents.

Method. The reader can perhaps foresee the basic methods that must be used in the study. Two kinds of data must be obtained; a measurement of the child's personality, and a measurement of the disciplinary methods used in the home. After these are obtained it is possible to determine whether or not there is any correlation between treatment and personality characteristics.

Data from the parents. The information concerning the methods of discipline were obtained from answers to a questionnaire composed of 127 items. The items were designed to obtain a description of the following principles and methods of authority and discipline in the home:

4 Marion J. Radke, *The Relation of Parental Authority to Children's Behavior and Attitude.* University of Minnesota Press, Minneapolis, 1946.

Philosophy of authority and discipline
Strictness or laxness of disciplinary policies
Severity or mildness of punishments
Amount and areas of parental supervision
Friction over discipline (mother-father, parent-child)
Mother's versus father's role in home discipline
Parents' rapport with child
Sibling differences related to discipline and intrafamily rapport
Techniques of discipline
Effectiveness of discipline

The questionnaire was taken in the presence of the experimenter, and it was followed by an interview in which the parents were encouraged to report further on the topic of authority and discipline.

Data on the personality of the children. Two kinds of data were obtained on the children. Each child was interviewed, and a series of questions were asked which were designed to throw light on the child's relation with his parents. Following this two projective tests were employed. The first was a series of pictures. These pictures were always presented in pairs. One of the pair would show a child and parent in a happy situation and the other the child and parent in an unhappy situation. Other pairs of pictures showed parents together either happily or unhappily. For each pair the child was asked to tell which picture was most like him or his father and mother.

Doll play constituted the other projective test. The child was given dolls representing each member of his family and was permitted to play with them for about twenty minutes. A record of his actions and verbalizations was recorded and evaluated.

The other source of data on the children came from the kindergarten and nursery-school teachers. Two teachers rated each child on twenty different traits of personality. These are some of the kinds of traits upon which they were rated: popularity, considerateness, leadership, sociability, emotional control, cautiousness.

Results.

(1) THE AUTOCRATIC HOME. When the children whose home disciplinary methods may be classified as autocratic were compared with those whose homes were democratic, the autocratic children were characterized as more unpopular, more given to quarreling,

more inconsiderate, more emotionally unstable, more daring, more insensitive to praise and blame, and less rivalrous.

(2) THE RESTRICTIVE HOME. Children who came from homes where there were many restrictions (even though the restrictions may be enforced by autocratic or democratic means) tended to be nonrivalrous, passive and unpopular.

(3) THE SEVERE HOME. The pattern of the personality traits of the children who came from homes wherein the discipline was severe was much the same as that of the children from the autocratic and restrictive homes and these children tended also to be hesitant to express themselves verbally and to be nonaffectionate.

Summary. It is well to interject a word of caution at this point. Questionnaire studies must always be viewed with a bit of skepticism, for whenever we ask a person what he does, his reply always consists of what he *thinks* he does. Sometimes what we think we do is quite different from what we actually do. Since the data on home disciplinary methods were obtained by means of a questionnaire, they are certainly not completely accurate. Similarly, the measurements of the personality traits of the children lack precision and leave much to be desired.

These statements are merely words of caution, and they should not be permitted to undermine the significance of the experiment. The data of the experiment do indicate, even with these crude methods of measurement, that there is some relationship between the technique of home discipline and the characteristic reactions of the children. It is impossible, however, from such an experiment as this to determine just what psychological mechanisms are operating to result in these relationships. Such words as "autocratic" or "severe" or "restrictive" simply refer to a general pattern of home disciplinary method; precisely what aspect of these general conditions the child reacts to and precisely which ones serve to develop these personality habits have not as yet been determined.

4. PERSONALITY REACTIONS AND THE PRESENT

In the search for the absolute, of which mankind is so mistakenly fond, we are often inclined to label someone as aggressive, rebellious, flighty, or some other such term. We imply that this is the true characteristic of the individual, that he carries around with him some trait that inevitably seeks expression regardless of the nature of the present situation. We disregard the immediate environment, and feel that the behavior springs only out of some source within the individual. Perhaps this is particularly true when the individual's behavior is undesirable; we are ready to condemn him and to attribute his undesirable action to some fault within himself.

When we do this we are neglecting to recognize that responses are always reactions to a situation. The response which is made is never determined solely by the nature of the reactor; it is determined also by the nature of the stimulus. It is true that a person may behave consistently in a particular manner, but his consistency may arise from an unchanging environment as well as from some basic personality trait.

If we accept the hypothesis that immediate environment is an influential factor in determining the nature of the response, then we would expect that the essential behavior characteristics in two different kinds of social environment would differ. This hypothesis was tested by Lewin, Lippett, and White.[5]

Method. In its broad outlines the experimental plan consisted of having boys' club work under three different conditions of society. One society was democratic, another authoritarian, and the third was laissez-faire.[6] The general working plan of these three "societies" is listed below.

Groups of five ten-year-old boys were the subjects for the experiment. They had been selected from a large group of volunteers through the use of various testing, rating, and observational techniques, which showed them to be highly similar in their intellectual, physical, socioeconomic, and personality characteristics. These children were then organized into clubs which met regularly in the club room-laboratory. Work materials were available so that they could engage in such activities as model airplane building, mask making, or painting. Careful observations during the play periods were made

[5] K. Lewin, R. Lippitt, and R. K. White, "Patterns of Aggressive Behavior in Experimentally Created 'Social Climates.'" *Journal of Social Psychology,* 1939, 10, 271-299.

[6] The student of economics will be familiar with a type of society. It is a society with a minimum of restraints, and where each individual is permitted to do as he pleases.

AUTHORITARIAN	DEMOCRATIC	LAISSEZ-FAIRE
1. All determination of policy by the leader	1. All policies a matter of group discussion and decision, encouraged and assisted by the leader	1. Complete freedom for group or individual decision, with a minimum of leader participation
2. Techniques and activity steps dictated by the authority, one at a time, so that future steps were always uncertain to a large degree	2. Activity perspective gained during discussion period. General steps to group goal sketched, and, where technical advice was needed, the leader suggested two or more alternative procedures from which choice could be made	2. Various materials supplied by the leader, who made it clear that he would supply information when asked. He took no other part in work discussion
3. The leader usually dictated the particular work task and work companion of each member	3. The members were free to work with whomever they chose, and the division of tasks was left up to the group	3. Complete nonparticipation of the leader
4. The dominator tended to be "personal" in his praise and criticism of the work of each member; remained aloof from active group participation except when demonstrating	4. The leader was "objective" or "fact-minded" in his praise and criticism and tried to be a regular group member in spirit without doing too much of the work	4. Infrequent spontaneous comments on member activities unless questioned and no attempt to appraise or regulate the course of events

by hidden observers, who recorded all conversation, kept a record of the social interactions, and wrote an interpretive account of the atmosphere of the group as a whole.

Each group of boys played in each of the three different social atmospheres, and, in addition to that, the leaders were varied so that it was not always the same adult who led in any particular social climate. Thus the reactions were not merely to an individual but to a situation.

453

Results. The results of the experiment are not treated in the statistical fashion which makes it possible to evaluate the reliability of differences of the various groups from each other, but trends can be noted. In general the morale in the democratic groups ran higher than in any of the other groups. Symptoms of this were to be found in more friendly remarks to each other and to the leader, fewer expressions of discontent, more group-minded remarks made to the leader, and less purposeful ignoring of the leader. To a greater extent than in the other groups, the autocratic atmosphere gave rise to aggressions against fellow group members, aggressions which arose when the leader left the room, or which reached a peak when the groups shifted from autocratic leadership to some other type. On the other hand, however, the autocratic group spent more of its time in intensive work.

These are perhaps the major results of the study; they are trends which indicate the importance of the immediate environment in determining the children's reactions. In one environment they behaved in one manner, and in another in a different fashion. One cannot definitely say of a misbehaving child that his behavior is the expression of some undesirable personality trait; it may be only a natural reaction to a particular type of environment. Change the environment and the behavior may also change.

This stress upon the immediate environment as a determinant of our social action does not deny that individuals have habits or traits that are unique to them and may find expression in many situations. Actually in the present experiment some of the children differed quite markedly from each other in their reactions to particular social climates. Several of the children showed no aggression in the autocratic group, and one child preferred this group to any of the others. Thus behavior is always an interaction between the situation that confronts us and the repertoire of habits which we carry with us and which we have learned in the past.

An interpretation of the differences in behavior in the three situations can be given only in fairly general terms; for each situation or social climate differed from the others in many respects. We cannot tell exactly what was basic to the situation. There is reason to believe, however, that frustration gives rise to aggression. The inevitable large amount of personal frustration in the autocratic groups may serve to explain the high incidence of aggression that these groups showed. Aggression was also frequent in the laissez-faire group, and this at first seems paradoxical, for the laissez-faire society is one with a minimum of restraints. The authors reason, however, that this was a frustrating society. It was frustrating because the nature of the work was not clearly structured, and for children who have been accustomed to clearer goals this may have been frustrating. The very nondirectedness would also permit the more frequent occurrence of unfruitful activity. It is a case of idle hands finding mischief to do.

All of these interpretations must be considered with reference to the children who served as subjects. They were children brought up in a moderate-sized city in the Midwest, they were products of this American culture and its school system. Thus they entered each social climate with certain past habits and this, interacting with the climate, produced the behavior. Children from England, Germany, Russia, Japan, France, or any other nation might well have shown somewhat different reactions.

Summary. This study points to the importance of the nature of the immediate environment as a determining factor in personality reactions. Without being able to show exactly what factors are operating, it indicates that the same children behave differently in autocratic, democratic, and laizze-faire cultures. The trend of the results is for higher morale and less aggression in the democratic culture, and a possible explanation of this is in the relative lack of frustration in this culture as compared with the others.

5. PROJECTION

When, in a previous chapter, the topic of perception was considered, it was pointed out that there is no perfect correlation between the physical nature of the environment and what the subject sees in the environment. Our perception of the world around us is distorted by our motivations, our present organic conditions, and the nature of our past habits. Characteristic reactions of the individual, personality traits if you wish, are habits which develop out of our past experience. These habits not only determine what we shall do in a given situation, but they should also determine how we shall perceive or structure the situation.

That our own personality traits and personal motivation can structure our environment for us has not passed unnoticed. Novelists, playwrights, and poets who are sometimes acute observers of human behavior, have pointed to this tendency. They have drawn pictures of the generous and honest soul who is easily duped because he sees all others as believing and acting as he does. At the other extreme are the sketches of the habitual aggressors who are quick to take offense because they read offensiveness into the slightest remark, and the dishonest who trust no man.

The significance of this tendency to project into others the kinds of motivations which characterize ourselves was especially emphasized by the great psychoanalyst Sigmund Freud. Time and time again while he was probing into the early history of his patients he discovered instances of this projecting. In many cases it was so strong the patients fully believed that some event had occurred although a careful investigation proved that it never had.

Such a personality mechanism as *projection* is not itself abnormal, although it may be associated with extreme personality maladjustments. The fact that it does operate among a group of more or less typical college students is shown in an experiment by Sears.[7]

Subjects. The subjects of the experiment were members of three fraternities, there being thirty-eight persons in one fraternity, thirty-seven in another, and twenty-two in the third. All of these persons had lived together for a minimum of two months, and hence knew each other at least moderately well.

Method

(1) COLLECTION OF DATA. Each member of the house rated each other member and himself on a group of personality traits. The traits on which the rating was done were *Stinginess–Generosity; Obstinacy–Acquiescence; Disorderliness–Orderliness; Bashfulness–Forwardness.* The rating was done on a scale from 1 to 7, with one representing one extreme of the trait and seven the other.

[7] Robert R. Sears, "Experimental studies of projection I. Attribution of traits," *Journal of Social Psychology*, 1930, **7**, 151-163.

All the ratings were made at the same time while the raters were alone in their rooms and the sheets were immediately returned to the experimenter. The subjects were assured that their ratings would be confidential.

(2) TREATMENT OF DATA. (A) The degree to which each individual demonstrated a given trait was determined by averaging the combined ratings assigned to him on that trait by all the others. (B) The amount of a given trait which each person attributed to the others was obtained by averaging the value of all the scores on that trait that he assigned to others. (C) A third measure was obtained and that was the difference between the rating on a trait that a person assigned to himself and the ratings which others assigned to him. This is called a measure of *insight*.

Let us see how these ratings can be used. Measure A gives us an indication of how much of a given trait a person possesses.[8] Measure B gives us an indication of how much of the trait he thinks others possess. If the mechanism of projection operates, those who are high in a given trait would rate others high, and those who are low would rate others low. There should, in other words, be a numerical agreement between a person's score on A and B. Measure C gives an additional bit of information whose significance will be referred to later.

Results. When the groups as a whole were considered, there was very little if any relationship between the scores on A and B. There was not, on the average, a tendency for persons high or low on a trait to rate others high or low respectively. The total group was then broken down into those who had insight and saw themselves as others see them, and those who lacked insight. This still resulted in no relationship for the insightful subjects, but the subjects who lacked insight *did* show such a relationship. These insight-lacking subjects were exhibiting the phenomenon of projection. They tended to see others as they themselves were.

There is one other result which should be mentioned. Does projection occur only if the particular trait is socially undesirable? There is some suggestion in the data of this experiment that such is

[8] This assumes that the combined judgments of others is a "true" estimate of the individual.

not the case. Persons who were high in generosity, for example, tended to consider others as generous, and at the opposite extreme the stingy saw others as stingy. This same trend was true for the other traits. These seem to be a perceptually distorting factor working for both the desirable and undesirable characteristics.

Summary. This study has given experimental evidence for the operation of the personality mechanism of projection. It has shown it to be a phenomenon closely related to the person's own ability to see himself as others see him, and to operate for traits that are desirable as well as undesirable.

6. BRAIN OPERATIONS AND PERSONALITY

Within recent years a very spectacular method for the treatment of personality disorders has been developed. The method is not a highly difficult one, but its drama lies in the fact that it consists of a surgical operation upon the brain. The surgeon enters the brain cavity by means of a small hole drilled near the temple and cuts the nerve fiber tracts connecting the front part of the brain and some of the nerve centers within the brain. The original report upon this operation[9] stressed the fact that patients treated in this manner recovered from excessive reactions of anxiety, worry, and despondency which had been characteristic of their abnormality.

This method of treatment is by no means 100 per cent effective. Cases occur in which there is no relief of symptoms. The operation is a drastic one, for intellectual loss may occur as an experiment on monkeys in the previous chapter has shown, and once the fiber tracts are destroyed they are gone forever. For this reason it is important to be able to predict who will profit by the operation and who will not. The following experiment by Peters[10] reports one of the first systematic efforts to make such a prediction.

Method. The basic hypothesis behind this study was that there might be a particular pattern or patterns of personality which could

[9] W. Freeman, and J. Watts, *Psychosurgery: Intelligence, Emotion and Social Behavior Following Prefrontal Lobotomy for Mental Disorders,* Springfield, Ill., Thomas, 1942.
[10] H. N. Peters, "Traits Related to Improved Adjustment of Psychotics after Lobotomy," *Journal of Abnormal and Social Psychology,* 1947, 42, 383-392.

obtain relief by such treatment, and others which could not. If such were the case, one might be able to discover consistent personality differences between the recoverers and the nonrecoverers. It was to this end that the experiment was directed.

An evaluation of the amount of recovery for seventy-one patients who had been operated on in this manner was made by means of interviews with the patients. The patients were divided into three classes: those showing no improvement, those showing limited improvement, and those showing clear signs of improvement. Actually about one third of the patients fell into each of these classes.

Then through case histories, and in some cases through preoperative interviews, the patients were rated on a group of personality traits which were characteristic of the improved patients as compared with those of the unimproved patients to determine whether or not there was any basic difference between the two.

Results. Actually, there seemed to be some evidence that the improvable and the unimprovable did differ from each other in their preoperative personality characteristics. They differed in the following basic ways:

(1) The improvables showed a high activity level characterized by such traits as restlessness, alertness, high energy, and excitability.

(2) The improvables also seemed to have a greater directness to their actions. They were more purposive, ambitious, aggressive, and showed greater initiative.

(3) Throughout their illness those who were to improve maintained a contact with reality and had not shown marked tendencies to withdraw from the world.

(4) The improvables tended also to be more sociable, and less given to unaccountable swings in mood.

Summary. The significance of the present experiment lies along several lines. In the first place it indicates that brain operations do not inevitably result in cures of psychotic disorders. In fact, these data indicate that only about one third of the patients showed satisfactory signs of recovery. This figure, however, does not permit the conclusion that one third of the psychotics can recover following such an operation; for the operation is performed only on those who the psychiatrists feel can profit thereby. Actually the operation is not even considered for many of the patients. Hence, the percentage of the psychotics who might be expected to recover as a result of the operation is far less than one third.[11]

Secondly, this experiment indicates what scientists do when a particular technique is successful some of the times and unsuccessful other times. They search for some characteristic variable which is associated with the successful case, and for another variable which is associated with failure. If consistent variables are found which are unique, then a prediction of success or failure can be made, and the employment of a technique which is useless and dangerous in a particular case can be avoided. The research can go even further than that; for by discovering these variables it may be possible to reach a better understanding of the working of the technique and the nature of the disorder itself.

In the present experiment variables of personality were discovered for the successful and the unsuccessful cases. We cannot be certain on the basis of this single experiment that this finding is generally true; more experimentation must be done to substantiate it. One of the major reasons for this is the fact that we do not have measures of personality which approximate perfection. Other persons when trying to evaluate personality might not have the same standards of judgments that this author used.

Summary of the chapter. The first and second sections describe some methods employed in the measurement of personality. The first section illustrates some of the projective techniques and points out some of the methods that are used to evaluate such tests. The second section is a description of the program of personality evaluation that was introduced during the war by the Assessment Staff of the Office of Strategic Services. The experiment in the third section

[11] The use of the term "recovery" does not mean that the individual is perfectly normal and has returned to his prepsychotic self. It simply means that some of his disabling symptoms may have left him. He may no longer be plunged into depression by some fancied act, or be racked with feelings of guilt; on the contrary he may become happy-go-lucky and even irresponsible. It means that the patients feel better, but he may become unpredictable and very trying to those who are close to him.

460

indicates the importance of parent-child relationships in the development of personality habits. It gives some evidence that the type of home environment develops habits of reaction which generalize to the school situation. The fourth experiment shows how the nature of the immediate environment may determine what types of "personality" reactions occur. The fifth experiment gives experimental identification to the clinical concept of projection. The final experiment evaluates a technique of treatment of abnormal subjects, and roughly identifies personality characteristics which are associated with those who recover and those who do not.

NAME INDEX

SUBJECT INDEX

A

Achievement, 53–57

African Bushmen, 141–142

Age and ability to learn, 369–373

Aircraft instruments, 18–20
  application of scientific method to problem of human efficiency, 18–19

Alcohol, effects of, on human behavior, 168–176
  Hollingsworth's experiment, 170–173
  Miles's study, 175–176
  practical application of study, 173–175

Alpha waves, 429–430

Amblystoma experiment, 94–98
  explanation, 96–98

Amnesia, 282, 284
  posthypnotic, 282, 283

Anatomy and Physiology of the Nervous System, 5

Anesthesia, 296–301

Anger, 245–251
  causes of, 246
  methods of dealing with, 246–251

Anger responses in children, 245–246

Animal experiments in heredity, 70–73

Anoxia, 176–181

Ape and the child, 75–87
  behavior dependent on human environment, 87
  conditions of experiment, 75–77
  development of behavior independent of human environment, 86–87
  manual dexterity, 84–86
  what they learned, 81–83

Appetites, 193–196
  preference of rats for salted water, 194–195

Aptitude, 41–43
  achievement and, 53–57
  artistic abilities, 64–68
  clerical, 43–50
  defined, 41

Aptitude, for flying, 57–64
  and heredity, 41
  individual diagnosis, 50–53

Army General Classification Test, 130–132

Artistic abilities, 64–68
  musical aptitude tests, 65–68

Aspiration, level of, 223–226
  and level of achievement, difference between, 223

Assessment of men, 439–448
  construction test, 441, 443–446
  Station S procedure, 440
  stress interview, 445–446
  validity of ratings, 446–448
  wall problem, 440–442

Auditory localization, 311–316

Auditory reversal, 316–319

Australian primitive people, 141–142

Aveyron, Wild Boy of, 73–75

B

Balland field test, 135–141

Behavior studies with rats, 411–416

Berger's investigations of brain waves, 429–431

Beta waves, 429–430

Binet scale, 118–121
  1937 revision of, 126–128

Blond and brunet traits, 12–15

Bonuses as incentives, 208–210
  limit of improbability, 209–210

Brain function studies, in higher animals, 416–420
  in lower animals, 411–416
  on monkeys, 417–420

Brain operations and personality, 458–460

Brain waves, 429–432

Briarsville, 136–140

Brogden's experiment in incentive conditions, 338–340

Brunet and blond traits, 12–15

Burtt's experiment, in previous learning, 381–384

467

471